2 6.29

Microsoft® Exchange Server 2010 Administration

Instant Reference

D1235998

Microsoft® Exchange Server 2010 Administration
Instant Reference

Ken St. Cyr

WILEY

Wiley Publishing, Inc.

Acquisitions Editor: Agatha Kim
Development Editor: Stef Jones
Technical Editor: Doug Fidler
Production Editor: Angela Smith
Copy Editor: Liz Welch
Editorial Manager: Pete Gaughan
Production Manager: Tim Tate
Vice President and Executive Group Publisher: Richard Swadley
Vice President and Publisher: Neil Edde
Book Designer: Maureen Forys, Happenstance Type-O-Rama
Compositor: Craig Woods, Happenstance Type-O-Rama
Proofreader: Rebecca Rider
Indexer: J & J Indexing
Project Coordinator, Cover: Lynsey Stanford
Cover Designer: Ryan Sneed
Cover Image: iStockPhoto

Copyright © 2010 by Wiley Publishing, Inc., Indianapolis, Indiana

Published simultaneously in Canada

ISBN: 978-0-470-53050-4

Library of Congress Cataloging-in-Publication Data
St. Cyr, Ken, 1979-
  Microsoft Exchange server 2010 administration instant reference / Ken St. Cyr. — 1st ed.
    p. cm.
  ISBN 978-0-470-53050-4 (pbk.)
1. Microsoft Exchange server. 2. Client/server computing. 3. Electronic mail systems. I. Title.
QA76.9.C55S763 2010
005.7'1376—dc22
                          2009047242

10 9 8 7 6 5 4 3 2 1

MAY 0 1 2010

Dear Reader,

Thank you for choosing *Microsoft Exchange Server 2010 Administration Instant Reference*. This book is part of a family of premium-quality Sybex books, all of which are written by outstanding authors who combine practical experience with a gift for teaching.

Sybex was founded in 1976. More than 30 years later, we're still committed to producing consistently exceptional books. With each of our titles, we're working hard to set a new standard for the industry. From the paper we print on, to the authors we work with, our goal is to bring you the best books available.

I hope you see all that reflected in these pages. I'd be very interested to hear your comments and get your feedback on how we're doing. Feel free to let me know what you think about this or any other Sybex book by sending me an email at nedde@wiley.com. If you think you've found a technical error in this book, please visit http://sybex.custhelp.com. Customer feedback is critical to our efforts at Sybex.

Best regards,

Neil Edde
Vice President and Publisher
Sybex, an Imprint of Wiley

Acknowledgments

There's no way I could have finished this book without my tremendously strong support system. At the top of that system is my amazing wife Brenna. She has the patience of a saint and is wise beyond her years. It's with her support and help that I was able to have the time to take on this project. Alongside her, tugging on her pants are my little crumb-snatchers, Lincoln and Nora. Even though they are both in diapers, their helpfulness was manifested in their cuteness and willingness to let me write.

It was a great pleasure to work with the wonderful group of professionals at Sybex. In particular, I would like to thank developmental editor Stef Jones; production editor Angela Smith; editorial manager Pete Gaughan; copyeditor Liz Welch; and the compositors at Happenstance Type-O-Rama. I would also like to thank my good friend and technical editor, Doug Fidler, who was kind enough to stand with me and bear the pain of writing about software that was still being developed. And I would like to give an extra special thanks to my acquisitions editor, Agatha Kim, who was a real treat to work with and was wonderful in coaching me along the way.

I would be remiss if I didn't thank my wonderful friends and coworkers at Microsoft. A big thanks goes out to the Exchange community and members of the product group who answered my questions and gave me great insight. I would also like to thank my many teachers, mentors, and encouraging friends: Scott Miller, Dan Quintiliano, Abe Berlas, Jim McBee, Andy Baratta, Jim Beasey, Jeff McMullen, Mike Hall, Jamie McClellan, Jim Hale, and many others.

And finally, I would like to give a special thanks to my wonderful friends and family at Grace Baptist Church in Bowie, MD, who offered their prayers and encouragement for me throughout this process. The Godly direction given by my pastors and teachers has been invaluable: Steve Lane, Dr. George Harton, Mark Tanious, and Dr. Tom Salem. There's no group of people more loving and caring than those at Grace.

About the Author

K en St. Cyr is a Solution Architect at Microsoft in the Public Sector Services CTO organization. Aside from Microsoft Exchange, Ken's areas of technical expertise are in directory services and identity management systems. Ken is a 12-year industry veteran, consulting with a broad range of organizations to design and deliver numerous large and complex messaging, directory, and identity management solutions. In addition to being a Microsoft Certified Master in Directory Services and Advanced Infrastructure, Ken has written for TechNet Magazine and Windows IT Pro Magazine.

In his leisure, Ken enjoys spending time with his wife Brenna and two children, Lincoln and Nora. As a lifelong learner and avid technology enthusiast, Ken enjoys researching the latest technologies and attempting to understand how they work. Ken is most enthusiastic about teaching and instructing others to realize their passion through the magic of software.

Contents

Introduction

The goal of this book is to give you quick answers in an easy-to-follow format so you can get in there and get the job done. I did not seek to answer your deepest and darkest questions about Exchange Server 2010. Instead my attempt is to give you a practice guide that you will want to keep out on your desk and carry with you in your backpack.

Perhaps the most exciting thing about the book that you are holding right now is how hands-on and practical it is. Rather than going into long and drawn-out discussions of messaging theory and minutiae, this book guides you, the Exchange administrator. Whether you are a one-person team in a small organization or a member of a larger team in a big email shop, this book is your own personal guide to installing, configuring, and managing Exchange Server 2010. This book is chock full of practical solutions and step-by-step procedures for scenarios that you face as an Exchange administrator. You can learn how to:

- Get the most out of using PowerShell to manage Exchange.
- Stop leaks of confidential information over email.
- Ensure that people's email is always there and always available.
- Get a better handle on the permissions that other administrators have.
- Keep your Exchange servers healthy.
- Eliminate PSTs by implementing archiving.

If you are new to Exchange and deploying it for the first time, you can start at the first chapter and read through the book to learn how to install it, manage it, configure it, and ensure that it continues to work right. Each chapter of this book deals with a different area of Exchange administration—everything from deployment to security. At the beginning of the chapter, you can glance at the topics covered and hone in on a particular area. You can quickly navigate to that area to find step-by-step procedures and guidance for the things you might encounter. My hope is that you'll keep coming back to this book and use it as a quick reference to remind you how to perform that task or use that PowerShell command. We look forward to being a well-used tool in your Exchange administration toolbox.

Who Should Read This Book

Though many ranks of IT professionals can get something out of this book, my target audience is primarily administrators who manage Microsoft Exchange Server 2010 environments. Whether or not you have experience with previous versions of Exchange Server, you can use this book.

In order to use this book to the fullest, you should possess:

- A rudimentary knowledge of Active Directory and Domain Name System (DNS)

- Some level of familiarity with Windows Server 2008 or Windows Server 2008 R2

- A basic understanding of Windows networking

This book may also prove useful to people who want to use hands-on examples with relevant narratives to play with Exchange Server 2010 in a lab environment. If you fall into this category, you can start at the first chapter and read your way through the book, following the examples and steps as you go along.

How to Contact the Author

I welcome feedback from you about this book or about books you'd like to see from me in the future. You can reach me by writing to ken@kenstcyr.com. For more information about my work, please visit my blog at www.kenstcyr.com.

Sybex strives to keep you supplied with the latest tools and information you need for your work. Please check their website at www.sybex.com, where we'll post additional content and updates that supplement this book if the need arises. Enter *Exchange 2010* in the Search box (or type the book's ISBN—9780470530504), and click Go to get to the book's update page.

PART I

Getting Started

IN THIS PART ◉

1

Deploying Exchange Servers

IN THIS CHAPTER, YOU WILL LEARN TO:

The first step along the journey of administering Microsoft Exchange Server 2010 is deploying the product. In many cases, deploying Exchange isn't a process that should be taken lightly. It is vital to build an Exchange infrastructure that can meet the needs of your business, ensure appropriate levels of availability, and support the growth of your organization. Therefore, this chapter starts out by explaining the factors that go into deploying Exchange before diving into the process of installing Exchange servers.

Prepare for Installation

Preparation is often a key to success. When you take the appropriate amount of time to prepare for a big change in your IT environment, you are in a better position to anticipate potential problems and you are more likely to be ready with a solution.

In preparation for the installation of Exchange, you need to focus on three stages. Without considering all three of these stages, you could encounter many setbacks during the deployment of Exchange. These three stages are as follows:

1. Properly planning the Exchange deployment
2. Preparing Active Directory
3. Preparing the server that runs Exchange

Plan the Exchange Deployment

Planning the deployment of Exchange is a crucial step that should be given heavy consideration. A properly planned Exchange deployment will help minimize the problems that you could run into during deployment. Many different frameworks exist for deployment planning. Regardless of your methodology for planning Exchange, the process encompasses three common elements:

1. Know where you are starting from, and weigh that against the requirements for Exchange.
2. Design a well-thought-out Exchange architecture.
3. Create a deployment plan that helps you understand how to get from where you are to where you want to be.

These three components are a required part of a solid deployment strategy for Exchange. If any of them are omitted, you are sure to encounter bumps along the way.

Understand the Server Roles

Exchange Server 2010 uses the concept of roles. A server with a particular role performs a specific functionality. In a typical Exchange installation, four roles are commonly used:

Hub Transport Server Role   The Hub Transport Server role is responsible for transporting email around the Exchange organization. Every message that is sent or received in the organization flows through at least one Hub Transport server. Because of this, the Hub Transport server provides the perfect location for virus scanning, transport rules, or other activities that would require every message to be touched.

In Exchange Server 2010, you are required to have at least one Hub Transport server in every site that contains Mailbox servers. It also makes sense to install additional Hub Transport servers in each site for redundancy and load balancing.

Client Access Server Role   The Client Access Server role is the connection point for your email clients. Because Exchange Server 2010 uses Client Access servers to perform MAPI (the Messaging Application Programming Interface) on the Middle Tier (MoMT), all connectivity from mail clients is funneled through these servers. MoMT is a feature that moves the client access point for all mailbox connections to a Client Access server instead of the Mailbox server. Therefore, it's important to ensure that you have enough Client Access servers to handle your expected load. Generally, Microsoft recommends three Client Access server processor cores for every four Mailbox server processor cores. (Your mileage may vary depending on the Exchange design.)

Like Hub Transport servers, Client Access servers are required in every site. In Chapter 10, "Maintaining Reliability and Availability," you'll learn how to load balance your Client Access servers to ensure that they are redundant.

Mailbox Role   Mailbox servers house all of the data for the users. In Exchange Server 2010, Mailbox servers contain databases with multiple users inside. Clients do not connect directly to the Mailbox servers. Rather, clients connect to the Client Access servers and the Client Access servers access the Mailbox servers on the clients' behalf.

In Exchange Server 2010, Mailbox server databases can be made highly available through the use of database availability groups (DAGs); therefore, you will likely install multiple Mailbox servers. DAGs are covered in more detail in Chapter 7, "Managing Mailbox Databases."

Edge Transport Server Role   The Edge Transport Server role is a unique role among the others. The Edge Transport server was designed to sit on the edge of your network and minimize the outside attack surface. Therefore, Edge Transport servers *cannot* be members of the Active Directory forest that your Exchange implementation resides in.

NOTE   Exchange Server 2010 also has a role called Unified Messaging. The Unified Messaging role is not covered in any depth in this book.

Understand Exchange Requirements

When thinking in terms of requirements for Exchange, you must take into account multiple facets. You need to think of requirements for Exchange in terms of both hardware and software.

The hardware requirements for Exchange Server 2010 are similar to those for Exchange Server 2007. Typically, you must consider three primary areas when selecting Exchange hardware:

- Amount and speed of processors
- Amount of memory
- Size, speed, and configuration of storage

As with previous versions of Exchange, the specifics of your hardware will vary depending on your design. Different roles require different hardware configurations.

Exchange Server 2010 supports only 64-bit processors in a production environment. Unlike with Exchange Server 2007, however, Microsoft has decided to not make the 32-bit version available. This means any workstations on which you install the Management Tools need to run 64-bit Windows as well as the servers that you use to perform the Active Directory preparation.

The number of processors required for Exchange will vary based on how you use Exchange. Table 1.1 shows the processor requirements based on role.

Table 1.1: Processor Requirements

Role	Minimum CPU Cores	Maximum CPU Cores
Client Access Server	2	12
Hub Transport Server	1	12
Edge Transport Server	1	12
Mailbox Server	2	12
Unified Messaging Server	2	12
Multifunction Server (CAS+Hub+Mail)	2	24

The memory requirements for Exchange are also dependent on the role of the server. Microsoft makes memory recommendations for most server roles based on the number of processor cores in the server. Table 1.2 shows the memory requirements for Exchange based on role.

Table 1.2: Memory Requirements

Role	Minimum Memory	Maximum Memory
Client Access Server	4 GB	16 GB
Hub Transport Server	4 GB	16 GB
Edge Transport Server	4 GB	16 GB
Mailbox Server	4 GB	64 GB
Unified Messaging Server	4 GB	16 GB
Multifunction Server (CAS+Hub+Mail)	8 GB	64 GB

Calculating the storage requirements for Exchange is always somewhat of an art. The storage used by Exchange will vary greatly between server roles. The Client Access (CA) role has a completely different storage requirement than the Mailbox (MB) role, which is heavily dependent on the amount of mailbox data that is being stored. However, there are some baseline storage requirements for every role. The Exchange software requires 1.2 GB of free space on the volume that you are installing it on. There should also be a minimum of 200 MB free on the operating system volume. Additional storage requirements will be necessary depending on the type of server, as shown in the following list:

Transport Servers Transport servers require enough space to store the message queue database. You need at least 500 MB, but the amount of storage needed will vary depending on how big you expect the queues to get.

Unified Messaging (UM) Servers UM servers require an additional 500 MB of disk space for each language pack installed.

Mailbox Servers The sizing of storage for mailbox servers is heavily dependent on the data that the server will hold. The common factors in considering this are the number of people on each Mailbox server, the limits of their mailboxes, and how long you expect to keep deleted mail and mailboxes for.

In terms of software, Table 1.3 illustrates the software requirements for Exchange Server 2010.

Table 1.3: Software Requirements

Component	Minimum Version Required
Operating system	Windows Server 2008 Standard Edition with SP2 x64 Windows Server 2008 Enterprise Edition with SP2 x64 Windows Server 2008 R2 Standard Edition Windows Server 2008 R2 Enterprise Edition Windows Vista with SP2 x64 (Management Tools only)
Transition from previous Exchange versions	Exchange Server 2003 SP2 Exchange Server 2007 SP2
Active Directory	Windows Server 2003 Forest-Functional Mode One Windows Server 2003 SP2 Global Catalog server in each site Writable domain controller in each site

Design the Exchange Architecture

You would not build a house without having a design first. In the same manner, you should not deploy Exchange without having a designed architecture. Putting together a design that represents the end state of your Exchange environment helps you anticipate the overall picture of what you will accomplish with Exchange. By laying this out on paper first, you will understand every aspect of your Exchange deployment. You will easily see where your strong points are as well as your deficiencies, and you can tweak your design to compensate for those areas. If you deploy Exchange first and then try to tweak your design, you will have a much tougher time and incur more setbacks.

When you're designing your Exchange architecture, here are a few areas you need to consider:

Message Routing   The first piece of the Exchange architecture that you should look at is the message routing component. You want to make sure that you fully understand the impact of the site topology in Active Directory and how it affects your plans for a routing architecture.

Server Placement   When deciding where to place servers, many factors come into play. Server placement has a large impact on your site architecture and is also usually tied into the message routing system. The idea is to understand where your servers are and how many of them there are at each site.

Capacity Planning   Another important aspect of the Exchange architecture is making sure that the servers can accommodate the number of people that you expect to be using them. With Exchange Server 2010 in particular, additional responsibilities are placed on the Client Access servers, so they will probably need to be upsized from Exchange Server 2007 architectures. Another area of capacity planning that is important is the Mailbox server. Ensure that you can provide enough storage for the Mailbox servers to satisfy user quotas, archiving requirements, and responsiveness metrics.

Disaster Recovery   The disaster recovery component is often overlooked in the design phase of the system. Ensure that you have in place a solid design and plan for disasters before you start implementing your design.

Anything that comes out of the design should be well documented. Write it down. Doing so will enable you to see the big picture and fill in any gaps that are missing before the deployment starts. Creating the documentation gives you a guide to follow. After the deployment is done, the documentation provides a record of what you did for others to reference as well.

Create a Deployment Plan

The final thing you will want to do to prepare for Exchange is to develop a deployment plan. A deployment plan should cover the entire lifespan of your Exchange deployment. Here, you will determine what all of the moving pieces are. You will orchestrate those moving pieces so that they can be executed with ease. A solid deployment plan accommodates the following areas:

- What is currently in the production environment?
- What does the end-state vision look like (design)?
- What do we need to do to get from where we are to where we want to be?

Coming out of your deployment plan should be a clear direction on how to get from the state that you are in now to the state that is described in your architecture documentation. Know which Exchange servers you should install first and where. Design a strategy for transitioning your routing topology from your legacy Exchange environment to Exchange Server 2010. If you are currently using something other than Exchange, know exactly what it takes to move off your current mail system.

Having this deployment plan in place and well communicated to the key players in your organization is a major time-saver.

Prepare Active Directory

Before Exchange Server 2010 can be installed in your domain, Active Directory must be updated to support it. The process of preparing Active Directory can be performed in one fell swoop with a single command. However, you can also perform the tasks individually so you can verify that each one was successful before moving on to the next one. This also allows you to install Exchange with as few permissions as possible and delegate the installation of certain components to other people. This might be helpful if you want to perform one of the tasks after hours and would prefer to have someone on the late shift do it for you. Some organizations have a group of administrators who are trusted to perform certain tasks, such as updating the schema. Performing certain tasks separately allows you to delegate those tasks to others.

NOTE   Exchange Server 2010 is the first version of Exchange that will not have a 32-bit install package. Therefore, all of the Active Directory preparation must be performed from a 64-bit system.

The Active Directory preparation process consists of a series of steps:

1. Prepare the legacy permissions if you're running Exchange Server 2003.

2. Update the Active Directory schema.

3. Update the Active Directory forest.

4. Update each of the domains that will house Exchange or mail-enabled users.

TIP   Before Active Directory can be prepared, the server that you are using to run the preparation steps must have PowerShell version 2.0 and Windows Remote Management (WinRM) version 2.0 installed. The steps for installing these updates are covered in the upcoming section "Prepare the Server."

Install the Active Directory Management Tools

If you are not using a domain controller to update Active Directory (AD) and are instead using a Windows Server 2008 member server, you must first install the AD Management Tools on the server. These tools are installed through the Server Manager on the member server. You can add these tools by either using the Server Manager graphical user interface (GUI) or by using the ServerManagerCmd command.

Installing the Management Tools with the GUI

To install the AD Management Tools with the GUI:

1. Click Start ➤ Administrative Tools ➤ Server Manager to open the Server Manager tool.

2. Once Server Manager is open, you will see a set of nodes in the left pane. Right-click on the node called Features and select Add Features from the menu, as shown in Figure 1.1. This launches the Add Features Wizard.

Figure 1.1: Launching the Add Features Wizard in Server Manager

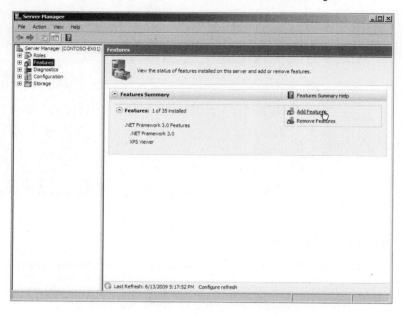

3. In the middle of the Add Features Wizard, scroll down the list of available features and click on the plus sign (+) next to the feature Remote Server Administration Tools to expand that feature. Then expand the Role Administration Tools feature, as shown in Figure 1.2.

4. Click the check box for the Active Directory Domain Services Tools option and click Next.

5. In the confirmation dialog box, verify that you are installing the Remote Server Administration Tools and then click the Install button.

Figure 1.2: Installing the Active Directory Domain Services Tools

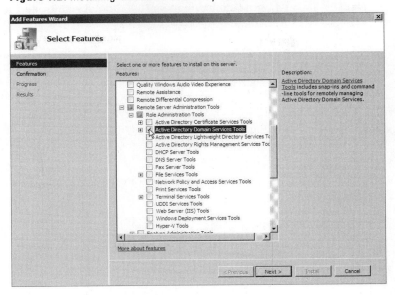

Installing the Management Tools at the Command Prompt

To install the AD Management Tools with the command prompt:

1. Open the command prompt. Click Start ➤ Accessories ➤ Command Prompt to open up a command prompt.

2. Run the following command from the command prompt:
   ```
   ServerManagerCmd -I RSAT-ADDS
   ```

Modify the Active Directory Schema

To update the schema, the account you use will need to be a member of the Schema Admins group in Active Directory. Also, the Schema Master Flexible Single Master Operation (FSMO) role must reside on a domain controller that is running on at least Windows Server 2003 Service Pack 2. To determine which domain controller hosts the Schema Master role, you can run the following command at the command prompt:

```
Netdom query fsmo
```

> **NOTE**   If you have existing Windows 2000 domain controllers in your AD environment, you will want to use the /DomainController switch to target a Windows Server 2003 SP1 domain controller.

When performing the schema updates, some Active Directory classes and attributes are updated to accommodate Exchange Server 2010. It's important that you only run the Exchange Server 2010 schema extensions in a forest that you expect to finish the AD preparation in. If you do not run the additional steps to prepare the forest for Exchange, you will run into some permissions problems.

To perform the schema update, run the following command from the Exchange media:

```
setup.com /PrepareSchema
```

Prepare the Active Directory Forest

Exchange must also make some additional updates to the configuration partition in Active Directory. This process needs to be completed only once for the entire forest, since the configuration partition is replicated among all domain controllers in the forest. When performing this update, Active Directory must contain information about the Exchange organization. If the Exchange organization does not already exist, you'll need to supply the organization name when you perform this process.

To prepare the Active Directory forest, run the following command:

```
setup.com /PrepareAD
```

Prepare the Active Directory Domains

In addition to preparing the schema and the forest, each domain that contains Exchange servers or mail-enabled users will also have to be updated. This process can be run on each domain individually or on all of the domains at the same time.

To prepare the Active Directory domains individually, open a command prompt and run the following command from the Exchange installation media:

```
setup.com /PrepareDomain:[Domain_Name]
```

For example, the contoso.com domain would be prepared with the command setup.com /PrepareDomain:contoso.com.

If you run the command with only the /PrepareDomain switch and do not specify a domain name, the command will run against the domain that you are currently logged in at. You do not need to perform this step in the domain that you ran /PrepareAD from.

To prepare all of the domains in the forest, run the following command from a command prompt:

```
setup.com /PrepareAllDomains
```

Prepare the Server

Before Exchange Server 2010 can be installed on a member server, there are some prerequisites that must be met. When using the installation interface, these prerequisites are outlined as a series of steps you need to take before you can start the installation of the Exchange server software. Figure 1.3 shows the necessary steps in the installation interface.

Figure 1.3: The Exchange Server 2010 installation interface

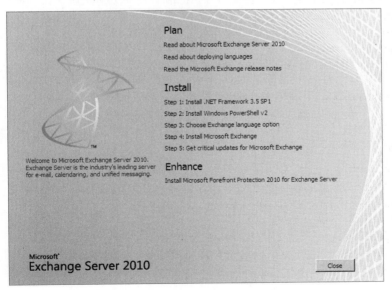

If you attempt to skip ahead to Step 4 and try to install Exchange, an error will be returned stating that you can't continue unless you install the prerequisite software. This software needs to be installed even if you are only installing the Exchange Management Tools on a workstation. This is because the Exchange Management Tools need the prerequisite software in order to manage Exchange remotely.

NOTE Throughout the installation process of Exchange, you may encounter User Account Control (UAC) prompts. UAC is a security mechanism that is built into newer versions of Windows to prevent unauthorized software from making changes to your computer. If you encounter UAC prompts at any point during Exchange installation, click the Yes button to continue and authorize Exchange to install.

Install .NET Framework 3.5 SP1

The first step to preparing the server is to install the Microsoft .NET Framework version 3.5 with SP1. The .NET Framework provides a framework for developers to use when developing applications. Exchange Server 2010 takes advantage of the 3.5 SP1 version of the framework. The process for installing .NET Framework 3.5 SP1 is different for Windows Server 2008 SP2 and Windows Server 2008 R2.

If you are using Windows Server 2008 SP2 for your Exchange servers, you can download the .NET Framework 3.5 SP1 in either an online or an offline installer. The online installer is smaller (around 3 MB), but the Exchange server must have access to the Internet in order to download the rest of the package. The other option is to download the offline installer, which is over 200 MB in size. It's a bigger package, but you can install it on an Exchange server that is not on the Internet.

Download the .NET Framework 3.5 with Service Pack 1 from

```
http://download.microsoft.com/download/2/0/e/20e90413-712f-
438c-988e-fdaa79a8ac3d/dotnetfx35.exe
```

To install the .NET Framework on Windows Server 2008 SP2:

1. Download and launch the `dotnetfx35.exe` installer package.

2. After the files extract, the setup wizard will launch. Accept the licensing agreement and click the Install button.

3. The package will download any necessary updates from the Internet (unless you are installing the full package) and will install the framework.

4. After installation is complete, click the Exit button to finish.

To install the .NET Framework on Windows Server 2008 R2, you can run the following command at a command prompt:

```
ServerManagerCmd -i NET-Framework-Core
```

Install the Windows Management Framework

The Windows Management Framework is a single download that contains PowerShell version 2 and Windows Remote Management 2.0. Windows Server 2008 R2 already contains the necessary components in this update, so this only needs to be applied to Exchange servers running on Windows Server 2008 with SP2.

PowerShell version 2 is used for running the Exchange Management Shell in Exchange Server 2010. PowerShell offers a great command-line interface for performing administrative tasks and running powerful scripts. Before installing PowerShell version 2, remove all previous versions of PowerShell that were installed on the server.

Windows Remote Management (WinRM) 2.0 is used to allow remote management capabilities on the Exchange server through PowerShell. Download the Management Framework from

```
http://go.microsoft.com/fwlink/?LinkId=157601
```

To install the Management Framework:

1. Download and launch the `Windows6.0-KB968930-x64.msu` installation package.

2. The Windows Update Standalone Installer dialog box will appear. Click OK to continue installation.

3. When the installer launches, click the I Accept button to accept the license terms.

4. When the update package completes, you will be asked to reboot the server. Click the Restart Now button and allow the system to reboot.

Install the Required Server Components

There are potentially several server components that you are required to install before you can install Exchange Server 2010. The components that need to be installed will depend on the roles that you select during installation. Table 1.4 shows the required components for each role. These features can be installed with the Add Roles or Add Features task in Server Manager.

Table 1.4: Required Components per Server Role

Role	Component
Hub Transport	IIS 6 Metabase Compatibility Web Server (IIS) Tools Windows Process Activation Service Process Model IIS 7 Basic Authentication IIS 7 Windows Authentication IIS 7 .NET Extensibility IIS 6 Management Console
Client Access	Internet Information Services World Wide Web Service (W3SVC) HTTP Activation IIS 6 Metabase Compatibility IIS 6 Management Console IIS 7 Dynamic Content Compression IIS 7 Static Content Compression Web Server (IIS) Tools Windows Process Active Service Process Model IIS 7 Basic Authentication IIS 7 Windows Authentication IIS 7 Digest Authentication IIS 7 .NET Extensibility
Unified Messaging	Windows Media Encoder Windows Media Audio Video Codec IIS 6 Metabase Compatibility Web Server (IIS) Tools Windows Process Activation Service Process Model IIS 7 Basic Authentication IIS 7 Windows Authentication IIS 7 .NET Extensibility IIS 6 Management Console

Table 1.4: Required Components per Server Role *(continued)*

Role	Component
Mailbox	Internet Information Services World Wide Web Service (W3SVC) 2007 Office System Converter: Filter Pack IIS 6 Metabase Compatibility IIS 6 Management Console Web Server (IIS) Tools Windows Process Activation Service Process Model IIS 7 Basic Authentication IIS 7 Windows Authentication IIS 7 .NET Extensibility
Edge Transport	Active Directory Lightweight Directory Services
Management Tools	Web Server (IIS) Tools IIS 6 Metabase Compatibility IIS 6 Management Compatibility IIS 6 Management Console

Rather than installing all of these components one at a time, Exchange Server 2010 setup provides `ServerManagerCmd` XML files for each set of components. Table 1.5 lists the package to install for each role.

Table 1.5: Server Component XML Files

Role	XML File
Hub Transport Server	`exchange-hub.xml`
Client Access Server	`exchange-cas.xml`
Unified Messaging Server	`exchange-um.xml`
Mailbox Server	`exchange-mbx.xml`
Edge Transport Server	`exchange-edge.xml`
Typical Exchange Installation	`exchange-typical.xml`
All Server Roles	`exchange-all.xml`

Getting Started

PART I

These XML files are located on the Exchange installation media under the \Scripts folder. To install the components with the XML file, run the following command:

```
ServerManagerCmd -ip <path and name of XML file>
```

For example, to install the server components for the Typical Exchange Installation, use the following command:

```
ServerManagerCmd -ip exchange-typical.xml
```

Configure the Net.Tcp Port Sharing Service

If you are installing the Client Access role on a server, you are required to set the Net.Tcp Port Sharing service to Automatic startup mode. Ensure that you only configure this setting on servers that have the Client Access role.

1. Open the Services management console by clicking on the Start menu and selecting All Programs ➢ Administrative Tools ➢ Services.

2. In the result pane in the management tool, scroll down to the Net.Tcp Port Sharing service and double-click on it to open the properties.

3. In the Properties dialog, ensure that the General tab is selected. In the drop-down menu for Startup Type, select Automatic.

4. Click OK to make the changes and close the Properties dialog.

Install Exchange Server 2010

After the preparations are complete, Exchange can be installed on the member server. There are many different options for installing Exchange. Exchange provides the capability to set up a server in a very basic configuration as well as advanced configurations.

Perform a Basic Installation

A basic installation of Exchange Server 2010 consists of a single server with the minimum roles installed. In the Exchange setup wizard, this is referred to as a Typical Exchange Installation. The Typical Exchange Installation consists of the following roles:

- Hub Transport Server
- Client Access Server
- Mailbox Server
- Management Tools

A basic installation can be performed either through the graphical installation wizard or through the setup command prompt. Before performing the installation, ensure that you complete the prerequisite work outlined in the "Prepare the Server" section earlier in this chapter.

Install Exchange Using the GUI

Installing Exchange using the GUI provides a walkthrough of the process. To perform a basic installation through the GUI, use the following steps:

1. Launch setup.exe from the Exchange installation media.

2. In the installation interface, ensure that steps 1and 2 are completed and click the link for Step 3: Choose Exchange Language Option. Two additional options will appear below this link.

    - The first option, Install All Languages From The Language Bundle, gives you the ability to load all of the language packs available for Exchange.

    - The second option is Install Only Languages From The DVD. If you are installing Exchange in English, click this option.

3. From the main menu in the Exchange setup program, select Step 4: Install Microsoft Exchange, under the Install section.

    This launches the Exchange Server 2010 installation wizard, which will walk you through the remainder of the installation.

4. When the installation wizard launches, click Next on the Introduction page.

5. On the License Agreement page, select the option "I accept the terms in the license agreement." and click Next.

6. On the Error Reporting page, choose whether or not you want to send error reports back to Microsoft and click Next.

7. On the Installation Type page, select the option for Typical Exchange Server Installation. If you want to install Exchange to a different location on your hard drive, you can choose that location here. After you're done, click Next.

    Figure 1.4 shows the Installation Type page of the wizard.

Figure 1.4: Selecting the type of Exchange installation

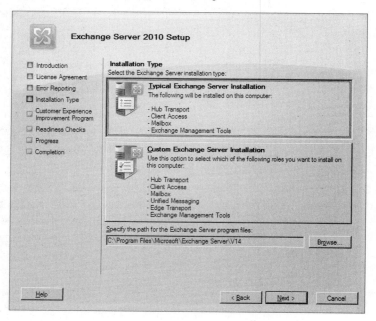

8. If this is the first Exchange server in your organization, you will see the Exchange Organization page next. If you see this page, you will need to enter a name for the Exchange organization that you are creating.

    If you don't see this option, then you are installing Exchange into an existing organization.

9. If this is the first Exchange server in your organization, then you will also see the Client Settings page. The question here is whether you want to install a public folder database. If you have older or legacy clients in your environment, then choose Yes. If you choose

No, you can go back and add a public folder database later. Click Next to continue.

Public folder databases are required for certain clients, such as Outlook 2003 and earlier, because those clients rely on the system information that is stored in public folders. However, newer clients such as Outlook 2007 don't require this functionality.

10. On the Configure Client Access Server External Domain page, you are asked whether this Client Access server will be exposed to the Internet. If you want your users to access their email from outside of your network, you should check the option The Client Access Server Role Will Be Internet-Facing. You will also need to enter the name that users will use when contacting this Client Access server from the Internet, such as `mail.contoso.com`. Click Next to continue.

11. On the Customer Experience Improvement Program page, choose whether or not you want to participate in the customer experience improvement program and click Next.

12. On the Readiness Checks page (see Figure 1.5), Exchange will perform a series of tests for each role that the server will install. Before Exchange installation can continue, these checks must pass without any errors. If errors are encountered, you will need to review them and correct them before continuing. If your server passes all of the readiness checks, then click the Install button to continue.

    These errors are also captured in the setup log. For more information on reviewing the setup log, see "Verify a Successful Installation," later in this chapter.

13. If you get this far, that means that the Exchange installation has been completed. Click Finish to close the setup wizard.

Install Exchange Using the Command Prompt

Exchange Server 2010 can also be installed with minimal interaction through the command prompt. Using the command prompt will still give you a verbose output like the GUI does, but some assumptions about installation options are made for you. You can specify additional installation options, but if you don't provide those options, you are not prompted to enter them. Instead, the default options are used.

Figure 1.5: Readiness Checks

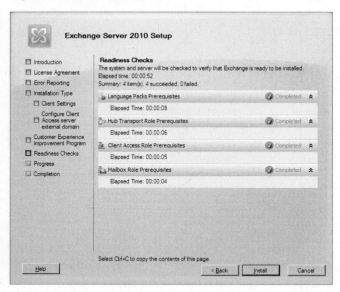

To perform a basic installation using the command prompt, take the following steps:

1. Open a command prompt in administrator mode by right-clicking on the Command Prompt icon and selecting Run As Administrator from the drop-down list.

2. Navigate to the folder that contains the Exchange installation media.

3. Run the following command:

```
setup.com /mode:install /role:mailbox,hubtransport,↵
clientaccess/OrganizationName:NameOfExchangeOrg
```

Perform an Advanced Installation

An advanced installation of Exchange requires you to more thoroughly think through your implementation path ahead of time. Exchange allows different servers to perform different roles. Exchange servers can host multiple roles or even just one role per server. Performing an advanced installation gives you more control over the roles that you will install.

Select Which Roles to Install

Some roles require more planning before being implemented, so before you can complete the advanced installation, you need to know what roles you are installing on the Exchange server. Before choosing to install roles, review the section "Prepare the Server," earlier in this chapter, and ensure that you have installed all of the prerequisites for the role.

In most cases, roles can be grouped together without discrimination. However, there are some situations where you will want a particular server to retain a single role rather than multiple roles. For example, your Client Access servers may be Internet-facing. In that situation, adding the Mailbox role to those servers may impose too much data exposure risk.

Start the Advanced Installation

The beginning of the process for performing an advanced installation of Exchange is the same for every role when you are using the graphical Exchange setup wizard. Use these steps to start the installation, and then use the following sections that pertain to the roles you want to install in order to complete the installation.

1. Launch setup.exe from the Exchange installation media.

2. In the installation interface, click on the link for Step 3: Choose Exchange Language Option. Two additional options will appear below this link:

   - The first option is labeled Install All Languages From The Language Bundle, and it gives you the ability to load all of the language packs available for Exchange.

   - The second option is labeled Install Only Languages From The DVD. If you are installing Exchange in English, click this option.

3. From the main menu in the Exchange setup program, select Step 4: Install Microsoft Exchange under the Install section.

   This launches the Exchange Server 2010 installation wizard, which will walk you through the remainder of the installation.

4. When the installation wizard launches, click Next on the Introduction page.

Getting Started

PART I

5. On the Licensing Agreement page, select the option "I accept the terms in the license agreement." and click Next.

6. On the Error Reporting page, choose whether or not you want to send error reports back to Microsoft and click Next.

7. On the Installation Type page, select the option for Custom Exchange Server Installation. If you want to install Exchange to a different location on your hard drive, you can choose that location here. After you're done, click Next.

8. Use the following sections to install specific roles on the server.

Installing the Hub Transport Server Role

To install the Hub Transport server through the graphical interface:

1. Follow the instructions in the earlier section "Start the Advanced Installation."

2. On the Server Role Selection page, check the box next to Hub Transport Role (see Figure 1.6). The Management Tools will automatically be checked as well. Click Next to continue.

Figure 1.6: Choosing to install the Hub Transport role

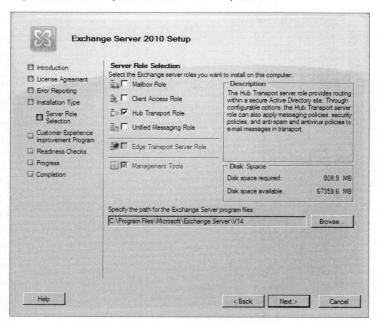

3. If this is the first Exchange server in your organization, you will see the Exchange Organization page next. If you see this page, you will need to enter a name for the Exchange organization that you are creating.

   If you don't see this option, then you are installing Exchange into an existing organization.

4. On the Customer Experience Improvement Program page, choose whether or not you want to participate in the customer experience improvement program and click Next.

5. On the Readiness Checks page, Exchange will perform a series of tests for the Hub Transport role. Before Exchange installation can continue, these checks must pass without any errors. If errors are encountered, you must review and correct them before continuing. If your server passes all of the readiness checks, then click the Install button to continue.

   These errors are also captured in the setup log. For more information on reviewing the setup log, refer to the section "Verify a Successful Installation," later in this chapter.

6. After the server is finished installing, click Finish to close the setup wizard.

Install the Client Access Server Role

To install the Client Access Server role through the graphical interface:

1. Follow the instructions in the earlier section, "Start the Advanced Installation."

2. On the Server Role Selection page, check the box next to Client Access Role (see Figure 1.7). The Management Tools will automatically be checked as well. Click Next to continue.

3. If this is the first Exchange server in your organization, then you will see the Exchange Organization page next. If you see this page, you must enter a name for the Exchange organization that you are creating. If you don't see this option, then you are installing Exchange into an existing organization.

Figure 1.7: Choosing to install the Client Access role

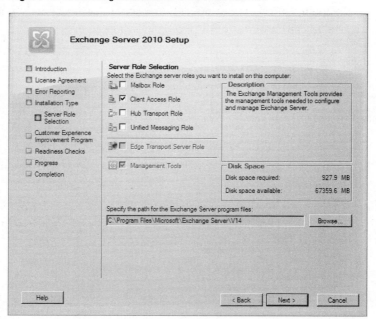

4. On the Configure Client Access server external domain page, you are asked whether this Client Access server will be exposed to the Internet. If you want your users to access their email from outside of your network, you should check the option The Client Access Server Role Will Be Internet-Facing. You will also need to enter the name that users will use when contacting this Client Access server from the Internet, such as mail.contoso.com. Click Next to continue.

5. On the Customer Experience Improvement Program page, choose whether or not you want to participate in the customer experience improvement program and click Next.

6. On the Readiness Checks page, Exchange will perform a series of tests for the Client Access role. Before Exchange installation can continue, these checks must pass without any errors. If errors are encountered, you will need to review and correct them before continuing. If your server passes all of the readiness checks, click the Install button to continue.

These errors are also captured in the setup log. For more information on reviewing the setup log, refer to the section called "Verify a Successful Installation," later in this chapter.

7. After the server is finished installing, click Finish to close the setup wizard.

Install the Mailbox Server Role

To install the Mailbox Server role through the graphical interface:

1. Follow the instructions in the earlier section, "Start the Advanced Installation."

2. On the Server Role Selection page, check the box next to Mailbox Role (see Figure 1.8). The Management Tools will automatically be checked as well. Click Next to continue.

Figure 1.8: Choosing to install the Mailbox role

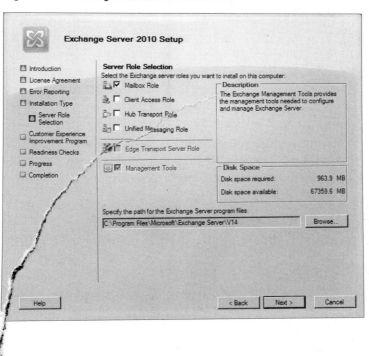

3. If this is the first Exchange server in your organization, then you will see the Exchange Organization page next. If you see this page, you must enter a name for the Exchange organization that you are creating. If you don't see this option, then you are installing Exchange into an existing organization.

4. If this is the first mailbox server in your organization, then you will also see the Client Settings page. The question here is whether you want to install a public folder database. If you have older or legacy clients in your environment, then choose Yes. If you choose No, you can go back and add a public folder database later. Click Next to continue.

   Public folder databases are required for certain clients, such as Outlook 2003 and earlier, because those clients rely on the system information that is stored in public folders. However, newer clients, such as Outlook 2007, don't require this functionality.

5. On the Customer Experience Improvement Program page, choose whether or not you want to participate in the customer experience improvement program and click Next.

6. On the Readiness Checks page, Exchange will perform a series of tests for the Mailbox role. Before Exchange installation can continue, these checks must pass without any errors. If errors are encountered, you will need to review and correct them before continuing. If your server passes all of the readiness checks, click the Install button to continue.

   These errors are also captured in the setup log. For more information on reviewing the setup log, refer to the section "Verify a Successful Installation," later in this chapter.

7. After the server is finished installing, click Finish to close the setup wizard.

Install the Edge Transport Server Role

To install an Edge Transport server using the graphical Exchange setup wizard:

1. Ensure that the server you are installing the Edge Transport role on is *not* a member of the Active Directory forest that Exchange is deployed in.

To verify this, open the System applet from Control Panel (Start ➢ Control Panel). Under the section labeled Computer Name, Domain, And Workgroup Settings, ensure that the Domain field is empty.

2. Follow the instructions in the earlier section, "Start the Advanced Installation."

3. On the Server Role Selection page, check the box next to Edge Transport Server Role (see Figure 1.9). The Management Tools will automatically be checked as well. Click Next to continue.

Getting Started

PART I

Figure 1.9: Choosing to install the Edge Transport Server role

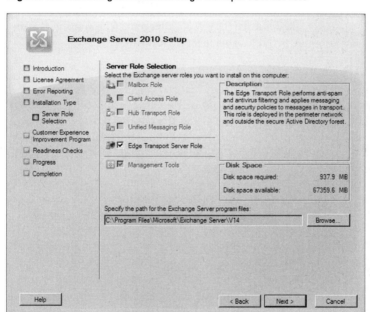

4. On the Customer Experience Improvement Program page, choose whether or not you want to participate in the customer experience improvement program and click Next.

5. On the Readiness Checks page, Exchange will perform a series of tests for the Edge Transport Server role. Before Exchange installation can continue, these checks must pass without any errors. If errors are encountered, you must review and correct them before continuing. If your server passes all of the readiness checks, click the Install button to continue.

These errors are also captured in the setup log. For more information on reviewing the setup log, refer to the section called "Verify a Successful Installation," later in this chapter.

6. After the server is finished installing, click Finish to close setup wizard.

Perform an Automated Installation

Installing Exchange through the setup wizard makes the Exchange installation process simple. However, when deploying multiple Exchange servers across a large enterprise, we need a repeatable process that is quick to execute and ensures consistency across servers. Automating the installation of Exchange provides this level of assurance.

Perform an Unattended Install

Performing an unattended setup of Exchange is accomplished with the setup command-line installer. Using the command-line installer, you can run setup and specify the options that you want to customize as parameters. For example, if you want to install a Mailbox server, you can use the following setup command:

```
setup.com /mode:install /roles:Mailbox
/OrganizationName:Contoso
```

Executing the command setup.com /? will give you a list of all of the supported setup parameters.

Error checking is performed during the install and the results are displayed on the screen. If errors are encountered, the unattended installer stops. You will then have to correct the errors before restarting the installation.

Install Using an Answer File

An answer file is a plain text file with the appropriate setup switches specified. The answer file can contain advanced options necessary for a more thorough Exchange configuration.

The answer file contains all of the information that the Exchange setup process is looking for so the setup program does not have to prompt the administrator for the answer. You only spend a few minutes creating the answer file up front, and once it's created installation is a repeatable process that requires very little attention.

Figure 1.10 illustrates a common answer file.

Figure 1.10: A common answer file for unattended installation

Using an answer file for unattended installation in Exchange is not a requirement. A capable administrator could just as easily run the setup. com installation program for Exchange and specify all of the options as switches in that one command. However, depending on the number of options that are configured during the install, this one command could be very long. Typing in a very long command even once is prone to error, but if you repeat it multiple times for many deployments in the enterprise then you are bound to improperly configure something on the server.

In many cases, therefore, creating an answer file makes a lot of sense. When executing the unattended installer with the answer file, you will use the /AnswerFile switch. In the following example, I'm installing Exchange using an answer file:

```
setup.com /mode:install /roles:mailbox
/AnswerFile:TypicalExchange.txt
```

Perform Post-Installation Tasks

After Exchange is installed, there are some post-installation tasks that you will want to run through to finish configuring Exchange and to get mail flowing properly in your organization.

Finalize the Installation

After installing the Exchange server, you should finalize the installation by performing some additional tasks.

Enter the Product Key

Exchange doesn't require you to enter the product key before installation. Until you enter a product key, Exchange runs in trial mode. In trial mode, the server functions as Exchange Standard edition. The unlicensed server will function in trial mode for 120 days. Exchange is more than happy to let you know that you have unlicensed servers. Every time the Exchange Management Console is started, you will get a list of unlicensed servers and the amount of time before trial mode expires. (See Figure 1.11.)

Figure 1.11: The unlicensed server dialog box presented by the Management Console

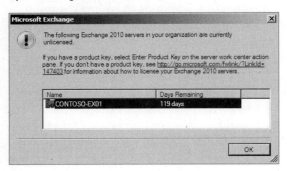

You can also obtain this same information using the Exchange Management Shell (EMS). The Exchange Management Shell is covered in detail in Chapter 2, "Using the Exchange Management Console and the Exchange Management Shell." To obtain licensing information, use the following one-liner:

```
Get-ExchangeServer | where-object
{$_.IsExchange2007TrialEdition -match $true}
```

An example result of the licensing information command is shown in Figure 1.12.

Figure 1.12: Licensing information obtained from the EMS

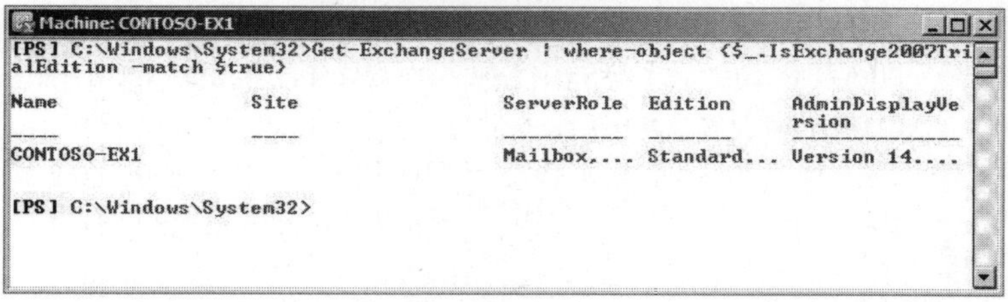

```
Machine: CONTOSO-EX1                                                    _ □ x
[PS] C:\Windows\System32>Get-ExchangeServer | where-object {$_.IsExchange2007Tri
alEdition -match $true}

Name                    Site              ServerRole  Edition    AdminDisplayVe
                                                                  rsion
----                    ----              ----------  -------    --------------
CONTOSO-EX1                               Mailbox,... Standard... Version 14....

[PS] C:\Windows\System32>
```

The product key is entered after the server is installed. To enter the key, you will use the Exchange Management Console.

1. Open the Exchange Management Console by clicking Start ➤ All Programs ➤ Microsoft Exchange Server 2010 ➤ Exchange Management Console.

2. In the left pane of the EMC, click on the Server Configuration Node.

3. In the center pane, select the server that is unlicensed.

4. In the right side under the Action pane, select Enter Product Key.

5. In the Product Key dialog box, type in the product key and click Enter.

6. Restart the Information Store service for the changes to take effect.

You can also use the EMS to enter the product key. With the EMS, you have ability to do this easily in bulk, or to script the product at the end of an automated installation. You can use the `Set-ExchangeServer` cmdlet to license the server:

```
Set-ExchangeServer -Identity MAILSRV1 -ProductKey ↵
XXXXX-XXXXX-XXXXX-XXXXX-XXXXX
```

If you want to enter a product key for all unlicensed servers in your Exchange organization, you can use the following one-liner:

```
Get-ExchangeServer | where-object
{$_.IsExchange2007TrialEdition-match $true} |
Set-ExchangeServer -ProductKey
XXXXX-XXXXX-XXXXX-XXXXX-XXXXX
```

Verify a Successful Installation

Another thing that you will want to do after Exchange is installed is to verify that the installation was completely successful. In particular, you will want to review the setup logs.

All of the setup logs for Exchange are found in a folder on the root of the system drive. If your system drive is C:, then the logs are stored in the folder C:\ExchangeSetupLogs.

The primary log that contains setup information about Exchange is ExchangeSetup.log. This log file records the status of every task that the installer performs when installing and configuring Exchange. This is especially useful when your system fails the readiness checks. The quickest way to view this log is to just review it in Notepad (see Figure 1.13).

Figure 1.13: Reviewing the Exchange setup log in Notepad

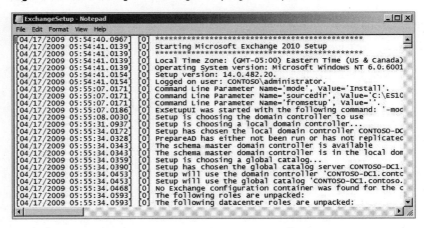

You can also review the setup logs using a PowerShell script that parses the output for you. You can find the Get-SetupLog.ps1 script from the C:\Program Files\Microsoft\Exchange\Scripts folder. Sample output is shown in Figure 1.14.

Check the Health of the Server

After you verify that the installation of Exchange was successful, you can check the overall health of the Exchange server. The primary method for checking the health of the server is the Application log in the Event Viewer and the Exchange Management Shell.

Figure 1.14: Reviewing the setup logs in PowerShell

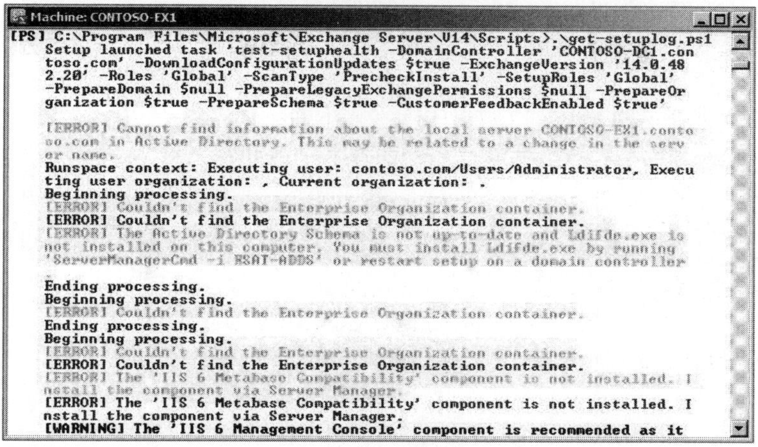

Any errors or warning processed by Exchange are reported in the Application log in Event Viewer. You can use the following procedures to review the Application log:

1. Click Start ➤ Administrative Tools ➤ Event Viewer to launch the Event Viewer tool.

2. In the left pane of Event Viewer, expand the Windows Logs node and select Application. This will display the Application log in the center pane of Event Viewer, as shown in Figure 1.15.

3. Review the list of application events for any errors or warnings that may pertain to Exchange Server.

You can also use the Exchange Management Shell to review the configuration of the Exchange server that you just installed. Open the Exchange Management Shell and run the `Get-ExchangeServer` cmdlet.

Install the Management Tools on a Different Computer

To help with the ongoing management of the Exchange server, you will want to install the Exchange Management Tools on another computer. Doing so will allow you to administer the Exchange Server without having to log into it.

One of the great improvements in Exchange Server 2010 in terms of administration is the powerful remote administration capabilities. These capabilities are exposed through the combination of the Exchange

Management Console and the Exchange Management Shell. Exchange Server 2010 uses Windows Remote Management (WinRM) to bring the power of the Exchange Management Shell to your workstation.

Figure 1.15: Reviewing the logs to ensure server health

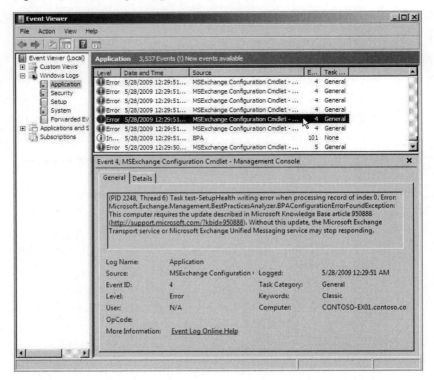

To run the Management Tools on your workstation, you need to run Windows Vista with Service Pack 1 or later. Also, there is no 32-bit release for Exchange Server 2010, so your workstation has to be running the 64-bit version of Vista. In addition, the system needs to have the following software installed:

- .NET Framework 3.5
- Windows Remote Management (WinRM)
- PowerShell version 2

Install the Management Tools Using the GUI

To install the Management Tools with the graphical user interface:

1. From the Exchange installation media, run `setup.exe` as an administrator.

2. In the installation interface, ensure that steps 1–3 are completed and click the link for Step 3: Choose Exchange Language Option. Two additional options will appear below this link.

   - The first option is Install All Languages From The Language Bundle, and it gives you the ability to load all of the language packs available for Exchange.

   - The second option is Install Only Languages From The DVD. If you are installing Exchange in English, click this option.

3. Next, in the installation interface click the link for Step 4: Install Microsoft Exchange (see Figure 1.16).

Figure 1.16: Launching Exchange setup from the GUI

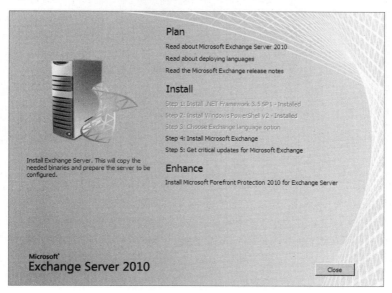

4. The Exchange setup wizard will launch. On the Introduction page, click Next.

5. On the Licensing Agreement page, review the license agreement and select "I accept the terms in the license agreement." Then click Next.

6. On the Error Reporting page, select your error reporting option and click Next.

7. On the Installation Type page, select the option Custom Exchange Server Installation and click Next.

8. On the Server Role Selection page, select the check box for the Management Tools (see Figure 1.17) and click Next.

Figure 1.17: Choosing to install the Management Tools

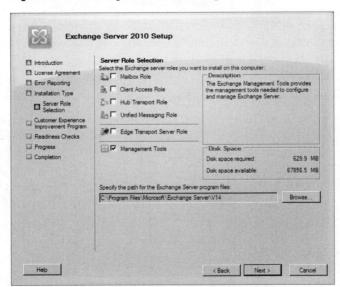

9. On the Exchange Organization page, enter the name of your Exchange organization and click Next.

10. On the next page, the readiness checks will run. This will ensure that your workstation meets the prerequisites for installing the Management Tools and the language packs you selected. If there are any errors reported, you must resolve those errors and rerun the setup. When this completes, click Install.

11. After installation is finished, click the Finish button on the completion page.

Install the Management Tools Using the Command Prompt

You can also use the command prompt to install the Management Tools in unattended mode:

1. Open the command prompt in administrator mode by right-clicking on the Command Prompt icon and selecting Run As Administrator from the drop-down list.
2. Navigate to the folder of the Exchange installation files.
3. Run the following command:

```
setup.com /mode:install /role:managementtools
```

4. Verify that the installation completed by reviewing the output of the command prompt for any errors. If any errors were encountered, correct them and rerun the unattended setup.

Configure Internet Mail Routing

After your Exchange server is installed, one of the more common tasks is to set up Internet mail routing. The depth of procedures to accomplish this will vary depending on your configuration of Exchange. When using the Typical Exchange Installation option in the Exchange setup, you can use the following set of procedures to get Internet mail routing configured. Note that this setup includes using the Hub Transport server to route Internet mail instead of an Edge Transport server.

Create the DNS MX Records

The Mail eXchanger (MX) records in DNS allow mail servers outside of your organization to figure out which server to send mail to. Without MX records, you can route mail inside your Exchange organization, but you will not be able to receive Internet mail.

In DNS, create a record with the type MX that points to the server that is going to route Internet mail for your organization; in this example it's the Hub Transport server. The following record will need to be created:

```
<Domain Name>.    IN    MX    <Priority>    <Server Name>
```

For the Hub Transport server in the contoso.com domain, the MX record would be:

```
contoso.com.    IN    MX    10    contoso-hub.contoso.com
```

To create this record using Windows DNS, follow these steps:

1. Open the DNS management snap-in by clicking Start ➢ Administrative Tools ➢ DNS.

2. In the left panel of the DNS Manager, browse down to the forward lookup zone that represents your domain (see Figure 1.18).

Figure 1.18: Opening the forward lookup zone for your domain in DNS Manager

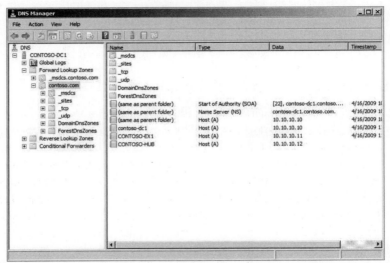

3. Right-click on the zone and select New Mail Exchange (MX) from the drop-down list.

4. For the domain name of the record, ensure that the fully qualified domain name (FQDN) points to the name of the domain that Exchange is authoritative for.

   To accomplish this for contoso.com, the Host Or Child Domain box is left empty. Enter the FQDN of the Hub Transport server in the Fully Qualified Domain Name (FQDN) Of Mail Server box. Then adjust the priority of the record in the Mail Server Priority box and click OK. (See Figure 1.19.)

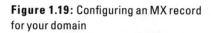

Figure 1.19: Configuring an MX record for your domain

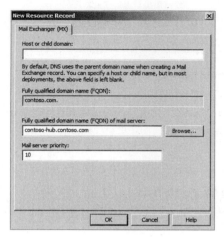

Create the Send Connector

To ensure that Exchange knows how to route outgoing mail, you need to set up at least one send connector. For our example in the Typical Exchange Installation, we'll create one send connector for the Hub Transport server that will route all messages sent to locations outside of the Exchange organization through DNS MX record resolution. The Hub Transport server will use DNS along with public MX records that were published by other mail systems to ensure that the messages are sent to the right place.

Create the Send Connector in the Exchange Management Console

To create the send connector in the Exchange Management Console, follow these steps:

1. Open the Exchange Management Console by clicking Start ➤ All Programs ➤ Microsoft Exchange Server 2010 ➤ Exchange Management Console.

2. In the left pane of the EMC, open the Organization Configuration node and choose Hub Transport.

3. In the center pane, choose the Send Connector tab.

4. In the right pane under Hub Transport Actions, choose the option New Send Connector (see Figure 1.20). The wizard launches.

Figure 1.20: Launching the New Send Connector wizard

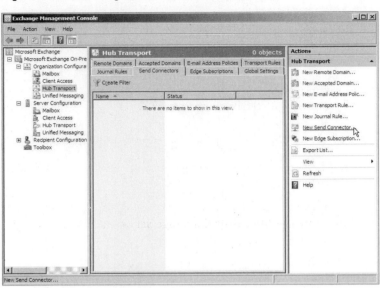

5. In the New Send Connector wizard, type the name of the connector and choose Internet for its intended use.

6. In the Address Space dialog box, click the Add button. This will add a new SMTP address space and open the SMTP Address Space dialog box.

7. In the Address field, enter an asterisk (*). Ensure that you check the box Include All Subdomains, as shown in Figure 1.21. Click OK. Click Next in the wizard.

Figure 1.21: Configuring the Send Connector options

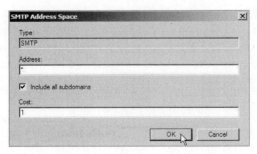

8. In the Network Settings dialog box, select the option Use Dynamic Name System (DNS) "MX" Records To Route Automatically. Click Next.

9. In the Source Servers dialog box, ensure that the correct Hub Transport server is selected and click Next.

10. In the New Connector dialog box, click New. After the new connector is created, click Finish to exit.

Create the Send Connector in the Exchange Management Shell

To create the send connector in the Exchange Management Shell, follow these steps:

1. Start the Exchange Management Shell by clicking Start ➤ All Programs ➤ Microsoft Exchange Server 2010 ➤ Exchange Management Shell.

2. Run the following command:

```
new-SendConnector –Name 'SendConnectorName' ↵
–Usage 'Internet' –AddressSpace 'SMTP:*;1' ↵
–IsScopedConnector $false –DNSRoutingEnabled $true ↵
–UseExternalDNSServersEnabled $false ↵
–SourceTransportServers '<SERVERNAME>'
```

Configure Receive Connector Permissions

Now that you can send email to other people on the Internet, you're halfway there. The Exchange servers also have to be configured to receive email. Since your MX records are published in DNS, other email systems can find you and know which server to send mail to for your domain. However, Hub Transport servers in Exchange are secured by default and do not allow other email systems to send mail to them. This is because in most configurations, Microsoft wants to encourage you to use Edge Transport servers rather than Hub Transport servers for receiving Internet mail. Edge servers offer a wide range of security features that you should consider taking advantage of.

If you are using the Typical Exchange Installation without Edge Transport servers, you can change the permissions on the receive connector for the Hub Transport servers. Receive connectors run on transport servers and listen for incoming mail on a specific port. You will need to modify the default receive connector for routing Internet mail, which listens on port 25 of your Hub Transport server.

Configure the Receive Connector Permissions Using the Exchange Management Console

To configure the receive connector permissions using the Exchange Management Console, follow these steps:

1. Open the Exchange Management Console by clicking Start ➢ All Programs ➢ Microsoft Exchange Server 2010 ➢ Exchange Management Console.

2. In the left pane of the EMC, open the Server Configuration node and choose Hub Transport.

3. At the bottom half of the center pane, choose the Default Receive Connector and in the right pane, select Properties, as shown in Figure 1.22. The Properties dialog box will appear.

Figure 1.22: Opening the properties for the default receive connector

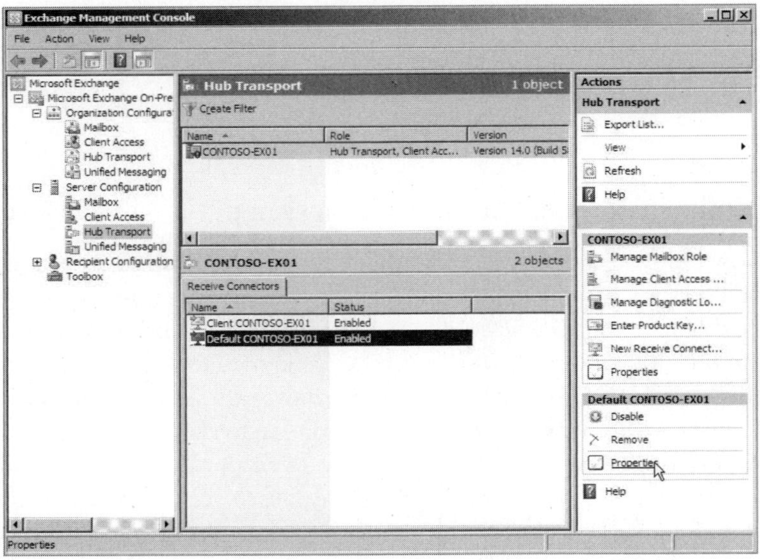

4. In the Properties dialog box, select the Permission Groups tab.

5. Check the box next to Anonymous Users and click OK.

Configure the Receive Connector Permissions Using the Exchange Management Shell

To configure the receive connector permissions using the Exchange Management Shell, follow these steps:

1. Start the Exchange Management Shell by clicking Start ➤ All Programs ➤ Microsoft Exchange Server 2010 ➤ Exchange Management Shell.

2. Run the following command in the EMS:

```
Set-ReceiveConnector -PermissionGroups AnonymousUsers,
ExchangeUsers, ExchangeServers, ExchangeLegacyServers
```

Getting Started

PART I

2

Using the Exchange Management Console and the Exchange Management Shell

IN THIS CHAPTER, YOU WILL LEARN TO:

The administrative aspects of Exchange went through a tremendous transformation in Exchange Server 2007. Exchange Server 2010 builds on this groundwork. At the heart of Exchange administration lies the Exchange Management Console (EMC) and the Exchange Management Shell (EMS). The EMC is graphical and takes the approach of the standard Windows management console tools. EMS, on the other hand, is based on Windows PowerShell. Any administrators who are intent on doing their job successfully must be intimately aware of these two tools. This chapter focuses on using these tools successfully.

Use the Exchange Management Console

As the graphical tool for administering Exchange Server 2010, the Exchange Management Console (EMC) is more commonly used by those who are new to administering Exchange. Many of the common administrative tasks can be performed in the EMC. In this section, you'll take a close look at the EMC and understand the basic features of the tool itself as well as some of the new advanced features in Exchange Server 2010.

Understand the EMC Basics

Understanding how to use the EMC is a key step to successfully administering Exchange. For most people, using the EMC is the first choice for completing an administrative task. So knowing how to use this tool is essential to an administrator's daily life.

Navigate the Management Console

The EMC is based on the Microsoft Management Console (MMC) version 3.0. The MMC is a framework for administrative tools. Any application (even non-Microsoft applications) can provide a snap-in for the MMC. Version 3.0 of the MMC added a new layout, which improves on what was available in version 2.0. Figure 2.1 uses the EMC to depict this layout.

Figure 2.1: The EMC and its components

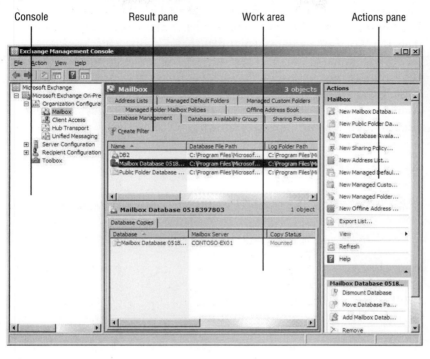

Four panels (also called panes) comprise this tool. The left panel is called the Console tree. The Console tree provides your main point of navigation throughout the snap-in. In the Console tree, you can drill down to different nodes and select the scope of what you are working on. For example, in the EMC, there is a node in the Console tree called Server Configuration. If you expand the Server Configuration node, you have the option to select which type of server you want to administer. Selecting the Mailbox node will populate the other panes with the options and information for administering Mailbox servers.

The middle of the EMC is split into two parts—the Result pane and the Work area. The Result pane is the top half, and it contains the results of what you selected in the Console tree. For example, when you select the Mailbox node in the Console tree, the Result pane will contain a list of Mailbox servers.

The Work area is at the bottom of the EMC. This area displays information about what you've selected in the Result pane. So if you select the Mailbox server EX-MBX1, the Work area will list the storage groups and databases available on that Mailbox server. What you see in the Work area depends on what type of item you select. For example, if you are working with Client Access servers and you select a server in the Result pane, the Work area will display things that pertain to that server.

The last panel on the right side of the EMC is the Actions pane. The Actions pane presents you with several actions that you can perform on the items you have selected in other panes, including the Console tree, Result pane, and Work area. The Actions pane will display a separate section for each of the panes, as shown in Figure 2.2.

Figure 2.2: The Actions pane provides separate sections for each area that you are working with.

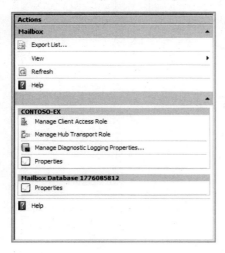

Get Help on a Topic

While working in the EMC, you can get help at any time on the topic that you are currently working with. To do so, select the appropriate Help link in the Actions pane in the EMC. The help files for Exchange Server 2010 are maintained on the Internet, so selecting the Help link will launch the web browser and go to the URL containing the relevant help information. The Help links are context sensitive. This means that you can access multiple Help links if you are working in multiple contexts.

In the following example, we are working in the Recipient node of the EMC. The list of recipients is displayed in the Result pane and we have a specific recipient selected. You'll notice in Figure 2.3 that two Help links are available. The Help link in the top half of the Actions pane will give you help for the Recipient Configuration node of the EMC. The Help link in the bottom half of the Actions pane will give you help on configuring the options for the recipient that you have selected in the Result pane.

Figure 2.3: Context-sensitive help links in the EMC

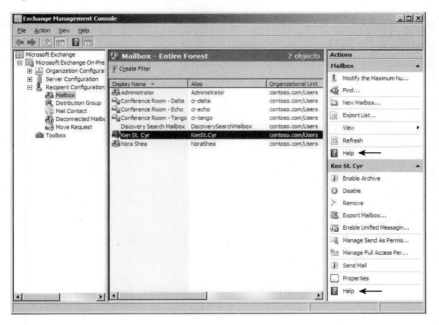

Export Data to a File

At any time in the EMC, you can export the list of data displayed in the Result pane to a file. You can save this list in either a tab-delimited file (columns are separated by tabs) or a comma-delimited file (columns are separated by commas). Both of these files can be imported into Microsoft Excel to give you a way to manipulate the data and run various charts and statistics against it.

To export the contents of the Result pane to a file:

1. In the Actions pane on the right side of the EMC, choose the option Export List.

2. A Save File dialog box will be displayed. Browse to the location where you want to save the file, and in the File Name text box, type the name of the file.

3. In the Save As Type drop-down list, select the type of file that you want to save the results as (tab delimited or comma delimited; text or Unicode text). Click the Save button.

Filter Results

If you have a lot of items in the Result pane, you may have trouble sorting through them all to get the information that you want. At any time, you can filter the list of results and narrow down your options. To do this, you can create a filter in the Result pane and specify the criteria that you want to display. In this example, we'll show all mailboxes on the server CONTOSO-EX.

To filter the results in the Result pane:

1. At the top of the Result pane, click the Create Filter button. This will create an expression for the filter and allow you to select the criteria for the expression.

2. In the first drop-down list in the expression, select Server to create an expression based on the server the mailbox is on.

3. In the middle drop-down list, select Equals.

4. Click the Browse button next to the last text box to select the server that you want to filter the results for. This will launch the Select Mailbox Server dialog box.

5. In the Select Mailbox Server dialog box, choose the server that you want to filter for and click OK.

6. Click the Apply Filter button to apply the filter and only display mailboxes on CONTOSO-EX. This is demonstrated in Figure 2.4.

Figure 2.4: Applying a filter in the EMC

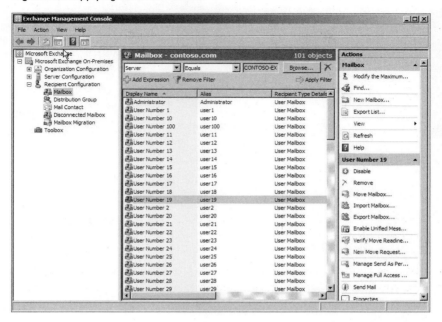

Change the Domain Controller Used for AD Operations

Domain controllers (DCs) are the servers that host Active Directory. Since Exchange uses Active Directory for many things, the EMC needs access to a domain controller on a regular basis. The DC that the EMC uses may not always be the one that you would prefer it to use.

While running the EMC, you can switch to a different domain controller. This is helpful if you are remotely running the EMC on a server and you want to make the changes on a different site's DC so the users in that site don't have to wait for Active Directory replication.

To change the current DC:

1. In the Console tree (the left pane) in the EMC, select the Organization Configuration node.

2. In the Actions pane (the right pane), select the option Modify Configuration Domain Controller. This will launch the Configuration Domain Controller dialog box.

3. In the Configuration Domain Controller dialog box, choose the option Specify A Domain Controller.

4. Click the Browse button next to the Domain text box to search for the domain. The Select Domain dialog box will launch. Click on the appropriate domain in the list of domains and click OK.

5. Click the Browse button next to the Configuration Domain Controller text box to browse for the DC that you want to use. The Select Domain Controller dialog box will launch and a list of DCs for the domain you selected will be available. Click on the DC that you want to use and click OK.

6. In the Configuration Domain Controller dialog box, click OK to switch the DC you selected.

Use Advanced Features

Advanced features of the EMC allow you to manage more complex aspects of the Exchange enterprise.

Manage Additional Exchange Forests

One of the most interesting new features of the EMC is the ability to manage other Exchange organizations in different Active Directory forests. To manage an additional forest, you need to have a trust in place between your Exchange forest and the forest you want to manage. This trust can either be a traditional Windows Active Directory trust or it can be a new Exchange federated trust. This topic is covered in more detail in Chapter 3, "Managing the Organization." To manage an additional forest, you must add that forest to the EMC.

To add an additional Exchange forest to the EMC:

1. In the EMC, select the top node called Microsoft Exchange in the Console tree.

2. In the Actions pane, select the option Add Exchange Forest. This will launch the Add Exchange Forest dialog box.

3. In the Add Exchange Forest dialog box, type the name that you want displayed in the EMC for domain in the "Specify a friendly name for this Exchange forest" text box.

4. Select the correct type of Exchange forest. If you are connecting to an Exchange forest over an Active Directory trust, select the option Microsoft Exchange On-Premises. If you are instead managing a hosted Exchange environment or Exchange over a federated trust, select the option Microsoft Exchange Online.

5. Type the username in the Administrator Identity text box and the password in the Password text box. The account that you use here needs to have permissions to administer the other Exchange organization. The administrative capabilities that you have depend on the role that the account is in. Role-based access is discussed more in Chapter 12, "Securing Exchange Server."

6. In the Remote PowerShell URL text box, enter the URL of the remote PowerShell session that you are connecting to in the other forest.

7. Click OK to close the Add Exchange Forest dialog box and add the Exchange forest to the EMC.

Collect Data about an Exchange Forest

In the EMC, you can view information about an Exchange forest that you are managing. This information is displayed in a summary view and contains data (number of databases, database copies, licenses, etc.) about your organization, servers, and recipients. There is also some limited information on the health of your environment, such as the number of failed database copies, but for the most part, this is statistical data. To view the data about a forest:

1. In the EMC, select an Exchange forest node in the Console tree. The Exchange Forest node is called Microsoft Exchange On-Premises by default and is found directly below the top node in the tree.

2. In the Finalize Deployment tab in the Result pane, you will see three sections: Organization Summary, Servers Summary, and Recipients Summary.

NOTE   If the data is unavailable, you need to gather the organizational information. Unavailable data is represented by a yellow sign with an exclamation point.

Getting Started

PART I

3. Click the Collect Organizational Health Data link in the Actions pane to gather the information to be displayed. This will launch the Collect Organizational Health Data wizard.

4. On the Welcome screen of the Collect Organizational Health Data wizard, select the Immediately option to gather the information now and click Next. You can also schedule the information to be gathered after hours.

5. On the confirmation screen, click the Gather button to collect the data. Depending on the amount of data you have, this may take several moments to complete.

6. After the information is collected, click the Finish button to exit the wizard. The Finalize Deployment tab in the Result pane will now display the organizational statistics that were collected.

Work with the PowerShell Command Log

The Exchange Management Console is nothing more than a front-end interface for PowerShell. When you perform an action in the EMC, the appropriate PowerShell command is launched in the background. Consequently, you can keep and review a log of the PowerShell commands that the EMC uses. To access the PowerShell command log, you must first enable command logging.

Enable PowerShell Command Logging

To enable PowerShell command logging:

1. In the EMC, click View ➢ View Windows PowerShell Command Log.

2. In the PowerShell Command Log window, click Actions ➢ Start Command Log.

3. You can safely close the PowerShell Command Log window now and the EMC will continue to log the commands. The log will remain enabled until you disable it.

After the log is enabled, you can launch the PowerShell Command Log window to access the logs.

View the PowerShell Command Log

To view the PowerShell command log:

1. In the EMC, click View ≻ View Windows PowerShell Command Log to launch the Command Log window.

2. When you are in the command log, you can select one of the entries to view the full command run, as shown in Figure 2.5.

Figure 2.5: Viewing the PowerShell command log

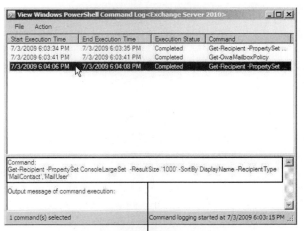

The executed PowerShell command

Review a PowerShell Command Before Use

Every time you make a change to an object in the EMC, there is a PowerShell command being executed in the background. These commands are logged in the command log, as discussed in the previous section. However, when you modify the properties of an object, you can view the PowerShell command that will be used before the change is made. This is a great feature if you want to script a change for a number of users but you aren't sure of the correct PowerShell command. You can open one user, configure the options, and view the command without committing the changes.

To view the PowerShell command used for a property change:

1. Open the object that you want to make changes to. In this example, we'll add a middle initial to a recipient.

    When the change is made in the dialog box, the PowerShell button at the bottom left of the dialog box is illuminated, as shown in Figure 2.6.

Figure 2.6: After a property is changed, the PowerShell button is illuminated.

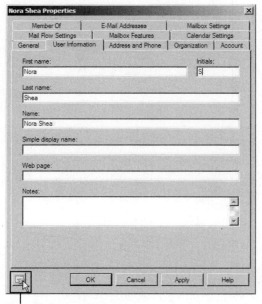

PowerShell command button

2. Click the PowerShell icon in the bottom left of the dialog box.

    This will launch the Exchange Management Shell Command dialog box (Figure 2.7), which will expose the PowerShell command that would be run if you clicked OK in the properties dialog box.

3. You can copy this command by pressing Ctrl+C and use it in a PowerShell script. Click OK to close the Exchange Management Shell Command dialog.

Figure 2.7: The Exchange Management Shell Command dialog box displays the command that will be run.

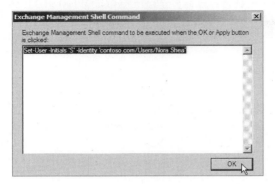

4. In the properties dialog box, click the Cancel button if you want to close the dialog box without saving the changes that you made.

WARNING If you are just changing a property to find out what the EMS command would be, make sure that you click Cancel instead of OK when you close the dialog box, unless you really want to change the property.

Use the Exchange Management Shell

The Exchange Management Shell (EMS) makes up the second half of the administration puzzle for Exchange Server. Unlike the EMC, the EMS is a command-based administrative tool. There is no mouse clicking and there are no pretty graphics. Typos are easy to make. The EMS is not for wimps—it's a tool for hardcore Exchange administrators who want raw power at their fingertips. While the EMC only exposes a fraction of the properties and actions available, the EMS exposes everything that can be changed. Since the EMS is command driven, batch jobs and scripts can be created and run both manually and on an automated schedule. This makes administration much easier in the long run, particularly when you have a task that may need to be repeated in the future. To use the power of the EMS, you need to know how to ask it for what you want. This part of the chapter will show you how to do that.

> **WARNING** Make sure that you know what the command is going to do before you run it. One wrong word and you could wipe out an entire database. Later in this chapter, I show you some ways to test a command before letting it run in the wild.

The EMS is based on Windows PowerShell. PowerShell version 1 was introduced with Windows Server 2008, though you had to install it through the Add Features wizard. (You can download it from www .microsoft.com and install it on Windows Server 2003, Windows XP SP2, and Vista as well.) In the most basic sense, PowerShell is a command interpreter. Much like you do with a command prompt, you type a command, press Enter, and the command executes. But beyond that, PowerShell has some amazing scripting capabilities that take it to the next level in terms of administrative usefulness.

Exchange Server 2010 uses PowerShell version 2, which has multiple enhancements over the version 1 product. The most prominent of the new features is the "remoting" capability, which allows you to use PowerShell remotely to administer computers across the network. This feature is discussed in more detail in the section "Manage Exchange Servers Remotely," later in this chapter.

Understand the Basics of PowerShell

Every effective Exchange administrator should know how to use the EMS. But before you can explore this topic more deeply, you should have a basic understanding of how to use PowerShell. Knowing the essentials of PowerShell will give you the tools that you need to get started with administering Exchange through the EMS. You can build on this knowledge later by learning how to do some of the more advanced administrative tasks with the EMS.

Execute Cmdlets

In PowerShell a cmdlet (pronounced *command-let*) is a precompiled command that you can run. There are several cmdlets built into PowerShell and even more built into the EMS that are geared specifically for Exchange. In Exchange Server 2010, there are over 350 Exchange-specific cmdlets for administration. That might sound daunting, but if you know the basics, then finding the right cmdlet for the right job is a tamable task.

Basic Cmdlet

Each cmdlet has a common structure. This structure is referred to as a *verb-noun pair.* The first part of the cmdlet consists of a verb and the second part consists of a noun. For example, in the Get-Mailbox cmdlet, the verb (Get) tells the cmdlet that it is retrieving information for the noun (Mailbox). As you can probably guess, the Get-Mailbox cmdlet retrieves information for a mailbox in Exchange. All cmdlets are singular, so you will never see a cmdlet called Get-Mailboxes.

To execute a cmdlet in the Exchange Management Shell, you would use the following steps:

1. Open the Exchange Management Shell by clicking Start ➢ All Programs ➢ Microsoft Exchange Server 2010 ➢ Exchange Management Shell.

   After the EMS loads, it will be ready to accept commands. The EMS window will be in the state shown in Figure 2.8.

Figure 2.8: Starting the EMS

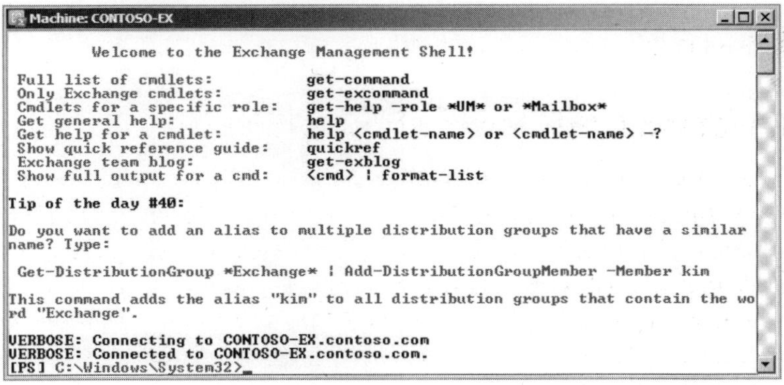

2. Type the cmdlet and press Enter. For example, to get a list of mailboxes in your Exchange organization, you can run the Get-Mailbox cmdlet, as shown in Figure 2.9.

Cmdlet Parameters

You can also feed parameters to cmdlets to use them against specific resources. To specify a parameter, you append the parameter to the end of the cmdlet. For example, if you want to get information on a specific mailbox in your Exchange organization, you can run the same Get-Mailbox cmdlet that you just ran, but this time specify the identity of the mailbox. Figure 2.10 shows the output of the Get-Mailbox cmdlet run against a specific mailbox using a parameter.

Figure 2.9: Running a cmdlet in the EMS

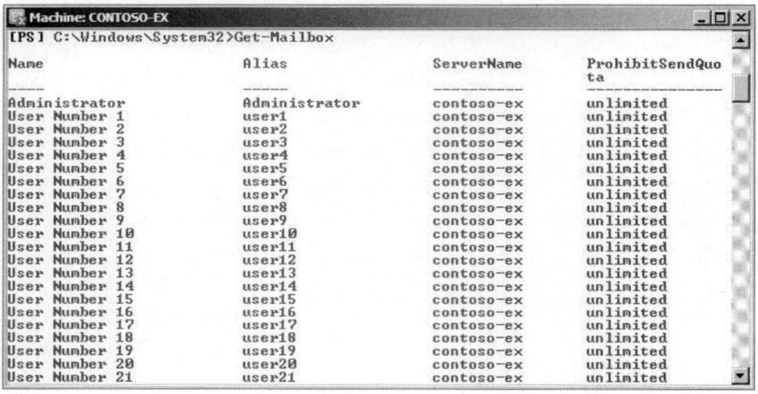

Figure 2.10: Adding a parameter to a cmdlet

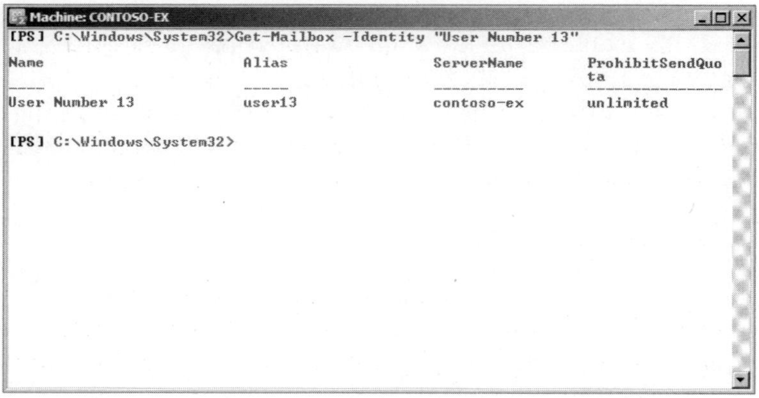

The Identity parameter shown in Figure 2.10 is used in the majority of cmdlets. In fact, if you just add a parameter and don't specify what the parameter is, the cmdlet will assume that it's an Identity parameter. For example, the following cmdlets both have the same output:

```
Get-Mailbox -Identity "Nora Shea"
Get-Mailbox "Nora Shea"
```

NOTE Cmdlets and their parameters are not case sensitive. However, it's a good practice to apply capitalization for cmdlets that other people might read, such as when writing scripts. This increases the readability of the command without affecting the syntax of the cmdlet.

Some of the more common cmdlets also have aliases, which are typically shorter and require you to type less. For example, if you want to clear the screen of all of the PowerShell output that is currently displayed, you can run the `Clear-Host` cmdlet. However, there is an alias for this cmdlet called `cls`. You will probably recognize the `cls` command from the command prompt. So to clear the PowerShell screen, you can run either `Clear-Host` or `cls`. You can get a list of aliased cmdlets by running the `Get-Alias` (or `gal`) cmdlet.

For Exchange administration, one of the more useful cmdlets is `Get-ExCommand`. `Get-ExCommand` retrieves a list of the Exchange cmdlets available.

String Cmdlets Together

By itself, a cmdlet can be a powerful tool. However, for more efficiency, you can string multiple cmdlets together using a process called *pipelining*. When you pipeline two cmdlets, the results of the first cmdlet are fed into the second cmdlet. In order to perform a pipeline, you use the *pipe character* (|). For example, if you want to enable all mailboxes in your organization, you would use the `Get-Mailbox` cmdlet and pipe its output into the `Enable-Mailbox` cmdlet. The cmdlet to accomplish this looks like this:

```
Get-Mailbox | Enable-Mailbox
```

A pipelined cmdlet is also sometimes referred to as a *one-liner*. Advanced Exchange administrators pride themselves on the length of their one-liners. Some consider a long one-liner an administrative badge of honor. One-liners can get complex, but when you start using the EMS regularly, they will become second nature. Some of the complex one-liners can be good substitutes for administrative tasks that require multiple steps. For example, the following one-liner can be run after a Hub Transport server is installed. This one-liner sets the permissions on the Receive connector to allow Internet traffic to it. In the EMC, this task would require multiple steps of opening various dialog boxes and clicking different buttons. Adding this one-liner into your server installation document is a lot easier than describing the EMC steps for accomplishing it.

```
Get-ReceiveConnector | where-object {$_.bindings —match ↵
"0.0.0.0:25"} | Set-ReceiveConnector -PermissionGroups ↵
AnonymousUsers, ExchangeUsers, ExchangeServers, ↵
ExchangeLegacyServers
```

Get Help on a Cmdlet

You can get help on executing any of the Exchange cmdlets using a special cmdlet in EMS called Get-Help. For example, if you're stuck on how to use the Get-Mailbox cmdlet, you can run Get-Help Get-Mailbox to get help on the Get-Mailbox cmdlet. Figure 2.11 shows the output of Get-Help Get-Mailbox cmdlet.

Figure 2.11: Output from the Get-Help Get-Mailbox cmdlet

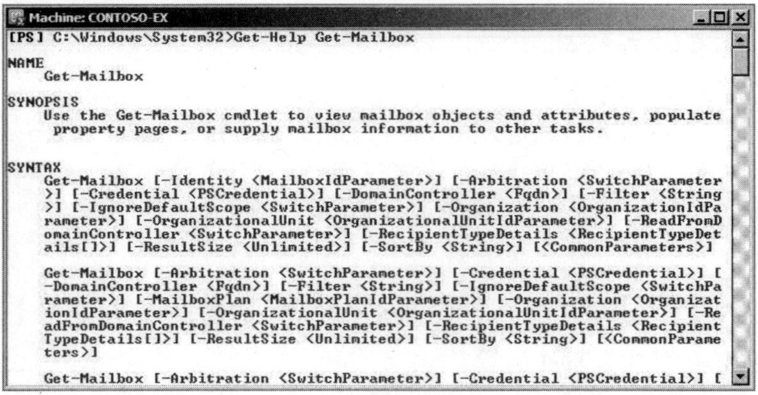

There are various types of help available for cmdlets. If you don't want to read through a large screen full of text just to find out the syntax for a particular command, you can add the Examples parameter to your Get-Help cmdlet. This will only print out examples for the cmdlet. Using the Get-Help Get-Mailbox cmdlet, Figure 2.12 shows the output with the Examples parameter.

Figure 2.12: Using Get-Help with the Examples parameter

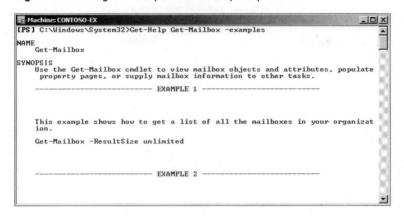

Table 2.1 outlines the various parameters available for use with the Get-Help cmdlet.

Table 2.1: Parameters for the Get-Help Cmdlet

Parameter	Description	Example
Examples	Displays various examples that demonstrate the use of the cmdlet	Get-Help Get-Alias -Examples
Detailed	Displays detailed information on the cmdlet, including a description of each parameter that is accepted	Get-Help Get-Mailbox -Detailed
Full	Displays the full output of the technical information for the cmdlet	Get-Help Get-User -Full

Format the Output of a Command

Sometimes when you run a command, the output is difficult to read or you may not get all of the information you wanted. You can change the output of the cmdlets that you run in various ways. This is accomplished using cmdlets beginning with Format-.

There are multiple Format- cmdlets that will format the output into multiple views. To use them, you simply pipeline the output from one cmdlet into the appropriate format cmdlet. For example, if you want to view the mailboxes in your organization in the format of a list, you can pipeline the output to the `Format-List` cmdlet:

```
Get-Mailbox | Format-List
```

To view the list of available format cmdlets, you can run the cmdlet `Get-Help Format-*`, as shown in Figure 2.13.

Figure 2.13: Getting help on the available formatting options

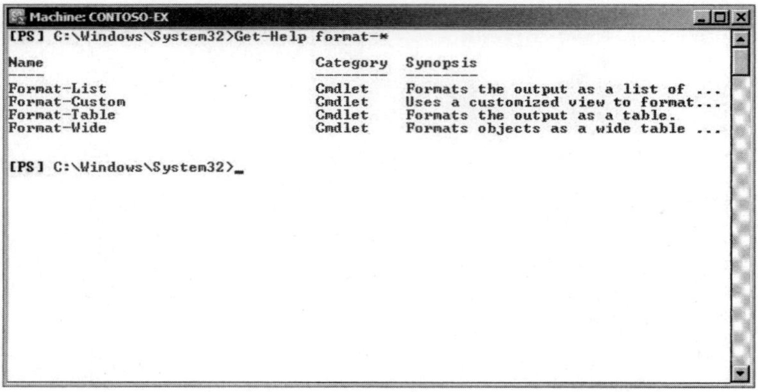

```
Machine: CONTOSO-EX                                                    _|□|x|
[PS] C:\Windows\System32>Get-Help format-*

Name                           Category   Synopsis

Format-List                    Cmdlet     Formats the output as a list of ...
Format-Custom                  Cmdlet     Uses a customized view to format...
Format-Table                   Cmdlet     Formats the output as a table.
Format-Wide                    Cmdlet     Formats objects as a wide table ...


[PS] C:\Windows\System32>_
```

Test What a Command Will Do

There may be times when you just want to see the output of a particular command to make sure that you have it right, without making the actual change in your environment. This is especially useful when writing PowerShell scripts, which is covered in the section "Script Administration Tasks," later in this chapter.

To find out what is affected by a command without actually running it, you can use the -WhatIf parameter. For example, Figure 2.14 illustrates what will happen if you run the `New-Mailbox` cmdlet.

Perhaps you're just trying to figure out if you have the syntax of a cmdlet right, but you don't want to accidentally run the cmdlet if you happen to get it right. In this case, you can use the -Confirm parameter. This adds a confirmation prompt to your command that requires additional input by the executor before it continues. Figure 2.15 applies the -Confirm parameter to a `Remove-Mailbox` command to prevent the administrator from accidentally deleting a mailbox.

Figure 2.14: Testing what a cmdlet will do before running it

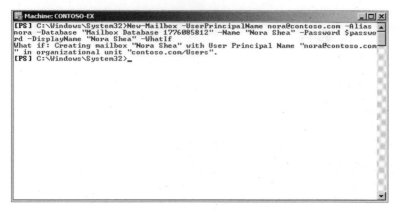

```
Machine: CONTOSO-EX                                                    _ □ x
[PS] C:\Windows\System32>New-Mailbox -UserPrincipalName nora@contoso.com -Alias
nora -Database "Mailbox Database 1776085812" -Name "Nora Shea" -Password $passwo
rd -DisplayName "Nora Shea" -WhatIf
What if: Creating mailbox "Nora Shea" with User Principal Name "nora@contoso.com
" in organizational unit "contoso.com/Users".
[PS] C:\Windows\System32>_
```

Figure 2.15: Using the -Confirm parameter to prevent an accidental change

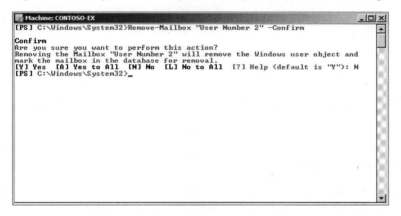

```
Machine: CONTOSO-EX                                                    _ □ x
[PS] C:\Windows\System32>Remove-Mailbox "User Number 2" -Confirm

Confirm
Are you sure you want to perform this action?
Removing the Mailbox "User Number 2" will remove the Windows user object and
mark the mailbox in the database for removal.
[Y] Yes  [A] Yes to All  [N] No  [L] No to All  [?] Help (default is "Y"): N
[PS] C:\Windows\System32>_
```

Script Administration Tasks

Aside from offering a robust environment for executing cmdlets, PowerShell also provides an integrated environment for writing scripts. Like one-liners, scripts allow you to execute a series of commands all at once, without having to enter each command individually. For example, if you have a list of commands that you run every time an Exchange Hub Transport server is installed, you can put those commands into a script. Then the next time you install a Hub Transport server, you just run the script once instead of executing each command.

Scripts are also useful if you want to apply some logic to a series of commands. For example, you could write a script to count the number of users in the mailbox databases on an Exchange Mailbox server and then create a new user in the database that has the least amount of users in it. The script would automatically make the decision about where to place the user.

Create PowerShell Scripts

PowerShell scripts are contained in files with the .ps1 extension. PowerShell version 2 provides a new Integrated Scripting Environment (ISE) for writing PowerShell scripts with more ease. The ISE provides some great capabilities that are typically found in expensive development environments. Full development environments offer additional features that justify the cost if you will be writing a lot of code, but if you're just looking for basic debugging and script writing, you need look no further than the ISE.

To launch the ISE:

1. Click on the Start menu and select All Programs ➢ Windows PowerShell V2 ➢ Windows PowerShell ISE.

   The ISE will be launched, as shown in Figure 2.16.

2. To use the Exchange commands in the ISE, you will need to establish a session to the Exchange Server, even if you are already logged on to the server locally. To do this, follow the procedures in the section "Connect Remotely Through PowerShell" later in this chapter.

The ISE consists of three panels that assist you in writing scripts.

Script Editor   The top panel is the script editor. This is where you type the script. The tab that you have selected in the editor is the current script that you are working in. The button with the arrow allows you to execute the script. One of the nice features of the ISE is that it allows real-time script debugging. This allows you to stop your script at certain points to examine the content inside of variables or step through the script one line at a time to troubleshoot it.

Command Pane   The bottom panel is the command pane. The command pane allows you to type in PowerShell commands and execute them just as if you were using a regular PowerShell session.

This can be helpful during scripting because it lets you check the syntax of your commands without having to debug your script.

Output Pane When you run the script or launch a command in the command pane, the output appears in the middle panel, which is called the output pane. The output pane will display the output of the commands just like in a typical PowerShell session. In the output pane, you have full copy and paste capabilities, so you can copy text from your output and place it in your script.

Figure 2.16: Launching the Integrated Scripting Environment

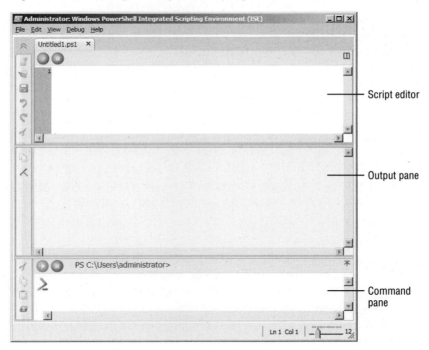

The ISE isn't the only way to create PowerShell scripts. PowerShell scripts can be created with any text editor. This includes the built in utilities such as Notepad and Wordpad, along with third-party development environments.

Use Variables in a Script

You could just write scripts to execute one command after another, but
PowerShell scripts can be more than mere substitutes for batch files. To
take your scripting to the next level and write more powerful scripts, you'll
need to learn some of the basics of scripting, starting with variables.

Variables are nothing more than a way to temporarily store data for
later use. In PowerShell, variables are easy to work with because they
can hold any type of data, such as text or numbers.

NOTE   Some other development languages require you to define
what kind of data your variables will hold up front, but this is not
the case with PowerShell.

Variables in PowerShell all begin with a dollar sign ($). For example,
if you wanted to create a variable and hold a sentence in it, you would
use the following PowerShell command:

```
$MySentence = "Exchange Server 2010 Rocks!"
```

What we just did in this example was store the text string "Exchange
Server 2010 Rocks!" in the variable called $MySentence. You can name
variables anything you want, as long as they begin with a dollar sign.
Here's another example, except this time we'll store a number:

```
$MyInteger = 1234567890
```

You'll notice that we didn't use the quotation marks this time. You
only use quotation marks for text strings. You have to use quotation
marks for text so PowerShell knows you are using text and not trying
to run a PowerShell cmdlet instead.

You can store data other than text and numbers in variables. For
example, the following command is valid in PowerShell:

```
$DirectoryListing = Dir
```

This command runs the PowerShell command Dir, which lists the files
and folders in the current directory and stores the output in the variable
called $DirectoryListing. $DirectoryListing doesn't just contain the text
of the output from the Dir command. Instead, $DirectoryListing stores
each of the files and folders as objects with their own properties. This

allows you to do some interesting things. For example, you could go through the file and folder objects in the $DirectoryListing variable and rename them.

Variables can contain many types of objects. The type of object that is stored in the variable depends on the output of the command that is populating the variable. The Dir command we used in the example works with files and folders, so it stores file and folder objects. If you used an Exchange command, such as Get-Mailbox, it would store the mailbox object and its associated properties into the variable.

You can see what variables are currently being used by running the Get-Variable cmdlet, as shown in Figure 2.17.

Figure 2.17: Listing the variables currently in use

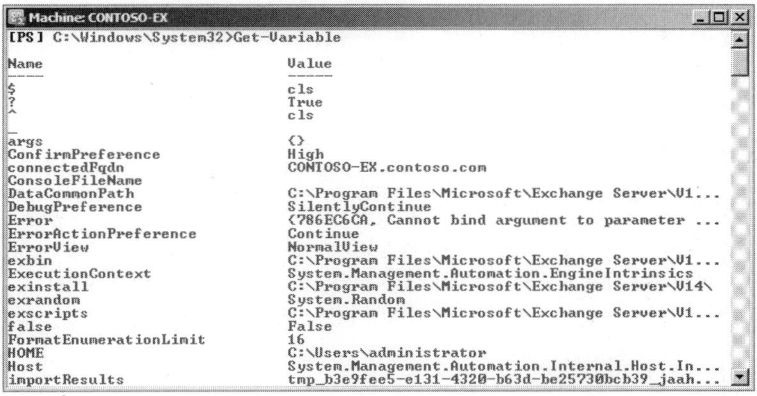

In addition to variables that you define yourself, there are special variables built into PowerShell called *shell variables*. Shell variables are automatically created by PowerShell. An example of a shell variable is the $null variable. $null always means that something has no value. For example, if you had an Exchange recipient object and you wanted to clear the Notes property, you could set the Notes property to $null. This can be accomplished with the following command:

```
Set-User "Lincoln Alexander" -Notes $null
```

There are many other shell variables in PowerShell. Table 2.2 lists some of the more common shell variables that you will encounter.

Table 2.2: Common Shell Variables

Variable	Description
$_	Refers to the current object that is being processed in a pipeline or a loop.
$Error	When an error is encountered in the command, the error is stored here.
$ExBin	Contains the location where Exchange Server is installed.
$ExScripts	Contains the location of the Exchange scripts.
$Home	The home directory of the current user.
$true	Represents the condition **True**.
$false	Represents the condition **False**.
$null	Represents a null entry, meaning the property is blank.

Add Logic to a Script

Logic allows your scripts to do things to the variables you're using and make decisions about what to do. There are two basic logic concepts that you need to know for writing PowerShell scripts: loops and conditionals.

Loops

Loops allow you to go through a collection of items and do something to each item. For example, if you just run the Get-Mailbox cmdlet on one of your Exchange Mailbox servers, the EMS displays a list of mailboxes on that server. However, you can assign the output of Get-Mailbox to a variable, using the following command:

```
$MailboxesOnServer = Get-Mailbox
```

In the $MailboxesOnServer variable, each mailbox is represented by a different object. I could loop through the objects in this variable and do something to each object, such as display the DisplayName of each mailbox. One way to accomplish this is with the ForEach-Object cmdlet:

```
$MailboxesOnServer | ForEach-Object { Write-Host ↵
$_.DisplayName }
```

By piping the $MailboxesOnServer variable into the ForEach-Object cmdlet, the ForEach-Object cmdlet can cycle through all of the objects. The command inside of the curly brackets ({...}) is executed for each of the objects processed by the loop. You may recognize the $_ variable from Table 2.2. The $_ variable references the current object that the loop is processing. So when $_.DisplayName is used, we're working with the DisplayName property on each of the objects in the variable. In this case, we're calling the Write-Host cmdlet to output the DisplayName of each mailbox to the screen.

Another type of loop that you can use is the Do loop. The Do loop allows you to loop until a specific condition is met. There are two types of Do loops: Do … While and Do … Until.

In a Do … While loop, a block of script code is executed over and over again as long as something is happening. For example, consider the following script code snippet:

```
$counter = 0
Do
{
    Write-Host "Current Number: $counter"
    $counter++;
} While ($counter -lt 3)
```

If you were to run this code in a .ps1 script, the output would read:

```
Current Number: 0
Current Number: 1
Current Number: 2
```

The Do statement loops through the code inside the curly brackets as long as the condition specified in the While statement is valid. In this example, the Do loop will keep going as long as the $counter variable is less than 3 (-lt 3). After $counter reaches 3, the loop stops and therefore only the numbers 0, 1, and 2 are displayed. So with a Do … While loop, the code inside the curly brackets is executed first and then the condition determining whether it should keep going is evaluated.

On the other hand, a Do … Until statement processes the condition first. To understand this, we'll turn the previous code into a Do … Until loop:

```
$counter = 0
Do
{
```

```
    Write-Host "Current Number: $counter"
    $counter++;
} Until ($counter -gt 3)
```

This time, the Do loop is going to continue to process until $counter is greater than 3. Before the code in the Do loop is processed even once, the condition is evaluated to make sure $counter is still 3 or lower. The following is the output if this code were run in a script:

```
Current Number: 0
Current Number: 1
Current Number: 2
Current Number: 3
```

After the script displays that the current number is 3, $counter is incremented to 4. This causes the condition ($counter -gt 3) to be met because 4 is greater than 3 and the Do loop is no longer processed.

Conditionals

In addition to loops, you can use conditionals to make decisions inside your scripts. One conditional that you will probably use often is the If … Else conditional. The If statement tests whether something is true. If it is, it executes some code. If not, the If statement can either end or test to see if something else is true. For example, consider the following If statement:

```
$MailStats = Get-MailboxStatistics -Database "DB1"
$MailStats | ForEach-Object
{
  If ($_.ItemCount -eq 0)
  {
    Write-Host $_.DisplayName ": Mailbox is Empty"
  }
  Else
  {
    Write-Host $_.DisplayName ":"$_.ItemCount "Items Found"
  }
}
```

If you were to execute this script, the output would list every empty mailbox on the database named DB1. The ForEach-Object command loops through all of the mailboxes on DB1. For each mailbox, the If statement is evaluated. The If statement checks to see if the number of items in the mailbox is equal to 0. If so, it writes to the screen that it found an empty mailbox and displays the name of the mailbox. If the number of items is not equal to zero, the Else statement is executed and instead the script outputs to the screen the name of the mailbox and the number of items it found.

The -eq parameter indicates that the If statement is checking whether $_.ItemCount and 0 are equal. In typical programming languages, this is usually accomplished with the symbols == or =. Instead, PowerShell uses the comparison operators listed in Table 2.3.

Table 2.3: PowerShell Comparison Operators

Comparison Operator	Description	Example
-eq	Determines if expression1 is equal to expression2	"Exchange 2010" -eq "Exchange 2K10" False
-ne	Determines if expression1 is not equal to expression2	"Exchange 2010" -ne "Exchange 2K10" True
-gt	Determines if expression1 is greater than expression2	1000 -gt 50 True
-ge	Determines if expression1 is greater than or equal to expression2	1000 -ge 1000 True
-lt	Determines if expression1 is less than expression2	1000 -lt 50 False
-le	Determines if expression1 is less than or equal to expression2	1000 -le 1000 True
-like	Determines if expression1 is equal to expression2 using the wildcard character (*)	"Exchange 2010" -like "Exch*" True
-notlike	Determines if expression1 is not equal to expression2 using the wildcard character (*)	"Exchange 2010" -notlike "Ex*10" False

Table 2.3: PowerShell Comparison Operators *(continued)*

Comparison Operator	Description	Example
-match	Uses a regular expression to determine if expression1 matches expression2	"Exchange 2010" -match "[abc]" True
-notmatch	Uses a regular expression to determined if expression1 does not match expression2	"Exchange 2010" -notmatch "[abc]" False
-contains	Determines if a specific item is in a group of items	"Exchange 2010", "Exchange 2007" -contains "Exchange 2007" True
-notcontains	Determines if a specific item is not in a group of items	"Exchange 2010", "Exchange 2007" -notcontains "Exchange 2007" False

In addition to the If statement, you can use the Where-Object command. Where-Object will evaluate the objects that are piped into it and filter out everything that doesn't meet the expression that you set. For example, you can use the following Where-Object command in a script to filter out all mailboxes that are empty:

```
Get-Mailbox -Database "DB1" | WhereObject { $_.ItemCount ↵
-gt 0 } | ForEach-Object { Write-Host "Size of" ↵
$_.DisplayName":" $_.TotalItemSize
```

In this command, the Where-Object cmdlet is passing through every mailbox that has more than zero items in it. The mailboxes that are passed through the filter are piped into the ForEach-Object cmdlet so they can be further processed and the information is displayed on the screen.

Run a Script Outside of PowerShell

When you write a .ps1 script, you can run that script anytime you are in a PowerShell session. But you can also run scripts without opening PowerShell manually. The process is similar to running a batch file outside of the command prompt. You can double-click on the script and PowerShell will be automatically opened, your script will run, and then PowerShell will close.

By default, when you double-click on a PowerShell .ps1 script file, the file opens in Notepad. You can use the following procedures to launch the file in PowerShell:

1. Browse to the PowerShell .ps1 script file that you want to launch.

2. Right-click on the file and select Run With PowerShell from the drop-down menu, as shown in Figure 2.18.

Figure 2.18: Launching a PowerShell script outside of PowerShell

The PowerShell script will launch and run in PowerShell. Power-Shell will be closed when the script completes.

You can also change the file association to PowerShell instead of Notepad. This will ensure that when you double-click on the script, it opens in PowerShell automatically.

To change the .ps1 file association:

1. Open Control Panel and run the Default Programs applet.

2. When the Default Programs applet launches, select the option Associate A File Type Or Protocol With A Program.

3. In the Set Associations dialog box, scroll down to the .ps1 file extension and click on it to select it. Click the Change Program button above the list of file types, as shown in Figure 2.19.

Figure 2.19: Changing the default program for PowerShell scripts

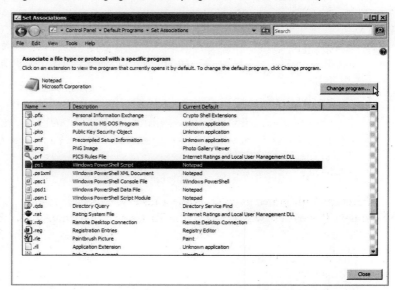

4. When the Open With dialog box opens, click the Browse button to locate the PowerShell executable. This executable is stored at C:\Windows\System32\WindowsPowerShell\v2.0\ powershell.exe. Select the powershell.exe file and click Open to choose it.

5. Click OK in the Open With dialog box to choose Windows PowerShell and set the file association.

6. Close the Default Programs applet and any remaining windows. Now when you double-click on a .ps1 file, it will launch with PowerShell instead of Notepad.

Schedule a Script to Run Later

Sometimes you will want to create a script and have it run repeatedly at a specified interval. Windows Server 2008 has a powerful task scheduler service that allows you set up programs to launch in a very flexible manner. If you want to schedule a script to run at a later time or after a specified interval, you can schedule the script to run with the Task Scheduler. A couple of things need to be in place beforehand to make this successful:

- PowerShell .ps1 script files need to be associated with the PowerShell.exe program, or you need to have the scheduler execute the command PowerShell.exe MyScript.ps1 to launch the script in the scheduled task.

- If you're executing a script that contains Exchange cmdlets, you need to have the script remotely connect to the Exchange PowerShell session first, even if the script is running on the Exchange server locally.

There are multiple ways to schedule a task with the Windows Task Scheduler. The easiest way is to use the Task Scheduler snap-in. In this example, we'll use the Task Scheduler to create a task that does the following things:

- Run a script every night that collects mailbox statistics for all mailboxes on a database. In this example, the script is named GetDB1Stats.ps1. This is a script that we created ourselves and it is not installed with Exchange. In our fake script, the statistics are saved in the file C:\Stats\DB1Stats.log.

- Email the statistics file to the mail-enabled distribution group called ExchangeTeam@contoso.com.

To create the scheduled task:

1. Click Start ➤ Administrative Tools ➤ Task Scheduler. The Task Scheduler launches.

2. In the Actions pane on the right side of the Task Scheduler snap-in, choose the option Create Task. This will launch the Create Task dialog box.

3. On the General tab, give the task a name and choose the option Run Whether User Is Logged On Or Not. Set the account that you want the script to run under using the Change User Or Group button. Ensure that the account running the script has the appropriate permissions for Exchange. Figure 2.20 shows these options.

Figure 2.20: Selecting the appropriate permissions for scheduling a script

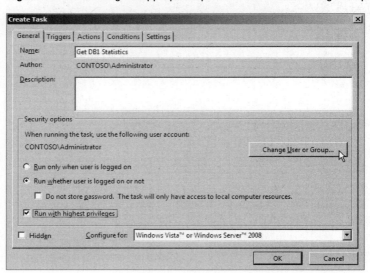

4. Click the Triggers tab and click the New button to create a new trigger for the task. We'll set this task to run every night at 1:00 a.m.

5. Click the Actions tab and choose the New button to create a new Action for this task to perform. In the Actions drop-down list, choose Start A Program. In the Program/Script text box, type **powershell.exe**. In the Add Arguments text box, type the location of the script:

   ```
   C:\Scripts\GetDB1Stats.ps1
   ```

   These options are shown in Figure 2.21. Click OK in the New Actions dialog box.

6. When you're back on the Actions tab, click the New button to add another action. In the New Actions dialog box, select Send An E-mail from the Actions list. Fill out the options for the email message. Type **C:\Stats\DB1Stats.log** in the Attachment text box and enter your Exchange SMTP server name in the SMTP Server text box. Click OK to add the action.

7. When you're back in the Create Task dialog box, click OK to create the task. You may be prompted to enter the password for the account that the task is going to run under.

Figure 2.21: Selecting the appropriate action for running a PowerShell script

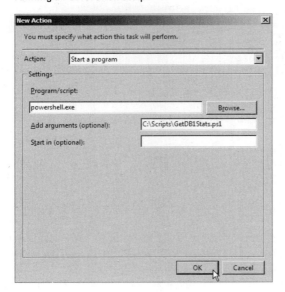

Manage Exchange Servers Remotely

One of the biggest enhancements in the Exchange Management Shell for Exchange Server 2010 is the ability to remotely administer Exchange servers. All Exchange servers except for the Edge Transport server can be managed through the remote management shell. To pull this off, Exchange uses a combination of PowerShell version 2 and Windows Remote Management (WinRM) 2.0. PowerShell provides the command-line interface for executing commands, and WinRM provides the transport from the local system to the remote system.

One of the big benefits of the remote management shell is that you do not have to install the Exchange Management Tools on the computer that you are managing Exchange from. The only things you need installed are PowerShell version 2 and WinRM 2.0. This saves administrators from having to install the Exchange Management Tools at each workstation they use or having to deploy the tools through software distribution mechanisms. Also, the remote management shell allows you to administer your 64-bit Exchange servers from a 32-bit workstation. (Since there is no 32-bit version of Exchange available, there is no 32-bit version of the Management Tools.)

Allow an Administrator to Use PowerShell Remotely

Before the remote shell can be used, administrators have to be given access to it. By default, only the account that you use to install Exchange will be enabled for the remote PowerShell capability. To enable this capability for additional users, you use the Set-User cmdlet with the RemotePowerShellEnabled parameter. The following example command gives remote capability to the user named "Nora Shea":

```
Set-User "Nora Shea" -RemotePowerShellEnabled $True
```

You can disable the remote shell for a user by setting the RemotePowerShellEnabled parameter to $False. The example disables remote shell for "Nora Shea":

```
Set-User "Nora Shea" -RemotePowerShellEnabled $False
```

To launch this command, open the EMS and run the following command, substituting for *UserName* the name of the user that you want to enable the remote management shell for:

```
Set-User UserName -RemotePowerShellEnabled $True
```

The things that you can do with remote shell are controlled using the new Role-Based Access Control (RBAC) capabilities in Exchange. Using RBAC, administrators are assigned management roles. The management role that an administrator is assigned will determine which cmdlets and settings the administrator has access to. If you enabled the remote PowerShell capability for an administrator and you assign her the Organization Management role, she can remotely use PowerShell to manage the organization. The topic of leveraging RBAC for managing permissions is discussed in more detail in Chapter 12.

Connect Remotely Through PowerShell

The connections for the remote shell are handled by Internet Information Services (IIS) running on the Exchange server. There is an IIS virtual directory for PowerShell. Even when you use the Exchange Management Shell locally, you are still connecting through IIS on the local server. Therefore, you will need to make sure that you can access the Exchange server over the HTTP Secure Sockets Layer (SSL) port, 443. Because you are using SSL, you must trust the certificate that the Exchange server is using. This is covered in the upcoming section, "Overcome the Certificate Check."

PowerShell uses the concept of *sessions*. A session is an instance of the shell that has its own portion of memory separate from other instances. For example, two cmdlets in a single session can access the same variables. When you use PowerShell on your workstation, you are using the *local session*. If you were to connect to an Exchange server remotely with PowerShell, you would be using the session on the Exchange server, which is referred to as the *server-side session*.

To connect your local PowerShell to an Exchange session remotely, you need to use the New-PSSession cmdlet. After you run this cmdlet, you have two sessions running:

- Your local session (the client-side session)

- The server-side session that is connected to Exchange

At this point, your sessions are still separate. To join them, you need to run an additional cmdlet called Import-PSSession. Running this cmdlet will give your local session access to everything that you are allowed to do through your assigned roles. You will be able to run an Exchange command in your local session and have it execute in the server-side session on the Exchange server.

Connect Remotely with Your Current Log-In Credentials

You can use the following steps to establish a remote PowerShell connection to Exchange with your current log-in credentials:

1. Run PowerShell from your workstation by clicking Start ➢ All Programs ➢ Windows PowerShell V2 ➢ Windows PowerShell V2.

2. When PowerShell opens, run the following command to create the remote session and store it in the variable called $Session. Replace contoso-ex1.contoso.com with the name of your Exchange Server 2010 computer:

```
$Session = New-PSSession -ConfigurationName ↵
Microsoft.Exchange -ConnectionUri ↵
https://contoso-ex1.contoso.com/PowerShell/ ↵
-Authentication NegotiateWithImplicitCredential
```

3. Import the remote session that you created by running the following command:

```
Import-PSSession $Session
```

4. After you are finished with your PowerShell session, run the following command to disconnect it:

```
Remove-PSSession $Session
```

Connect Remotely with Different Credentials

If your administrator account is separate from the one you are using to log in to your workstation, you would previously have needed to run PowerShell with the Run As command in order to run the administrator tools. This approach is limited because the workstation must be joined to the domain or be in a domain that is trusted. If you're administering your Exchange server from your home computer, however, this is not always possible. Instead, you can supply your credentials remotely with PowerShell.

To connect remotely using different credentials:

1. Run PowerShell from your workstation by clicking Start ➣ All Programs ➣ Windows PowerShell V2 ➣ Windows PowerShell V2.

2. When PowerShell opens, run the following command to create the remote session, instruct PowerShell to prompt you for different credentials, and have PowerShell store the session in the $Session variable (replace contoso-ex1.contoso.com with the name of your Exchange server):

```
$Session = New-PSSession -ConfigurationName ↵
Microsoft.Exchange -ConnectionUri ↵
https://contoso-ex1.contoso.com/PowerShell/ ↵
-Credential Get-Credential
```

3. The Windows PowerShell Credential Request dialog box is displayed. Enter your username and password and click OK.

4. Import the remote session that you created by running the following command:

```
Import-PSSession $Session
```

5. After you are finished with your PowerShell session, run the following command to disconnect it:

```
Remove-PSSession $Session
```

Overcome the Certificate Check

When you use remote PowerShell, you are connecting to a service running in IIS on the Exchange server. This service communicates with your client securely using SSL on port 443. In order for you to trust the Exchange server, you have to trust the certificate that it's using. By default, the Exchange server uses a self-signed certificate. To trust the self-signed certificate, you must import it into the Trusted Root Certificate Authorities on your client. This is a two-step process:

1. You must export the certificate from the Exchange server into a file that your client can import.

2. You must import the certificate file into the client.

You can also bypass the certificate check. All these procedures are covered in this section.

Export the Certificate into a File

To export the certificate from the Exchange server, follow these steps:

1. Log into the Exchange server and run mmc.exe from the command prompt. Press Ctrl+M to add a new snap-in to the MMC.

2. In the Add Or Remove Snap-ins dialog box, select the Certificates snap-in and click the Add button.

3. A dialog box will launch asking you which certificates you want to manage. Select the option Computer Account and click the Next button.

4. In the Select Computer dialog box, ensure that Local Computer is selected and click the Finish button.

5. Back in the Add Or Remove Snap-ins dialog box, click OK to close the dialog box.

6. In the left pane of the snap-in, browse down to Personal\ Certificates.

7. In the right pane, select the certificate that corresponds to the Exchange server. The name of the Exchange server will show up in the Issued To column, as shown in Figure 2.22.

8. Right-click on the certificate and choose All Tasks ➤ Export from the context menu. This will launch the Certificate Export Wizard. You will use this wizard to save the certificate to a file.

Figure 2.22: Exporting the Exchange server's certificate

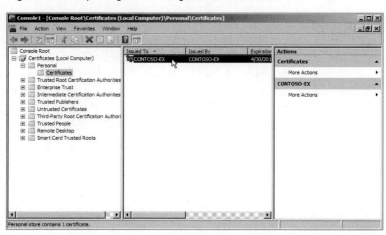

9. When the wizard launches, click Next on the Welcome screen.

10. At the Export Private Key screen, ensure that "No, do not export the private key" is selected and click Next.

11. At the Export File Format screen, select the option Cryptographic Message Syntax Standard - PKCS #7 Certificates (.P7B) and click Next.

12. At the File To Export screen, type the name of the file that you want to save the certificate to—for example, `c:\users\public\contoso-ex.p7b`.

13. On the last screen of the certificate wizard, click the Finish button to save the certificate to the file. When this is completed successfully, you'll get a confirmation screen stating that the export was successful.

Import the Certificate File into the Client

The certificate file can be on a network share or can be copied manually to your client. Since it's just the public key of the server, there are no security concerns with transferring this file across the network.

To import the file into a Windows Vista SP1 client:

1. Log into your Windows Vista SP1 client, and using Windows Explorer, browse to the location of the certificate file that you exported from the Exchange server.

2. Right-click on the file in Windows Explorer and select Install Certificate from the context menu. This will launch the Certificate Import Wizard.

3. At the Welcome screen of the Certificate Import Wizard, click the Next button.

4. At the Certificate Store screen, select "Place all certificates in the following store" and then click the Browse button.

5. At the Select Certificate Store screen, select the Trusted Root Certification Authorities store, as shown in Figure 2.23, and click OK. Click the Next button when you're back in the Certificate Store screen.

Figure 2.23: Importing the certificate into the correct certificate store

6. In the completion screen of the wizard, click the Finish button to import the certificate into your Trusted Root Certification Authorities store. If the import was successful, you will see a confirmation screen.

Disable the Remote PowerShell Certificate Check

You can disable the remote PowerShell certificate check entirely. Bypassing the check means you will not be required to trust the certificate from the Exchange server. The remote PowerShell session will still communicate with SSL over port 443, but you will not validate the certificate on the Exchange server.

WARNING Bypassing the certificate check poses a security risk. An attacker could redirect you to a rogue Exchange server with the same name by using a name resolution exploit.

The certificate check is disabled when you create the remote connection using the New-PSSession cmdlet. You can set the options for skipping the certificate check and store the command in a variable that you pass into the New-PSSession cmdlet. You can do this manually each time you open a PowerShell session, or you can insert the command into your PowerShell profile.

Manually Disable the Certificate Check

To disable the certificate check manually, perform these steps every time you open a new PowerShell session:

1. Run PowerShell from your workstation by clicking Start ➣ All Programs ➣ Windows PowerShell V2 ➣ Windows PowerShell V2.

2. When PowerShell opens, run the following command to set the variable for skipping the certificate check:

```
$SkipCertCheck = New-PSSessionOption -SkipCACheck
-SkipCNCheck -SkipRevocationCheck
```

3. Follow the steps in the section, "Connect Remotely Through PowerShell," for establishing a remote PowerShell session. But this time, when you create the session object with the New-PSSession cmdlet, append -SessionOption $SkipCertCheck to the end of the command. The following command demonstrates this:

```
$Session = New-PSSession -ConfigurationName ↵
Microsoft.Exchange -ConnectionUri ↵
https://contoso-ex1.contoso.com/PowerShell/ ↵
-Authentication NegotiateWithImplicitCredential ↵
-SessionOption $SkipCertCheck
```

Every time you open PowerShell, you will have to repopulate the $SkipCertCheck variable because it's not saved.

Disable the Certificate Check in Your PowerShell Profile

Instead of disabling the certificate check manually every time you open a PowerShell session, you can insert the command into your PowerShell profile. Then when you open PowerShell, your profile is run and the variable will be set for you. When you create the session to the Exchange server, you can specify the SessionOption parameter with the variable.

To store the command in your PowerShell profile:

1. Run PowerShell from your workstation by clicking Start ➤ All Programs ➤ Windows PowerShell V2 ➤ Windows PowerShell V2.

2. When PowerShell opens, run the following command to edit your profile:

   ```
   Notepad.exe $Profile.CurrentUserAllHosts
   ```

3. The profile will open in Notepad. If you receive a message stating that the file doesn't exist, that means that your profile hasn't yet been created. You'll save it in step 5.

4. In your PowerShell profile script, add the commands shown in Figure 2.24. (Replace contoso-ex1.contoso.com with the name of your Exchange server.)

Figure 2.24: Adding the remote session commands to your PowerShell profile script

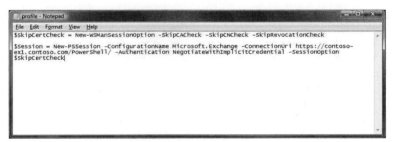

5. In Notepad, click File ➤ Save. If you're prompted for a filename, browse to the folder C:\%HOMEPATH%\. In this folder, create the folder called WindowsPowerShell if it doesn't already exist. Save the profile as profile.ps1 in the WindowsPowerShell folder.

Getting Started

PART I

Create a LaunchRemoteShell Script

Instead of adding a $SkipCertCheck variable to your profile and individually typing the commands to create the remote PowerShell session, you can create a custom script to do all of this for you. You can type the following script into a .ps1 file, such as LaunchRemoteShell.ps1. Then when you want to connect to Exchange remotely, just run LaunchRemoteShell.ps1.

In your script, be sure you tailor the New-PSSession command to the authentication method that you want to use. Also, make sure that the ConnectionUri property of the session object points to your Exchange server. This script will run the shell under the context of the currently logged-in user.

Example LaunchRemoteShell.ps1 Script

```
## File Name: LaunchRemoteShell.ps1
## Description: Launches a remote PowerShell connection
## for Exchange with the appropriate parameters.
$SkipCertCheck = New-PSSessionOption -SkipCACheck ↵
    -SkipCNCheck -SkipRevocationCheck
## Use the cached credentials in the session
$Session = New-PSSession -ConfigurationName ↵
    Microsoft.Exchange -ConnectionUri ↵
    https://your_exchange_server.com/PowerShell/ ↵
    -Authentication NegotiateWithImplicitCredential ↵
    -SessionOption $SkipCertCheck
## Use Basic Authentication
## $Session = New-PSSession -ConfigurationName
##     Microsoft.Exchange -ConnectionUri
##     https://your_exchange_server.com/PowerShell/
##     -Authentication Basic -Credential Get-Credential
##     -SessionOption $SkipCertCheck
## Use LiveID Credentials
## $Session = New-PSSession -ConfigurationName
```

```
##      Microsoft.Exchange -ConnectionUri
##      https://your_exchange_server.com/PowerShell/
##      -Authentication Negotiate -Credential
##      Get-Credential -SessionOption $SkipCertCheck
Import-PSSession $Session
```

3

Managing the Organization

IN THIS CHAPTER, YOU WILL LEARN TO:

▷ **MANAGE RELATIONSHIPS WITH OTHER ORGANIZATIONS (Pages 96 – 112)**

- Enable Data Sharing with Other Organizations (Page 96)
- Define Which Information Users Can Share (Page 107)

▷ **MANAGE ADDRESS LISTS (Pages 112 – 129)**

- Manage Address List Content (Page 113)
- Manage Address List Distribution (Page 122)

The organization is what Exchange considers to be the scope of its boundaries—that is, the organization defines what's in Exchange's purview. When you install Exchange into a fresh environment, you are required to name the organization up front, because the organization sets the context around the entire Exchange infrastructure.

Controlling things at the organization level can have an impact on every Exchange resource in the environment. Likewise, administrators who have administrative permissions at the organization level also have (or can grant themselves) permissions to all Exchange resources in the organization. This can be a dangerous or powerful position in which to find yourself. This chapter focuses on managing at the organization level.

Manage Relationships with Other Organizations

Among the many enhancements brought to the table by Exchange Server 2010, the ability to share data outside the typical boundaries of Exchange is welcomed by many administrators. Integration with external or third-party systems has always been a challenge. Exchange Server 2010 takes a positive step in the right direction.

Enable Data Sharing with Other Organizations

In Exchange Server 2010, you can share data with other Exchange organizations. Most people would agree that this is a good thing; however, there must be some management of what kind of data the users can share. Having unrestricted sharing capabilities could circumvent internal confidentiality controls and cause data spillage. Therefore, it's important to appropriately manage sharing policies and Exchange Server 2010 gives you a way to do that.

Understand Federation Trusts

Exchange allows you to share your calendar, free/busy information, and contacts through a *federation trust.* In a typical Windows Active Directory trust, users from one domain can authenticate from computers in another domain and use those authentication credentials to access resources in the other domain. A federation trust is different from an Active Directory trust in that it's based on web services standards and provides the capability for two parties to exchange Security

Assertion Markup Language (SAML) tokens, which are sets of claims used in federation scenarios.

In Exchange Server 2010, two Exchange organizations do not establish federation trusts with each other explicitly. Instead, the Windows Live service is used as a *trust broker*. Both Exchange organizations establish a federation trust with Windows Live. After the federation trust is established, a sharing policy is defined that establishes the relationship between the two Exchange organizations. Because of the dependency on Windows Live, if your Exchange organization is not exposed to the Internet, you cannot take advantage of this feature.

There are some prerequisites that you will need before you can set up the federation trust with Windows Live:

- The certificate used for the trust needs to have been issued by a certification authority that is trusted by Windows Live. You cannot use a self-signed certificate. The certificate must also be installed on all of the Exchange Server 2010 Client Access servers.

- The federation uses an authoritative domain name that you define. All users who will participate in the federation need to have an SMTP address configured for this domain. This domain does not have to be the primary SMTP address for your Exchange organization. For example, if your primary address space is @contoso .com, the SMTP addresses you can use for federation could be @federation.contoso.com. If you use an SMTP address that is different from your existing primary address, you will need to create an email address policy or add the address manually to accounts that you want to allow federation on.

- The domain name you use for federation must be resolvable from the Internet. Also, it cannot contain any of the domain names that are blocked by Windows Live.

After you have these things in place, you can establish a federation trust and share data with other Exchange organizations that also have federation trusts. The process of federating Exchange consists of the following high-level steps:

1. Create the federation trust.
2. Configure DNS for federation.
3. Configure the Organization Identifier.
4. Create a sharing relationship.

The following sections walk you through setting up this federation.

Create the Federation Trust

The federation trust establishes a trusted connection between your Exchange organization and the Microsoft Federation Gateway (MFG). Both organizations in the federation establish a trust with the MFG, and the MFG acts as a trust broker. Both you and the organization you are federating with will need to follow these steps. Regardless of how many other Exchange organizations you federate with, you will only need to set up the federation trust with the Microsoft Federation Gateway once per Exchange organization.

Create the Federation Trust in the Exchange Management Console

To create the federation trust in the Exchange Management Console (EMC):

1. Open the Exchange Management Console by clicking Start ➢ All Programs ➢ Microsoft Exchange Server 2010 ➢ Exchange Management Console.

2. In the EMC, select the Organization node from the Console tree in the left pane.

3. In the Actions menu in the right pane, select New Federation Trust.

4. The New Federation Trust wizard will launch, as shown in Figure 3.1. In the Certificate Thumbprint field, click the Browse button to look for a certificate that you can use for federation. Remember that you cannot use a self-signed certificate and that the certificate has to be from an authority chain that is trusted by the MFG. Choose the certificate that you want to use and click OK to close the certificate dialog box.

5. Back in the New Federation Trust wizard, click the New button to create the trust.

6. After the trust is created, the Completion screen will be displayed. Click Finish to close the wizard.

Create the Federation Trust in the Exchange Management Shell

To create the federation trust with the Exchange Management Shell:

1. Launch the Exchange Management Shell by clicking Start ➢ All Programs ➢ Microsoft Exchange Server 2010 ➢ Exchange Management Shell.

Figure 3.1: The New Federation Trust wizard will launch.

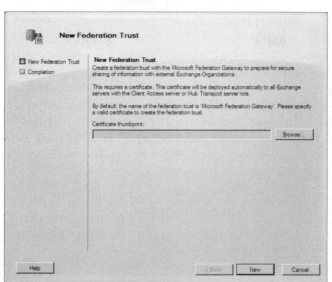

2. Get the thumbprint of the certificate that you will use for the federation trust by running the following command:

    ```
    Get-ExchangeCertificate
    ```

3. Decide on a name that uniquely identifies this federation trust, such as Microsoft Federation Gateway. This name is referenced as [*TrustName*] in the next step.

4. Type the following command to establish the federation trust with the MFG. For [*ThumbPrintString*] you can copy and paste the thumbprint from step 2 above or manually type it in:

    ```
    New-FederationTrust -Name [TrustName] -Thumbprint ↵
    [ThumbPrintString]
    ```

5. For example, the following command will create a trust called Microsoft Federation Gateway and use the thumbprint ABCDEF0123456789:

    ```
    New-FederationTrust -Name "Microsoft Federation Gateway" ↵
    -Thumbprint ABCDEF0123456789
    ```

Configure DNS for Federation

After the federation trust is configured, you will need to prove to the MFG that you own the domain that you want to share data for. To prove this, you will create a DNS record with some information that only you and the MFG know. When you created the federation trust, an Application Identifier was created during the process. You will need to create a DNS TXT record in the domain you are federating with the Application Identifier as the data for the DNS record. The fact that you can create this text record proves to the MFG that you own the domain.

If you are running Windows DNS, you can use the following steps to retrieve the Application Identifier and create the DNS TXT record:

1. Launch the EMS (Start ➤ All Programs ➤ Microsoft Exchange Server 2010 ➤ Exchange Management Shell).

2. Retrieve the Application Identifier for the trust by running the `Get-FederationTrust` command.

   For example, the following command retrieves the Application Identifier for the federation trust named Microsoft Federation Gateway:

   ```
   Get-FederationTrust -Identity "Microsoft Federation ↵
   Gateway"
   ```

3. Open the DNS management tool by clicking Start ➤ All Programs ➤ Administrative Tools ➤ DNS.

4. In the DNS Manager, browse down to the forward lookup zone that represents the domain you are federating. Right-click on the zone and select Other New Records from the context menu.

5. In the Resource Record Type dialog box, scroll down to the bottom of the record list, select Text (TXT), and click the Create Record button, as shown in Figure 3.2.

6. The New Resource Record dialog box will launch. Leave the Record Name field empty. In the Text field, enter the following string, replacing [*ApplicationIdentifier*] with the Application Identifier that you retrieved in the previous set of steps:

   ```
   AppID=[ApplicationIdentifier]
   ```

7. Click OK to finish creating the TXT record.

Figure 3.2: Adding a DNS TXT record in Windows DNS

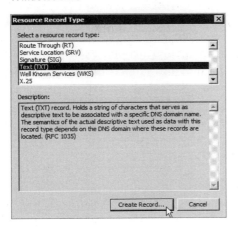

Configure the Organization Identifier

At this point, you will have created the federation trust and created the DNS record that you will use to prove to the Microsoft Federation Gateway that you own the domain. The next step is to create the Organization Identifier for the domain. This establishes that the domain is enabled for federation.

Before you can configure the Organization Identifier for a domain, the domain must first be on the Accepted Domains list for your Exchange organization. You can do this either in the EMC or the EMS.

Add an Accepted Domain

To add an accepted domain in the EMC:

1. Open the Exchange Management Console (Start ➤ All Programs ➤ Microsoft Exchange Server 2010 ➤ Exchange Management Console).

2. In the Console tree in the left pane, browse to Organization Configuration ➤ Hub Transport.

3. In the Work Area pane, choose the Accepted Domains tab to view the list of domains that your Exchange organization can accept.

4. If the domain you are federating isn't listed in the Accepted Domains list, select New Accepted Domain from the Actions

pane on the right side of the console. This launches the New Accepted Domain wizard.

5. In the Name field, type a name that describes the accepted domain. In the Accepted Domain field, type in the DNS name of the domain that you are federating—for example, **federation. contoso.com**. Figure 3.3 illustrates this configuration.

Figure 3.3: Adding an accepted domain namespace

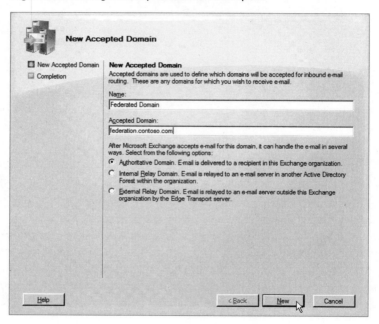

6. Ensure that the Authoritative Domain option is selected and click the New button to create the accepted domain. When the Completion screen appears, click the Finish button.

To add an accepted domain in the EMS, run the New-AcceptedDomain command. For example, use the following command to add the accepted domain federation.contoso.com:

```
New-AcceptedDomain -Name "federation.contoso.com" ↵
-DomainName "federation.contoso.com" -DomainType ↵
"Authoritative"
```

After you have added the federation domain to the list of accepted domains, you can configure the Organization Identifier for the domain. This process needs to be completed for each domain that you are federating. You can complete this process in either the EMC or the EMS.

Configure the Organization Identifier

To configure the Organization Identifier in the EMC:

1. Open the EMC (Start ➤ All Programs ➤ Microsoft Exchange Server 2010 ➤ Exchange Management Console).

2. In the Console tree in the left pane, browse to the Organization Configuration node.

3. In the Actions pane on the right, select Manage Federation.

4. In the Manage Federation wizard, the first screen, Manage Federation Certificate, allows you to modify the certificate that you are using for the federation trust. To continue and use your current certificate, click the Next button.

5. In the Manage Federated Domains list, click the Add button to add your domain to the list of federated domains. A screen will launch that allows you to select the domain that you are federating. Click OK after you have selected the domain.

   If the domain you want to use isn't in the list, ensure that the domain is configured as an accepted domain for your Exchange organization as described earlier in this section.

6. In the field E-mail Address Of Organization Contact, type the email address of the organization's contact.

   Figure 3.4 shows the configuration of the parameters on the Manage Federated Domains screen.

7. Select the Enable Federation check box and click Next to continue.

8. In the Manage Federation screen, click the Manage button to complete the configuration of the Organization Identifier.

9. At the Completion screen, click the Finish button to complete the configuration of the federated domain.

To configure the Organization Identifier using the EMS, you can use the Set-FederatedOrganizationIdentifier command.

Getting Started

PART I

Figure 3.4: Selecting a domain on the Manage Federated Domains screen

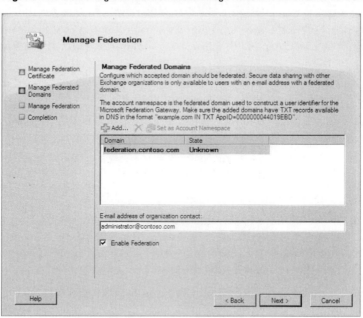

For example, if your namespace is federation.contoso.com and the federation trust that you created earlier is called Microsoft Federation Gateway, you would use the following command:

```
Set-FederatedOrganizationIdentifier -AccountNamespace ↵
"federation.contoso.com" -DelegationFederationTrust ↵
"Microsoft Federation Gateway" -Enabled $True
```

Create an Organizational Relationship

You now have a domain namespace that is enabled for federation through the Microsoft Federation Gateway. To share data with another organization, you need to create an organizational relationship. In an organizational relationship, you are defining what can be shared with the partner organization. You can share the following features:

Free/Busy Calendar Information   Allows users in a trusted organization to view the free/busy information for your user. This feature aids in scheduling meetings between trusted organizations.

Federated Message Delivery   With federated delivery, messages destined for a trusted organization are treated the same way as messages routed inside the Exchange organization. This option allows the messages to be encrypted during transport and the data relating to trusted activities, such as filtering, is preserved.

Move Mailbox Capability   Enabling this capability allows mailboxes to be moved between trusted organizations.

NOTE   Organizational relationships only work in one direction. If you want to share your data with a partner organization and if the partner organization wants to share their data with you, then both your organization and the partner organization need to establish an organizational relationship.

Create an Organizational Relationship Using the Exchange Management Console

To create an organizational relationship using the EMC:

1. Open the EMC (Start ➤ All Programs ➤ Microsoft Exchange Server 2010 ➤ Exchange Management Console).

2. In the Console tree in the left pane, browse to the Organization Configuration node.

3. In the Actions pane on the right, select New Organizational Relationship.

    This will launch the New Organizational Relationship wizard.

4. In the first screen of the wizard, give the relationship a name.

    You may want to identify the name of the organization that you are sharing within the name—for example, **TailSpin Toys Organizational Relationship**.

5. Select the option Enable This Organizational Relationship and then check the features that you want to enable sharing for. Click the Next button to continue.

6. In the External Organization screen of the wizard, ensure that the Automatically Discover Configuration Information box is checked.

7. In the field Specify A Federated Domain Of The External Exchange Organization, enter the domain namespace of the partner organization. Click Next to continue.

For example, if Contoso is sharing data with TailSpin Toys and the domain namespace for TailSpin Toys is `federation.tailspintoys.com`, then you would enter **federation.tailspintoys.com** in this field, as shown in Figure 3.5.

Figure 3.5: Configuring the external organization settings

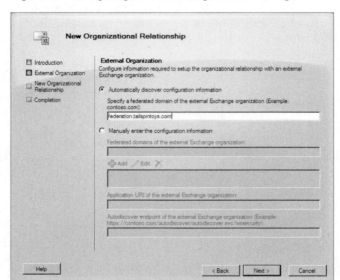

8. At the Configuration Summary screen, review the options that you selected and click New to create the organizational relationship.

Create an Organizational Relationship Using the Exchange Management Shell

You can also create an organizational relationship through the EMS. When you do so, you will want to specify the features that you are enabling sharing for. Table 3.1 shows the parameters you can use with the `New-OrganizationRelationhip` cmdlet to enable or disable sharing capabilities.

Table 3.1: EMS Parameters for Sharing Relationship Features

Feature	EMS Cmdlet Parameter
Free/Busy Calendar Sharing	FreeBusyAccessEnabled
Federated Message Delivery	FederatedDeliveryEnabled
Move Mailbox Capability	MailboxMoveEnabled

To create an organizational relationship using the EMS, run the New-OrganizationRelationship command. Specify the name of the organizational relationship and the address namespace of the partner organization that you are sharing data with.

For example, if you name the organizational relationship **TailSpin Toys Organizational Relationship** and the domain namespace that TailSpin Toys has enabled for federation is federation.tailspintoys.com, you would use the following command to establish an organizational relationship and enable Free/Busy sharing:

```
New-OrganizationRelationship -Name "TailSpin Toys Sharing ↵
Relationship" -DomainName "federation.tailspintoys.com" ↵
-FreeBusyAccessEnabled $true
```

NOTE When establishing an organization relationship, you only need to specify the domain namespace of the organization you are sharing with. Exchange will automatically collect the necessary server data. However, you have the option to enter this data manually in the External Organization screen of the New Organizational Relationship wizard, in case you have issues resolving this information through AutoDiscover.

Define Which Information Users Can Share

After the federation is set up and the organizational relationship is configured, users then have the means to share data. The final step is to create and apply sharing policies to users. A *sharing policy* defines the level of detail that users can share between federated organizations. You may want to allow specific users only the ability to share free/busy data, while giving other users the capability to share more details about the appointments on their calendar. Table 3.2 outlines what can be controlled in the sharing policy.

Table 3.2: Sharing Policy Actions

Sharing Policy Parameter	Description
CalendarSharingFreeBusySimple	Shares free/busy information only. Users in trusted partner organization cannot see any details about the calendar appointment; they can only see that the user is not available during this time.
CalendarSharingFreeBusyReviewer	Shares the Subject and Location fields of the calendar appointment. Users in trusted partner organizations can view these fields, but not the body of the appointment.
CalendarSharingFreeBusyDetail	Shares the details of the calendar appointment, including the subject, location, and the message body. This is the least restrictive of the options.
ContactsSharing	Shares contacts with the trusted partner organization.

After you create the sharing policy, you apply it to users. The policy will be enforced on the users that it is applied to. You can modify the list of users who receive the sharing policy at any time.

Create a Sharing Policy

Before the sharing policy can be applied to users, you must first create it. Sharing policies can be created in either the EMC or the EMS.

Create a Sharing Policy with the Exchange Management Console

To create a sharing policy with the EMC:

1. Open the EMC (Start ➤ All Programs ➤ Microsoft Exchange Server 2010 ➤ Exchange Management Console).

2. In the Console tree in the left pane, browse to the Organization Configuration ➤ Mailbox node.

3. In the Actions pane on the right, select New Sharing Policy.

This launches the New Sharing Policy wizard.

4. At the Introduction screen, enter the name of the sharing policy in the Name field. In the field Assign Actions To A Domain That This Sharing Policy Should Enforce, click the Add button to add federated domain namespaces to the list.

This launches the Add Action to Sharing Policy Domain screen.

5. In the Add Action to Sharing Policy Domain screen, enter the federated domain namespace—for example, `federation` `.tailspintoys.com`.

6. Select the sharing actions that you want to enable. Click OK to close the screen.

You can choose calendar sharing and/or contact sharing. If you choose calendar sharing, you will need to specify the level of detail that can be shared. Refer to Table 3.2 for more details about these options.

7. Back at the Introduction screen of the New Sharing Policy wizard, make sure that the option Enable Sharing Policy is checked. Click Next to continue.

Figure 3.6 illustrates the configuration of this screen.

Figure 3.6: Configuration of the New Sharing Policy wizard

8. In the Mailboxes screen, click the Add button to add mailboxes to the list. The mailboxes listed here will have this sharing policy applied to them. Click Next when you've finished adding mailboxes to the sharing policy.

9. At the New Sharing Policy screen, check the configuration summary and click the New button.

10. The sharing policy will be created and you will be taken to the Completion screen when it's finished. Click Finish to complete the process.

Create a Sharing Policy in the Exchange Management Shell

To create a sharing policy in the EMS, run the New-SharingPolicy command. You will need to specify the name of the policy and the actions that the policy will allow.

For example, the following command will create a sharing policy called TailSpin Toys Sharing Policy and give the federation.tailspintoys.com users the ability to see free/busy information:

```
New-SharingPolicy "TailSpin Toys Sharing Policy" -Domains ↵
"federation.tailspintoys.com:CalendarFreeBusySimple" ↵
-Enabled $true
```

When specifying the actions, the format is *DomainName:Action*. For example, if you want to share contacts with Tail Spin Toys, you would specify **federation.tailspintoys.com:ContactsSharing**.

Apply Sharing Policies to Recipients

After creating the sharing policy, you can apply it to users. The sharing policy will only apply to the users under the following conditions:

- The user mailbox must be configured to use the specific sharing policy.

- The sharing policy must be enabled.

- The sharing relationship must be correctly configured between the organizations that want to share data.

There are two ways to apply the sharing policy with the EMC: on the sharing policy or on the user mailbox.

Apply a Policy to Multiple Mailboxes Using the Exchange Management Console

To specify the mailboxes on the policy using the EMC, use the following steps:

1. Open the EMC (Start ➤ All Programs ➤ Microsoft Exchange Server 2010 ➤ Exchange Management Console).

2. In the Console tree in the left pane, browse to the Organization Configuration ➤ Mailbox node.

3. In the Work area in the center of the MMC, select the Sharing Policies tab.

4. Right-click on the sharing policy that you want to apply and select Properties from the context menu.

5. When the properties dialog box for the sharing policy is displayed, click the Mailboxes tab.

6. Use the Add button to add affected mailboxes to the list. Click OK when you are finished to make the configuration changes.

Configure the Sharing Policy for a Mailbox

To set the sharing policy on the mailbox directly using the EMC:

1. Open the EMC (Start ➤ All Programs ➤ Microsoft Exchange Server 2010 ➤ Exchange Management Console).

2. In the Console tree in the left pane, browse to the Recipient Configuration ➤ Mailbox node.

   The mailboxes in the Exchange organization will be displayed in the Work area.

3. Select the mailbox that you want to apply the sharing policy to. Right-click on the mailbox and select Properties from the context menu.

4. When the properties dialog box of the mailbox opens, choose the Mailbox Settings tab. In the list of mailbox settings, choose Federated Sharing and click the Properties button above the list, as shown in Figure 3.7. This will open the Federated Sharing dialog box.

Figure 3.7: Accessing the federated sharing options for a mailbox

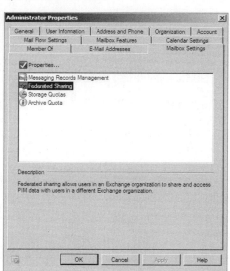

5. In the Federated Sharing dialog box, use the Browse button to browse through the sharing policies that you have configured and select the one you want to use.

6. Click OK to close the Federated Sharing dialog box. When back in the user properties dialog box, click OK to apply the changes and close the window.

To configure the sharing policy for a mailbox using the EMS, run the Set-Mailbox cmdlet and specify the SharingPolicy parameter.

For example, to set the TailSpin Toys Sharing Policy, you could run the following command:

```
Set-Mailbox "Nora Shea" -SharingPolicy "TailSpin Toys ↵
Sharing Policy"
```

Manage Address Lists

In Exchange, address lists are defined at the organization level. Often, the customization of address lists is overlooked and the address lists are left at their default settings. Exchange Server 2010 provides robust address list capabilities that need to be managed. There are two aspects to managing address lists.

- Managing the content of the address list
- Managing the distribution of the address list

Manage Address List Content

Address lists contain collections of users, contacts, mail-enabled groups, and other types of recipients as well. The data for the address list is stored in Active Directory. Therefore, any objects in Active Directory that meet the Lightweight Directory Access Protocol (LDAP) filter criteria of the address list will be included in the list. When managing address list content, you will need to know how to create and manage custom address lists and change the settings on address lists.

Create an Address List

By creating an address list, you can keep lists of recipients separated for particular users. This is usually helpful when you have a large Global Address List (GAL) and users have to scroll through many entries that may not necessarily be relevant to them before they find the entry they were looking for.

Create an Address List in the Exchange Management Console

To create an address list in the EMC:

1. Open the EMC (Start ➢ All Programs ➢ Microsoft Exchange Server 2010 ➢ Exchange Management Console).

2. In the Console tree in the left pane, browse to the Organization Configuration ➢ Mailbox node.

   The mailbox options will be displayed in the Work area.

3. In the Work area, select the Address Lists tab.

   The list of default address lists will be displayed.

4. In the Actions pane on the right side of the EMC, select New Address List.

The New Address List wizard will launch.

5. At the Introduction screen of the wizard, type a name for the address list in the Name field. Click Next to continue.

6. At the Filter Settings screen, click the Browse button to browse to the base OU that contains the user accounts that will be included for this address list.

7. In the Include These Recipient Types field, select the type of recipients that will be included in this address list and click Next.

8. If you chose to filter some users, you will be taken to the Conditions screen, where you will specify some additional criteria for filtering users. After you select your criteria, you can click the Preview button to preview what the address list will look like. Click Next to continue.

9. At the Schedule screen, choose when the address list will be applied. If the address list is exceptionally large and you expect it to have an impact on the performance of Active Directory or Exchange, you can choose to apply the address list after business hours. Click Next to continue.

10. At the next screen, review the options that you set and click the New button to create the address list. After the address list is added, you will see a confirmation window. Click Finish to complete the process and close the wizard.

Create an Address List in the Exchange Management Shell

If you want to use the EMS to create the address list, you use the New-AddressList cmdlet. You need to specify a filter that will determine which entries are added to the address list. One way of accomplishing this is to use the predefined parameters in the cmdlet.

Exchange has a list of predefined properties that you can specify in the cmdlet. If you are building a simple address list, this prevents you from having to write a custom filter for getting a simple address list created. Table 3.3 lists New-AddressList properties that have predefined parameters.

Table 3.3: Predefined Properties for the New-AddressList Cmdlet

Property	Cmdlet Parameter	Description
Company	`ConditionalCompany`	This is the **company** attribute on the user in Active Directory. When there are many recipients from different companies, you can use this parameter to create an address list for each company.
Custom Attributes	`ConditionalCustomAttribute1 - ConditionalCustomAttribute15`	The custom attributes map the **extensionAttribute1 - extensionAttribute15** attributes on the Active Directory user account. This consists of 15 attributes that you can fill with custom data and create an address list based on that data.
Department	`ConditionalDepartment`	In the Active Directory user account, this is the **department** attribute. This attribute is commonly used for storing the department that a user is in. You can use this to create address lists based on departments in your organization.
State (or Province)	`ConditionalStateOrProvince`	This property maps to the **st** attribute on the Active Directory user account. This attribute is commonly used for storing the state (or province) that the user is located in. This property will allow you to build address lists based on physical locations.
Type of Entry	`IncludedRecipients`	This property allows you to define what types of recipients can be included in the address list. For example, you may want to include users and contacts but not mail-enabled groups.

Getting Started

PART I

To create an address list in the EMS using predefined parameters:

1. Run the New-AddressList cmdlet to create an address list. Use the techniques described previously to create a filter for the address list.

   For example, to create an address list called "Everyone in Maryland" using a predefined parameter, you can use the following command:

   ```
   New-AddressList -Name "Everyone in Maryland" ↵
   -IncludedRecipients MailboxUsers ↵
   -ConditionalStateOrProvince Maryland
   ```

2. Apply the address list by running the Update-AddressList cmdlet. This will refresh the address list membership.

   The following example updates the Everyone in Maryland address list:

   ```
   Update-AddressList -Identity "Everyone in Maryland"
   ```

Use a Custom Recipient Filter

Aside from using a predefined parameter, you could instead create a custom filter. The filter uses logic that is similar to the logic discussed in Chapter 2, "Using the Exchange Management Console and the Exchange Management Shell." For example, if you want the address list to contain user mailboxes whose last name begins with *S*, the following filter would be appropriate:

```
{((RecipientType -eq 'UserMailbox') -and (LastName -like ↵
'S*'))}
```

After you have determined what your filter is going to be, you can use the RecipientFilter property of the New-AddressList cmdlet to apply it to a new address list.

To create an address list in the EMS using a custom filter:

1. Run the New-AddressList cmdlet to create an address list. Use the techniques described in Chapter 2 to create a filter for the address list.

For example, to create an address list called "Everyone in Baltimore" using a custom filter, you can use the following command.

```
New-AddressList -Name "Everyone in Baltimore" ↵
-RecipientFilter {((RecipientType -eq 'UserMailbox') ↵
-and (Location -eq 'Baltimore'))}
```

2. Apply the address list by running the Update-AddressList cmdlet. This will refresh the address list membership. The following example updates the Everyone in Baltimore address list:

```
Update-AddressList -Identity "Everyone in Baltimore"
```

Restrict Access to an Address List

By default, all authenticated users can view the contents of an address list. You can remove this permission from the address list and allow only specific accounts to view the address list. This task can be performed in the Exchange Management Shell using the following steps:

1. Run the Remove-ADPermission cmdlet to remove the user rights from the address list.

   For example, to remove authenticated user rights from the address list Everyone in Baltimore, run the following cmdlet:

```
Remove-ADPermission "Everyone in Baltimore" -User ↵
"Authenticated Users" -ExtendedRights "Open Address ↵
List" -Confirm:$false
```

2. After you have removed the Authenticated Users group, no users have access to the address list. Now add only those users that you want to have access using the Add-ADPermission cmdlet.

   For example, to add the Everyone in Baltimore group back to the address list, you would run the following cmdlet:

```
Add-ADPermission "Everyone in Baltimore" -User ↵
"Baltimore Users" -ExtendedRights "Open Address List" ↵
-Confirm:$false
```

Retrieve the Members of an Address List

Sometimes you may need to retrieve a list of the members of an address list. You can do this without having to log on to a mailbox. You can use the EMS to view and export address list membership.

To retrieve the address list entries, run the `Get-AddressList` cmdlet. For example, to retrieve a list of all of the entries in the address list Everyone in Baltimore, run the following cmdlet:

```
Get-AddressList "Everyone in Baltimore"
```

To export the address list entries, you can pipe the results of the `Get-AddressList` cmdlet into another command, just like any other collection of data in the EMS. For example, you would use the following command to export the Everyone in Baltimore address list entries into a CSV file:

```
Get-AddressList "Everyone in Baltimore" | export-csv ↵
c:\AddressListMembers.csv
```

Force an Address List to Update Using the Exchange Management Shell

After you create an address in the EMS, the address list object is created in Active Directory, but the membership has not yet been calculated. When you create an address list in the EMC, the wizard will update the address list automatically, but if you are using the EMS, you will need to force the address list to update its membership.

You can do this by running the `Update-AddressList` cmdlet. For example, to update the membership of the Everyone in Baltimore address list, run the following cmdlet:

```
Update-AddressList -Identity "Everyone in Baltimore"
```

When specifying the identity of the address list, you should include the full path if the address list is not at the top of the hierarchy. For example, if there is an address list called Service Desk under the IT Support address list container, the identity would be IT Support\ Service Desk.

WARNING   If you are updating an address list that contains a lot of members, Active Directory may have to update many objects, which might take some time. To reduce the impact to your AD environment, you can specify a less-utilized domain controller to run the update against. To do this, specify the -DomainController parameter in the Update-AddressList cmdlet.

Modify the Address List Template for Outlook Clients

When a user opens an address list in Outlook and views the properties on an entry, a dialog box is presented that contains information about the entry. If you have custom fields that you want to display in this box, you can modify what the dialog box looks like. You can edit the template dialog boxes for each of the object types that are displayed in the Global Address List. In this example, we'll edit the dialog box for users, but you could also modify it for groups, public folders, contacts, and searches.

The tool used to update the address list template for Outlook is the Details Templates Editor. You can find the Details Templates Editor in the toolbox node in the Exchange Management Console.

To launch the Details Templates Editor:

1. Open the EMC (Start Menu ➤ All Programs ➤ Microsoft Exchange Server 2010 ➤ Exchange Management Console).

2. In the Console tree in the left pane, browse to the Toolbox node. The different tools in the Toolbox will be displayed in the Work area.

3. In the Work area, double-click on the tool called "Details Templates Editor" to launch the tool, as shown in Figure 3.8.

Before you can edit a dialog template, you need to know the name of the attribute on the Active Directory object that will be displayed in the dialog box. For example, if you want to display the recipient's employee number, you need to know that the name of the attribute where the employee number is stored is called Employee-Number. You can gather this information from Active Directory using the Schema Management tool.

Figure 3.8: Launching the Details Templates Editor

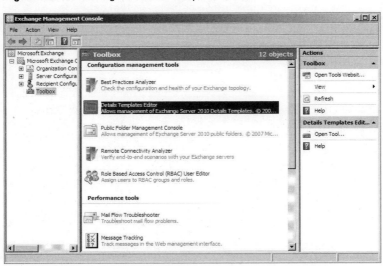

TIP To run the Schema Management tool on a computer that is not an Active Directory domain controller, you must install the Remote Server Administration Tools (RSAT) for Active Directory Domain Services in Windows Server 2008 or install the Support Tools in Windows Server 2003. In Windows Server 2008, you can install the RSAT tools by running the command ServerManagerCmd -i RSAT-ADDS.

In the following example, the Assistant field for the Recipient Details dialog box is replaced with the Employee Number field.

1. In the Details Templates Editor, the list of available templates is in the Work area in the center of the tool. Select the User template from the list and choose Edit in the Actions pane on the right. The template will open in a new window with a visual editor.

2. In the template editing window, select the Assistant text. On the right side of the tool is a list of properties for the Assistant text that you just selected. Modify the Text parameter to read **Employee Number** instead of Assistant. After you click off the parameter, the text in the Assistant field will change to Employee Number.

3. Select the text box next to the Employee Number text field. On the right side of the tool in the list of parameters, change the Attribute Name parameter from its current value to read Employee-Number. This is shown in Figure 3.9.

Figure 3.9: Setting the attribute displayed in the new field

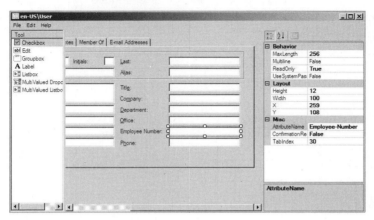

4. Choose File ➢ Save to save the dialog edits. You can now close the dialog editor and the Details Templates Editor tool. The next time you open Outlook and view the details for the recipient from the address list, the new dialog box will be used.

TIP   You can allow users to update their address list information directly from the Recipient Details dialog box. To make a field editable in the Details Templates Editor, change the Read Only parameter of the text box to False. The user also needs "write" permission to the attribute on their Active Directory user account. If they do not have this, they will get an access denied error when editing the information.

There are many other ways you can customize the Recipient Details dialog box. You can add tabs to the tab list, add check boxes, include additional text boxes, add menus, and so forth. If you want to revert back to the original version, you can select the dialog box in the tool and choose Restore in the Actions pane.

Manage Address List Distribution

You need to manage how address lists are distributed to users. To allow users to view address lists when they are not connected to the server, Exchange uses an Offline Address Book (OAB). The OAB is generated by a server and the files are made available for clients to download.

There are two ways the OAB can be downloaded by a client. Clients running Outlook 2007 and later can use the web-based distribution method, which uses web services to allow Outlook to download the OAB. Clients that run Outlook 2003 (or earlier) must rely on public folders to download the OAB. The OAB files are stored in a system public folder and the client downloads these files from that public folder.

There are multiple versions of OABs available. The newer versions add some features, but they work with different versions of Outlook. Table 3.4 outlines the differences in OAB versions. When choosing the versions of OAB that you will make available, ensure that you cover all of the Outlook versions available in your environment.

Table 3.4: Comparison of OAB Versions

Version #	Supported Outlook Versions	OAB Description
Version 2	Outlook 98 SP1 and earlier	ANSI; used starting in Exchange 5.5
Version 3	Outlook 98 SP2 and later	Unicode; reduction in RPC traffic; improved sorting and language features
Version 4	Outlook 2003 SP2 and later	Unicode; OAB download improvements; additional sorting improvements

Create an Offline Address Book

An OAB containing the Global Address List is created by default. You can create additional OABs for other purposes. For example, you can assign OABs to specific groups of users. Also, additional OABs give users a smaller set of files to download.

There are two ways to distribute an OAB: via public folders or via web services. Web-based distribution is enabled by default, but both distribution methods can be used at the same time.

NOTE If you choose a web-based method, only Outlook 2007 or later clients can download the OAB.

Create an OAB in the Exchange Management Console

To create an OAB in the EMC:

1. Open the EMC (Start ➢ All Programs ➢ Microsoft Exchange Server 2010 ➢ Exchange Management Console).

2. In the Console tree in the left pane, browse to the Organization Configuration ➢ Mailbox node.

3. In the Work area, select the Offline Address Book tab.

4. In the Actions pane, select New Offline Address Book.

   This will launch the New Offline Address Book wizard.

5. At the Introduction screen of the wizard, enter the name of the OAB in the Name field. Click the Browse button next to the Offline Address Book Generation Server field to find a server that the OAB will be generated on.

6. Still on the Introduction screen, select the address lists that you want included in this OAB. To specify an additional address list besides the default GAL, check the box Include The Following Address Lists and use the Add button to browse for and add the address lists that you want to use. Click Next to continue.

7. At the Distribution Points screen, select the distribution method for the OAB. If you choose a web-based method, you will be required to select an existing virtual directory that the OAB can use, as shown in Figure 3.10. Click Next to continue.

8. At the next screen, click the New button to create the OAB.

9. At the Completion screen, click Finish to close the wizard.

Create an OAB in the Exchange Management Shell

Before you can create an OAB in the EMS, you need to know what address lists will be included in the OAB and the distribution method you will use.

Figure 3.10: Configuring the distribution points for a new OAB

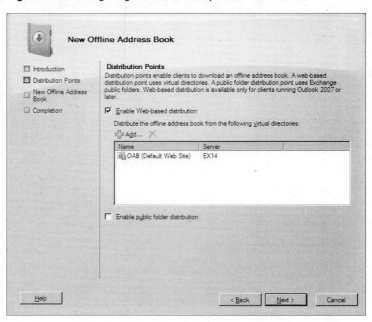

To create a public folder–distributed OAB in the EMS, run the New-OfflineAddressBook cmdlet to create a new OAB.

For example, the following command creates an OAB for public folder distribution:

```
New-OfflineAddressBook -Name "PF OAB" -AddressLists ↵
"Default Global Address List" -PublicFolderDatabase ↵
"Public Database" -PublicFolderDistributionEnabled $true
```

To create an OAB that uses web-based distribution in the EMS, run the New-OfflineAddressBook cmdlet without specifying a public folder database and without using the -PublicFolderDistributionEnabled option to create a new OAB.

When you don't specify public folder distribution, the distribution method defaults to web-based distribution. For example, the following command creates an OAB for web-based distribution:

```
New-OfflineAddressBook -Name "Web Based OAB" -AddressLists ↵
"Default Global Address List"
```

Change the Default OAB for New Users

The Offline Address Book that is designated as the Default OAB is the OAB that is associated with new mailboxes. You can modify which OAB is the default, which will control what address lists are in the OAB for new users, and what versions are available for them to download.

To modify the Default OAB in the EMC:

1. Open the EMC (Start ≻ All Programs ≻ Microsoft Exchange Server 2010 ≻ Exchange Management Console).

2. In the Console tree in the left pane, browse to the Organization Configuration ≻ Mailbox node.

3. In the Work area, click the Offline Address Book tab. The list of available OABs is displayed. Select the OAB that you want to make the default.

4. In the Actions pane under the menu for the OAB that you selected, choose the option Set As Default (Figure 3.11).

Figure 3.11: Setting the Default OAB for new users

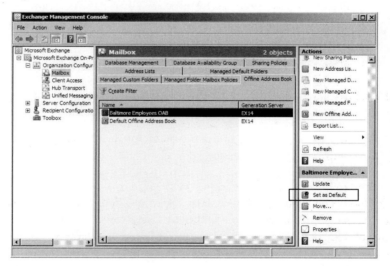

5. A dialog box will be displayed asking you to confirm the new default OAB. Click Yes and the Default OAB will be changed.

You can also change the Default OAB in the EMS. Run the Set-OfflineAddressBook cmdlet and specify the IsDefault parameter to set the default OAB.

For example, the following command makes the PF OAB the default OAB for new mailboxes:

```
Set-OfflineAddressBook -Identity "PF OAB" -IsDefault $true
```

Distribute an OAB to Specific Users

There are two ways to specify which OAB users receive:

- Attach the OAB to a mailbox database.
- Specify the OAB for individual users.

Apply an OAB to a Mailbox Database

To apply an OAB to a mailbox database using the EMC:

1. Open the EMC (Start ➤ All Programs ➤ Microsoft Exchange Server 2010 ➤ Exchange Management Console).

2. In the Console tree in the left pane, browse to the Organization Configuration ➤ Mailbox node.

3. In the Work area, click the Database Management tab. The top half of the Results pane lists the databases available in the Exchange organization. Select the database that you want to apply the OAB to.

4. In the Actions pane under the menu for the database that you selected, click Properties.

   This will open the Properties dialog box for the database.

5. In the Properties dialog box, click the Client Settings tab. In the Offline Address Book field, select the Browse button, as shown in Figure 3.12, to browse for the OAB that you want to assign to the database.

6. After you select the OAB, click OK to apply the OAB to the database and close the Properties dialog box.

To apply an OAB to a mailbox database using the EMS, run the Set-MailboxDatabase cmdlet and specify the OfflineAddressBook parameter to set the OAB.

Figure 3.12: Assigning an OAB to a mailbox database

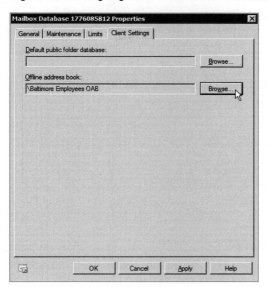

For example, the following command makes the PF OAB the OAB for the Mailbox DB1 database:

```
Set-MailboxDatabase -Identity "Mailbox DB1" ↵
-OfflineAddressBook "PF OAB"
```

Specify an OAB for an Individual User Using the Exchange Management Shell

When specifying the OAB on a per-user basis, you must use the EMS. There is no option available in the EMC to set the OAB for a particular user.

To apply an OAB to a specific user, run the `Set-Mailbox` cmdlet and specify the `OfflineAddressBook` parameter to set the OAB.

For example, the following command makes the PF OAB the OAB for the user Lincoln Alexander:

```
Set-Mailbox "Lincoln Alexander" -OfflineAddressBook "PF OAB"
```

Secure Address Book Distribution

By default, OABs distributed using web-based distribution methods have SSL enabled. However, the virtual directory does not disallow unencrypted OAB download. You can strengthen the security of OAB by setting it to require only SSL connections. This will ensure that the OAB is encrypted when you are downloading it over the Web.

WARNING Ensure that the Client Access server that is distributing the OAB has a valid certificate installed that is trusted by the client.

There are two ways to configure the OAB web service to require an SSL connection:

- Using IIS Manager on the Exchange Server
- Using the EMS

Configure an SSL Connection Using the IIS Manager

To configure an SSL connection using the IIS Manager:

1. Launch the IIS Manager tool by clicking Start ➢ All Programs ➢ Administrative Tools ➢ Internet Information Services (IIS) Manager.

2. In the Console tree of the IIS Manager tool, browse to the Sites ➢ Default Web Site ➢ OAB.

3. In the Work area, double-click the SSL Settings icon under the IIS grouping.

    The properties for the SSL settings will be displayed.

4. In the SSL Settings window, check the Require SSL box.

5. In the Actions pane, click Apply.

    This configuration is shown in Figure 3.13.

Configure an SSL Connection Using the Exchange Management Shell

To configure SSL requirements using the EMS, run the `Set-OABVirtualDirectory` cmdlet and specify the `RequireSSL` parameter to enforce SSL-only connections to the OAB.

The following command can be used if your OAB virtual directory is the default virtual directory that was installed with Exchange.

```
Set-OABVirtualDirectory "OAB (Default Web Site)" ↵
-RequireSSL $true
```

Figure 3.13: The SSL Settings window for the OAB virtual directory

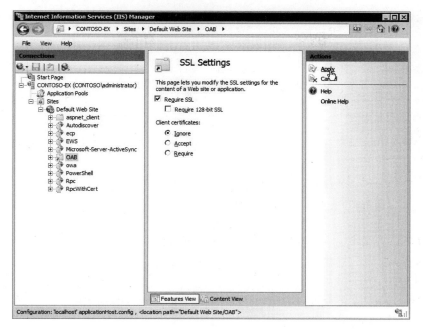

4

Administering Recipients

IN THIS CHAPTER, YOU WILL LEARN TO:

M any people think of recipients as being people. But in Exchange
Server 2010, a recipient can be a variety of things. A physical person
reading mail in Outlook is definitely one possibility, but other types of
recipients include:

- Distribution lists

- Conference rooms

- Pieces of equipment (such as projectors or cars)

- Nonphysical entities, such as a "Helpdesk" mailbox

When administering recipients, there are usually two aspects to consider. The first part is the account, which provides the identity for the
recipient. The account is stored in Active Directory, and in most situations
it is the same account that users log on to their computer with. The second
part to consider is the mailbox. The mailbox is stored in Exchange and
contains the email and other data that Exchange keeps for the recipient,
such as contacts, tasks, and calendars. Not every recipient has a mailbox,
however. Some recipients, such as contacts, only exist in Active Directory.

Exchange brings account administration and mailbox administration together into common tools, such as the Exchange Management
Console (EMC). The advantage is that for the most common tasks,
administrators don't need to flip back and forth between the management tools of Exchange and those of Active Directory. When administering recipients, you have several tools at your disposal. However, this
chapter focuses on using the EMC and the Exchange Management Shell
(EMS) for recipient administration.

Manage Recipient Accounts

The account provides the identity of the recipient. Accounts are stored
in Active Directory as various types of objects, such as user objects or
contact objects. Not every account has a mailbox associated with it, but
every usable mailbox must have an account that it is tied to. The recipient account contains important information in its attributes that are
used by Exchange. This includes data such as contact information for
the recipient and data that ties the account to the mailbox.

This portion of the chapter explores various account-related tasks
that many Exchange administrators will likely encounter regularly.

Manage User Accounts

Recipients with user accounts have an actual mailbox linked to the account. Therefore, these recipients will require administration both on their account and on their mailbox. In this section you will learn to create a new user with a mailbox, enable mail, modify user information, and hide users so they don't appear in the address list.

Create a New User with a Mailbox

When you create a new user with a mailbox, you are creating the user account in Active Directory and the mailbox on the Exchange server. You will need to know basic information about the user in order to create their account. You may also want to decide which mailbox database you will be storing the account in. If you are using the EMC, you have the ability to browse the available databases when creating the mailbox. But whether you use the EMC or the EMS, if you don't tell it what database to use, Exchange will decide for you.

Use the Exchange Management Console to Create a New User with a Mailbox

To use the EMC to create a new user with a mailbox:

1. Open the EMC (Start ➢ All Programs ➢ Microsoft Exchange Server 2010 ➢ Exchange Management Console).

2. In the Console tree in the left pane, browse to the Recipient Configuration ➢ Mailbox node.

   The current list of mailboxes in your organization will be displayed in the Results pane.

3. In the Actions pane on the right, select the New Mailbox option to launch the New Mailbox wizard.

4. At the Introduction screen of the wizard, select User Mailbox as the type of mailbox that you are creating and click Next.

5. At the User Type screen, select New User and click Next.

6. At the User Information screen (Figure 4.1), enter the user information for the new mailbox and then click Next. You can browse and select an Organizational Unit (OU) to place the account in if you don't want to use the default OU for new accounts.

7. At the Mailbox Settings screen, enter an alias for the user. You can also specify additional options here, such as which mailbox database

to put the user in or what managed folder policy applies to the user, as shown in Figure 4.2.

Figure 4.1: Supplying information for a new user mailbox

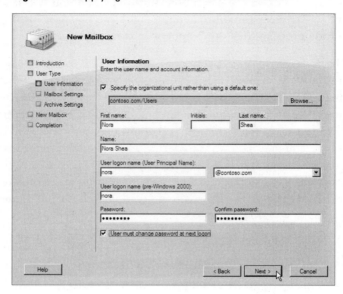

Figure 4.2: Specifying a database for a new mailbox

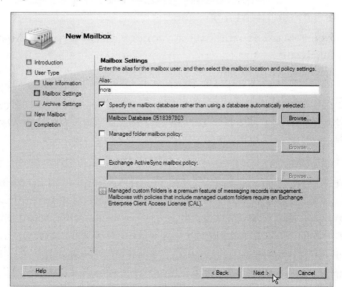

For more information about managed folders, see Chapter 9, "Administering Mailbox Content." If you do not select a database, the database used will be determined automatically.

8. At the Archive Settings screen, determine whether you will give this user an online archive and click Next.

   For more information about archiving, see Chapter 9.

9. The next screen displays the options that will be used to create the user mailbox. If you are satisfied with these options, click New to create the account.

10. At the Completion screen, confirm that the user mailbox was created successfully and click the Finish button.

Use the Exchange Management Shell to Create a Room Mailbox

To create a user mailbox in the EMS:

1. Run the New-Mailbox cmdlet with the following parameters:

```
New-Mailbox -Alias [MailAlias] -Name [FullName] ↵
-FirstName [FirstName] -LastName [LastName] ↵
-UserPrincipalName [UPN]
```

   For example, to create the same mailbox that we created in the EMC, use the following command:

```
New-Mailbox -Alias 'nora' -Name 'Nora Shea' -FirstName ↵
'Nora' -LastName 'Shea' -UserPrincipalName ↵
'nora@contoso.com'
```

2. When you run this command, you will be prompted to enter a password for the account. The password you type in will be the password of the new user, as shown in Figure 4.3.

Create a Mail-Enabled Contact

Contacts are recipients that don't have a mailbox in your Exchange organization. You typically want to create a contact when you have a recipient that you want to appear in an address list, but that recipient doesn't live in your Exchange organization. This situation often arises when two companies merge. Two separate Exchange organizations can

Getting Started

PART I

have a similar Global Address List (GAL) if both organizations create contacts in their Active Directory forest that represent the users in the other system. Typically, these contacts would have an SMTP address associated with them, such as eleanor@contoso.com. Once the contact is created and mail-enabled, it shows up in the GAL and can be selected just like recipients that have mailboxes in your Exchange organization.

Figure 4.3: Creating a new user mailbox in the EMS

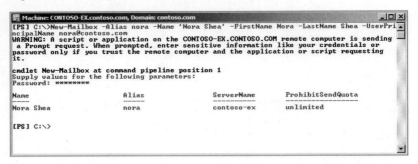

Create a Mail-Enabled Contact in the Exchange Management Console

To create a mail-enabled contact in the EMC:

1. Open the EMC (Start ➤ All Programs ➤ Microsoft Exchange Server 2010 ➤ Exchange Management Console).

2. In the Console tree in the left pane, browse to the Recipient Configuration ➤ Mail Contact node.

   The current list of contacts in your organization will be displayed in the Results pane.

3. In the Actions pane on the right, select the New Mail Contact option to launch the New Mail Contact wizard.

4. At the Introduction screen of the wizard, select whether you are creating a new contact or mail-enabling an existing contact. In this example, we'll create a new contact. Click Next to continue.

5. At the Contact Information screen, fill in the name, alias, and email address of the contact, as shown in Figure 4.4, and click Next.

6. At the New Mail Contact screen, verify that the information is accurate and click New to create the contact.

7. At the Completion screen, click Finish to complete the process.

Figure 4.4: Creating a new mail-enabled contact

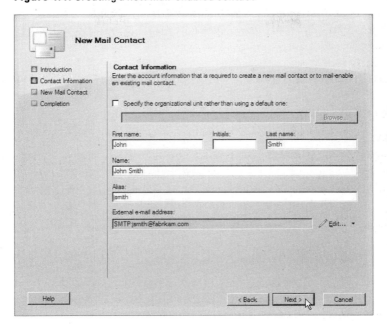

Create a Mail-Enabled Contact in the Exchange Management Shell

To create a mail-enabled contact in the EMS, run the New-MailContact cmdlet with the following parameters:

```
New-MailContact [FullContactName] -ExternalEmailAddress ↵
[SMTPAddress]
```

Mail-Enable an Existing User

There may be cases where you have an existing account in Active Directory that does not have an Exchange mailbox. You can mail-enable this account, thereby creating a mailbox for the user in Exchange and associating the account with that mailbox.

Mail-Enable an Existing User in the Exchange Management Console

To mail-enable a user in the EMC:

1. Open the EMC (Start ➤ All Programs ➤ Microsoft Exchange Server 2010 ➤ Exchange Management Console).

2. In the Console tree in the left pane, browse to the Recipient Configuration ➤ Mailbox node.

   The current list of user mailboxes in your organization will be displayed in the Results pane.

3. In the Actions pane on the right, select the New Mailbox option to launch the New Mailbox wizard.

4. At the Introduction screen of the wizard, select User Mailbox as the type of mailbox that you are creating and click Next.

5. At the User Type screen, you can choose to create a new account for the user mailbox or choose an existing account to attach the mailbox to. We're going to create a mailbox for an existing user, so select Existing Users and click Add.

6. In the next screen, you can select users that you want to create mailboxes for. Select the users that you want and click OK. Click Next at the User Type screen.

7. At the Mailbox Settings screen, enter the alias for the user and select the database and policies for the user, if you choose to. Click Next to continue.

8. At the Archive Settings screen, choose whether you want to give the user an online archive and click Next.

9. At the next screen, click the New button to mail-enable the accounts you selected.

10. At the Completion screen, click Finish to complete the process.

Mail-Enable an Existing User in the Exchange Management Shell

To create a mailbox for an existing user in the EMS, run the `Enable-Mailbox` cmdlet with the following parameter:

```
Enable-Mailbox [Name]
```

The *Name* parameter can be specified in many different forms. For example, you can use the username, or user's name in quotes, or even the distinguished name of the account. The following commands are all valid:

```
Enable-Mailbox joesmith
Enable-Mailbox "Joe Smith"
Enable-Mailbox "cn=Joe Smith,cn=Users,dc=contoso,dc=com"
```

Modify a User's Contact Information

The contact information about users that appears in address lists is
stored on the user account. Each account in Active Directory has a series
of attributes associated with it, where information about the account
is stored. For example, there is an attribute called `telephoneNumber` that
contains the phone number of the user. When you open a user's contact
information from the GAL in Outlook, the information displayed on the
form is stored in these attributes. You can modify this information in
the EMC or the EMS.

Modify Contact Information in the Exchange Management Console

To modify a user's contact information in the EMC:

1. Open the EMC (Start ➤ All Programs ➤ Microsoft Exchange
   Server 2010 ➤ Exchange Management Console).

2. In the Console tree in the left pane, browse to the Recipient
   Configuration ➤ Mailbox node. The current list of user mailboxes in your organization will be displayed in the Results pane.

3. Select the user mailbox that you want to modify and click the
   Properties option for the user in the Actions pane on the right.

   The properties dialog box for the user will open.

4. In the properties dialog box for the user mailbox, select the tab with
   the information that you want to edit, as shown in Figure 4.5. After
   you edit this information, click OK to save the changes.

   These changes are made to the user's account and will be reflected
   in the address lists accessed by Outlook clients.

Modify Contact Information in the Exchange Management Shell

To modify a user's contact information in the EMS, run the `Set-User`
cmdlet with parameters that specify the information you want to
change. For example, the following cmdlet can be used to change the
address for a user:

```
Set-User 'John Smith' -StreetAddress '123 Oak Street' -City ↵
'Redmond' -State 'WA'
```

If you don't know what parameter to use when updating an attribute,
you can update the attribute in the EMC and preview the PowerShell
command as described in Chapter 2, "Using the Exchange Management

Console and the Exchange Management Shell." You can also use the
`Get-Help` cmdlet to view a list of all of the parameters that the `Set-User`
cmdlet accepts. Some of the more common parameters for updating user
information are provided in Table 4.1.

Figure 4.5: Editing the contact information for a user

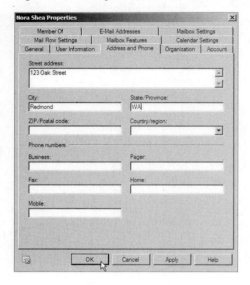

Table 4.1: Common Parameters When Updating Contact Information in the EMS

Type of Information	Cmdlet Parameter
Street address	StreetAddress
City	City
State	State
Zip code	PostalCode
Country	CountryOrRegion
Business telephone number	Phone
Home telephone number	HomePhone
Mobile telephone number	MobilePhone
Fax number	Fax

Table 4.1: Common Parameters When Updating Contact Information in the EMS *(continued)*

Type of Information	Cmdlet Parameter
Pager number	`Pager`
Title	`Title`
Department	`Department`
Office	`Office`

Getting Started

PART I

Hide a User from the Address Lists

You have the ability to prevent recipients from showing up in an address list. When you choose to do this for an account, an attribute called `msExchHideFromAddressLists` is set to `$True`. Setting this attribute to `$True` excludes the recipient from all address lists. You should note that when an account is hidden, it can't be verified as an active account when you are setting up an Outlook profile. Therefore, if you need to create an Outlook profile for the account so you can open its mailbox, you need to unhide it, create the Outlook profile, and then rehide it.

Hide a User from Address Lists in the Exchange Management Console

To hide a user from the address lists using the EMC:

1. Open the EMC (Start ➤ All Programs ➤ Microsoft Exchange Server 2010 ➤ Exchange Management Console).

2. In the Console tree in the left pane, browse to the Recipient Configuration ➤ Mailbox node.

   The current list of user mailboxes in your organization will be displayed in the Results pane.

3. Select the user mailbox that you want to modify and click the Properties option for the user in the Actions pane on the right.

   The properties dialog box for that user will be displayed.

4. In the properties dialog box, ensure that the General tab is selected and check the Hide From Exchange Address Lists option. Click OK to make the change.

Hide a User from Address Lists in the Exchange Management Shell

To hide a user from the address lists using the EMS, run the `Set-Mailbox` cmdlet with the `HiddenFromAddressListsEnabled` parameter. The following cmdlet prevents the user account John Smith from showing up in address lists:

```
Set-Mailbox 'John Smith' -HiddenFromAddressListsEnabled $true
```

Manage Resource Accounts

Resource accounts are different from user accounts. You generally want special functionality with resource accounts that wouldn't typically apply with user accounts. For example, someone might use a conference room mailbox to schedule a conference room. In this situation, you would want the request accepted or rejected automatically. (In a user account, the user needs to explicitly approve or reject a meeting invitation.) Resource mailboxes allow you to use this type of specialized functionality.

Convert an Existing Mailbox into a Resource Mailbox

In Exchange Server 2003, resource mailboxes didn't exist. Instead, many organizations used shared mailboxes that were monitored by people for scheduling resources such as conference rooms. When you move to Exchange Server 2010, you will want to convert those Exchange 2003 shared mailboxes into resource mailboxes so you can take advantage of the automatic booking feature. Converting an existing mailbox into a resource mailbox can only be performed in the EMS. To do the conversion, you will use the `Set-Mailbox` cmdlet and specify a `Type` parameter on the mailbox. Table 4.2 describes the types of mailboxes that can be specified.

Table 4.2: Valid Resource Mailbox Types

Type Parameter	Description
`Equipment`	A mailbox that represents a piece of equipment, such as a projector
`Room`	A mailbox that represents a room that can be booked
`Shared`	A single mailbox that is shared between multiple people

The syntax for converting a mailbox to a resource mailbox is as follows:

```
Set-Mailbox [MailboxName] -Type [ResourceType]
```

Create a Mailbox for a Conference Room

A conference room mailbox is a special type of mailbox that represents a room that users can schedule. These mailboxes can be included in meeting requests and can take advantage of automatic scheduling. Like every other mailbox, room mailboxes have an account in Active Directory with an email address associated with it. However, this account is disabled and can't be logged in to.

Create a Room Mailbox in the Exchange Management Console

To create a room mailbox in the EMC:

1. Open the EMC (Start ➢ All Programs ➢ Microsoft Exchange Server 2010 ➢ Exchange Management Console).

2. In the Console tree in the left pane, browse to the Recipient Configuration ➢ Mailbox node.

   The current list of mailboxes in your organization will be displayed in the Results pane.

3. In the Actions pane on the right, select the New Mailbox option to launch the New Mailbox wizard.

4. At the Introduction screen of the wizard, select Room Mailbox as the type of mailbox that you are creating and click Next.

5. At the User Type screen, you can choose to create a new account for the room mailbox or choose an existing account. In this example, we'll create a new account. Select New User and click Next.

6. At the User Information screen, fill out the appropriate information for the account that represents the conference room, as shown in Figure 4.6. The password that you enter here can be a random password that you don't need to remember. This account will be disabled, so you will not need to use this password. Click Next.

7. At the Mailbox Settings screen, enter an alias for the mailbox and then click Next.

8. At the Archive Settings screen, click Next.

Getting Started

PART I

Figure 4.6: Account information for new room mailboxes

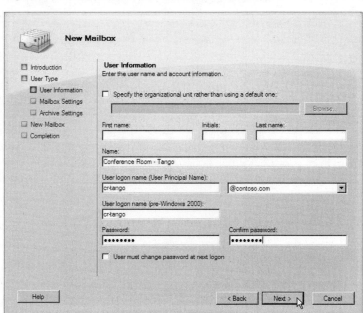

9. The next screen displays the options for the room mailbox that will be created. If you are satisfied with these options, click New to create the mailbox.

10. At the Completion screen, confirm that the room mailbox was created successfully and click Finish.

Create a Room Mailbox in the Exchange Management Shell

To create a room mailbox in the EMS, run the New-Mailbox cmdlet with the following parameters:

```
New-Mailbox [MailboxName] -UserPrincipalName [UPN] -Room
```

The following command creates a mailbox with the name Conference Room - Delta and the username cr-delta:

```
New-Mailbox 'Conference Room - Delta' -UserPrincipalName ↵
cr-delta@contoso.com -Room
```

Book Resources Automatically

When a resource is requested, the booking of that resource can be automatically accepted. This is accomplished using the Resource Booking Attendant, which acts on behalf of the resource mailbox and automatically approves resource requests.

Turn On Automatic Resource Booking in the Exchange Management Console

To turn on automatic resource booking in the EMC:

1. Open the EMC (Start ➤ All Programs ➤ Microsoft Exchange Server 2010 ➤ Exchange Management Console).

2. In the Console tree in the left pane, browse to the Recipient Configuration ➤ Mailbox node.

    The current list of mailboxes in your organization will be displayed in the Results pane.

3. In the Results pane, select the resource mailbox that you want to enable automatic booking on. In the Actions pane, click the Properties button that corresponds to the resource that you selected, as shown in Figure 4.7.

Figure 4.7: Choosing the resource mailbox to update

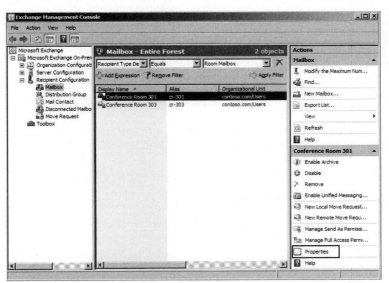

4. In the properties dialog box for the resource, select the Resource General tab. Check the box Enable The Resource Book Attendant option. Click OK to make the change.

Control Automatic Resource Booking in the Exchange Management Shell

When you enable or disable automatic resource booking in the EMS, you need to provide the correct `AutomateProcessing` parameter in the `Set-CalendarProcessing` cmdlet. This setting impacts both the Resource Booking Attendant (the process that automatically accepts booking requests based on the policies defined) and the Calendar Attendant (the process that updates meeting requests and responses). The `AutomateProcessing` parameter can be set to three possible values:

-AutomateProcessing None   Turns off both the Resource Booking Attendant and the Calendar Attendant

-AutomateProcessing AutoAccept   Enables both the Resource Booking Attendant and the Calendar Attendant

-AutomateProcessing AutoUpdate   Disables the Resource Booking Attendant, but leaves the Calendar Attendant enabled

To enable resource booking in the EMS, run the `Set-CalendarProcessing` cmdlet and set `AutomateProcessing` to `AutoAccept`:

```
Set-CalendarProcessing [MailboxName] -AutomateProcessing ↵
AutoAccept
```

Customize the Response to Resource Requests

When the resource mailbox schedules a resource booking, you have the option of replying to the requestor with a custom message.

Customize the Response Message in the Exchange Management Console

To define the custom response message in the EMC:

1. Open the EMC (Start ➢ All Programs ➢ Microsoft Exchange Server 2010 ➢ Exchange Management Console).

2. In the Console tree in the left pane, browse to the Recipient Configuration ➢ Mailbox node.

   The current list of mailboxes in your organization will be displayed in the Results pane.

3. In the Results pane, select the resource mailbox that you want to add the custom message to. In the Actions pane, click the Properties button that corresponds to the resource that you selected.

4. In the properties dialog box for the resource, select the Resource Information tab. Select the Add Additional Text check box. In the Additional Text field, enter the text that you want sent in response to booking this resource and then click OK. This process is shown in Figure 4.8.

Figure 4.8: Adding custom text to a resource-booking response

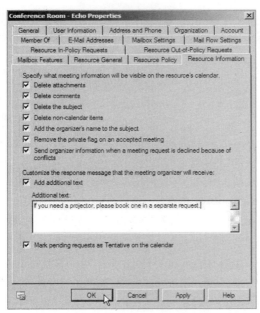

Customize the Response Message in the Exchange Management Shell

To customize the response message in the EMS, run the Set-CalendarProcessing cmdlet with the following parameters:

```
Set-CalendarProcessing [MailboxName] -AddAdditionalResponse ↵
$true -AdditionalResponse [TextToRespondWith]
```

Manage Recipient Addresses

When an email is sent, that message is routed to the organization that owns the address space. (The address space consists of everything after the @ symbol in the address.) Therefore, to successfully manage addresses for that address space, you must own the address space. You can specify an email address for an address space that you don't own, but unless that message is configured as an accepted address space and can be routed to your organization, that user will never receive messages based on that address.

Add an Email Address Manually

You can give users additional addresses in namespaces that you own. Any email sent to these addresses will go to the user who you configured the address for.

Add an Email Address in the Exchange Management Console

To specify additional addresses manually with the EMC, follow these steps:

1. Open the EMC (Start ➤ All Programs ➤ Microsoft Exchange Server 2010 ➤ Exchange Management Console).

2. In the Console tree in the left pane, browse to the Recipient Configuration ➤ Mailbox node.

   The current list of user mailboxes in your organization will be displayed in the Results pane.

3. Select the user mailbox that you want to modify and click the Properties option for the user in the Actions pane on the right.

   The properties dialog box for that user will be displayed.

4. In the properties dialog box, select the E-Mail Addresses tab. The list of current addresses is displayed for the user. The SMTP address that is listed in bold is the default address for the account, meaning that this address is used when an email is replied to.

5. Click the Add button to add an additional SMTP address.

6. In the SMTP Address dialog box, type in the email address that you want to add and click OK, as shown in Figure 4.9.

Figure 4.9: Adding an additional SMTP address for a user

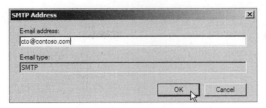

7. The new SMTP address will show up in the list of addresses for that user. Click OK to make the changes and to close the properties dialog box.

Add an Email Address in the Exchange Management Shell

You can also use the EMS to add an additional email address for the user. Run the `Set-Mailbox` cmdlet with the `EmailAddresses` parameter. Specify each SMTP address with a prefix of `smtp:`. For example, if you want to use the address `cto@contoso.com`, you would enter it as `smtp:cto@contoso.com`. For the address that you want to make the primary address (the one used for email replies), use an uppercase `SMTP:` in front of the address. Separate each address by a comma.

The following cmdlet adds two addresses to the John Smith mailbox. Replies will come from the `john.smith@contoso.com` address.

```
Set-Mailbox 'John Smith' -EmailAddresses ↵
'smtp:cto@contoso.com', 'SMTP:john.smith@contoso.com'
```

Create an Email Address Policy

If you don't want to manually specify addresses for each recipient, you can use an email address policy to apply email addresses to multiple recipients. When you define the email address policy, you specify how you want to format the email address that you are creating and which recipients this style of address applies to.

NOTE You can create a policy only for an address that you have configured as an accepted domain.

You can choose a predefined email address for the policy, or you can build a custom address. When defining a custom address, you use variables to build the email address. For example, `%g.%s@contoso.com` would form the email address *firstname.lastname@contoso.com* for the user that the policy is applied to. Table 4.3 outlines each of the available variables.

Table 4.3: Email Address Policy Variables

Variable	Description
%m	Email alias
%s	Last name
%g	First name
%i	Middle initial
%d	Display name
%#s	The character # stands for an integer representing the number of characters that you specify for the last name. For example, if the last name is Smith, then `%3s` would equal `smi`.
%#g	The character # stands for an integer representing the number of characters that you specify for the first name. For example, if the first name is John, then `%2g` would equal `jo`.

Configure a Predefined Email Address Policy in the Exchange Management Console

To create a new email address policy in the EMC:

1. Open the EMC (Start ➤ All Programs ➤ Microsoft Exchange Server 2010 ➤ Exchange Management Console).

2. In the Console tree in the left pane, browse to the Organization Configuration ➤ Hub Transport node.

3. In the Actions pane on the right, click New E-Mail Address Policy. This launches the New E-Mail Address Policy wizard.

4. At the Introduction screen, enter a name for the new policy and click the Browse button to select the container of recipients who you want to apply the policy to. You can also choose which types of recipients you want to apply the policy to. Click Next when you are finished.

For example, if you want to apply the policy only to users with mailboxes, choose the Users With Exchange Mailboxes option, as shown in Figure 4.10.

Figure 4.10: Choosing recipient types to which an address policy applies

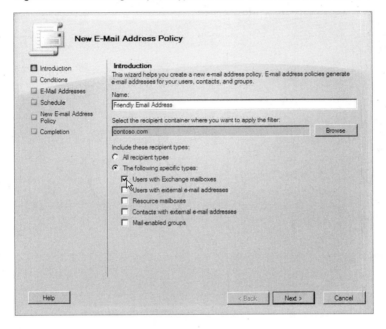

5. At the Conditions screen, you can specify detailed criteria for filtering which recipients receive the policy. For example, you can specify that all users in a particular department get a certain address policy. This configuration is shown in Figure 4.11. Click Next to continue.

6. At the E-Mail Addresses screen, click the Add button to add an address to the policy.

   The SMTP E-Mail Address dialog box will appear.

7. Select a predefined address. Figure 4.12 demonstrates choosing an address policy of firstname.lastname@contoso.com. Click OK after you have defined your address.

Figure 4.11: Filtering recipients for an address policy

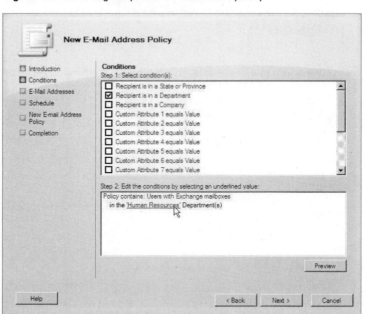

Figure 4.12: Choosing a predefined address policy

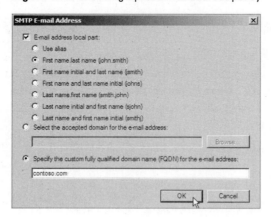

8. At the next screen, click Next to continue.

9. At the Schedule screen, you can specify when you want to apply the new policy. Click Next to continue.

    If the scope of your policy is a container with many recipients, it might take some time for the policy to update each recipient's addresses. You can choose to apply the policy now to those users or schedule it to run after hours when it will have less of an impact. You can also specify the maximum number of hours the update will work by choosing the option Cancel Tasks That Are Still Running After (Hours).

10. At the Configuration Summary screen, verify that the options you selected are accurate and click New to create the new policy.

    If you choose to apply the policy now, the policy will be applied before you can continue.

11. At the Completion screen, review the results and click the Finish button to close the wizard.

Build a Custom Email Address Policy in the Exchange Management Shell

If you want to create a custom address policy, you can use the EMS. When you do, you will need to specify the `IncludedRecipients` parameter to select which recipient types are included in the policy. Table 4.4 shows the possible values for this parameter.

Table 4.4: Values for Filtering the Recipient Type in a New Email Address Policy

Value	Description
AllRecipients	Every recipient type available
MailboxUsers	User recipients with a mailbox in the organization
Resources	Resource recipients, such as rooms and equipment
MailContacts	Mail-enabled contacts
MailGroups	Mail-enabled distribution groups
MailUsers	Mail-enabled users that don't have mailboxes in the organization
None	No recipients

Getting Started

PART I

To create a new email address policy in the EMS, run the New-EmailAddressPolicy cmdlet with the following parameters. Use the address policy variables outlined in Table 4.4 to build the custom address policy.

The following example creates a policy named Friendly Address that applies to mailbox users:

```
New-EmailAddressPolicy 'Friendly Address' ↵
-IncludedRecipients MailboxUsers ↵
-EnabledPrimarySMTPAddressTemplate 'SMTP:%g.%s@contoso.com'
```

Apply an Address Policy

If you don't apply an email address policy when you create it, you will need to apply it at a later date. You can apply the policy through the EMC or through the EMS.

Apply an Address Policy Using the Exchange Management Console

To apply an address policy through the EMC:

1. Open the EMC (Start ➤ All Programs ➤ Microsoft Exchange Server 2010 ➤ Exchange Management Console).

2. In the Console tree in the left pane, browse to the Organization Configuration ➤ Hub Transport node.

3. In the Work area, click on the E-Mail Address Policies tab to display the list of address policies that exist. Select the policy that you want to apply and click Apply in the Actions pane.

   This launches the Apply E-Mail Address Policy wizard.

4. At the Introduction screen, select when you want to apply the policy. You can apply it now or schedule it to run later. You can also choose how many hours you want to let the policy run for. If the task exceeds the number of hours that you specify, the task will be terminated. Click Next to continue.

5. At the Configuration Summary screen, click Apply to apply the policy.

6. At the Completion screen, click Finish to close the wizard.

Apply an Address Policy Using the Exchange Management Shell

To apply an address policy using the EMS, run the `Update-EmailAddressPolicy` cmdlet and specify the policy that you want to apply. The following example updates the policy `Friendly Address Policy` immediately:

```
Update-EmailAddressPolicy 'Friendly Address Policy'
```

Manage Recipient Mailboxes

Managing the mailboxes of your recipients is the second part that makes up the recipient administration aspects of Exchange. When managing the mailboxes of your recipients, you are affecting the data stored in Exchange and how that data is accessed.

Manage Mailbox Growth

One of the most important jobs an Exchange administrator can perform is to manage the growth of mailboxes. There is a finite amount of storage available for users, so it's important to keep an eye on how storage space is used and enforce quotas on mailboxes when necessary.

Impose Storage Quotas on Specific Users

Storage quotas can be set on the mailbox database as a whole as well as on the individual mailboxes. When setting storage quotas on the database, every mailbox on that database adheres to that quota. However, you can also choose to set the quota specifically on the mailbox, which overrides the quotas set on the database.

Impose a Storage Quota on a Specific User with the Exchange Management Console

1. Open the EMC (Start ➤ All Programs ➤ Microsoft Exchange Server 2010 ➤ Exchange Management Console).

2. In the Console tree in the left pane, browse to the Recipient Configuration ➤ Mailbox node.

The current list of user mailboxes in your organization will be displayed in the Results pane.

3. Select the user mailbox that you want to modify and click the Properties option for the user in the Actions pane on the right.

The properties dialog box for that user will be displayed.

4. Select the Mailbox Settings tab and choose Storage Quotas from the list of available settings. Click the Properties button to open the storage quota options.

5. In the Storage Quotas dialog box, you can deselect the option to use the database defaults and instead specify storage quotas directly to that user. Figure 4.13 demonstrates this capability. Click OK when you are finished.

Figure 4.13: Specifying storage quotas for a mailbox

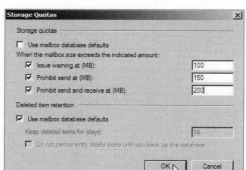

6. Back in the properties dialog box for the mailbox, click OK to apply the quotas and close the dialog box.

Impose a Storage Quota on a Specific User with the Exchange Management Shell

When using the EMS to set quotas, you will need to specify which quotas you are setting. To do this, you must use the appropriate parameter. Table 4.5 shows the various quota parameters and describes when they should be used.

Table 4.5: Quota Parameters Used in the EMS

Parameter	Description
ProhibitSendQuota	When this quota is exceeded, users cannot send messages.
ProhibitSendReceiveQuota	When exceeded, users cannot send or receive messages.
IssueWarningQuota	This limit defines when the user will begin receiving messages telling them that they are getting close to their quotas.
UseDatabaseQuotaDefaults	When set to $false, indicates that the mailbox should use its own quotas instead of obeying the quotas set on the database.

To apply storage quotas using the EMS, run the Set-Mailbox cmdlet and specify the quota parameters that you want to configure, using Table 4.5. The following example sets all three specific quotas on the John Smith mailbox:

```
Set-Mailbox 'John Smith' -ProhibitSendQuota 150MB
-ProhibitSendReceiveQuota 200MB -IssueWarningQuota 100MB
-UseDatabaseQuotaDefaults $false
```

Set Message Size Limits on a User

When you set message size limits on mailboxes, you can control how large the messages are that a mailbox can both send and receive. The larger the number, the more potential exists for one message to consume a large chunk of available storage, which might cause users to reach their quotas faster. Also, larger messages take longer to deliver, so several large messages have the potential of backing up the mail queues and slowing down the delivery of other messages.

Set Message Size Limits on a Mailbox Using the Exchange Management Console

To set message size limits on a single user's mailbox using the EMC:

1. Open the EMC (Start ➤ All Programs ➤ Microsoft Exchange Server 2010 ➤ Exchange Management Console).

2. In the Console tree in the left pane, browse to the Recipient Configuration ➢ Mailbox node.

   The current list of user mailboxes in your organization will be displayed in the Results pane.

3. Select the user mailbox that you want to modify and click the Properties option for the user in the Actions pane on the right.

   The properties dialog box for that user will be displayed.

4. Select the Mail Flow Settings tab and choose Message Size Restrictions from the list of available settings. Click the Properties button to configure the size restrictions for the individual mailbox.

5. In the Message Size Restrictions dialog box, choose whether to restrict the message send limit or the message receive limit and enter the size that you want to restrict it to. For example, Figure 4.14 demonstrates limiting both the send size and the receive size to 10,240 KB (10 MB) for this individual mailbox.

Figure 4.14: Limiting the message size for a mailbox

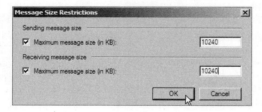

6. Click OK to close the Message Size Restrictions dialog box. When back in the properties dialog box for the mailbox, click OK to apply the size restriction and close the dialog box.

Set Message Size Limits on a Mailbox Using the Exchange Management Shell

To apply message size limits using the EMS, run the Set-Mailbox cmdlet and specify the MaxSendSize and MaxReceiveSize parameters that indicate the maximum size limit of sent and received messages. The following example limits the John Smith mailbox to send and receive messages no larger than 10 MB:

```
Set-Mailbox 'John Smith' -MaxSendSize 10MB -MaxReceiveSize ↵
10MB
```

Manage Mailbox Access

Although mailboxes are tied to individual accounts in Active Directory, other users can be granted access to the data in the mailbox. You can remove access to mailboxes as well. This section shows you how to disable a user's access to their mailbox and how to give other people access to mailboxes.

Disable a User's Mailbox

When a mailbox is disabled, two things happen:

- The account that is tied to the mailbox is stripped of all of the Exchange-specific attributes. This effectively disconnects the mailbox from the account. However, the account is not deleted and remains in Active Directory.

NOTE The behavior when you disable a mailbox is different from the behavior when you choose the Remove option. When you remove a mailbox, the associated Active Directory account is deleted in addition to the mailbox being deleted.

- The mailbox is scheduled for deletion.

  See Chapter 10, "Maintaining Reliability and Availability," for details on how to recover a deleted mailbox.

Disable a Mailbox Using the Exchange Management Console

To disable a mailbox using the EMC:

1. Open the EMC (Start ➤ All Programs ➤ Microsoft Exchange Server 2010 ➤ Exchange Management Console).
2. In the Console tree in the left pane, browse to the Recipient Configuration ➤ Mailbox node.

The current list of user mailboxes in your organization will be displayed in the Results pane.

3. Select the mailbox and click the Disable option for the user in the Actions pane on the right.

   This will remove the account from the mailbox and mark the mailbox for deletion.

4. When prompted for confirmation, click the Yes button.

Disable a Mailbox Using the Exchange Management Shell

To disable a mailbox using the EMS, run the `Disable-Mailbox` command and specify the mailbox that you want to disable. The following example disables the `John Smith` mailbox. By specifying the `Confirm` parameter, you are telling the EMS command not to prompt you for confirmation. This is useful when you are disabling many mailboxes at the same time, because you won't have to keep confirming after every mailbox is processed.

```
Disable-Mailbox 'John Smith' -Confirm:$false
```

Give a User Access to a Mailbox

You can give other users different levels of access to mailboxes other than their own. When using the EMC, you have the option of giving SendAs Access or Full Access.

Give a User Access to a Mailbox Using the Exchange Management Console

To use the EMC to give another user Full Access to a mailbox:

1. Open the EMC (Start ➤ All Programs ➤ Microsoft Exchange Server 2010 ➤ Exchange Management Console).

2. In the Console tree in the left pane, browse to the Recipient Configuration ➤ Mailbox node.

   The current list of user mailboxes in your organization will be displayed in the Results pane.

3. Select the mailbox for which you want to modify the permissions and choose the Manage Full Access Permission option in the Actions pane.

4. In the Manage Full Access Permission screen, you can add and remove users that have access to this mailbox. Click the Add button to add a user to the mailbox.

5. In the Select A User Or Group dialog box, choose the user or group that you want to grant access for and click OK.

6. Back in the Manage Full Access Permission screen, click the Manage button to grant permissions to the users and groups that you specified.

7. In the Completion screen, click the Finish button to complete to the change.

Give Users Access to a Mailbox Using the Exchange Management Shell

When you give someone access to another mailbox with the EMS, you will need to determine what level of access they need. Table 4.6 outlines the appropriate values to use with the `AccessRights` parameter to give the corresponding level of access.

Table 4.6: Mailbox Access Rights Parameters

Parameter	Permission Granted
ChangePermission	Gives the user the ability to change other permissions on the mailbox.
ChangeOwner	Allows the user to change the owner of the mailbox.
DeleteItem	The user will have the ability to delete content from the mailbox.
ExternalAccount	Specifies that the account is not in the same domain as the mailbox.
FullAccess	Gives the user full permissions to the mailbox.
ReadPermission	Gives the user the ability to read the mailbox.
SendAs	Allow the user to send messages under the identity of this mailbox.

To allow a user to gain access to a mailbox using the EMS, run the `Add-MailboxPermission` command and specify the user that you want to give permissions to and access rights that you want them to have. The available access rights are outlined in Table 4.6. The following example gives user Nora Shea full access to the John Smith mailbox:

```
Add-MailboxPermission 'John Smith' -User 'Nora Shea' ↵
-AccessRights FullAccess
```

Manage Mailbox Data

When managing the mailbox data, administrators need to be familiar with two primary functions:

- Moving the data around
- Gathering statistical information on the mailbox data

Moving the data is important because you will need to continuously monitor your mailbox databases and make sure that they don't grow so large that backups and maintenance windows can't be completed. If they get too large, you may need to move mailboxes to other databases or other servers to balance them out.

The statistical information that you can gather is also important because you can use this data for determining information about last mailbox access times, size of the mailbox, number of deleted items, and so forth. Knowing this information helps you manage your Exchange organization more effectively and efficiently.

This section shows you how to use Exchange 2010 to move mailbox data and gather information about it.

Obtain Information About a User's Mailbox

You can use the Exchange Management Shell to gather statistical information about a user's mailbox. Here is some of the useful information that you can gather:

- The number of items in the mailbox
- The number of deleted items
- The total size of the mailbox
- The last time a user logged on to the mailbox
- The last person to access the mailbox
- Information about the server and database the mailbox is currently hosted on
- The history of which databases the mailbox has moved between

> **NOTE** You can only gather this information through the EMS, and only after the user has already logged into the mailbox at least once.

To gather information about a user's mailbox using the Exchange Management Shell, run the `Get-MailboxStatistics` command and specify the mailbox that you want to gather statistics for. The following example gathers information about the `John Smith` mailbox and pipes it to the `FormatList` command (`fl` for short):

```
Get-MailboxStatistics 'John Smith' | fl
```

If you want to include the move history for the mailbox, you can use the `IncludeMoveHistory` parameter. The following command shows how to gather the move history for a user:

```
Get-MailboxStatistics 'Abe Berlas' -IncludeMoveHistory | fl ↵
DisplayName, MoveHistory
```

Export Messages from a User's Mailbox

In previous versions of Exchange, you had to use the ExMerge tool to export and import mail to and from a mailbox. This functionality is built into Exchange 2010. You can export messages from one mailbox into another using varying options, filters, and conditions. For example, you can choose to export only messages that contain certain words or that are from specific individuals.

> **NOTE** In order for you to have the ability to export messages, you need to have the Mailbox Import Export role. For steps on adding users to roles, refer to the "Manage Permissions" section in Chapter 12, "Securing Exchange Server."

Export Messages Using the Exchange Management Console

To use the EMC to export data from a mailbox:

1. Open the EMC (Start ➤ All Programs ➤ Microsoft Exchange Server 2010 ➤ Exchange Management Console).

2. In the Console tree in the left pane, browse to the Recipient Configuration ➤ Mailbox node.

The current list of user mailboxes in your organization will be displayed in the Results pane.

3. Select the mailbox that you want to export data from and click the Export Mailbox option in the Actions pane to launch the Export Mailbox wizard.

4. At the Introduction screen, click the Browse button to choose the mailbox that you want to export the messages into. In the Target folder field, type the name of the folder that you want the messages stored in. Click Next to continue.

5. At the Conditions screen, choose the conditions that will determine whether a message is exported. You have multiple options to choose from, including messages sent to or from a specific person, messages that contain certain words, or messages sent on a certain date.

6. At the Export Options screen, you can specify how messages that are exported are handled. For example, you may want to delete messages from the source mailbox if you are manually archiving messages into another mailbox. If you don't want source messages modified, just click Next.

7. At the Summary screen, click the Export button to export the messages.

8. At the Completion screen, click Finish to close the wizard.

Export Messages Using the Exchange Management Shell

To export data from a mailbox using the EMS, run the `Export-Mailbox` command and specify the mailbox that you want to export from as well as the mailbox you want to export the data into. The following example exports messages from the `John Smith` mailbox into the `Under Investigation` folder of the `Security Admin` mailbox:

```
Export-Mailbox 'John Smith' -TargetMailbox 'Security ↵
Admin' -TargetFolder 'Under Investigation'
```

Import Data into a User's Mailbox from PST Files

Exchange Server 2010 provides a cmdlet for importing data from one or more PST files in a folder into mailboxes. You need to use the EMS to perform this task.

To import mail from a PST into a mailbox, run the `Import-Mailbox` command and specify the PST file or folder containing the mail along with the mailbox that you want to import the mail into. The following command imports the file `johnsmith.pst` into the `John Smith` mailbox:

```
Import-Mailbox 'John Smith' -PSTFolderPath ↵
D:\MailPSTs\johnsmith.pst
```

Move a Mailbox to a Different Database

Mailbox moves in Exchange Server 2010 are handled differently from previous versions of Exchange. The new client access architecture in Exchange 2010 includes the capability to perform online mailbox moves, which allows users to maintain access to their mailboxes even while mailboxes are moved around. Mailbox moves are now asynchronous. They are performed by the Mailbox Replication Service (MRS). The MRS runs on Client Access servers and can move mailboxes inside of an organization and to other organizations over the Internet.

When moving mailboxes between different versions of Exchange, only the following versions are supported:

- Exchange Server 2010

- Exchange Server 2007 SP2

- Exchange Server 2003 SP2

In Exchange 2010, mailbox moves are requested by the administrator and then carried out by the Client Access servers. When you specify to move a mailbox, you are actually creating a move request and then monitoring the status of the request to see if it has been fulfilled yet.

Move a Mailbox to a Different Local Database Using the Exchange Management Console

To move a mailbox to a different database within the organization using the EMC:

1. Open the EMC (Start ➢ All Programs ➢ Microsoft Exchange Server 2010 ➢ Exchange Management Console).

2. In the Console tree in the left pane, browse to the Recipient Configuration ➢ Mailbox node.

   The current list of user mailboxes in your organization will be displayed in the Results pane.

3. Select the mailbox that you want to move and choose the New Local Move Request option in the Actions pane to launch the New Local Move Request wizard.

4. At the Introduction screen, click the Browse button to select the database that you want to move the mailbox to. Click Next to continue.

5. At the Move Options screen, choose whether you want to skip the entire mailbox if there are errors or just skip the messages that produced the errors. Click Next to continue.

6. At the Configuration Summary screen, click the New button to start the mailbox move.

7. At the Completion screen, click Finish to close the wizard.

Move a Mailbox to a Different Database Using the Exchange Management Shell

To move a mailbox to a different database within the organization using the EMS, run the New-MoveRequest command and use the TargetDatabase parameter to specify which database to move the mailbox to. The following example moves the John Smith mailbox to the database named VIPDatabase:

```
New-MoveRequest 'John Smith'  -TargetDatabase VIPDatabase
```

Verify That a Move Request Was Completed

After you create the move request, you will need to go back and verify that the request was fulfilled and that the move was completed. You can check the status of the move request in the EMC using the following step:

1. Open the EMC and browse to the Recipient Configuration ➤ Move Request node in the Console tree.

View the list move requests displayed in the Results pane. The status of the move request is noted in the Move Request Status column. When the status reads Completed, the move request has finished.

Clear an Uncompleted Move Request

While the move request is in the list, the mailbox will function as normal, but you will not be able to move the mailbox again until you clear the request. Also, the mailbox will have a green arrow icon on it when you view it in the EMC. This notes that there is a move request on record for the mailbox. Once you clear the move request, this green arrow disappears and the mailbox icon resets to its usual icon. You can clear the move request by following these steps:

1. Open the EMC and browse to the Recipient Configuration ➤ Move Request node in the Console tree.

2. Select the move request that you want to clear.

3. Click the Clear Move Request task from the Actions pane for the request you selected.

4. When you are prompted with the dialog box asking you if you are sure that you want to clear the request, click the Yes button.

Manage Distribution Groups

Distribution groups enable collections of recipients to be gathered into a single unit. Rather than having to email each recipient individually, a message can be sent to a group and each member of that group receives the message.

Exchange Server 2010 brings about some new functionality in distribution groups. Among these is the ability to have self-managed groups and moderated messaging.

Manage Basic Distribution Group Functionality

The basics of distribution group management include creating new distributions groups, mail-enabling existing ones, and modifying the memberships of distribution groups.

Create a Distribution Group

When you create a new distribution group, you create a universal group object in Active Directory. These groups contain the Exchange attributes that give them email addresses and the appropriate data to ensure they appear in address lists. Distribution groups can be security enabled, which allows them to be used for assigning permissions to resources, such as files or folders. When you create the group, you can decide whether you want the group to be used for distribution or security. Choosing the Security option allows you to still use the group for distribution, but it also security-enables the group.

Create a Distribution Group in the Exchange Management Console

To create a distribution group in the EMC:

1. Open the EMC (Start ➤ All Programs ➤ Microsoft Exchange Server 2010 ➤ Exchange Management Console).

2. In the Console tree in the left pane, browse to the Recipient Configuration ➤ Distribution Group node.

3. Click the New Distribution Group option in the Actions pane to start the New Distribution Group wizard.

4. At the Introduction screen, ensure that New Group is selected and click Next.

5. At the Group Information screen, select whether this group will be used for distribution only or if it will be security enabled as well. Enter the name and alias of the group and click Next.

6. At the Configuration Summary screen, click the New button to create the group.

7. At the Completion screen, click Finish to close the wizard.

Create a Distribution Group in the Exchange Management Shell

To create a new distribution group using the EMS, run the New-DistributionGroup command and include the Type parameter to specify the options that you want to set for the group. If you don't specify the type of group you are creating (Distribution or Security), the group defaults to a distribution group. The following example creates a security-enabled distribution group named HR Personnel:

```
New-DistributionGroup 'HR Personnel' -Type Security
```

Mail-Enable an Existing Group

When you mail-enable an existing group, you are taking a group that was already created in Active Directory, assigning an email address to it, and attaching Exchange attributes to it.

> **NOTE**   Groups have different scopes, which define various membership options and resource usage options for security-enabled groups. The three possible scopes for a group are universal groups, global groups, or domain local groups. You can only mail-enable existing groups if they are universal groups. Domain local groups and global groups must be converted to universal groups before they can become mail-enabled.

Mail-Enable an Existing Group in the Exchange Management Console

To mail-enable an existing group in the EMC:

1. Open the EMC (Start ≻ All Programs ≻ Microsoft Exchange Server 2010 ≻ Exchange Management Console).

2. In the Console tree in the left pane, browse to the Recipient Configuration ≻ Distribution Group node.

3. Click the New Distribution Group option in the Actions pane to start the New Distribution Group wizard.

4. At the Introduction screen, ensure that Existing Group is selected and click the Browse button.

5. The Select Group dialog box will open, allowing you to select the existing group that you want to mail-enable. Select the group and click OK to close the dialog box. Click Next at the Introduction screen to continue.

6. At the Group Information screen, type in a unique alias for the group and click Next.

7. At the Configuration Summary screen, click the New button to mail-enable the group.

8. At the Completion screen, click Finish to close the wizard.

Mail-Enable an Existing Group in the Exchange Management Shell

To mail-enable an existing group using the EMS, run the `Enable-DistributionGroup` command and specify the existing group that you want to mail-enable. The following command mail-enables the `IT Support` group:

```
Enable-DistributionGroup 'IT Support'
```

Manage Distribution Group Membership

The membership of the distribution group defines which recipients receive messages that are sent to that group's email address. Groups can contain as many members as you want to include. But when managing distribution groups with a large number of people, simple tasks become more difficult. When using the EMC, you have to scroll through multiple pages of users to find the one that you want to remove, and when visually searching through a lot of members, it's easy to pass members by without noticing them. Therefore, it's useful to know how to manage distribution groups in both the EMC and the EMS.

Add and Remove Distribution Group Members Using the Exchange Management Console

To manage the membership of a distribution group using the EMC:

1. Open the EMC (Start ➤ All Programs ➤ Microsoft Exchange Server 2010 ➤ Exchange Management Console).

2. In the Console tree in the left pane, browse to the Recipient Configuration ➤ Distribution Group node.

   The list of distribution groups is displayed in the Results pane in the middle.

3. Select the distribution group that you want to manage and click the Properties option in the Actions pane.

4. In the properties dialog box for the distribution group, click the Members tab.

   This tab lists the current members of the distribution group and allows you to add and remove members.

5. If you want to add a new member, click the Add button above the member list. This will launch the Select Recipient dialog box and allows you to choose who you want to add to the group.

6. If you want to remove a member, select the member in the list and click the red X button.

7. After you are finished editing the list of members, click OK to save the changes.

Add or Remove Distribution Group Membership Using the Exchange Management Shell

You can add or remove members from a distribution group using the EMS:

- The `Add-DistributionGroupMember` command adds members to a distribution group:

      Add-DistributionGroupMember 'HR Personnel' -Member ↵
      'John Smith'

- The `Remove-DistributionGroupMember` command removes members from a distribution group:

      Remove-DistributionGroupMember 'HR Personnel' -Member ↵
      'John Smith'

Administer Access to Distribution Groups

In previous versions of Exchange, distribution group management had to be performed by users using administrative tools or custom-built group management applications. In Exchange Server 2010, distribution group management is built into Outlook Web App (OWA). This section takes you through enabling users to manage their own distribution groups as well as setting up moderated distribution groups.

Give Management Responsibility for a Distribution Group to a User

You can allow users to manage the membership of distribution groups. Managers must have an Active Directory account in the forest and have a valid email address. Therefore, only user mailboxes and mail-enabled users can be managers of groups.

Add Distribution Group Managers Using the Exchange Management Console

To configure group managers with the EMC:

1. Open the EMC (Start ➢ All Programs ➢ Microsoft Exchange Server 2010 ➢ Exchange Management Console).

2. In the Console tree in the left pane, browse to the Recipient Configuration ➢ Distribution Group node.

   The list of distribution groups is displayed in the Results pane in the middle.

3. Select the distribution group that you want to delegate management to and click the Properties option in the Actions pane.

4. In the properties dialog box for the group, select the Group Information tab.

   The Managed By field displays the list of people who currently manage the group.

5. Click the Add button to launch the Select Mailbox Or Mail-Enabled User dialog box. From this dialog box, select the mailbox that you want to designate as a manager of this group and click OK.

6. Click OK to apply the manager changes and close the dialog box.

Specify Distribution Group Managers Using the Exchange Management Shell

To set the managers of a distribution group using the EMS, run the `Set-DistributionGroup` command with the `ManagedBy` parameter. List the group managers separated by commas. The following example sets the John Smith and Ann Yuki users as managers of the HR Personnel distribution group:

```
Set-DistributionGroup 'HR Personnel' -ManagedBy ↵
'John Smith','Ann Yuki'
```

Moderate Messages Sent to a Distribution Group

Messages that are sent to distribution groups can be moderated. When a group is moderated, the group moderators must approve certain messages before they are sent to the group. Moderation can be performed on all messages or specific users can be excluded from moderation. You can determine whether users are informed if their messages are not approved.

Set Up Message Moderation Using the Exchange Management Console

The following steps can be used to configure a distribution group for moderation with the EMC:

1. Open the EMC (Start ➤ All Programs ➤ Microsoft Exchange Server 2010 ➤ Exchange Management Console).

2. In the Console tree in the left pane, browse to the Recipient Configuration ➤ Distribution Group node.

The list of distribution groups is displayed in the Results pane in the middle.

3. Select the distribution group that you want to change the moderation options on and click the Properties option in the Actions pane.

4. In the properties dialog box for the group, select the Mail Flow Settings tab. In the list of settings, select the Message Moderation option and click the Properties button.

    This will launch the Message Moderation dialog box.

5. In the Message Moderation dialog box, select the option Messages Sent To This Group Have To Be Approved By A Moderator.

6. There are two list boxes enabled. The first list box contains the list of moderators who can approve messages. Click the Add button to launch the Select Recipient dialog box and choose a moderator.

7. The second list includes senders that don't require moderation. Messages from people who are in this list are sent immediately and are not subject to moderation. Click the Add button to launch the Select Recipient dialog box and choose the unmoderated recipients.

8. In the Select Moderation Notifications field, select how senders are notified about their messages not being approved. Figure 4.15 demonstrates the configuration of the message moderation options. Click OK to close the Message Moderation dialog box.

Figure 4.15: Message Moderation options for a distribution group

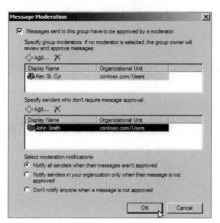

9. Click OK to close the properties dialog box for the distribution group and save the changes.

Set Up Message Moderation Using the Exchange Management Shell

When configuring moderation in the EMS, there are a few parameters you will want to set. Table 4.7 outlines these parameters.

Table 4.7: Distribution Group Moderation Parameters for the EMS

Parameter	Description
ModerationEnabled	Determines whether moderation is enabled on the distribution group. Set to $true or $false.
ModeratedBy	List of users that moderate this group. Separate the users in this list with commas.
BypassModerationFrom	List of senders that bypass the moderation rules. Separate the users in this list with commas.
BypassModerationFromDLMembers	Allows members of specified distribution groups to bypass moderation.

To set the message moderation options for a distribution group using the EMS, run the Set-DistributionGroup command and specify any of the moderation parameters outlined in Table 4.7. The following command turns on moderation and sets John Smith as a moderator.

```
Set-DistributionGroup 'HR Personnel' -ModerationEnabled ↵
$true -ModeratedBy 'John Smith'
```

Configure Distribution Groups That Update Automatically

Dynamic distribution groups are groups that have no set membership. The membership of dynamic distribution groups is determined by the filter and conditions that are active on the group. The primary advantage of this approach is that you don't have to manage group memberships.

On the other hand, if you want to have granular control over who is a member of a group, you need to create and manage complex filters.

Create a Dynamic Distribution Group

When creating a dynamic distribution group, you must specify the filter and conditions for group membership. This filter defines which recipients are included as members of this group.

Create a Dynamic Distribution Group Using the Exchange Management Console

To create a dynamic distribution group using the EMC:

1. Open the EMC (Start ➤ All Programs ➤ Microsoft Exchange Server 2010 ➤ Exchange Management Console).

2. In the Console tree in the left pane, browse to the Recipient Configuration ➤ Distribution Group node.

3. Click the New Dynamic Distribution Group option in the Actions pane to start the New Dynamic Distribution Group wizard.

4. At the Introduction screen of the New Dynamic Distribution Group wizard, enter the name of the dynamic distribution group and a valid unique email alias. Click Next.

5. At the Filter Settings screen, click the Browse button to launch the Select Organizational Unit dialog box and select the OU of recipients that this group encompasses. You can also filter by the recipient type and choose only certain recipients, such as resource mailboxes only. Click Next to continue.

6. At the Conditions screen, you can specify the conditions that are required for recipients to be a member of this dynamic group. Click Next to continue.

7. At the Configuration Summary screen, click the New button to create the dynamic distribution group.

8. At the Completion screen, click Finish to close the wizard.

Create a Dynamic Distribution Group Using the Exchange Management Shell

To create a dynamic distribution group using the EMS, run the New-DynamicDistributionGroup command and specify the filtering options for the new group using the `IncludedRecipients` parameter. For example, the following command creates an IT Support group that includes all of the mailboxes in the IT Support OU in Active Directory:

```
New-DynamicDistributionGroup 'IT Support' ↵
-IncludedRecipients MailboxUsers ↵
-RecipientContainer 'contoso.com/IT Support'
```

View the Membership of a Dynamic Distribution Group

When you create a dynamic distribution group, you set a filter that is used to determine who its members are. Therefore, there is no particular attribute that you can look at on the group to see who its members are as you can with regular distribution groups. If you want to view the membership of a dynamic distribution group at any one point in time, you can use one of the following methodologies.

View the Members of a Dynamic Distribution Group Using the Exchange Management Console

To view the membership of a dynamic distribution group using the EMC:

1. Open the EMC (Start ➤ All Programs ➤ Microsoft Exchange Server 2010 ➤ Exchange Management Console).

2. In the Console tree in the left pane, browse to the Recipient Configuration ➤ Distribution Group node.

    The list of distribution groups is displayed in the Results pane in the middle.

3. Select the dynamic distribution group that you want to view the membership of and click the Properties option in the Actions pane.

4. In the properties dialog box of the dynamic distribution group, select the Conditions tab.

5. On the Conditions tab, click the Preview button to view the list of members.

View the Members of a Dynamic Distribution Group Using the Exchange Management Shell

To view the members of a dynamic distribution group using the EMS, run the following commands, specifying the name of the dynamic distribution group:

```
$ddg = Get-DynamicDistributionGroup GroupName
Get-Recipient -RecipientPreviewFilter $ddg.RecipientFilter
```

PART II

Managing Exchange Server Roles

IN THIS PART ▶

Managing Exchange
Server Roles

PART II

5

Managing Client Access

Managing Exchange
Server Roles

Exchange Server 2010 makes significant advancements in client access technology by brokering clients through the Client Access Server role, including direct remote procedure call (RPC)-based Messaging Application Programming Interface (MAPI) connections used by on-site Outlook clients. Instead of talking directly to the servers that hold the mailbox databases, all clients talk to the Client Access server (CAS) and the CAS talks to the Mailbox server on behalf of the client. By moving client access away from the Mailbox servers, you expose better failover capabilities. Now, databases can move from one Mailbox server to another without the client even knowing. A single mailbox can be moved between databases while the end user is online using their mail client, and the only impact to users is that they might receive a notice asking them to close Outlook and reopen it.

There are many ways for clients to connect to Exchange, but in this chapter, we'll cover the three most common forms of client connection:

- Web-based email
- Mobile devices
- Microsoft Office Outlook

Each of these access methodologies has a unique set of considerations for configuration, deployment, and administration. While a lot needs to be considered, this chapter focuses on the essentials of managing client access across these methodologies.

Manage Web-Based Email Access

Exchange Server 2010 allows users to use a web browser to access their email through an interface called Outlook Web App (OWA). While this capability existed in Exchange Server 2007 as well, significant enhancements have been made in the Exchange Server 2010 version. Some of these enhancements are

- Redesigned user interface
- The fact that browsers other than Internet Explorer can use the Premium functionality in OWA
- Email conversation view
- Integrated chat capabilities with Office Communications Server
- Seamless browser redirection when users connect to the wrong OWA URL

From a management standpoint, we'll look at what it takes to configure OWA for production environments and how to enable some of the features offered by the web-based email client. There are three management tools that you will use when working with OWA:

- Exchange Management Console
- Exchange Management Shell
- Internet Information Services (IIS) Manager

The EMC and the EMS are the same tools that we use to manage many other aspects of Exchange, and they are introduced in Chapter 2, "Using the Exchange Management Console and the Exchange Management Shell." IIS Manager, however, might be new to you. IIS Manager is the Windows Server 2008 management tool for services hosted by IIS. In this case, OWA is a website that runs from the Client Access server. So some of the web-specific settings on OWA will need to be configured using IIS Manager.

Configure OWA Connectivity

OWA is enabled by default on Client Access servers. Although OWA is usable in its default configuration, there are probably some changes you will want to make to optimize the way you use OWA.

Configure OWA URLs

Some services on a CAS use the concept of internal and external URLs. When Exchange is installed, the internal URL is automatically populated using the name of the server. During setup you are prompted to decide if the CAS is exposed to the Internet. If you choose not to make the CAS Internet-facing, the external URL is kept blank (Figure 5.1).

The external URL is used for redirecting the client to a server in the same site as the user's mailbox. Here's an example of how that works:

1. The user browses to `https://seattle.contoso.com/owa`.

2. The CAS in Seattle queries AD and determines that the user's mailbox is in Baltimore.

3. The Seattle CAS finds a CAS that is located in Baltimore and retrieves the external URL for OWA on that CAS.

4. The user is redirected to the external URL of the CAS in Baltimore, `https://baltimore.contoso.com/owa`.

Figure 5.1: In OWA, a non-Internet-facing CAS has no external URL setting.

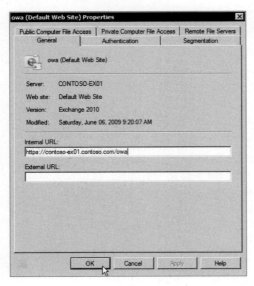

If the Baltimore CAS does not have an external URL defined, the Seattle CAS will proxy connections to the Baltimore CAS instead of redirecting the user to another URL. In this case, the user remains connected to the Seattle CAS and the Seattle CAS accesses the Baltimore CAS on behalf of the user.

Set the Same External Name for All Services on a Client Access Server

In Exchange Server 2010, there are multiple ways to configure the URLs for OWA and other client services. If you want to set the same external DNS name for all of the services on a particular CAS, the Configure External Client Access Domain interface can be used. You do not need to perform this process if you chose to expose the CAS to the Internet when you installed Exchange.

Following this process sets the external URLs for OWA, ActiveSync, the Offline Address Book, Exchange Web Services, and the Exchange Control Panel.

1. Open the Exchange Management Console and browse to the Server Configuration ➢ Client Access node in the Console tree.

2. In the Actions pane on the right, click the Configure External Client Access Domain option, as shown in Figure 5.2.

Figure 5.2: Opening the Configure
External Client Access Domain interface

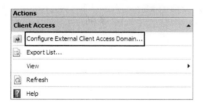

3. In the Configure External Client Access Domain interface, enter
    the external DNS name of the CAS in the text box. In the list box,
    use the Add button to add Client Access servers that will be con-
    figured to use this external DNS name. This is demonstrated in
    Figure 5.3.

Figure 5.3: Configuring the external DNS name for Client Access servers

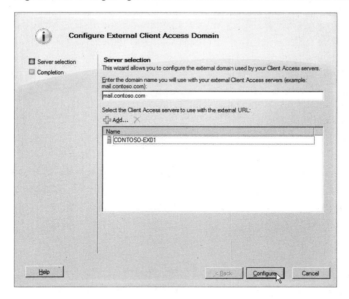

4. Click the Configure button to set the external URLs on all of the
    Client Access Servers in the list.

    You may receive a warning notification when configuring the
    OWA URLs, indicating that you should ensure that the ECP URL
    has the same domain name. The ECP should also be automatically

Managing Exchange
Server Roles

PART II

configured during this process, but to ensure that everything is working properly, do not change the ECP URL domain name to something different from the OWA URL domain name.

Configure an External URL on OWA Manually

Aside from using the configuration dialog box to configure the external URLs for all of the virtual directories, you can set independent external URLs manually for each of the virtual directories. The only exception to this capability is that the OWA URL and the ECP URL should have the same domain name associated with them.

To manually set the external URL for OWA using the EMC:

1. Open the EMC and browse to the Server Configuration ➤ Client Access node in the Console tree.

2. In the Results pane in the middle, select the Client Access Server that you want to set the external URL on.

3. In the Work area beneath the Results pane, select the Outlook Web App tab and click on the OWA website. In the Actions pane on the right, click the Properties option for the OWA website that you selected.

4. In the OWA Properties dialog box, ensure that you are on the General tab. In the External URL box, type the full URL that users outside the network will use to access OWA and click OK (see Figure 5.4).

5. Use the steps in the next section, "Configure the Exchange Control Panel External URL," to configure the ECP external URL to ensure that external users can access the Exchange Control Panel from OWA.

Aside from using the EMC, you can also configure the default OWA URL using the EMS:

1. Open the Exchange Management Shell.

2. Use the Set-OWAVirtualDirectory command with the ExternalURL parameter to configure the external URL:

```
Set-OWAVirtualDirectory ↵
"CONTOSO-EX01\owa (Default Web Site)" ↵
-ExternalURL "https://baltimore.contoso.com/owa"
```

Figure 5.4: Setting the external URL for OWA using the OWA Properties dialog box

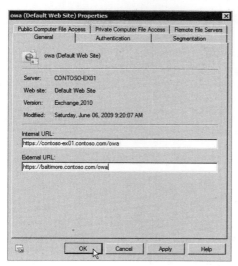

3. Use the Set-ECPVirtualDirectory command to set the external URL on the Exchange Control Panel virtual directory as well. As with the OWA command, you will use the ExternalURL parameter to specify the URL.

```
Set-ECPVirtualDirectory -Identity ↵
"CONTOSO-EX01\ecp (Default Web Site)" ↵
-ExternalURL "https://baltimore.contoso.com/ecp"
```

Configure the Exchange Control Panel External URL

The ECP is the user configuration interface that is used in conjunction with OWA. When you configure OWA with an external URL, you also want to ensure that the external URL is configured for the ECP, so users can access it when they click the Options button from OWA.

To configure the ECP using the Exchange Management Console:

1. Open the EMC and browse to the Server Configuration ➤ Client Access node in the Console tree.

2. In the Results pane, select the Client Access server that you want to modify the ECP external URL for.

3. In the Work area for the CAS that you selected, select the Exchange Control Panel tab.

4. Select the ECP virtual directory and choose Properties from the Actions pane on the right.

5. In the properties dialog box for the ECP virtual directory, enter the external URL that you want to use into the External URL box and click OK. Ensure that you use the /ecp virtual directory instead of the /owa virtual directory that you used previously. For example, the URL might be https://baltimore.contoso.com/ecp.

Redirect the Default Server URL to OWA

To access web mail, users will type the URL to the Client Access server into their browser. By default, the URL that is set up for OWA is https:// <FQDN of CAS>/owa. If a user browses to https://contoso-ex01.contoso.com without the /owa at the end of the URL, they will see the default IIS 7 website. Also, SSL is required on OWA by default, so if a user browses to the nonsecure site, http://contoso-ex01.contoso.com/owa, they are met with an Access Denied error.

By customizing the OWA URLs, we'll do the following things:

- Ensure users are redirected to the OWA site if they leave /owa off the URL.

- Redirect users to the SSL-enabled site if they use http instead of https.

WARNING   By default, when a Client Access server is installed, it uses a self-signed certificate to secure communications for its virtual directories. Unless this self-signed certificate is trusted by the client workstations, users will receive a warning when accessing OWA. The correct way to resolve this is to install a certificate on your CAS that is issued by a certificate authority (CA) that is trusted by your clients. Steps for installing certificates from a trusted CA are covered in Chapter 12, "Securing Exchange Server."

To ensure that users are redirected to the correct location if they don't type /owa at the end of the URL, you will configure the default IIS site with an HTTP redirection. Follow these steps on the Client Access server to configure this redirection:

1. Open the IIS Manager tool by clicking Start ➢ All Programs ➢ Administrative Tools ➢ Internet Information Services (IIS) Manager.

2. When IIS Manager opens, browse to the Default Web Site node in the Console tree, as shown in Figure 5.5.

Figure 5.5: Browse to the Default Web Site node in IIS Manager.

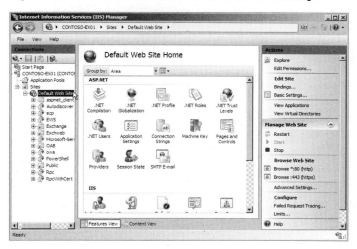

3. In the Work area, double-click the HTTP Redirect icon in the IIS section, as shown in Figure 5.6.

Figure 5.6: Double-click the HTTP Redirect icon.

4. When the HTTP Redirect options are displayed, check Redirect Requests To This Destination. For the destination, enter **/owa**.

Using only the /owa location will ensure that the URL is redirected appropriately regardless of whether the user is accessing OWA from an internal URL or an external URL. Figure 5.7 demonstrates the configuration of the HTTP Redirect options.

Figure 5.7: Configuring HTTP Redirect

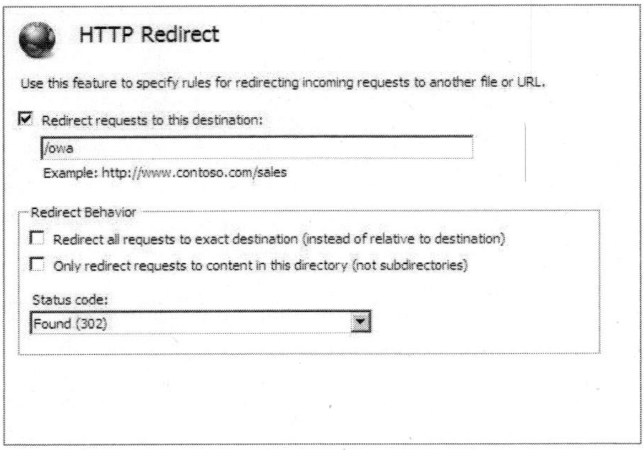

5. Click the Apply button in the Actions pane on the right to apply the HTTP Redirect configuration change.

WARNING   When you set the HTTP Redirect at the root in the default website, the HTTP Redirect settings will be inherited by every virtual directory and application beneath it. Therefore, you will need to remove the HTTP Redirect settings for OWA from each of these virtual directories and applications individually.

---

6. You must now remove the inherited HTTP Redirect settings from each site under the default website. Repeat steps 2–5 for each virtual directory and application beneath the default website. However, in step 4, be sure to *uncheck* the option Redirect Requests To This Destination. This option should not be configured for anything other than the default website. Remember to click Apply (step 5) after configuring each virtual directory. At a minimum, this set-

ting should be removed for the following virtual directories and applications:

- Autodiscover
- ecp
- EWS
- Microsoft-Server-ActiveSync
- OAB
- OWA
- PowerShell
- RPC
- RpcWithCert

Redirect from HTTP to HTTPS

In addition to redirecting users from the default website to the OWA virtual directory, you should also set up a redirection from the non-secure HTTP URL to the SSL-enabled HTTPS URL. To do this, you will create a custom error for when a user accesses the URL without SSL. This custom error will redirect the user to the HTTPS OWA URL instead of displaying an error page. To configure this, you will need to use the IIS Manager tool on the Client Access server.

1. Open IIS Manager by clicking Start ➢ All Programs ➢ Administrative Tools ➢ Internet Information Services (IIS) Manager.

2. In the IIS Manager tool, browse to the Default Web Site node in the Console tree.

3. In the Work area, double-click on the Error Pages icon in the IIS menu to bring up the list of custom error pages.

4. In the Actions pane, click the Add button to add a new custom error page.

   This will launch the Add Custom Error Page dialog box.

5. In the Add Custom Error Page dialog box, enter **403.4** in the Status Code field.

6. In the Response Action box, click the option Respond With A 302 Redirect. In the absolute URL field, enter the full HTTPS URL to OWA. For example, this could be `https://mail.contoso.com/owa`.

7. Click OK to make the changes and close the dialog box.

Configure OWA Features

OWA comes with many features that allow you to exercise granular control over user accounts. Many of these features enable functionality that resembles the full-featured Outlook desktop client. This section shows you how to configure some of these features in your OWA implementation.

Modify Basic OWA Features

There are many features in OWA that you can enable or disable for users. In Exchange, these are called *segmentation options*. All of the segmentation options can be enabled and disabled through the EMC or through the EMS.

Modify Segmentation Options in the Exchange Management Console

To modify segmentation options in the EMC:

1. Open the EMC and browse to the Server Configuration ➤ Client Access node in the Console tree.

2. In the Work area, select the Outlook Web App tab to display a listing of available OWA virtual directories.

3. Select the virtual directory that you are using from the list and click the Properties option in the Actions pane.

   This will bring up the properties dialog box for that virtual directory.

4. In the properties dialog box, click the Segmentation tab.

   The list of segmentation options are displayed in the dialog box.

5. Select the option that you want to enable or disable and click the Enable or Disable button above the list, as shown in Figure 5.8.

6. After modifying the segmentation options, click OK to make the changes and close the properties dialog box.

Figure 5.8: Segmentation options in OWA

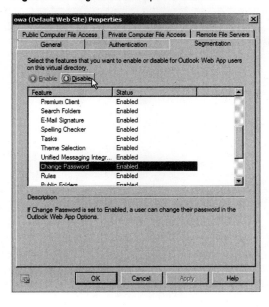

Modify Segmentation Options in the Exchange Management Shell

To modify the segmentation options in the EMS, you will use the Set-OWAVirtualDirectory command. To enable or disable a particular segmentation option, you will need to supply the correct parameter, displayed in Table 5.1.

Table 5.1: EMS Parameters for OWA Segmentation Options

Feature	Parameter
All Address Lists	AllAddressListsEnabled
Calendar	CalendarEnabled
Change Password	ChangePasswordEnabled
Contacts	ContactsEnabled
Email Signature	SignaturesEnabled
Exchange ActiveSync Integration	ActiveSyncIntegrationEnabled

Table 5.1: EMS Parameters for OWA Segmentation Options *(continued)*

Feature	Parameter
Journal	`JournalEnabled`
Junk Email Filtering	`JunkEmailEnabled`
Notes	`NotesEnabled`
Premium Client	`PremiumClientEnabled`
Public Folders	`PublicFoldersEnabled`
Recover Deleted Items	`RecoverDeletedItemsEnabled`
Reminders and Notifications	`RemindersAndNotificationsEnabled`
Rules	`RulesEnabled`
S/MIME	`SMimeEnabled`
Search Folders	`SearchFoldersEnabled`
Spell Checker	`SpellCheckerEnabled`
Tasks	`TasksEnabled`
Theme Selection	`ThemeSelectionEnabled`
Unified Messaging Integration	`UMIntegrationEnabled`

For example, to disable the ability for users to change their password from OWA, you can use the following command:

```
Set-OWAVirtualDirectory "CONTOSO-EX01\owa ↵
(Default Web Site)" -ChangePasswordEnabled $false
```

Manage Web-Based Document Viewing

OWA users can view Microsoft Office attachments and PDFs in OWA without having to install the Office or PDF viewer software. This feature is known as *web-ready document viewing*. Table 5.2 lists the file types that are supported with web-ready document viewing.

Table 5.2: File Types Supported in Web-Ready Document Viewing

File Type	Extension
Microsoft Word 2003 and earlier	`.doc`
Microsoft Word 2007 and later	`.docx`
Microsoft Word Template	`.dot`
PowerPoint SlideShow	`.pps`
Microsoft PowerPoint 2003 and earlier	`.ppt`
Microsoft PowerPoint 2007 and later	`.pptx`
Microsoft Excel 2003 and earlier	`.xls`
Microsoft Excel 2007 and later	`.xlsx`
Rich Text Format	`.rtf`
PDF Documents	`.pdf`

Managing Exchange Server Roles

PART II

Use the Exchange Management Console to Enable Web-Ready Document Viewing

You can enable web-ready document viewing in the EMC using the following steps:

1. Open the EMC and browse to the Server Configuration ➤ Client Access node.

2. In the Work area, click the Outlook Web App tab to show the list of OWA virtual directories.

3. Select the OWA virtual directory and click the Properties option in the Actions pane.

4. In the properties dialog box, select the Private Computer File Access tab. Check the Enable WebReady Document Viewing option.

   If you want users to be able to use web-ready document viewing when accessing OWA on public computers, use the Public Computer File Access tab.

5. Click OK to close the dialog box and make the changes.

Use the Exchange Management Shell to
Enable Web-Ready Document Viewing

You can also enable WebReady Document Viewing with the EMS
using the `Set-OWAVirtualDirectory` command. To enable WebReady
Document Viewing for private computers using OWA, use the
`WebReadyDocumentViewingOnPrivateComputersEnabled` parameter. For public
computers, use the `WebReadyDocumentViewingOnPublicComputersEnabled`
parameter. The following example enables both on the default OWA site:

```
Set-OWAVirtualDirectory -Identity "OWA (Default Web Site)" ↵
-WebReadyDocumentOnViewingPrivateComputersEnabled $true ↵
-WebReadyDocumentOnViewingPublicComputersEnabled $true
```

Manage Access for Mobile Devices

Exchange comes out of the box with features that allow you to connect mobile devices to compose and read messages and other items.
The technology that Exchange uses for mobile device access is called
ActiveSync. ActiveSync is based on HTTP and is designed for Internet-
based connections. The following types of items can be accessed with
mobile devices using ActiveSync:

- Email messages
- Calendar
- Contacts
- Tasks

When managing mobile device access for Exchange, it's important
that you know how to configure access for the devices, how to manage
the features and settings that are imposed on the devices, and—since
these devices are accessing email primarily over their public cellular-
based Internet connection—how to secure and protect the devices and
the data that is stored on them.

Configure Mobile Device Connectivity

Configuring mobile device connectivity is a straightforward task. Most
of the settings are preconfigured out of the box, and will only require a
little tweaking if you want to enable or disable certain aspects.

Enable or Disable Exchange ActiveSync

ActiveSync is enabled by default when the Client Access role is installed. Since it uses HTTP as its protocol, the only firewall ports that need to be opened are port 80 for HTTP or port 443 for HTTPS.

NOTE   As with most HTTP-based communications, HTTPS provides an extra layer of protection by encapsulating the connection in a Secure Sockets Layer (SSL). Since credentials are exchanged over this protocol, it is highly recommended that you require the use of HTTPS for ActiveSync and disable HTTP without SSL. This is the default configuration on the CAS.

To enable or disable ActiveSync on a CAS, you will need to stop the application pool for the IIS virtual directory that ActiveSync uses. You can use the following steps to enable or disable ActiveSync on an Exchange server:

1. Open the IIS Manager tool.

2. In the Console tree, select the Application Pools node.

   The list of available application pools for this server appears in the Results pane in the middle.

3. Find the application pool called MSExchangeSyncAppPool. This is the application pool for ActiveSync.

4. Click the MSExchangeSyncAppPool application pool and choose the Stop command from the Application Pool Tasks menu in the Actions pane on the right, as shown in Figure 5.9. Choosing Stop will disable ActiveSync. Conversely, choosing Start will enable ActiveSync access.

Enable Mobile Device Access for Users

Mobile device access can also be enabled and disabled on a per-user basis. If you have multiple users and you want only a select few to be able to access email with their mobile devices, you can use the following steps.

NOTE   ActiveSync is turned on by default for all users. You will need to explicitly turn it off if you don't want to allow mobile device access for a user.

Figure 5.9: Stopping the ActiveSync application pool

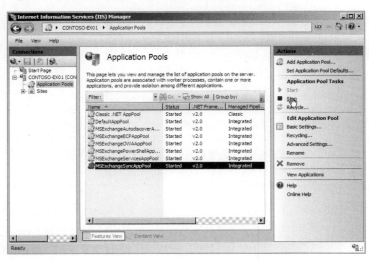

Use the Exchange Management Console to Enable or Disable Mobile Device Access

To enable or disable mobile device access through the EMC:

1. Open the EMC.

2. In the Console tree, browse to the Recipient Configuration ➤ Mailbox node.

   The list of mailboxes is displayed in the Results pane.

3. Click on the mailbox that you want to enable or disable mobile device access for and choose Properties from the Actions pane on the right.

   This will launch the properties dialog box for the recipient that you selected.

4. Select the Mailbox Features tab.

   The Exchange ActiveSync feature controls mobile device access to the mailbox.

5. Select the Exchange ActiveSync feature in the list and select either Enable or Disable to allow or disallow mobile device access for this mailbox.

Use the Exchange Management Shell to Enable or Disable Mobile Device Access

To enable or disable mobile device access using the EMS, you will use the `Set-CASMailbox` command. For example, to enable mobile device access for John Smith, you would use the following EMS command:

```
Set-CASMailbox "John Smith" -ActiveSyncEnabled $true
```

Similarly, to disable mobile device access for John Smith, you would use

```
Set-CASMailbox "John Smith" -ActiveSyncEnabled $false
```

Restrict Devices

By default users can synchronize any ActiveSync-capable device with Exchange. However, mobile device settings in Exchange can get very granular. One option that you have is preventing users from connecting with specific devices. You can disable mobile device connectivity for a device by obtaining the device ID.

To obtain the device ID for a user's mobile device, use the `Get-ActiveSyncDeviceStatistics` command in the Exchange Management Shell. The following command can be used to display the devices used by a user along with the device IDs, model names, and the phone numbers of the devices:

```
Get-ActiveSyncDeviceStatistics -Mailbox:[alias] | ↵
ft DeviceModel, DeviceID, DevicePhoneNumber
```

NOTE   The device ID for a mobile device can be obtained only after the user has synchronized the device at least once.

After you obtain the device ID, you can add the device to the block list. To do this, you use the `Set-CASMailbox` command with the `ActiveSyncBlockedDeviceIDs` parameter. The following command adds John Smith's device ID to the block list:

```
Set-CASMailbox "John Smith" -ActiveSyncBlockedDeviceIDs ↵
32194329043269432874
```

In a similar manner, you can also block every device *except* for the device IDs that you deem acceptable. To do this, you would use the `Set-CASMailbox` command again, but use the `ActiveSyncAllowedDeviceIDs` parameter instead. If this parameter is not specified as a `null` value, then every device is blocked expect those listed in this parameter.

```
Set-CASMailbox "John Smith" -ActiveSyncAllowedDeviceIDs ↵
32194329043269432874
```

If you want to clear the device IDs that are currently in the allowed and blocked lists, run the previous commands, except pass the parameter the `$null` value instead of the device ID:

```
Set-CASMailbox "John Smith" -ActiveSyncBlockedDeviceIDs $null
```

Manage Mobile Device Features and Settings

Exchange allows many different types of mobile devices to connect and download data from the server. However, the features and settings available are different for each type of device. For example, the iPhone Exchange allows only basic PIN control and remote wipe capabilities, whereas Exchange allows Windows Mobile phones a much richer set of functionality and control.

Use Mobile Device Policies

Mobile device policies allow you to specify many settings and apply them all to multiple users. The following high-level steps are required to use mobile device policies:

1. Create the policy.
2. Set up the features and settings in the policy.
3. Apply the policy to users or groups.

Create a Mobile Device Policy

Use the following steps to create a mobile device policy in the EMC:

1. In the EMC, browse to the Organization Configuration ➤ Client Access node in the Console tree.
2. In the Actions pane on the right, click the option New Exchange ActiveSync Mailbox Policy.

3. In the New Exchange ActiveSync Mailbox Policy dialog box, type the name of the policy you are creating and select the basic requirements for the mobile device password for these users.

4. Click the New button to create the policy.

5. When the Completion dialog box is displayed, click the Finish button.

To create a policy in the EMS, you can use the `New-ActiveSyncMailboxPolicy` command. The following command creates a policy called Executive Policy with the default options set:

```
New-ActiveSyncMailboxPolicy 'Executive Policy'
```

Configure Features and Settings

There are many features and settings that you can define in ActiveSync policies. Many of these options are covered later in this chapter. After you have created your mobile device policy, follow the steps in the section that corresponds to the features that you want to use. For example, if there is a feature that you want to disable, follow the steps in the "Disable Mobile Device Functionality" section.

Set a Mobile Device Policy on One or More Users

After the policy is created and configured, you can apply the policy to users. Policies can be applied to single users with the EMC or to groups of users in a batch with the EMS. Each user can only have one mobile device policy applied.

To set the policy on an individual user with the EMC:

1. Open the EMC and browse to the Recipient Configuration ➤ Mailbox node in the Console tree.

2. The list of mailboxes is displayed in the Results pane in the center of the EMC. Select the mailbox that you want to apply the mobile device policy to and click the Properties option in the Actions pane on the right.

3. In the properties dialog box for the mailbox, select the Mailbox Features tab.

    A list of features is displayed for the mailbox.

4. Select the Exchange ActiveSync feature and click the Properties button above the feature list.

This will allow you to set the ActiveSync mobile device policy on the mailbox.

5. In the Exchange ActiveSync Properties dialog box, click the Browse button to open a window that enables you to browse through existing mobile device policies. Select the policy that you want to apply and click OK.

6. Click OK to close the Exchange ActiveSync Properties dialog box. Then click OK to close the mailbox properties and apply the device policy.

You can also set the ActiveSync mailbox policy through the EMS by running the Set-CASMailbox command with the ActiveSyncMailboxPolicy parameter. The following example enables the policy called Executive Policy on each user that is in the Executive Users group:

```
Get-DistributionGroupMember "Executive Users" | ↵
Set-CASMailbox -ActiveSyncMailboxPolicy "Executive Policy"
```

Disable Mobile Device Functionality

You can control which functionality mobile devices have enabled using the ActiveSync Mailbox Policy that you previously created. When you disable one of the components in the ActiveSync Mailbox Policy, the component is disabled for the entire device, and not just for use in Outlook. The following features can be disabled for devices:

- Removable storage (SD cards, compact flash cards, etc.)
- Camera
- Wireless network adapter
- Infrared port
- Internet sharing functionality
- Remote desktop from the device
- Synchronization with a desktop computer
- Bluetooth capabilities (can be disabled completely or set to hands-free only)

Use the Exchange Management Console to Enable or Disable Mobile Device Features

To turn functionality on and off using the EMC:

1. Open the EMC and browse to the Organization Configuration ➤ Client Access node in the Console tree.

2. In the Work area in the center of the EMC, select the Exchange ActiveSync Mailbox Policies tab.

3. In the ActiveSync Mailbox Policies list, select the policy that you want to configure the features for.

4. After selecting the policy that you want to modify, either double-click on it or select the Properties option from the Actions pane on the right of the EMC.

    This will bring up the properties dialog box for the policy.

5. In the properties dialog box, click the Device tab. The list of features is displayed in this tab as check boxes. Check and uncheck the appropriate boxes to configure functionality for this device policy.

6. Click OK to make the changes to the policy.

> **WARNING** Make sure that this policy is applied to the appropriate users or you may inadvertently disable functionality for the wrong person!

Use the Exchange Management Shell to Enable or Disable Mobile Device Features

You can configure mobile device functionality options for the policy using the EMS as well. In the EMS, you should use the Set-ActiveSyncMailboxPolicy command with the parameters shown in Table 5.3.

Table 5.3: Parameters for Configuring Mobile Device Policies in the EMS

Functionality	Command Parameter	Possible Values
Removable Storage	AllowStorageCard	$true, $false
Camera	AllowCamera	$true, $false

Managing Exchange Server Roles
PART II

Table 5.3: Parameters for Configuring Mobile Device Policies in the EMS *(continued)*

Functionality	Command Parameter	Possible Values
Wireless Adapter	`AllowWiFi`	`$true, $false`
Infrared Port	`AllowIrDA`	`$true, $false`
Internet Sharing	`AllowInternetSharing`	`$true, $false`
Remote Desktop from the device	`AllowRemoteDesktop`	`$true, $false`
Synchronization with a Desktop PC	`AllowDesktopSync`	`$true, $false`
Bluetooth Settings	`AllowBluetooth`	`Allow, Disable, HandsFreeOnly`

For example, to turn off Internet sharing and configure Bluetooth for hands-free only operation, you can run the following EMS command:

```
Set-ActiveSyncMailboxPolicy "Executive Policy" ↵
-AllowInternetSharing $false -AllowBluetooth ↵
'HandsFreeOnly'
```

Manage Synchronization Settings

In addition to controlling the available features on mobile devices, you can control how the device synchronizes data with Exchange. The synchronization settings that you can specify through the ActiveSync policy are as follows:

- How old synchronized email and calendar items are before they are no longer synchronized

- The maximum size of email and attachments

- Direct Push usage when a user is in a "roaming" area on their mobile phone. Direct Push is a feature that allows mobile devices to receive email as soon as it arrives at the server. Without Direct Push, devices have to initiate a synchronization either manually or on a predefined interval.

- The formatting of synchronized messages (HTML or text)

> **NOTE**   Not all of these synchronization features are available for every phone.

Use the Exchange Management Console to Manage Synchronization Settings

To manage synchronization settings in the EMC:

1. Open the EMC and browse to the Organization Configuration ➤ Client Access node in the Console tree.

2. In the Work area, click the Exchange ActiveSync Mailbox Policies tab.

3. Double-click on the policy that you want to configure synchronization settings for. You can also select the policy and click the Properties option in the Actions pane on the right.

4. The properties dialog box for the policy will open. Click the Sync Settings tab.

5. Configure the synchronization settings to your liking and click OK to make the changes to the policy.

Use the Exchange Management Shell to Manage Synchronization Settings

To configure these settings with the EMS, you can use the Set-ActiveSyncMailboxPolicy command. Table 5.4 lists the appropriate parameters to use with this command.

Table 5.4: Parameters for Configuring Sync Settings in the EMS

Sync Setting	Command Parameter	Possible Values
Include Past Calendar Items	MaxCalendarAgeFilter	All, TwoWeeks, OneMonth, ThreeMonths, SixMonths
Include Past Email Items	MaxEmailAgeFilter	All, OneDay, ThreeDays, OneWeek, TwoWeeks, OneMonth
Limit Email Size To (KB)	MaxEmailBodyTruncationSize	Numeric value measured in KB

Managing Exchange
Server Roles

PART II

Table 5.4: Parameters for Configuring Sync Settings in the EMS *(continued)*

Sync Setting	Command Parameter	Possible Values
Allow Direct Push When Roaming	`RequireManualSyncWhenRoaming`	`$true`, `$false`
Allow HTML-Formatted Email	`AllowHTMLEmail`	`$true`, `$false`
Allow Attachments To Be Downloaded To Device	`AttachmentsEnabled`	`$true`, `$false`
Maximum Attachment Size (KB)	`MaxAttachmentSize`	Numeric value measured in KB

As an example, the following command will set the maximum message size to 50 KB and disable attachment synchronization:

```
Set-ActiveSyncMailboxPolicy "Executive Policy" ↵
-MaxEmailBodyTruncationSize 50 -AttachmentsEnabled $false
```

Protect Mobile Devices

One of the dangers of mobile device usage is that if a user loses the device, they lose control of all the data on it. Exchange allows you to take many precautions to keep this loss at a minimum. This section explores those protection capabilities and shows you how to implement them.

Enforce Password Requirements

One of the simplest ways to protect your mobile devices is through password requirements. Many users will look on this protection mechanism as an annoyance, but it's easy to implement and extremely effective.

By setting a password requirement on your devices, you force the user to enter the password after the device hasn't been used for a specified period of time. You then determine how many failed password attempts you want to allow. If the wrong password is entered more times than you allow, the device is wiped clean, which destroys all the data that was stored on the device.

The password requirements can be controlled at a granular level. The following password options are available:

- Require both letters and numbers
- Allow usage of a simple PIN number
- Set minimum length of the password
- Set number of days before a password expires and the user is forced to change it
- Specify number of previous passwords that can't be used again

In addition to setting requirements on how the password is composed, you can control additional features related to security management and what happens when the wrong password is entered. The following settings can be configured:

- Whether the password can be recovered if the user forgets it
- Encryption requirements on the device and the storage card
- The number of wrong passwords before the device is wiped
- The number of minutes between uses of the device before the user must enter the password

The password settings are enforced through the device policy, which was discussed earlier in this chapter. If you don't have a device policy configured, following the steps in the section "Use Mobile Device Policies" earlier in this chapter.

Use the Exchange Management Console to Change Password Requirements

To change the password requirements in the EMC:

1. Open the EMC and browse to the Organization Configuration ➤ Client Access node in the Console tree.
2. In the Work area, select the Exchange ActiveSync Mailbox Policies tab.
3. In the ActiveSync Mailbox Policies list, select the policy that you want to configure the password settings on.
4. After selecting the policy that you want to modify, either double-click on it or select the Properties option from the Actions pane on the right of the EMC.

   This will bring up the properties dialog box for the policy.

5. In the properties dialog box, click the Password tab.

   The list of password options is displayed on this tab.

6. Select the Require Password check box. This will turn on the password requirement for devices using this policy. Check and uncheck the appropriate boxes to configure the password rules for this device policy.

7. After configuring the password options, click OK to make the changes.

Use the Exchange Management Shell to Change Password Requirements

If you use the EMS to configure password options, you can configure some of the options more granularly than in the EMC. For example, you can set a device to lock after 15 minutes and 30 seconds, instead of just 15 minutes. To set a password policy in the EMS, you use the `Set-ActiveSyncMailboxPolicy` command. Table 5.5 shows the parameters to use with this command to set the various password options.

Table 5.5: Parameters for Mobile Device Password Requirements in the EMS

Password Option	Command Parameter	Possible Values
Require Password	`DevicePasswordEnabled`	$true, $false
Require Alphanumeric Password	`AlphaNumericDevicePasswordRequired`	$true, $false
Minimum Number Of Complex Characters	`MinDevicePasswordComplexCharacters`	A number between 1 and 4
Enable Password Recovery	`PasswordRecoveryEnabled`	$true, $false
Require Encryption On The Device	`RequireDeviceEncryption`	$true, $false
Require Encryption On Storage Card	`RequireStorageCardEncryption`	$true, $false
Allow Simple Password	`AllowSimpleDevicePassword`	$true, $false

Table 5.5: Parameters for Mobile Device Password Requirements in the EMS *(continued)*

Password Option	Command Parameter	Possible Values
Number Of Failed Attempts Allowed	MaxDevicePasswordFailedAttempts	Unlimited or a number between 4 and 16
Minimum Password Length	MinDevicePasswordLength	$null to disable or a number between 1 and 16
Time Without User Input Before Password Must Be Re-entered (In Minutes)	MaxInactivityTimeDeviceLock	Unlimited or a time value between 1 minute and 1 hour
Password Expiration (Days)	DevicePasswordExpiration	Unlimited or a time value between 1 and 730 days
Enforce Password History (Prevent The User From Repeating Passwords Used Previously)	DevicePasswordHistory	A number between 0 and 50

For time values, the format is entered as *dd.hh:mm:ss* (*days .hours:minutes:seconds*). For example, if you want to use 15 minutes and 30 seconds as the time value, that would be represented as 00.00:15:30.

The following example command turns on the password requirement and sets the password to expire in 90 days, 4 hours, 10 minutes, and 13 seconds:

```
Set-ActiveSyncMailboxPolicy "Executive Policy" ↵
-DevicePasswordEnabled $true ↵
-DevicePasswordExpiration 90.04:10:13
```

Managing Exchange Server Roles

PART II

Recover the Password for a Device

If users are required to set passwords on their devices, the potential exists for them to forget their passwords. Therefore, Exchange gives you the ability to recover their device password for them. If you enable password recovery for mobile devices, a secondary password is generated and stored in Exchange. An administrator can gain access to this password via the steps in this section. A user can also access their secondary password themselves using the ECP in OWA.

TIP   If the user forgets their password, they can enter password recovery mode on their mobile device and establish a new password. To enter recovery mode on a Windows Mobile device, the user should select the Menu ➢ Reset Password option from the device.

To access the recovery password via the EMC:

1. Open the EMC and browse to the Recipient Configuration ➢ Mailbox node.

2. In the list of mailboxes displayed in the Results pane, select the mailbox of the user that you want the recovery password for.

3. In the Actions pane, click the Manage Mobile Phone option.

4. In the Manage Mobile Device dialog box, the recovery password is displayed in the Recovery Password field, as shown in Figure 5.10. Give this password to the user and instruct them to enter it in the Recovery Password field on their device.

The recovery password can also be accessed through the EMS using the `Get-ActiveSyncDeviceStatistics` command. You must specify the `ShowRecoveryPassword` parameter in order for the password to be displayed. Users can have multiple devices, so it is useful to also display the phone number of the device so you know what device the recovery password belongs to. The following command can be used to get the recovery password for a device. It lists the phone numbers and recovery passwords for all the devices associated with the John Smith mailbox.

```
Get-ActiveSyncDeviceStatistics -Mailbox "John Smith" ↵
-ShowRecoveryPassword | fl DevicePhoneNumber, ↵
RecoveryPassword
```

Figure 5.10: Obtaining the mobile device recovery password

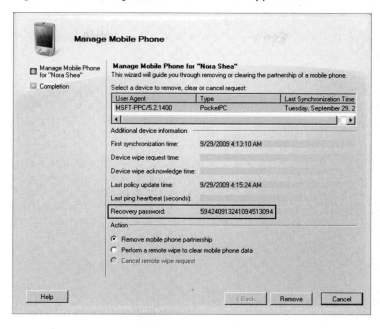

Control Application Usage

When a user has physical control over their device, they can install any application that they want to run. Because of this, the possibility exists for malicious or inappropriate applications to be used. As the Exchange administrator, you can control application usage on the mobile device by blocking certain applications.

You can disable applications and application installers that are not signed by the developer as well as specific applications.

Use the Exchange Management Console to Disable Mobile Device Applications

To disable unsigned applications and installation packages in the EMC:

1. Open the EMC and browse to the Organization Configuration ➢ Client Access node.

2. Select the policy that you want to restrict unsigned applications for and either double-click it or click the Properties option in the Actions pane.

3. In the properties dialog box for the policy, click the Device Applications tab.

4. Uncheck the options Allow Unsigned Applications and Allow Unsigned Installation Packages.

5. Click OK to make the changes to the policy.

Installing a Custom CAB File

When using some of the features discussed in this section, you may find that they don't consistently work across all devices. In order for a device to apply features such as blocking application usage, the mobile operator must provision the mobile device with the Enterprise security role. If this didn't happen, you can make the changes yourself with a custom CAB file. Follow these steps:

1. Paste the following text into a blank file with Notepad and save the file as _setup.xml:

```
<wap-provisioningdoc>
  <characteristic type="SecurityPolicy">
    <!--Grant Enterprise Policy:-->
    <parm name="4119" value="252" />
  </characteristic>
</wap-provisioningdoc>
```

2. Then make this XML file into a CAB file by performing the steps at the following website:

   http://technet.microsoft.com/en-us/library/cc182267.aspx

3. Install the CAB file on the mobile devices, re-sync the mail, and perform a soft reset of the device.

To block specific applications by name in the EMC:

1. Open the EMC and browse to the Organization Configuration ➤ Client Access node.

2. Select the policy that you want to block applications on and either double-click it or click the Properties option in the Actions pane.

3. In the properties dialog box for the policy, click the Other tab.

4. In the Block Applications list, click the Add button to add a blocked application.

    A dialog box will be displayed that asks for the application name.

5. In the Add Blocked Application dialog box, enter the filename of the application that you are blocking and click OK.

    For example, if you are blocking Google Maps, enter **GoogleMaps.exe**.

6. Click OK to close the properties dialog box and make the changes to the policy.

Use the Exchange Management Shell to Disable Mobile Device Applications

Applications can be restricted and blocked using the EMS as well. To disallow unsigned applications and block specific applications, you use the `Set-ActiveSyncMailboxPolicy` command. For disabling unsigned applications, use the `AllowUnsignedApplications` and the `AllowUnsignedInstallationPackages` parameters. For blocking a specific application, use the `UnapprovedInROMApplicationList` parameter.

The following command disables unsigned applications and blocks Google Maps from running on the device:

```
Set-ActiveSyncMailboxPolicy "Executive Policy" ↵
-AllowUnsignedApplications $false ↵
-AllowUnsignedInstallationPackages $false ↵
-UnapprovedInROMApplicationList GoogleMaps.exe
```

Remotely Wipe a Device

If a mobile device is stolen or missing, the owner's email, contacts, and other personal data can be in the hands of the wrong person. Therefore, for mobile devices, you can wipe a device remotely (over the Internet) to ensure that the data is cleaned off it. This doesn't aid in the recovery of the physical device, but it does help protect the data that was on it. You can remotely wipe a device and any storage cards attached to it through either the EMC or the EMS.

> **WARNING**   Remotely wiping a device not only deletes the data on the device, but also deletes all of the data on the storage cards in the device. If you are testing this functionality on your own phone, you may want to remove the storage card beforehand to prevent losing your data.

Use the Exchange Management Console to Remotely Wipe a Mobile Device

To remotely wipe a device in the EMC:

1. Open the EMC and browse to Recipient Configuration ➢ Mailbox in the Console tree.

2. In the Results pane, select the user whose device you want to wipe from the list of recipients.

3. Select the option Manage Mobile Phone from the Actions pane.
   If the Manage Mobile Phone option doesn't appear, that means the user does not have any mobile devices.

4. In the Manage Mobile Device wizard, select the device that you want to wipe from the device list.

5. Click the option Perform A Remote Wipe To Clear Mobile Phone Data.

6. Click the Clear button. You will be prompted with a dialog box asking whether you are sure that you want to clear the device. Click the Yes button to proceed.

7. In the Completion screen, click the Finish button to close the wizard.

Use the Exchange Management Shell to Remotely Wipe a Mobile Device

You can also wipe a device using the EMS:

1. Open the Exchange Management Shell.

2. Get a list of devices for a user and determine which device you want to wipe. To retrieve a list of devices, use the Get-ActiveSyncDeviceStatistics command.

The following example lists the Identity parameters of all devices associated with the Nora Shea mailbox:

```
Get-ActiveSyncDeviceStatistics -Mailbox "Nora Shea" | ↵
fl Identity
```

3. You will need the Identity parameter acquired in Step 2 to perform the wipe. Run the Clear-ActiveSyncDevice command and specify the device's identity:

```
Clear-ActiveSyncDevice -Identity [DeviceIdentity]
```

When wiping the device using the EMS, you can also opt to send the owner a notification email indicating that the device was wiped. To do this, specify the NotificationEmailAddresses parameter with the Clear-ActiveSyncDevice command.

Sometimes the device identity parameter can be long and arduous to enter. Using the EMS, however, there are ways to pipeline the command so you don't need to re-enter the device identity. The following EMS command will clear the device associated with the John Smith mailbox that has a phone number ending with 1234 and will email a notification to jsmith@contoso.com:

```
Get-ActiveSyncDeviceStatistics -Mailbox "John Smith" | ↵
where {$_.DevicePhoneNumber -like '*1234'} | ↵
Clear-ActiveSyncDevice -NotificationEmailAddresses ↵
"jsmith@contoso.com"
```

Monitor Mobile Device Usage

When users can freely add and remove mobile devices that are in their possession, it is difficult to get a handle on what's in use. Exchange comes with some basic monitoring functionality that can help you understand who is using the device and in what ways.

Retrieve a List of Devices for a User

Users can potentially connect more than one device to Exchange. If you want to perform activities on a single device, you need to ensure you are targeting the right one. For example, if the user has two devices and one

Managing Exchange Server Roles

PART II

of them is lost, you don't want to accidentally wipe the wrong device. To do this, you can retrieve the list of devices for a user.

To retrieve the list of devices for a user through the EMC:

1. Open the EMC and browse to the Recipient Configuration ➤ Mailbox node.

2. From the list of mailboxes in the Results pane, select the mailbox that you want to retrieve a list of mobile devices for.

3. In the Actions pane, select the Manage Mobile Phone option. This will launch the Manage Mobile Device dialog box.

4. In the Manage Mobile Device dialog box, a list of devices for the mailbox is presented. Click on a device to have the dialog box populated with the device's information.

You can also retrieve a list of mobile devices for a user from the EMS using the `Get-ActiveSyncDeviceStatistics` command. You will need to specify the `Mailbox` parameter and point it to the user's mailbox that you want the devices for. For example, the following command prints the list of devices for a user in a table:

```
Get-ActiveSyncDeviceStatistics -Mailbox "John Smith" | ↵
ft
```

Generate Device Reports

To stay on top of your usage trends, you should regularly examine client access logs. ActiveSync stores its logs in IIS. However, when it comes time to collect the logs, it can be difficult to read through them all and weed out the right information. Therefore, Exchange 2010 offers an ActiveSync command that goes through the IIS logs and creates reports based on those logs for you.

Six different reports are generated:

Usage Report (users.csv) Shows a detailed usage report for each user

Hourly Report (hourly.csv) Shows the number of unique devices and how many synchronizations were requested for each hour of the day

Policy Compliance Report (policycompliance.csv) Shows the number of fully compliant, partially compliant, and noncompliant devices

Server Report (`servers.csv`)   Shows the device connection statistics broken down for each server

HTTP Status Report (`statuscodes.csv`)   Shows the HTTP status codes encountered by the devices

User Agent (`useragents.csv`)   Shows the various user agents used by the devices

Generate Reports for a Single Day

The reports can only be generated with the EMS. To run the report, you use the `Export-ActiveSyncLog` command. When you run the command, you must use the `FileName` parameter to specify the location of the IIS logs from which you want to gather the report data. The following example will create reports from the IIS log file `u_ex090608.log` and store them in `c:\reports`:

```
Export-ActiveSyncLog -FileName ↵
C:\inetpub\logs\LogFiles\W3SVC1\u_ex090608.log ↵
-OutputPath c:\reports
```

Change How Often New Log Files Are Created

By default, Exchange uses daily IIS logs. If you want to retrieve statistics for ActiveSync based on a larger collection period, you can modify the log settings generated by ActiveSync. For example, these steps will enable you to generate monthly logs instead of daily logs:

1. Open the IIS Manager tool by clicking Start ➢ All Programs ➢ Administrative Tools ➢ Internet Information Services (IIS) Manager.

2. Browse to the Default Web Site node in the Console tree. If you are hosting the ActiveSync virtual directory in another site instead of the default site, browse to that site instead.

3. In the Work area, double-click the Logging icon under the IIS section.

4. In the Log File Rollover box, change the Schedule option to Monthly.

5. Click Apply in the Actions pane.

After making this change, the logs are recorded in a single file each month. When you run the Export-ActiveSyncLog command and specify that file, it will generate reports for the entire month instead of just the one day. Note that previously the log file was dated with the year, month, and day that the logs were captured (u_ex090609.log). After you change it to a monthly log, the file name changes to just the year and the month (u_ex0906.log).

Manage Outlook Client Access

Microsoft Outlook is the email client application that was designed with Exchange in mind. In the most common implementations of Exchange, end users will be accessing their mailboxes with Outlook. Therefore, it's important to ensure that email access through the Outlook client is easy to set up and use. This section shows you how to accomplish some of the common tasks related to managing client access through the Outlook application and through third-party applications.

Configure Outlook Anywhere

When an Outlook client is on the same network as the Exchange server, the client can connect to the server using the MAPI protocol through a RPC connection. RPC uses a service called an endpoint mapper. The job of the endpoint mapper is to determine which port both endpoints of the RPC connection will talk on. RPC requires that ports 1024 through 65535 be accessible because the endpoint mapper will dynamically select one of those ports to use. Few organizations will allow this port range to be exposed to the Internet, so users can't connect Outlook from outside the network to their Exchange mailboxes over RPC unless they use a VPN tunnel.

Outlook Anywhere solves this problem by encapsulating the RPC traffic into HTTPS communications. Because Outlook Anywhere wraps RPC inside HTTPS, the data is transferred as HTTPS traffic and can easily traverse firewalls without opening up a wide port range. If users can get to a secure website, they can get to their email using Outlook.

Enable Outlook Anywhere

Outlook Anywhere is not enabled by default. If you decide to use it, you will need to enable it on one or more Client Access servers. When you enable Outlook Anywhere, you must specify an external hostname that clients will use to connect to their mailboxes.

Configure Outlook Anywhere in the Exchange Management Console

To configure Outlook Anywhere in the EMC:

1. Open the EMC and browse to the Server Configuration ➢ Client Access node in the Console tree.

2. Select the Client Access server for which you want to enable Outlook Anywhere, and click the option Enable Outlook Anywhere in the Actions pane.

3. In the Enable Outlook Anywhere configuration screen, enter the external hostname that users will use to connect to their mailboxes through the Outlook client.

   This hostname needs to resolve to the Client Access servers in DNS and have a valid certificate associated with it. For steps on configuring certificates on a CAS, refer to Chapter 12, "Securing Exchange Server."

4. Click the Enable button to enable Outlook Anywhere.

5. In the Completion screen, click the Finish button.

   The configuration of Outlook Anywhere can take up to 15 minutes to take effect.

6. To determine if it is enabled, open the Application event log by clicking Start ➢ Administrative Tools ➢ Event Viewer.

7. In the Console tree inside Event Viewer, browse to Windows Logs ➢ Application.

8. In the Results pane, look for the Information event with Event ID 3006 with the source of the event MSExchange RPC Over HTTP Autoconfig. This signifies that Outlook Anywhere installed successfully.

Enable Outlook Anywhere Using the Exchange Management Shell

To enable Outlook Anywhere using the EMS, you can run the Enable-OutlookAnywhere command. When you run the command, you should specify the authentication method, the name that users will use to connect their Outlook clients from outside your network, and whether or not you'll use SSL offloading.

```
Enable-OutlookAnywhere -DefaultAuthenticationMethod Basic ↵
-ExternalHostname:mail.contoso.com -SSLOffloading:$false
```

Configure SSL Offloading

When using Outlook Anywhere, the HTTPS connections are secured using a Secure Sockets Layer (SSL) connection. This ensures that any data that is passed back and forth from the client to the server is encrypted, to prevent other people from viewing the data or modifying it. To secure this connection with SSL, the CAS uses an existing certificate. Certificates are covered in more detail in Chapter 12.

The work that the CAS performs to encrypt and decrypt the SSL communications can place an additional load and burden on the server. Therefore, Exchange has the ability to offload SSL. When SSL is offloaded, the CAS allows another system that it trusts, such as a firewall, to do the encryption and decryption. Instead of the client talking directly to the CAS, the client now has a secured connection to the firewall, and the firewall has an unsecured connection to the CAS.

Enable SSL Offloading Using the Exchange Management Console

You can use the following steps to enable SSL offloading in the EMC:

1. Open the EMC and browse to the Server Configuration ➤ Client Access node in the Console tree.

2. In the list of Client Access servers presented in the Results pane, click the CAS that you want to enable SSL offloading on.

3. Click the Properties option in the Actions pane to bring up the properties dialog box for the CAS.

4. In the properties dialog box, click the Outlook Anywhere tab.

5. Place a check mark beside the option Allow Secure Channel (SSL) Offloading.

6. Click OK to close the properties dialog box and make the changes.

Modify SSL Offloading Using the Exchange Management Shell

You can modify the SSL offloading setting in the EMS using the `Set-OutlookAnywhere` command. When you run the command, specify the `SSLOffloading` parameter and set it to $true, as shown here:

```
Set-OutlookAnywhere -Identity ↩
"CONTOSO-EX1\Rpc (Default Web Site)" -SSLOffloading $true
```

Modify the Authentication Method

The authentication method used in Outlook Anywhere determines how users present their username and password to the server. There are two authentication options that you can use for Outlook Anywhere:

- Basic authentication
- NTLM authentication

When Basic authentication is used, the user is prompted by the Outlook client for the username and password that it needs to connect to Exchange. Both the username and the password are sent to the server to validate the credentials of the user. Although the connection is secured with SSL, it's not generally a good idea to send a password over the Internet. Therefore, I recommended that you use NTLM authentication if possible.

NT LAN Manager (NTLM) authentication does not send the password over the Internet. Instead, NTLM sends a hashed value of the user's credentials. This means that the credentials are never sent over the Internet, making the connection more secure. If the client computer is a member of the forest that Exchange is in, and if the user is logged in with their domain account (a common scenario when users have company-owned laptops), NTLM authentication can use the current credentials of the user and does not need to prompt the user for their username or password. This provides another advantage over Basic authentication. However, NTLM authentication may not work through every firewall.

Configure the Authentication Method Using the Exchange Management Console

You can use the EMC to configure the authentication method using the following steps:

1. Open the EMC and browse to the Server Configuration ➤ Client Access node in the Console tree.

2. In the list of Client Access servers presented in the Results pane, click the CAS that you want to set the authentication method on.

3. Click the Properties option in the Actions pane to bring up the properties dialog box for the CAS.

4. In the properties dialog box, click the Outlook Anywhere tab.

5. In the Client Authentication Method section, select either Basic Authentication or NTLM Authentication.

6. Click OK to close the properties dialog box and make the changes.

Configure the Authentication Method Using the Exchange Management Shell

You can set the authentication method with the EMS using the Set-OutlookAnywhere command. When you use this command, you will specify the DefaultAuthenticationMethod parameter and specify either NTLM or Basic as its value. The following example turns on NTLM authentication for Outlook Anywhere.

```
Set-OutlookAnywhere "CONTOSO-EX1\Rpc (Default Web Site)" ↵
-DefaultAuthenticationMethod NTLM
```

Configure Automatic Client Configuration

Starting in Exchange Server 2007, email clients were given the ability to automatically configure their mail profiles. Before this time, the configuration of Outlook and mobile devices was a manual process. To accomplish automatic configuration, Exchange provides a service called AutoDiscover. The job of AutoDiscover is to provide an XML file to the email client that contains all the information it needs to connect to Exchange.

There are two ways that clients connect to AutoDiscover. If the client is coming from the internal network, it uses Active Directory to find the server it should talk to in order to get the client configuration data. On the other hand, if the client is coming from the Internet, it uses DNS to determine which server to get the AutoDiscover data from.

AutoDiscover runs as an IIS virtual directory on the Client Access server. The AutoDiscover virtual directory is installed and configured by default when the Client Access server is installed. Also, Active Directory is updated with the correct AutoDiscover service location information when the CAS is installed.

Understand AutoDiscover for Outlook Anywhere

When clients access email through Outlook Anywhere, AutoDiscover helps alleviate configuration problems by configuring the Outlook client automatically. To access the AutoDiscover service, the external user provides their email address and password and the AutoDiscover server is found using external DNS lookups.

Once the AutoDiscover server is found, the client uses SSL to exchange information with the server. To ensure that this is successful, your clients need to trust the certificate authority that issued the SSL certification that your CAS is using. Because of this requirement, you will not be able to use the self-signed certificate issued by the CAS during install, unless the client trusts the certificate. For steps on trusting the certificate authority that issued the CAS certificate, see Chapter 12.

Configure a DNS SRV Record for AutoDiscover

Outlook 2007 clients were initially created with the ability to choose from predefined URLs when discovering the AutoDiscover service. These early methods required some additional planning and cost for organizations implementing AutoDiscover. A later enhancement to Outlook allowed Outlook to query an SRV locator record in DNS for the AutoDiscover service. If Outlook has trouble obtaining information from the predefined URLs, it tries the SRV record.

NOTE   A service locator (SRV) record in DNS is a DNS entry that provides information about a network service instead of a name or IP address resolution. The SRV record can return information such as which host the service is running on, which port it is listening on, and the weighting and priority of the servers hosting the services.

To configure the SRV record for AutoDiscover on a Windows-based DNS server, you will need to use the DNS Manager tool. The SRV locator record should contain the information shown in Table 5.6:

Table 5.6: SRV Record Information for AutoDiscover

Setting	Value
Service	_autodiscover
Protocol	_tcp

Table 5.6: SRV Record Information for AutoDiscover *(continued)*

Setting	Value
Port Number	443
Hosts	External FQDNs that AutoDiscover provides

To configure the SRV record on a Windows DNS server:

1. Open the DNS Manager tool by clicking Start ≻ All Programs ≻ Administrative Tools ≻ DNS.

2. In the Console tree, browse to the zone that represents the SMTP domain name used in the email address. For example, if the email address is john@contoso.com, you need to find the contoso.com forward lookup zone.

3. After you browse to the zone, click the Action menu in the DNS Manager snap-in and select New Other Records from the menu.

4. The Resource Record Type window will appear and allow you to define which type of record you want to create.

5. Scroll down in the list and select Service Location (SRV) from the list of available record types. Then click the Create Record button.

6. In the New Resource Record dialog, type `_autodiscover` in the service field, `_tcp` in the protocol field, and `443` in the port field.

7. In the field Host Offering This Service, type the name of the server that will provide AutoDiscover services, such as `mail.contoso.com`. Figure 5.11 shows how the DNS record should be configured.

8. Click OK to create the record. Then click Done when you are back in the Resource Record Type dialog box.

Test AutoDiscover Configuration in the Exchange Management Shell

The Exchange Management Shell provides a command that you can use to test the configuration of AutoDiscover. You can run the `Test-OutlookWebServices` command to determine if any issues exist with AutoDiscover and report what those issues are. To run the test, you must specify an email address that AutoDiscover is run against.

Figure 5.11: Creating the SRV record for AutoDiscover

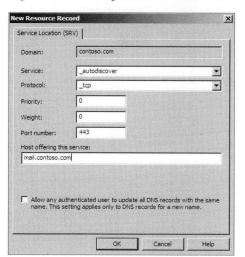

The report that is generated by the test is a line-by-line printout of the service information that should have been received. The test will report successes and failures and give you enough information to start troubleshooting AutoDiscover issues. The following example demonstrates the use of the `Test-OutlookWebServices` command:

```
Test-OutlookWebServices john.smith@contoso.com
```

Configure Access for Third-Party Clients

Exchange supports not only Outlook clients, but also other third-party clients that use the POP3 or IMAP4 protocols instead of MAPI. There are many reasons why MAPI would be the preferred client solution, but many clients have limited options and must use POP3 or IMAP4.

POP3 was designed to be an offline email protocol. When you use POP3, the default configuration is to download messages from the server to the client and remove the messages from the server. This places the burden of managing and backing up email on the end user.

IMAP4 is more robust than POP3. IMAP4 was designed to access mail both online and offline. IMAP4 also has some additional advantages over POP3, such as the ability to access public folders.

To allow clients to connect to Exchange using POP3 or IMAP4, you'll need to follow these high-level steps:

1. Enable the services.

2. Turn on access for the user explicitly.

3. Ensure that users can access mail via one of the protocols.

Enable the POP3 and IMAP4 Service

The POP3 and IMAP4 services are disabled by default in Exchange 2007. To turn them on, you need to set the service to the Automatic state. You can do this in either the Services MMC snap-in or the Exchange Management Shell.

To enable POP3 or IMAP4 using the Services MMC snap-in:

1. Open the Services snap-in by clicking Start ➤ All Programs ➤ Administrative Tools ➤ Services.

2. In the Services snap-in, select either the Microsoft Exchange IMAP4 or the Microsoft Exchange POP3 service, depending on whether you want to enable IMAP4 or POP3 connections.

3. Double-click on the service to bring up its properties dialog box. In the Startup Type section, change the setting to Automatic and then click OK.

4. Back in the list of services, right-click on the service and select the Start option from the menu.

To enable the service in the EMS, you can use the `Set-Service` command to configure the service, followed by the `Start-Service` command to start the service. The following EMS commands will enable the IMAP4 service:

```
Set-Service MSExchangeIMAP4 -StartupType automatic
Start-Service MSExchangeIMAP4
```

Turn On POP3 and IMAP4 for Users

After you have enabled the POP3 or IMAP4 service, you need to allow users to access their mail using those protocols. To enable POP3 or IMAP4 for individual users using the EMC:

1. Open the EMC and browse to the Recipient Configuration ➤ Mailbox node.

2. Select the mailbox that you want to enable POP3 or IMAP4 access for and click the Properties option in the Actions pane on the right.

3. In the properties dialog box for the mailbox, click the Mailbox Features tab.

4. In the list of mailbox features, select either the POP3 or IMAP4 feature and click the Enable button above the feature list. This will enable access through this protocol.

5. Click OK to make the changes and close the properties dialog box.

To configure POP3 or IMAP4 access using the EMS, you can use the Set-CASMailbox command. For configuring POP3, use the PopEnabled parameter, and for IMAP4, use the ImapEnabled parameter. The following example turns on both POP3 and IMAP4 access for the John Smith mailbox:

```
Set-CASMailbox "John Smith" -PopEnabled $true ↵
-ImapEnabled $true
```

Use Certificates with POP3 and IMAP4

You can use SSL with your POP3 and IMAP4 deployment to make it more secure. By default, POP3 and IMAP4 are installed using the self-signed certificate generated by Exchange. If you want your users to be able to access email over POP3 or IMAP4 from outside your organization using SSL, you need a certificate issued by a certificate authority (CA) that is trusted by your clients. Therefore, you should install a certificate obtained from a trusted CA. You then need to modify the POP3 or IMAP4 parameter to tell it to use the trusted certificate instead of the default self-signed certificate.

To modify the certificate used in the EMC:

1. Open the EMC and browse to the Server Configuration ➤ Client Access node in the Console tree.

2. Click the POP3 And IMAP4 tab.

3. Select either POP3 or IMAP4 from the protocol list and click the Properties option in the Actions pane.

4. In the properties dialog box, click on the Authentication tab.

5. In the field X.509 Certificate Name, enter the subject name of the certificate—for example, `mail.contoso.com`.

6. Click OK to make the changes and close the properties dialog box.

To set the certificate name using the EMS, you will use either the `Set-PopSettings` command or the `Set-ImapSettings` command. Specify the `x509CertificateName` parameter followed by the subject name of the certificate. The following example sets the IMAP4 certificate for Contoso:

```
Set-ImapSettings -x509CertificateName mail.contoso.com
```

6

Managing Message Routing

Managing Exchange
Server Roles

PART II

M any times during the day, people click the Send button on their email and trust that the person they are writing to will get the email quickly and in good order. People expect email to flow quickly and without issues. It's very seldom that email users understand and appreciate what happens behind the scenes to make sure that the email they just sent not only makes it to the other party, but also makes it there quickly and undamaged.

In Exchange Server 2010, email is moved by servers running the Transport role. The primary job of a Transport server is to receive mail, figure out where it's supposed to go, and send it on its way. The Transport server is truly the electronic version of the postal delivery worker.

There are two types of Transport roles:

- Hub Transport role
- Edge Transport role

Both roles are similar in that their primary job is to transport mail. However, the implementation of each role is very different. Servers hosting the Hub Transport role sit inside an email organization and play an active role in delivering mail throughout the intranet. Servers hosting the Edge Transport role, however, were designed to sit on the edge of the network, where there is potential exposure to hackers, viruses, and other bad things. The Edge Transport role cannot run on computers joined to a domain with an Exchange organization. Edge servers send and receive email to other servers on the Internet directly. You can look at the Edge Transport role as your first line of defense against spam, viruses, and attackers entering your Exchange organization.

In this chapter, you'll learn how to manage message flow in Exchange. We'll be working primarily with the Hub Transport and the Edge Transport role in doing so.

Manage the Routing Topology

The routing topology defines how email is passed from one Transport server to another. The routing topology for an organization has a strong tie-in to Active Directory (AD). The AD site topology defines how Exchange moves mail from servers in one site to servers in another site. In Active Directory, a site is a collection of computers that are on a well-connected and low-latency network. Generally speaking, an AD site typically maps to a physical site. For example, if your organization has an office in Seattle and an office in Baltimore, a common design pattern in AD would be to create a separate AD site for each of those offices.

For every site that a Mailbox server exists in, there must also be a Hub Transport server. The Mailbox server sends and receives all mail to and from a Hub Transport server in the same AD site. Every piece of mail that flows through an Exchange organization must pass through a Hub Transport server before it is delivered.

When you manage the routing topology, you manage how those Transport servers behave when they route mail to each other, to different sites, and to different email systems.

Configure How Exchange Sends and Receives Email

In order for a Transport server to send or receive messages, it needs to have a connector defined. The connector defines how the Transport server connects to other systems to transport messages. Two types of connectors are used in Exchange Server 2010:

Send Connectors   Send connectors define how a Transport server sends messages to another Transport server or to other systems. For example, a send connector could be defined so that every message sent to contoso.com would be routed to a specific IP address instead of looking for Mail Exchanger (MX) records in Contoso's public Domain Name System (DNS) server.

Receive Connectors   Receive connectors define how messages are received from other Transport servers or other email systems. The settings defined on the receive connector directly impact how a server is listening for messages. For example, you could configure a receive connector to accept email on a nonstandard Transmission Control Protocol (TCP) port.

Change the Port and IP Address on Which a Server Receives Mail

When a Transport server is installed, default receive connectors are created by the installation process. These receive connectors ensure that Hub Transport servers in the same Exchange organization can exchange messages. The administrator does not need to do anything further to ensure that messages can be sent from one Hub Transport server to another.

There are some instances where you might want to receive mail on a specific port or IP address. For instance, if you have multiple network cards in your Transport server, you may decide to prioritize connections from partner organizations over a dedicated network connection.

Use the Exchange Management Console to Change the Port and IP Address of a Receive Connector

To modify the port and IP address of a receive connector in the Exchange Management Console (EMC):

1. Open the EMC and browse to the Server Configuration ➤ Hub Transport node in the Console tree. If you are performing this on an Edge Transport server without an Edge Subscription, select the Edge Transport node in the EMC.

2. In the list of Hub Transport servers presented in the Results pane, select the server that has the connector on which you want to change the port or IP address. After selecting the server, the list of receive connectors configured on the server appears in the bottom half of the Results pane.

3. Select the receive connector that you want to modify and choose Properties from the Actions pane.

4. In the properties dialog box for the receive connector, click the Network tab. A list of IP addresses and ports are presented. Select the entry that you want to modify and click the Edit button, as shown in Figure 6.1.

5. In the Edit Receive Connector Binding dialog box, choose the IP address on which you want to listen for messages by clicking the Specify An IP Address button and entering the IP address in the text box.

6. In the Port field, type the updated port number on which you want to listen for mail.

7. Click OK to close the edit dialog box.

8. When back in the properties dialog box, click OK to make the changes and close the dialog box.

Use the Exchange Management Shell to Change the Port and IP Address of a Receive Connector

You can also use the EMS to change the IP address and port on a receive connector. To do so, use the Set-ReceiveConnector command

and specify the Bindings parameter. This parameter takes a list of one or more IP address and ports and ensures that the receive connectors listen for incoming connections on those IP addresses and ports. Specify the Bindings parameter in the form of IPAddress:Port. If you want the receive connector to listen on all IP addresses allocated to the server, use 0.0.0.0 as the IP address. The following example binds the receive connector to all IP addresses on port 25:

```
Set-ReceiveConnector "Contoso Receive Connector" ↵
-Bindings 0.0.0.0:25
```

Figure 6.1: Modifying the IP address and port of a receive connector

Configure How Mail Is Routed to a Specific Email Domain

When mail is sent from an Exchange user, Exchange uses send connectors to determine how that mail gets to its destination. If the message is sent to a recipient within the same Exchange organization, then Hub Transport servers send the message to other Hub Transport servers until the message reaches the site that the recipient's mailbox is in. This happens automatically when you install Exchange. Therefore, no additional configuration is needed to enable Exchange to send mail inside the organization.

When routing messages outside the organization, however, you must have a send connector in place. Send connectors define how mail is sent, how to look up the server to send the messages to, and how to authenticate to receiving servers.

You can create a send connector with settings geared specifically for a particular domain namespace. For example, if you have a partner organization, you can set up a send connector to bypass the typical DNS-based mailbox server lookup and instead send messages directly to specific server or IP address. This is called a smart host.

Use the Exchange Management Console to Configure a Send Connector to Use a Smart Host

The EMC steps to setting up a send connector to send messages directly to a specific location are as follows. You can configure the settings either on the Hub Transport server or on the Edge Transport server.

1. Open the EMC.

2. If you are performing the task on the Hub Transport server, browse to the Organization Configuration ➤ Hub Transport node in the Console tree. If you are performing it on an Edge Transport server without an Edge Subscription, select the Edge Transport node in the EMC.

3. In the Actions pane, click the New Send Connector option.

   This will launch the New Send Connector wizard.

4. On the Introduction screen of the wizard, type the name of the connector, for example, **Fabrikam Connector**. In the field Select The Intended Use For This Send Connector, select Custom from the list. Click Next to continue.

5. On the Address Space screen, click the Add button to add a domain name that this connector routes mail for.

6. Enter the email domain name in the Address field, as shown in Figure 6.2. Click OK to add the entry to the list. Click Next when back in the wizard.

7. On the Network Settings screen, choose Route Mail Through The Following Smart Hosts and click the Add button.

This allows you to enter the name or IP address of the server at fabrikam.com that you'll be sending messages to.

Figure 6.2: Adding an address space to route mail for

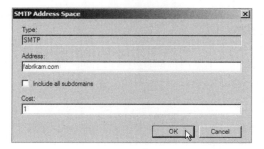

8. In the Add Smart Host dialog box, enter the IP address or fully qualified domain name (FQDN) of the receiving server (see Figure 6.3). Click OK to close the dialog box.

Figure 6.3: Adding a smart host for domain-specific mail routing

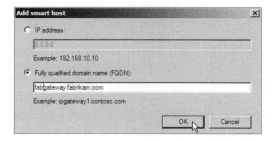

9. When back in the wizard, click Next. On the Configure The Smart Host Authentication Settings screen, choose how your Exchange server is going to authenticate to the receiving mail server. If your server won't use authentication, choose None and click Next.

10. If you are performing these steps on a Hub Transport server, you will see the Source Server screen. Ensure that the send connector is associated with the correct Hub Transport or Edge Transport servers. If not, you can add and remove servers from the association list using the Add and Remove buttons above the list. Click Next.

If you are performing these steps on an Edge Transport server, you will not see the Source Server screen. You can safely skip this step.

11. On the New Connector screen, click the New button to create the send connector.

12. On the Completion screen, click Finish to complete the process and close the wizard.

Use the Exchange Management Shell to Configure a Send Connector to Use a Smart Host

You can also create this send connector with the EMS. When doing so, you use the New-SendConnector command. You'll need to specify the AddressSpaces parameter and specify the domain name that you want this send connector to route mail to. You also need to use the SmartHosts parameter if you want to route to a specific server. When specifying the smart host, if you use an IP address, you need to enclose it in the format of [x.x.x.x]. The following example demonstrates this command:

```
New-SendConnector "Fabrikam Connector" -AddressSpaces ↵
fabrikam.com -SmartHosts [192.168.1.120]
```

Manage Message Flow Inside the Forest

When Exchange is configured out of the box, internal message flow tends to work with little or no tweaking. However, there are some changes you can make to get a better handle on how messages flow internally. This section steps you through some of the common things that you might configure to better manage message flow inside the forest.

Examine the Active Directory Site Topology

Exchange uses the Active Directory site topology to determine how sites are connected to each other. Using this information, Exchange can figure out how a message should be sent from one site to another.

In the Active Directory site topology, each site is composed of one or more IP address ranges. The site that a computer is in is determined by the IP address of the computer. For example, if the BAL site has an IP address range of 192.168.0.0–192.168.0.255, then a computer with the IP address of 192.168.0.10 would be in the BAL site.

When more than one site exists in the AD forest, sites are connected together with site link objects. Site links represent a logical connection between the sites. For example, if the sites BAL and HOU have WAN connectivity to each other, you might create a BAL-HOU site link and place the BAL and HOU sites in that site link. There are properties on the site link that define how good the network connection is. This is defined with an arbitrary number called the site link cost. Any number can be used for the cost; if there is more than one route between sites, the route with the lower cost is used. For example, Figure 6.4 shows a simple site topology with two possible routes from the BAL site to the SEA site.

Figure 6.4: Simple site topology with multiple routes

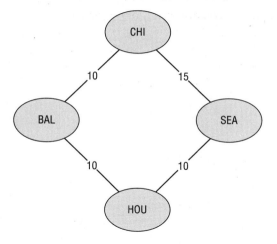

BAL can connect to SEA through either CHI or HOU. The total cost of the route is the sum of all of the site link costs along the way. When BAL connects to SEA using the CHI site, the total cost is 25, or 10 + 15. However, when BAL connects to SEA using HOU, the total cost is 20, or 10 + 10. What this means for Exchange is that if a message is sent from a user in BAL to a user in SEA, Exchange may need to send the message to HOU along the way. Whether the message is sent to HOU first or not depends on a variety of scenarios, such as whether HOU is designated as a hub site or if message bifurcation (splitting a message with multiple recipients to deliver it to different servers) needs to happen at HOU.

There are multiple tools you can use to view the site topology.

View the Site Topology Using the Sites and Services Tool

In the built-in Active Directory administration tools, you can use the Active Directory Sites and Services snap-in to view the site topology. If you installed the Remote Server Administration Tools outlined in Chapter 1, you should have the AD Sites and Services tool available already.

1. Launch the tool by selecting Start ➤ All Programs ➤ Administrative Tools ➤ Active Directory Sites And Services.

2. When the tool opens, browse to the Sites node in the Console tree and you will see a list of sites as child nodes (Figure 6.5).

Figure 6.5: Viewing the list of Active Directory sites

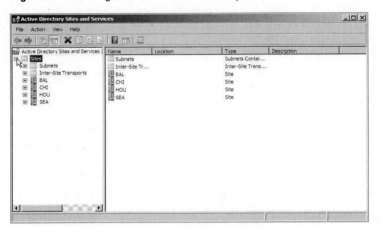

3. View the site links that connect the sites together by browsing to the Sites ➤ Inter-Site Transports ➤ IP node.

   The list of site links is in the Results pane, as shown in Figure 6.6. For each of the site links listed you can see the cost of the link.

4. View the list of IP address ranges and see what sites they are attached to by browsing to the Sites ➤ Subnets node in the Console tree.

   Figure 6.7 illustrates a list of IP subnets.

Use the Exchange Management Shell to Get Site Topology Information

In addition to using the AD Sites and Services tool, you can get the site topology information from the EMS. The Get-ADSite and Get-ADSiteLink

commands will gather that information. You can use these commands to
display a list of sites and site links in the EMS. By piping the commands
to a formatted list, you can view the advanced parameters configured specifically for Exchange. The following command will display the information for the BAL-HOU site link:

```
Get-ADSiteLink BAL-HOU | fl
```

Figure 6.6: Viewing the site links defined in Active Directory

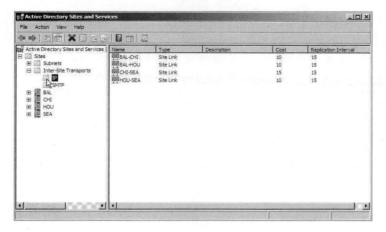

Figure 6.7: Viewing the list of IP subnets for Active Directory sites

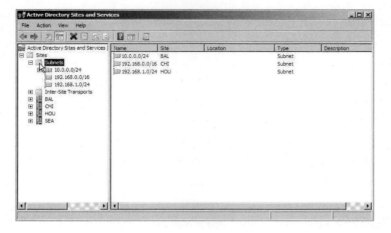

Modify How Mail Flows Through AD Sites

When determining the routing path that messages take, Exchange adds up the cost of every site link in each possible route from the source site to the target site and chooses the lowest cost. The cost defined on site links is determined by the Active Directory administrators. AD uses site link costs to determine the most efficient replication path for Active Directory domain controllers.

Although this costing model is typically a snapshot of the network conditions between sites, it's not always a good idea for email message flow to use these costing numbers.

Therefore, Exchange allows you to define an Exchange-specific site link cost. AD administrative permissions are not required to define this cost. This feature was developed with the idea that Exchange administrators would be setting this cost independently of the AD administrators. The Exchange-specific site link cost has no impact on Active Directory replication or client affinity; it only impacts how Exchange routes mail. To understand how this works, consider the example in Figure 6.8.

Figure 6.8: Understanding Exchange-specific site link costs

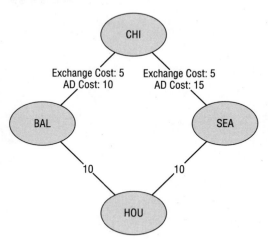

If an Exchange-specific cost were not defined on these site links, the message transport route from BAL to SEA would be BAL-HOU-SEA, because the cost of the route is 20, which is lower than the cost of the other route. However, with Exchange-specific costs defined on the

BAL-CHI and CHI-SEA site links, the cost of the BAL-CHI-SEA route becomes 10 instead of 25. Therefore, Exchange will route messages through the BAL-CHI-SEA route because it is cheaper. However, Active Directory replication will still prefer the BAL-HOU-SEA route.

To configure an Exchange-specific site link cost on an existing Active Directory site link, you can use the Set-ADSiteLink command in the EMS. When doing so, specify the ExchangeCost parameter along with the numeric cost value that you will be assigning to the site link. For example, the following command will modify the Exchange-specific cost on the BAL-CHI link to 5:

```
Set-ADSiteLink BAL-CHI -ExchangeCost 5
```

If you want to remove the existing cost on a site link, set the cost value to $null instead of a numeric value.

Force Mail to Route Through a Hub Site

When messages are routed through an organization, Exchange sends the message down the path that has the lowest cost. One of the options you have is to designate a site as a hub site. If a hub site exists in the routing path, messages are routed to the hub site instead of being relayed directly to the destination site. For example, consider the routing topology illustrated in Figure 6.9.

Figure 6.9: Sample routing topology

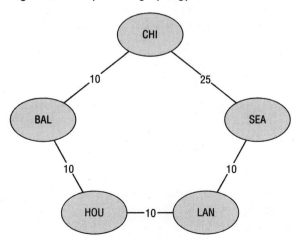

Because Exchange uses the least-cost path, mail will route from the BAL site to the SEA site using the path BAL-HOU-LAN-SEA. Even though the routing topology has a path defined through other sites, the Hub Transport server in BAL will attempt to establish a direct connection to the Hub Transport server in SEA and transfer the message directly. If a connection cannot be established, the BAL server will attempt to send to the next closest server according to the routing topology, or LAN in this example. This makes message routing faster since messages don't always have to be sent to the HOU and LAN sites before they are received in SEA.

When you designate a hub site, an attempt is made for messages to be sent to that site instead of being sent directly to the destination site. For example, if HOU is a hub site, BAL will send the message to HOU, and HOU will send the message to SEA. Hub sites are only used if they are in the least-cost routing path. If CHI were a hub site in this scenario, then BAL would not route messages through CHI because it's not in the least-cost path.

You can designate an AD site as a hub site using the `Set-ADSite` command in the EMS. Specify the `HubSiteEnabled` parameter to make the site a hub site.

```
Set-ADSite HOU -HubSiteEnabled $true
```

Manage Internet Message Flow

After you install Exchange Server 2010, mail flow in your organization will work with little to no additional configuration. Internet message flow, however, may require some additional work.

Configure the Domains for Which Exchange Is Responsible

Exchange maintains a list of domains for which it can receive email. This list is referred to as accepted domains. There are three types of accepted domains:

- Authoritative domain
- Internal relay domain
- External relay domain

When a domain is added as an authoritative domain, Exchange expects a mailbox to exist for those recipients. For example, if contoso.com is configured as an authoritative domain in Exchange, any messages sent to bill@contoso.com will only be accepted by Exchange if Bill has an Exchange mailbox. If a message for joe@contoso.com is received and Joe doesn't have an Exchange mailbox, a nondelivery report (NDR) is sent back to the sender, indicating that the email address they sent the message to is invalid.

WARNING   When the first HubTransport server is installed, Exchange creates an authoritative accepted domain entry for the root domain in your forest. If you are using a nonroutable domain name internally (such as domain.local), then you will need to add an accepted domain entry for your public domain name—**domain.com**, for example.

When a domain is configured as a relay domain, Exchange does not need to have a matching mailbox for the recipient. In the case of an internal relay domain, Exchange will first check for a mailbox for the recipient, and if one doesn't exist, it will send the message to a send connector that represents the domain address space. This is useful in situations where Exchange is sharing the domain namespace with another email system. You can route mail through Exchange first, and then if Exchange doesn't own the mailbox it will pass the message on to the server that is configured on the send connector.

Aside from an internal relay domain, you can also have an external relay domain. With an external relay domain, Exchange will not check for the mailbox in the organization, but rather will just forward the message to the send connector that represents the domain namespace. You could use this configuration to make an Edge Transport server a smart host and have it do the virus scanning and spam filtering for multiple domains before forwarding the message on to the server that is authoritative for the domain namespace.

Use the Exchange Management Console to Configure an Accepted Domain

To configure an accepted domain for Exchange using the EMC:

1. Open the EMC and browse to the Organization Configuration ➤ Hub Transport node in the Console tree.

2. In the Actions pane, click the option New Accepted Domain. This will launch the New Accepted Domain wizard.

3. In the Name field, type a friendly name for this accepted domain, such as **Contoso Email.**

4. In the Accepted Domain field, type the name of the domain, such as **contoso.com**.

5. Select what Exchange will do with messages that are received for this domain name.

   As outlined earlier, you can choose an authoritative domain, an internal relay domain, or an external relay domain.

6. Click the New button to create the accepted domain entry.

7. On the Completion screen, click the Finish button to complete the changes and close the wizard.

Use the Exchange Management Shell to Configure an Accepted Domain

You can also create the accepted domain in the EMS using the `New-AcceptedDomain` command. When doing so, you are required to specify the `DomainName` parameter and the `Name` parameter. You can also optionally use the `DomainType` parameter with one of the options listed in Table 6.1. When you don't specify the `DomainType` parameter, the accepted domain is created as an authoritative domain.

Table 6.1: Possible Domain Types When Creating an Accepted Domain from the EMS

Type	Parameter
Authoritative Domain	`Authoritative`
Internal Relay Domain	`InternalRelay`
External Relay Domain	`ExternalRelay`

The following example creates an internal relay domain for contoso.com:

```
New-AcceptedDomain -Name "Contoso Email" -DomainName ↵
contoso.com -DomainType InternalRelay
```

Configure the DNS Records for Receiving Email

When email systems outside your organization need to send you messages, they have to find out what server to send them to. The most common method of accomplishing this across the Internet is through Mail Exchanger (MX) records configured in DNS.

When an email is sent from an outside system across the Internet, the sending system looks up the MX records for your domain in your public DNS zone. You can have multiple MX records published for load balancing and redundancy of servers that receive Internet email. If there is more than one MX record published, the sending server chooses the record with the lowest priority number. For example, you could have multiple MX records published in the configuration shown in Table 6.2.

Table 6.2: Example MX Record Design

Host Server	Priority Number
contoso-mx1.contoso.com	10
contoso-mx2.contoso.com	20
contoso-mx3.contoso.com	20

Since contoso-mx1 has the lowest priority value (10), mail will always be sent to it when an external domain sends a message to someone@contoso.com. Since contoso-mx2 and contoso-mx3 both have higher priority values (20), they are used solely for backup in the event that contoso-mx1 goes offline.

If you are using Windows DNS, you can use the following steps to create MX records for your mail domain:

1. Log onto a server that has the DNS Manager console installed, such as a domain controller.

2. Open DNS Manager by choosing Start ➤ All Programs ➤ Administrative Tools ➤ DNS.

3. In the DNS Manager tool, browse to the zone that represents your email domain. When you select the zone, the list of records for that zone is displayed in the right pane.

4. Right-click on the zone name in the Console tree, and select Other New Records from the context menu. The Resource Record Type dialog box will open.

5. In the Resource Record Type dialog box, scroll down and select the Mail Exchanger (MX) record entry. Then click the Create Record button, as shown in Figure 6.10.

Figure 6.10: Creating an MX record in DNS

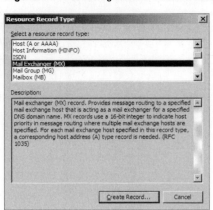

6. The New Resource Record dialog box will be displayed. In this dialog box, leave the field Host Or Child Domain empty. In the field for the FQDN of the server, type the FQDN of the Transport server that will be receiving Internet mail. Adjust the Mail Server Priority field as you see fit. This dialog box is shown in Figure 6.11.

Figure 6.11: DNS MX record properties

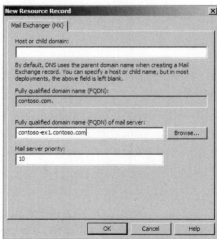

7. Click OK to create the record. When back in the Resource Record Type dialog box, click Done.

Manage Message Settings for Remote Domains

Remote domains are domains that Exchange isn't authoritative for. When a user from your Exchange organization sends a message to a remote domain, you can control the settings that are applied to that message. These remote domain settings are configured for the entire Exchange organization. So regardless of what Transport server delivers the message, the same settings will be applied.

Define a Remote Domain

You start off by defining a remote domain that you want to configure settings for. You can define one using the New-RemoteDomain command in the EMS, or you can use the following steps in the EMC:

1. Open the EMC and browse to the Organization Configuration ➢ Hub Transport node. Click the Remote Domains tab in the Work area.

   The list of currently defined remote domains is displayed.

2. To add a new remote domain, click the New Remote Domain option in the Actions pane.

   The New Remote Domain wizard will launch.

3. In the Name field, give the Remote Domain a friendly name and type the domain name into the Domain Name field. If you check the Include All Subdomains option, then settings specified on this domain will also be applied to messages sent to all subdomains under this domain as well.

4. Click the New button to create the remote domain.

5. On the Completion screen, click the Finish button.

   After the remote domain is added, it will appear in the list of remote domains in the EMC.

Configure Remote Domains

You will notice that a remote domain called Default is listed in the EMC. The Default entry is automatically created when you install the first Hub Transport server, and it includes all domains outside the Exchange organization. The message settings that you apply on the Default entry will be applied to every domain unless there is a more specific remote domain entry defined.

There are primarily two things for which you can modify remote domain settings:

- Out-of-office (OOF) messages
- Message Format settings

You can restrict how OOF messages are sent to a remote domain. For example, there may be a particular domain that you want no out-of-office messages sent to. You can modify the OOF settings by selecting the remote domain and choosing Properties in the Actions pane. The OOF settings are all listed on the General tab, as shown in Figure 6.12.

Figure 6.12: Out-of-office setting options for remote domains

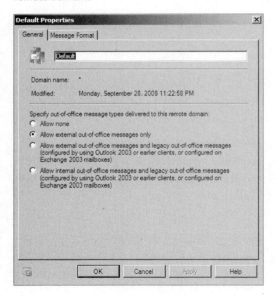

You can also configure the OOF settings using the Set-RemoteDomain command in the EMS. You will need to specify the AllowedOOFType parameter. Table 6.3 shows the available options for this setting and how they relate to the settings in the EMC.

Table 6.3: Remote Domain OOF Settings

EMC Setting	Description	EMS Parameter
Allow None	No out-of-office messages will be sent to this domain.	`None`
Allow External Out-Of-Office Messages Only	Only out-of-office messages created in Outlook 2007 (or newer client) or OWA in Exchange Server 2007 or 2010 and marked as External will be sent to this domain. This is the default setting.	`External`
Allow External Out-Of-Office Messages And Legacy Out-Of-Office Messages (Configured Using Outlook 2003 Or Earlier Clients, Or Configured On Exchange 2003 Mailboxes)	Out-of-office messages created in Outlook 2007 (or newer client) or OWA in Exchange Server 2007 or 2010 and marked as External will be sent to this domain. Also, all out-of-office messages created on older clients and older versions of OWA will be sent.	`ExternalLegacy`
Allow Internal Out-Of-Office Messages And Legacy Out-Of-Office Messages (Configured Using Outlook 2003 Or Earlier Clients, Or Configured On Exchange 2003 Mailboxes)	Out-of-office messages created in Outlook 2007 (or newer client) or OWA in Exchange Server 2007 or 2010 and marked as Internal will be sent to this domain. Also, all out-of-office messages created on older clients and older versions of OWA will be sent.	`InternalLegacy`

In addition to out-of-office settings, you can configure message format settings for remote domains. This is particularly useful in cases where you don't trust email coming from a certain domain and you want to ensure that things like NDRs or automatic replies don't get sent back. In some cases, these messages can confirm to spammers that the email address they sent the message to is valid or invalid.

The message settings can be changed in the EMS using the `Set-RemoteDomain` command. Table 6.4 outlines some of the common settings and their EMS parameters.

Managing Exchange Server Roles

PART II

Table 6.4: Message Format Settings for Remote Domains

EMC Setting	Description	EMS Parameter
Allow Automatic Replies	If enabled, automatic replies to emails set through client rules are allowed.	`AutoReplyEnabled`
Allow Automatic Forward	If enabled, messages can be auto-forwarded to the remote domain if client rules are set up for it.	`AutoForwardEnabled`
Allow Delivery Reports	Allows message delivery confirmations to be sent back to the sender from the remote domain.	`DeliveryReportEnabled`
Allow Non-Delivery Reports	Allows NDR messages to be sent back to the sender from the remote domain.	`NDREnabled`

To modify the message format settings in the EMC:

1. Open the EMC and browse to the Organization Configuration ➤ Hub Transport node in the Console tree.

2. Click the Remote Domains tab in the Work area. The list of currently configured remote domains is displayed.

3. Click the remote domain that you want to change the message format settings on.

   If the remote domain is not in the list, follow the steps at the beginning of this section for adding a new remote domain entry.

4. In the Actions pane, click the Properties option to bring up the properties dialog box for the remote domain.

5. In the properties dialog box, click the Message Format tab.

6. After making changes to the message format options, click OK to save the changes and close the properties dialog box.

Configure Mail to Flow Through an External Gateway

An external gateway can be used to provide services for outgoing and incoming messages. These services could be many things, such as email filtering, virus and spam protection, and high availability. If you want messages to go through a gateway when entering and exiting the Exchange organization, then you'll need to set up a send connector and a receive connector to the gateway.

In addition, you'll need to understand the authentication requirements of the gateway. Some gateways may require that you enter a username and password, while others may allow you send mail through them without credentials. There are three authentication options for use with an external gateway. These options are explained in Table 6.5.

Table 6.5: Authentication Options for External Gateways

Authentication Type	Description
None	No authentication is used. Messages are submitted to the gateway through anonymous mail relay.
Basic	Username and password authentication is used.
Externally Secured	No authentication is used, but there is an external source securing the connection, such as IPSec.

If you use Externally Secured authentication for the gateway, make sure that you really do have some form of external security. When messages come through an externally secured gateway, they are treated as if they originated inside the Exchange organization.

To configure mail flow through the gateway, you will need to create a send connector and a receive connector for the gateway. You can use the following steps to configure an external gateway that uses Basic authentication:

1. Open the EMC and browse to the Organization Configuration ➤ Hub Transport node in the Console tree.

2. Create the send connector for the gateway by clicking the New Send Connector option in the Actions pane on the right.

3. In the New Send Connector wizard, type the name of the send connector in the Name field.

4. In the Select The Intended Use For This Send Connector field, select Custom from the drop-down list and click Next.

5. In the Address Space screen, click the Add button to add an address space for the connector.

   The SMTP Address Space dialog box will appear.

6. In the SMTP Address Space dialog box, type * (an asterisk) in the Address field. Click Next.

7. In the Network Settings screen, click the option Route Mail Through The Following Smart Hosts. Click the Add button to display the Add Smart Host dialog box.

8. In the Add Smart Host dialog box, enter the IP address or FQDN of the smart host. Click OK when you are finished. When back in the New Send Connector wizard, click Next.

9. On the Configure Smart Host Authentication Settings screen, click the option Basic Authentication. In the User Name and Password fields, enter the username and password required to connect to the smart host. Click Next when finished.

10. On the Source Server screen, click Next if you are satisfied with the list of Transport servers associated with the connector. If you want to add Transport servers, click the Add button and browse for the server in the Select Hub Transport And Subscribed Edge Transport Server dialog box.

11. On the New Connector screen, click New to create the send connector.

12. On the Completion screen, click Finish.

13. Back in the EMC, browse to the Server Configuration ➤ Hub Transport node in the Console tree.

14. Select the Transport server that will be receiving mail from the external gateway and click the New Receive Connector option in the Actions pane.

15. On the Introduction screen of the New Receive Connector wizard, type the name of the receive connector in the Name field.

16. In the Select The Intended Use For This Receive Connector field, choose Custom from the drop-down list. Click Next when ready.

17. On the Local Network Settings screen, click Next to accept the default setting of listening for mail from the connector on all IP addresses.

18. On the Remote Network Settings screen, you have the option of configuring this connector to receive mail only from your external gateway's IP address. To do this, select the existing IP address range in the wizard and click the red X button to delete it. Then click Add to create a new IP address range.

19. In the Add IP Addresses Of Remote Servers dialog box, type an IP subnet and the bit mask for the range. If you want to accept email only from the IP address of the external gateway, you can enter the IP address of the gateway and specify a 32-bit mask. For example, you could enter `192.168.53.82/32`.

   Click OK to close the dialog box and add the range to the list in the wizard.

20. When back on the Remote Network Settings screen of the New Receive Connector wizard, click Next.

21. On the New Connector screen, click the New button to create the receive connector.

22. In the Completion dialog box, click the Finish button to close the wizard.

Configure a Hub Transport Server to Receive Internet Email

By default, Hub Transport servers cannot receive mail from the Internet. The most secure way to receive Internet email is from an Edge Transport server. Therefore, if you want to take the riskier route, you must consciously configure a Hub Transport server to receive Internet email.

TIP Even though an Internet-facing Hub Transport server introduces more risk, it's sometimes worth it. Some organizations will opt for this solution instead of using Edge Transport servers because they have another mail gateway or firewall that takes care of the messaging security for them. Some organizations may decide to use Internet-facing Hub Transport servers so they don't have to buy additional hardware for Edge Transport servers and spend time and money managing them.

When configuring a Hub Transport server to receive Internet email, you are modifying the receive connector on the server. The receive connecter determines who can send messages to the server. Receive connectors have a set of permissions assigned as well as a number of authentication mechanisms. These authentication mechanisms define how the identity of the sending party is verified. When a sender connects to a receive connector, the session starts out as anonymous and the sender has the permissions that are given to anonymous connections. If the sender authenticates after that, the permissions are changed to reflect those of the identity that it authenticated with.

Receive connectors have an access control list (ACL) that contains multiple entries. Each entry represents an identity and what permissions that identity has. Therefore, to control who has permissions to send mail to the receive connector, you need to modify the ACL on the receive connector. In the case of Internet email, you need to allow anonymous connections to submit SMTP messages to the receive connector on your Hub Transport server.

To allow anonymous SMTP submissions in the EMC:

1. Open the EMC and browse to the Server Configuration ➢ Hub Transport node in the Console tree.

2. From the list of Hub Transport servers in the Results pane, select the server that you want to receive Internet email on.

3. In the list of receive connectors for that server, select the connector labeled Default <*ServerName*> and click the Properties button in the Actions pane.

4. In the properties dialog box for the receive connector, click the Permission Groups tab.

5. Select Anonymous Users, as shown in Figure 6.13, and click OK to make the change and close the properties dialog box.

Figure 6.13: Allowing a Hub Transport server to receive Internet email

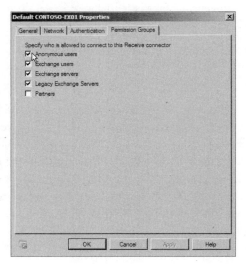

You can also make this configuration change using the EMS. To do so, you will use the `Set-ReceiveConnector` command along with the `PermissionGroups` parameter. In this parameter, you will need to specify that anonymous users can send mail to this connector. In the following example, a receive connector's permission groups are set to include `AnonymousUsers`, `ExchangeUsers`, `ExchangeServers`, and `ExchangeLegacyServers`.

```
Set-ReceiveConnector "Default CONTOSO-EX01" ↵
-PermissionGroups 'AnonymousUsers, ExchangeUsers, ↵
ExchangeServers, ExchangeLegacyServers'
```

Manage Mail Transport Servers

The Transport server in Exchange is responsible for moving the message to the next hop along the path of delivery. When troubleshooting mail delivery the most likely place you will start is at the Transport servers. When managing these servers, the message queues are of vital importance.

There are differences between the management of Hub Transport servers and the management of Edge Transport servers. So far in this chapter, we've been focused primarily on the management tasks in common between the two server roles, but with more of a focus on the Hub Transport role. In this part of the chapter, in addition to learning how to administer message queues, we will also look at Edge Transport server management specifically.

Administer Transport Server Message Queues

When messages are handled by Transport servers, they are placed into queues and processed in a particular order. Exchange has five different types of queues:

Submission Queue   The Submission queue is where messages are queued when they are first processed by a Transport server. When a message enters the Submission queue, the categorizer determines how these messages get to their destinations. Messages are processed out of the Submission queue and moved to one of the other queues.

Unreachable Queue   The Unreachable queue contains messages for which a routing path can't be determined. Messages in the Unreachable queue do not get resubmitted automatically. If you've fixed the routing issue, you will have to go back into the Unreachable queue and manually resubmit the messages. At that point, they are moved back into the Submission queue for reprocessing.

Mailbox Delivery Queue   The Mailbox Delivery queue consists of messages whose next step in the routing path is to the recipient's mailbox. Messages queued here will be on a Hub Transport server in the same site as the recipient's Mailbox server.

Remote Delivery Queue   The Remote Delivery queue contains messages that are queued up for SMTP delivery to an external domain, a smart host, or another Active Directory site.

Poison Message Queue   The Poison Message queue contains messages that could potentially be harmful to Exchange—for example, messages that failed processing through a transport agent due to message corruption, or another possible event.

Messages progress through different queues in order to be delivered. For example, if a user were to successfully send a message inside the organization to a user in a different site, the message would progress through the following queues in this order:

1. Submission queue on the Hub Transport server in the same site as the sender

2. Remote Delivery queue on the Hub Transport server in the same site as the sender

3. Submission queue on the Hub Transport server in the recipient's site

4. Mailbox Delivery queue on the Hub Transport server in the same site as the recipient

To better illustrate this, consider the following scenario where Tom sends Sarah an email. Sarah and Tom are in different AD sites. Figure 6.14 shows the queues that the message passes through.

Move the Message Queue Database to a Different Location

Although there are multiple queues on a Transport server, the messages are kept in a single queue database as they pass through the Transport server. The queue database is similar to mailbox databases on Mailbox servers. Therefore, if you have large volumes of messages coming through the Transport server, you may be able to get a performance increase if you move the queue database to a separate set of hard disks.

Figure 6.14: How messages flow through the queues inside an organization

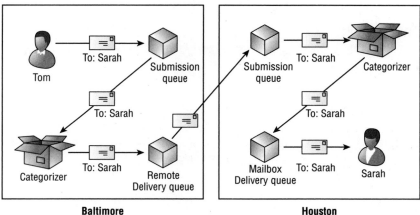

Baltimore   **Houston**

Managing Exchange
Server Roles

NOTE   Using additional hard disks increases the throughput of data transfers for Exchange databases. For more details on this process, see Chapter 7, "Managing Mailbox Databases."

You can modify the location of the queue database using the following steps on the Transport server:

1. Stop the Exchange Transport service. To do so, open a command prompt and run the command net stop MSExchangeTransport.

2. Next you'll edit the transport configuration file with the new queue location. Open the file C:\Program Files\Microsoft\Exchange Server\V14\Bin\EdgeTransport.exe.config in Notepad.

3. Browse to the section of the file labeled <appSettings> and find the following line:

```
<add key="QueueDatabasePath" value="C:\Profile Files ↵
\Microsoft\Exchange Server\V14\TransportRoles\data ↵
\Queue" />
```

4. Replace the `value` property with the new location of the queue database.

Figure 6.15 shows the changes that are made when the queue is moved to the location Q:\QueueDB.

Figure 6.15: Modifying the transport configuration file with the new queue database location

5. Save the file and close Notepad.

6. Ensure that the folder where you want to move the queue exists.

7. From the command prompt, move all of the files from the old queue database location to the new location by running the following command:

```
move "C:\Program Files\Microsoft\Exchange Server\V14\ ↵
TransportRoles\data\Queue\*.*" "Q:\QueueDB"
```

8. Start the Exchange Transport service back up. Open a command prompt and type **net start MSExchangeTransport**.

Force a Message Queue to Retry

When a message can't be moved out of a queue and on to the next hop toward its destination, the queue is placed into a retry state. When a queue is in retry, you can either force it to try its next hop again, or wait until the retry timer counts down, at which point it retries automatically.

You can manually force a retry in either the Queue Viewer or the EMS. To retry a queue using the Queue Viewer, you can use the following steps:

1. Run the Queue Viewer by opening the EMC and clicking on the Toolbox node in the Console tree. In the Work area, double-click the Queue Viewer icon under the Mail Flow Tools area.

2. In the Queue Viewer, ensure that the Queues tab is selected.

    The Results pane lists all the queues that are available on the server.

3. Select the queue that is current in the retry state.

4. In the Actions pane, click the Retry Queue option.

To force a retry in the EMS, you can use the `Retry-Queue` command. When you run the command, you need to specify the name of the queue that you want to retry. The following example demonstrates the command:

```
Retry-Queue CONTOSO-EX1\Queue
```

Export Messages Out of a Queue Using the Exchange Management Shell

You can export messages straight from a queue so you can examine them or place them in the replay directory for resubmission to the Transport server. Having the ability to examine messages in a queue can help troubleshoot potential issues. This is particularly helpful when dealing with messages in the Poison Message queue.

To export a message out of the queue and to a file, you can use the `Export-Message` command from the EMS. To export a single message from the queue, you need to specify the message ID and the path of the file that you want to export it to. The exported message will be saved with an `.EML` extension. You can open this message with any text editor, such as Notepad. The following command demonstrates exporting a message from the Poison Message queue to a file:

```
Export-Message CONTOSO-EX1\Poison\1 -Path C:\ExportedMsgs
```

You can retrieve a list of messages in the queue by running the `Get-Message` command. This command will retrieve a list of messages currently queued on the Transport server, along with the message

Managing Exchange Server Roles

PART II

ID. You can also pipeline the Get-Message command into the Export-Message command and export all of the messages in queues to EML files. Use the following command, substituting your own path:

```
Get-Message | Export-Message -Path C:\ExportedMsgs
```

Suspend a Message Queue

When you suspend a message queue, you freeze the processing of the queue. Suspending a queue does not change the state of the messages in the queue. You then have the option of suspending individual messages and resuming the queue.

You can suspend a queue either through the Queue Viewer in the EMC or through the EMS.

To suspend a queue using the Queue Viewer:

1. Run the Queue Viewer by opening the EMC and clicking the Toolbox node in the Console tree. In the Work area, double-click the Queue Viewer icon under the Mail Flow Tools area.

2. In the Queue Viewer, ensure that the Queues tab is selected.

   The Results pane lists all the queues that are available on the server.

3. Click on the queue that you want to suspend. In the Actions pane, select the Suspend option to suspend the queue.

To suspend the message queue using the EMS, you can use the Suspend-Queue command. Specify the name of the queue that you want to suspend. For example, the following command suspends the Submission queue:

```
Suspend-Queue CONTOSO-EX1\Submission
```

The Suspend-Queue command also accepts a filter. This allows you to specify logic when suspending queues. You can filter on things such as message count and message status. For example, if you want to suspend any queue that has more than 10 messages in the retry state, you can use the following command (substituting the name of your server):

```
Suspend-Queue -Server CONTOSO-EX2010 -Filter ↵
{MessageCount -gt 10 -and Status -eq "Retry"}
```

Manage the Edge Transport Server

Management practices for the Edge Transport server are different from those for the Hub Transport servers inside the organization. By placing Edge servers at the perimeter of your network, you can make them your first line of defense for protecting your organization against email-related threats.

To reduce the attack surface, Edge Transport servers are not members of the Active Directory forest that Exchange is in. However, Edge Transport servers require information from Active Directory in order for the Edge Transport server to perform some of its key functions. To get this information, the Edge servers run Active Directory Lightweight Directory Services (AD LDS), which is a portable directory service that is based on the same technology as Active Directory. AD LDS is installed on each Edge Transport server, and a service called EdgeSync runs on a Hub Transport server in the site that the Edge server is subscribed to. EdgeSync synchronizes the recipient data, routing topology data, and Exchange configuration data to the Edge Transport server.

NOTE   The synchronization from Active Directory to AD LDS on the Edge Transport server is a one-way sync. This sync is initiated by the Hub Transport server. Data in the AD LDS directory will never be merged with or replicated to AD.

This section of the chapter will take you through some common administrative functions of managing Edge Transport servers.

Subscribe an Edge Transport Server to an Active Directory Site

To use an Edge Transport server as a basic SMTP relay device, you don't need to subscribe it to an Active Directory site. However, if you do subscribe the Edge Transport server to an AD site, the settings for the Edge Transport server are managed within your Exchange organization and then synchronized to the Edge Transport server using the EdgeSync service. This allows you to utilize the data in the Active Directory environment for antispam features, which offers you the advantage of features such as recipient lookup or safe list aggregation, which uses safe sender lists stored in Outlook to determine the validity of messages. You can use the following steps to subscribe the Edge Transport server to a site.

Managing Exchange
Server Roles

PART II

Step 1: Ensure That the Correct Ports Are Open in Your Firewall

The AD LDS directory service uses port 50636 by default to communicate with the Hub Transport servers that are replicating the directory data. This port is secured with SSL, and the synchronization process is authenticated using LDAP bind authentication over SSL.

In order for the Hub Transport and the Edge Transport servers to communicate, you will need to ensure that any firewalls that exist between the Hub and the Edge servers allow TCP traffic on port 50636. To test this connectivity, a service needs to be actively listening on 50636. If you don't have an existing AD LDS instance listening on that port, you will need to check with your communications network administrators to verify that the port is open.

Step 2: Ensure That Name Resolution Works Between the Hub Transport Servers in the Site and the Edge Transport Server

You need to ensure that the Hub Transport server and the Edge Transport server can both resolve each other through DNS name resolution.

Often in a perimeter network, DNS is configured in a split-brain design. This allows you to use internal DNS servers and separate, independent external DNS servers that both provide name resolution for the domain name.

You will want to ensure that the DNS servers used by the Hub Transport servers can resolve the names of the Edge Transport servers. Likewise, the DNS servers that the Edge Transport servers are using will need to resolve the names of the Hub Transport servers. This may require additional record registrations if the Edge Transport server is using an Internet-facing DNS server.

You can verify that name resolution works using the following procedures:

1. Log on to the Hub Transport server and open a command prompt by clicking Start ➤ All Programs ➤ Accessories ➤ Command Prompt.

2. At the command prompt, type **nslookup** and specify the name of the Edge Transport server. For example, if the name of the Edge Transport server is contoso-edge1.contoso.com, you would use the following command:

```
C:\> nslookup contoso-edge1.contoso.com
```

3. Log out of the Hub Transport server.

4. Log on to the Edge Transport server and open a command prompt.

5. Run the `nslookup` command again, but this time specify the name of the Hub Transport server in the site that the Edge Transport server will be subscribed to—for example:

```
C:\> nslookup contoso-hub1.contoso.com
```

6. Use `nslookup` to test name resolution for each Hub Transport server in the site.

Step 3: Export the Subscription XML File from the Edge Transport Server

The Edge Subscription XML file is generated on the Edge Transport server. The file will need to be manually copied over to the Hub Transport server that you will configure EdgeSync on.

To export the Edge Subscription XML file, you can use the `New-EdgeSubscription` command in the EMS. Make sure that you run the command from the Edge Transport server that you are subscribing, and include the `FileName` parameter in the command to define the name and location of the XML file that the information is output to. The following example illustrates this command:

```
New-EdgeSubscription -FileName "C:\EdgeSubscription.xml"
```

You will receive a warning message, indicating that some custom settings on the Edge Transport server may be overwritten with data by the EdgeSync service, since the configuration will now be managed within the Exchange organization instead of on the Edge Transport servers. Type **Y** and press Enter to continue.

Step 4: Create the Subscription on the Hub Transport Server and Import the XML File That Was Exported in Step 3

After you have the Edge Subscription XML file created, you manually move it over a Hub Transport server in the target site and delete the original file from the Edge Transport server. After the file is moved, you can use the EMC or the EMS to create the Edge Subscription by importing the XML file. After the `EdgeSynchronization.xml` file is created, you have up to 1,440 minutes (24 hours) to create the edge subscription on the Hub Transport server.

To create the Edge Subscription using the EMC:

1. Log into the Hub Transport server and open the EMC.

2. From the EMC, browse to the Organization Configuration ➤ Hub Transport node in the Console tree.

3. In the Actions pane on the right, click the New Edge Subscription option to launch the New Edge Subscription dialog box.

4. In the New Edge Subscription dialog box, click the Browse button next to the Active Directory site field to choose the site that the Edge server will be subscribed to.

5. In the Subscription File field, click the Browse button and find the XML file that you moved over to the server.

6. Place a check mark in the option Automatically Create A Send Connector For This Edge Subscription.

   Figure 6.16 demonstrates the settings used for creating an Edge Subscription.

Figure 6.16: Creating an Edge Subscription

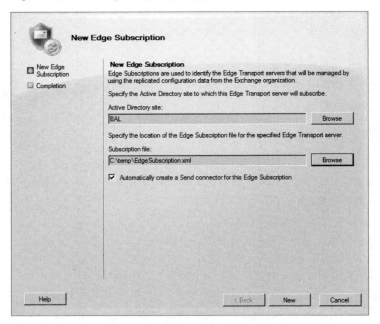

7. After you've entered your configuration, click the New button to create the Edge subscription.

8. On the Completion page, click the Finish button.

You can also use the EMS to create the edge subscription. To do so, you would use the `New-EdgeSubscription` command on the Hub Transport server. In addition to specifying the name of the site, you will need to import the XML file for the Edge Subscription into a byte-encoded data object. The following example demonstrates this command:

```
New-EdgeSubscription -FileData ([byte[]]$(Get-Content -Path ↵
"C:\EdgeSubscription.xml" -Encoding Byte -ReadCount 0)) ↵
-Site "BAL" -CreateInternetSendConnector $true ↵
-CreateInboundSendConnector $true
```

Force the Synchronization of Edge Transport Server Data

The data that is synchronized between Active Directory on a Hub Transport server and AD LDS on the Edge Transport server follows a regular interval. For recipient data, the Hub Transport server must not allow more than four hours to pass between synchronization cycles. For configuration data, no more than one hour can pass. And for routing topology information, the data needs to be synchronized at least every five minutes.

Instead of waiting for these time cycles to complete, you can force the immediate synchronization of an Edge Transport server by issuing the `Start-EdgeSynchronization` EMS command from the Hub Transport server. If you are running the command from a server other than a hub in the site that the Edge server is subscribed to, you will need to specify the `Server` parameter and point it to a Hub Transport server that participates in the EdgeSync. The following example starts synchronization on a server in another site:

```
Start-EdgeSynchronization -Server contoso-hub1
```

Test Edge Transport Server Synchronization

Exchange provides a way for you to test the synchronization of the Active Directory data from the Hub Transport server to the AD LDS instance on the Edge Transport server. The `Test-EdgeSynchronization`

Managing Exchange Server Roles

PART II

command in EMS allows you to test this synchronization without having to force synchronization to see if it's working. Run this command from the Hub Transport server in the site that the Edge Transport server is subscribed to:

```
Test-EdgeSynchronization
```

With the Test-EdgeSynchronization command, you can single out a specific recipient and test whether that recipient has replicated. To do this, you use the VerifyRecipient parameter with the command. For example, the following command tests whether the account nora@contoso.com has synchronized to the Edge Transport server:

```
Test-EdgeSynchronization -VerifyRecipient nora@contoso.com
```

When you test the synchronization of a specific recipient, the output field RecipientStatus will report whether the recipient is synchronized. If the recipient is synchronized to the Edge Transport server, the status will read Synchronized. Otherwise, it will report NotSynchronized.

7

Managing Mailbox Databases

D atabases are at the heart of information storage in Exchange. The database is the primary place that user data is kept, and there are two types: Mailbox databases and Public Folder databases. This chapter is mostly about managing Mailbox databases.

Each Mailbox server can contain only one Public Folder database, but it can contain multiple Mailbox databases. You can place as many mailboxes as you'd like in a Mailbox database, but if the database grows too big, backing it up effectively becomes difficult. Also, bigger databases introduce more opportunity for corruption.

The way data is written to and read from databases is controlled by the Extensible Storage Engine (ESE). The ESE is an impressive piece of technology. There are many challenges to overcome when designing a database system that can hold hundreds of gigabytes of data that is heavily accessed and must be reliable enough to hold data as important as email. And Exchange meets this challenge with ease. This chapter shows you how to manage these databases and how to use the new database redundancy technologies in Exchange Server 2010.

Perform Essential Database Management

The management aspects of maintaining databases in Exchange aren't very complex. However, an elementary knowledge of the ESE is a necessity. The ESE controls how data is written to and read from the databases. Data isn't written to databases directly. Instead, Exchange holds the data in memory and writes it to transaction logs first. The data in memory and in the transaction log files are then periodically written to the database. This design is referred to as *write-ahead logging*, and is illustrated in Figure 7.1.

Manage the Database Files

A single database is kept in one file, which has the extension .EDB. The EDB contains the actual data for the database. If a Mailbox server has many databases, then there are many EDB files.

Create a New Mailbox Database

When creating Mailbox databases in Exchange, you must make a couple of decisions. The first thing to decide on is the name of the database. This name must be unique across your Exchange organization. In Exchange Server 2010, databases exist at the organization level so new availability options can be leveraged. Therefore, you should ensure that your database naming scheme gives each database a unique name. Another thing to consider is that since databases can now move between servers, you may not want to tie the database name to the server name. For example, the name Server1Database wouldn't make a lot of sense if the database was hosted on Server2.

Figure 7.1: How data is written in Exchange

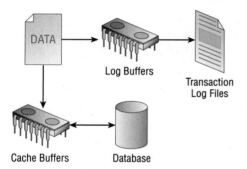

Log Buffers

Transaction Log Files

Cache Buffers   Database

The second and perhaps the most important thing you should decide on is the location of the database. Disk performance in Exchange Server 2010 is more efficient than in previous versions, so it's not as critical that the databases exist on fast, high-performance hard drives. It's completely acceptable to use slower local disks as long as the recoverability and availability concerns are addressed. When you plan your database storage, ensure that you have used drives that have enough space for the size that you anticipate your databases to be with any additional growth.

TIP   To help in planning your databases and their storage needs, I highly recommend that you download the Exchange Mailbox Server Role Storage Requirements Calculator from the Exchange Team's blog. You can find the download on the Exchange Team's Blog at http://msexchangeteam.com/archive/2007/07/05/445802.aspx. The calculator requires Microsoft Excel to run.

Managing Exchange Server Roles

You can create a new database in the Exchange Management Console (EMC):

1. Open the EMC and browse to the Organization Configuration ➢ Mailbox node in the Console tree.

2. In the Actions pane, click the option New Mailbox Database, which is in the list of Mailbox actions.

   This will launch the New Mailbox Database wizard.

3. At the Introduction screen, type the name of the database into the Mailbox Database Name field.

4. Click the Browse button under the Server Name field to browse for a Mailbox server that will be the active host of the database. After you have selected a Mailbox server and are back in the wizard, click the Next button.

5. At the Set Paths screen, type the location of the database and log files for this Mailbox database. Remember that this location could also be used on other Mailbox servers that have a copy of this database, so be sure the path is unique. Click Next to continue.

6. At the Configuration Summary screen, verify the settings for the new database and click the New button.

   The database is created and the Completion screen appears.

7. Verify the results and then click the Finish button to close the wizard.

You can also create databases using the `New-MailboxDatabase` cmdlet in the Exchange Management Shell (EMS). You will need to specify the server holding the database and the name of the database. The `EdbFilePath` parameter can be used to tell Exchange where you want to put the database file. You will also need to use the `LogFolderPath` parameter to specify the folder for the Transaction Log files for this database:

```
New-MailboxDatabase "DB01" -Server CONTOSO-EX01 ↵
-EdbFilePath "D:\DB01.edb" -LogFolderPath "E:\DB01Logs\"
```

NOTE When you create a new database in the EMC, the database is automatically mounted. If you use the EMS, you will need to mount the database manually afterward. The topic of mounting databases is covered in the next section.

Mount a Mailbox Database

Before a database can be used, it must be mounted. The process of mounting the database locks down the files and allows data to be read from and written to the database.

Check Whether a Database Is Mounted Using the Exchange Management Console

You can determine if a database is already mounted using the following steps in the EMC:

1. Open the EMC and browse to the Organization Configuration ≻ Mailbox node in the Console tree.

2. In the Work area, select the Database Management tab.

   The top half of the Database Management tab lists all the databases in the organization.

3. Look at the Mounted column in the list of databases. This column will tell you if the database is mounted.

   You can also look at the Mounted On Server column to see what server the database is mounted on (Figure 7.2).

Figure 7.2: Determining if a database is already mounted

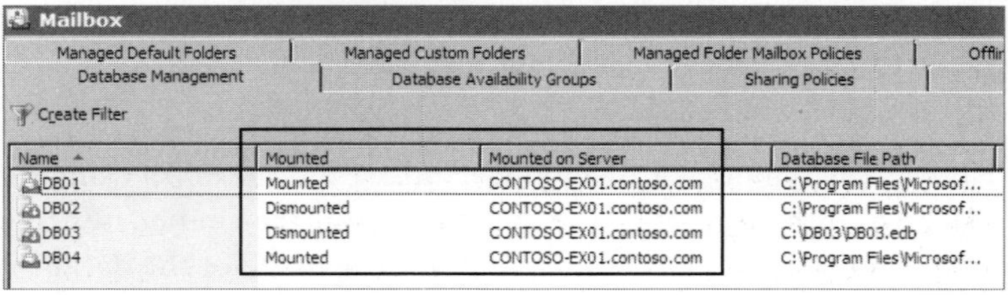

Mount a Mailbox Database Using the Exchange Management Console

To use the EMC to mount a database that is not currently mounted, use the following steps:

1. Open the EMC and browse to the Organization Configuration ≻ Mailbox node in the Console tree.

2. In the Work area, select the Database Management tab.

3. In the list of databases, select the database that you want to mount. The Mounted column should show that the database is currently Dismounted.

4. In the Actions pane for the database, click the Mount Database option, as shown in Figure 7.3.

Figure 7.3: Mounting a dismounted database

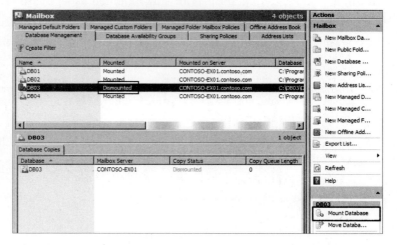

Mount and Dismount Mailbox Databases Using the Exchange Management Shell

You can also mount or dismount databases in the EMS using the Mount-Database cmdlet or the Dismount-Database cmdlet. When using these cmdlets, you only need to specify the name of the database that you want to mount or dismount. The following example commands mount and dismount the database named DB01:

```
Mount-Database "DB01"
Dismount-Database "DB01"
```

Move a Database to a Different Location

When you create a new database, you must specify the location where you want to place the database file. However, you can change this location afterward by moving the database. While the database is being moved, the database is dismounted. The database will be remounted after it is moved, if it was already mounted prior to starting the move.

NOTE   During the period that the database is dismounted, users will not be able to access the information in the database.

To move the database to a different location in the EMC, follow these steps:

1. Open the EMC and browse to the Organization Configuration ≻ Mailbox node in the Console tree.

2. Select the Database Management tab to view a list of the databases.

3. In the list of databases, select the database that you want to move.

4. In the Actions pane for the database that you have selected, click the Move Database Path option.

    The Move Database Path wizard will open.

5. Type the new location of the database file in the Database File Path field. Also type the new location of the logs in the Log Folder Path field, as shown in Figure 7.4.

Figure 7.4: Moving the database files

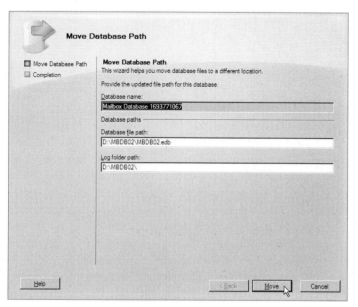

6. Click the Move button to move the database files to the new location.

7. If the database is mounted, you will be prompted with a message informing you that it must be dismounted before moving. If you see this message, click the Yes button if you want to continue moving the database files.

8. At the Completion screen, click the Finish button.

You can also move the database with the EMS, using the Move-DatabasePath cmdlet. When executing the command, you will need to include the new location for the database with the EdbFilePath parameter. You can also use the LogFolderPath parameter to specify the new location for the transaction logs.

WARNING   You cannot move the database files of a database that has multiple copies. You must first remove the database replicas, move the database files, and then re-create the replicas.

When running the Move-DatabasePath cmdlet, you may be prompted with a message explaining that the database has to be temporarily dismounted to move it. You can continue by pressing Y. You can bypass the message about dismounting the database by using the Force parameter.

```
Move-DatabasePath "DB01" -EdbFilePath F:\DB01\DB01.edb ↵
-LogFolderPath F:\DB01 -Force
```

Configure the Online Maintenance Window

During the online maintenance process, Exchange performs several tasks to clean up data in the database. In previous versions of Exchange, an online defrag of the database was performed at the end of the maintenance process. The defrag moved pieces of the database around on the disk so that the various blocks of data making up the database file were located closer together, thereby increasing performance. The defrag itself often took several hours to complete, particularly with large databases. In Exchange Server 2010, the option to run the defrag was moved out of the online maintenance window and the process now runs in the background all the time. This dramatically reduces the time needed for online maintenance, and you can adjust your maintenance window accordingly.

Adjust the Online Maintenance Window

To adjust the online maintenance window in the EMC, follow these steps:

1. Open the EMC and browse to the Organization Configuration ➢ Mailbox node in the Console tree.

2. Click the Database Management tab to bring up a list of databases.

3. Select the database that you want to configure the maintenance window on. Click the Properties option in the Actions pane for the database that you selected.

   This will open the properties dialog box for the database.

4. In the database's properties dialog box, click the Maintenance tab.

5. From the Maintenance Schedule drop-down list, select the pre-defined maintenance period you want to use or select Use Custom Schedule to define your own. See Figure 7.5.

6. Click OK to close the properties dialog box and make the changes to the maintenance window.

Figure 7.5: Selecting the maintenance window for a database

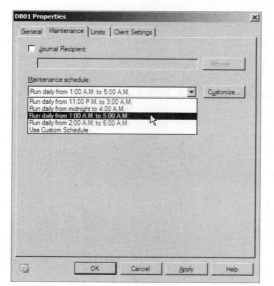

You can also modify the window in the EMS using the `Set-MailboxDatabase` cmdlet with the `MaintenanceSchedule` parameter. The following command turns on maintenance for only Sundays between 1 and 3 a.m.:

```
Set-MailboxDatabase DB01 -MaintenanceSchedule ↵
"Sun.1:00 AM-Sun.3:00 AM"
```

Change the Timing for Database Checksumming

There is also a process called database checksumming, which ensures that the database is scanned against corruptions. This process is performed in the background by default. If your database is relatively small (less than 500 GB), you can perform this checksumming at the end of your maintenance process instead, which gives the process a specific time window to run in. If the checksumming process doesn't finish within a three-day period, a warning event will be posted to the logs. You can enable this with the EMS using the `Set-MailboxDatabase` cmdlet. Specify the `BackgroundDatabaseMaintenance` parameter as `$False` to turn off background scanning and have it completed during online maintenance instead:

```
Set-MailboxDatabase DB01 -BackgroundDatabaseMaintenance ↵
$false
```

After this command is run, you must dismount and remount the database to enable the change.

Manage the Transaction Log Files

As I mentioned earlier, all data that is written to a database is first recorded in transaction log files. Each set of logs files is unique to a database. On disk, transaction log files are 1 MB files that are stored in the same location. Figure 7.6 shows a typical folder containing transaction logs.

In addition to log files, the database uses a checkpoint file, which records the last transaction that was successfully written to the database. The checkpoint file ends in the .CHK extension and is stored with the log files.

The log files are kept on disk until a backup is completed. After the logs are successfully backed up, they can be safely deleted from the server. If a database needs to be restored, the last full backup of the database and any log files that were created since the full backup are restored. When the database starts, the transactions inside the logs will be applied to the database.

Figure 7.6: Transaction logs viewed in Windows Explorer

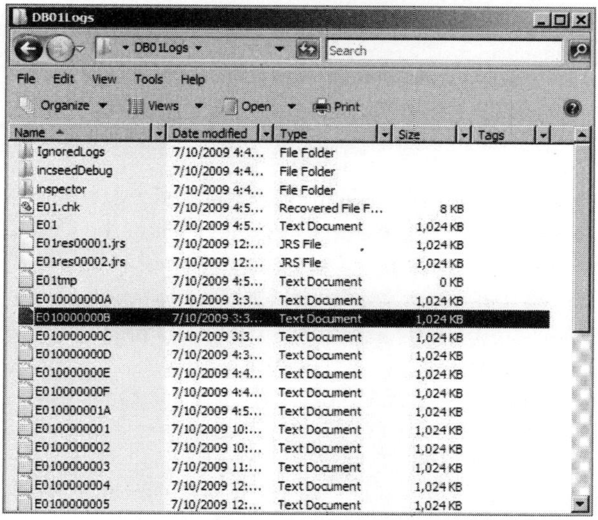

Managing Exchange
Server Roles

PART II

Move the Transaction Logs to a Different Location

In previous versions of Exchange, it was always a good idea to separate transaction logs and the database onto different hard disks. There were two primary reasons for this. First, the input/output (I/O) patterns are different for transaction log data than for database data. When transaction logs are written to the disk, the data is written sequentially because the data is written in contiguous blocks as it is streamed in from memory. This means that the disk head on the drive moves very little. On the other hand, when database data is written, the I/O is random and the disk head moves frequently across the disk because it is writing data in different places. Therefore, putting transaction logs on the same disks as the database means that you will lose some disk performance as that disk head moves back and forth.

The second reason for separating transaction logs involves recovery. If you lose the disks that the database is on, the transaction logs are still intact if they are on different disks. You can restore the last full backup and any transaction logs with it. Along with the transaction logs that are already on the server, you have a full set of data that you can restore.

TIP   In most cases, the database performance enhancements in Exchange 2010 obviate the need to separate logs from the database for performance reasons. If you have multiple copies of the database on different servers, you may not be concerned about losing the disks with the transaction logs. Therefore, in many scenarios it will be better to keep the database and log files on the same set of hard disks in Exchange 2010.

If you didn't move the transaction logs when you created the database, you can still do it afterward. To move the transaction logs using the EMC, follow the steps in the section "Move a Database to a Different Location," earlier in this chapter. When you are prompted for the new location of the files, only change the location of the log folder. This will move only the transaction logs.

You can also move the logs with the EMS using the `Move-DatabasePath` cmdlet. You can specify that you want to move the transaction logs by including the `LogFolderPath` parameter, as in this example:

```
Move-DatabasePath -Identity DB01 -LogFolderPath T:\Logs
```

Reuse Transaction Logs

Exchange gives you the option of reusing transaction logs that have already been committed to the database. This is called *circular logging*. In previous versions of Exchange, it was a best practice to minimize the use of circular logging in production environments. You usually wanted to keep transaction logs until the database or the logs had been backed up so that the data could be recovered. If you lost a database and didn't have the logs, all the data since the last backup was gone.

In Exchange Server 2010, circular logging plays a more integral role. If you decide to use a backup-less configuration, as discussed in Chapter 10, "Maintaining Reliability and Availability," then you must use circular logging to ensure that transaction logs are regularly truncated.

However, there may be other circumstances where you might want to use circular logging. If your transaction log drive is filling up quickly and you can't provision additional space, circular logging is a possible solution to ensure that the drive doesn't fill up, which would cause the database to shut down. Some organizations will enable circular logging for periods of time, such as during a large mailbox migration. Of course, there is a period of risk during the time that circular logging is enabled. But if you make a full backup after you turn circular logging off, the risk is minimized.

Set Up Circular Logging Using the Exchange Management Console

You can enable or disable circular logging through the EMC:

1. Open the EMC and browse to the Organization Configuration ➢ Mailbox node in the Console tree.

2. Click the Database Management tab to bring up a list of databases.

3. Select the database that you want to enable circular logging on and choose Properties from the database's Action menu in the Actions pane.

4. In the properties dialog box for the database, click the Maintenance tab.

5. Select the Enable Circular Logging check box, as shown in Figure 7.7.

Figure 7.7: Enabling circular logging in the EMC

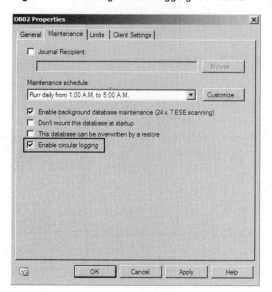

Managing Exchange Server Roles

PART II

6. If the database is mounted, you will receive a warning informing you that the database must be remounted before the circular logging setting will take effect. Click OK at this warning window.

7. When back in the properties dialog box, click OK to save the changes and close the dialog box.

8. You will need to dismount and remount the database in order for circular logging to take effect. When back in the EMC, make sure that you have the database selected and click the Dismount Database option in the database's Action menu in the Actions pane.

   When you are prompted to continue, click Yes.

9. After the database is dismounted, click the Mount Database option in the database's Action menu. This will remount the database.

Set Up Circular Logging Using the Exchange Management Shell

To configure circular logging through the EMS, use the Set-MailboxDatabase cmdlet with the CircularLoggingEnabled parameter, as shown in the following example. Set the parameter to $True to enable circular logging or $False to disable it:

```
Set-MailboxDatabase DB01 -CircularLoggingEnabled $True
```

Manage Database Settings

In addition to managing the database files themselves, there are some settings that you will want to understand and know how to configure. These settings affect the database and some of the features that it uses. The settings that you will want to know how to configure are the database indexing settings, the size limits, and the associated Client Access server.

Configure Exchange Search

Exchange Search creates a full-text index on Mailbox databases. This gives users the ability to search across their email very quickly. Items are added to the index as they arrive, which means that the index is always up-to-date.

Enable and Disable Exchange Search

You can enable or disable Exchange Search for individual Mailbox databases or for the entire Mailbox server. By default, the index is enabled on all Mailbox databases. To disable Exchange Search for a database, you can use the Set-MailboxDatabase cmdlet in the EMS with the IndexEnabled parameter. Set the parameter to $True to enable Exchange Search or $False to disable it. The following example disables Exchange Search:

```
Set-MailboxDatabase "DB01" -IndexEnabled $False
```

To enable or disable Exchange Search for the entire Mailbox server, you just disable the service. You can disable the Exchange Search service using the EMS. Open the EMS and run the following commands to disable the service:

```
Stop-Service MSExchangeSearch
Set-Service MSExchangeSearch -StartupType Disabled
```

You can reenable the service by setting the StartupType parameter to Automatic and manually starting it. The following EMS commands will accomplish this:

```
Set-Service MSExchangeSearch -StartupType Automatic
Start-Service MSExchangeSearch
```

NOTE Exchange Search is extremely efficient in Exchange Server 2010, and the Discovery feature relies on it being enabled. Before deciding to disable Exchange Search, ensure that you understand the implications.

Rebuild the Search Index

There may be times, such as in a data recovery scenario, where you will need to rebuild the Exchange Search index. The easiest way to rebuild this index is to use the PowerShell script that the Exchange team released with Exchange Server 2010.

This script is called ResetSearchIndex.ps1 and it's included in Exchange in the Program Files\Microsoft\Exchange Server\Scripts folder. Run the script with the -Force parameter and either specify the database that you want to reset the index on or specify All if you want to rebuild the indexes

Managing Exchange Server Roles

PART II

on the entire server. The following example rebuilds the indexes on the database DB01:

```
cd "C:\Program Files\Microsoft\Exchange Server\V14\Scripts"
.\ResetSearchIndex.ps1 -Force DB01
```

In the following example, all indexes on the current Mailbox server are rebuilt:

```
cd "C:\Program Files\Microsoft\Exchange Server\V14\Scripts"
.\ResetSearchIndex.ps1 -Force -All
```

Configure Limits on a Database

In Exchange Server, you can set a hard limit on a database, and if that database reaches that limit, it is dismounted. By default on Exchange Server 2010 Standard Edition, there is a 50 GB limit on databases. On the Enterprise Edition of Exchange, there is no defined limit. However, you can use these steps to set one or raise the 50 GB limit in Standard Edition.

NOTE If the database is in a database availability group (DAG), this limit is set on all copies of the database. DAGs are covered in more detail in the next section of this chapter.

---

1. Log into a Mailbox server that contains a copy of the database.

2. Open the EMS and run the following command to get the GUID of the database:

```
Get-MailboxDatabase DB01 | ft Name, GUID
```

Example output is shown in Figure 7.8.

Figure 7.8: Getting the GUID of a database

3. Open the Registry Editor by running `regedit.exe` from an elevated command prompt.

4. In the Registry Editor, browse to the following key:

   ```
   HKEY_LOCAL_MACHINE\SYSTEM\CurrentControlSet\Services\ ↵
   MSExchangeIS\NameOfServer\Private-DatabaseGUID
   ```

5. Look for the Registry value Database Size Limit In GB.

   - If it already exists, you can simply edit the value to be the maximum size that you want the database to grow.

   - If the Registry value does not exist, you can create it by following the remainder of these steps.

6. In the Registry Editor, select Edit ➢ New ➢ DWORD (32-Bit) Value. When the value is created, name it **Database Size Limit In GB**, as shown in Figure 7.9.

Figure 7.9: Creating the Registry key to set the database size limit

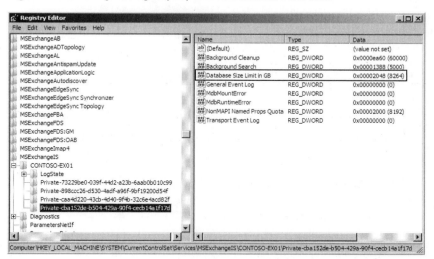

7. Double-click the Database Size Limit In GB Registry value to bring up the Edit dialog box. In the Value Data field, enter the database size limit that you want to use and click OK.

Associate a Client Access Server with a Mailbox Database

In Exchange 2010, Outlook clients now connect to Client Access servers instead of Mailbox servers. The Client Access server establishes a Remote Procedure Call (RPC) connection with the Mailbox server. Each database specifies the Client Access server that its users will use when connecting to it. When a Client Access server goes offline, you will need to ensure that the database is associated with a different Client Access server in the same site as the database, unless you are using a Client Access Server (CAS) array. CAS arrays are covered in Chapter 10.

You can change the Client Access server that is associated with a mailbox database manually in the EMS using the Set-MailboxDatabase cmdlet with the RpcClientAccessServer parameter. When you specify this parameter, you can specify the name of a particular Client Access server, or you can specify the name of the load-balanced Client Access array.

The following command changes the Client Access server that connects to the database:

```
Set-MailboxDatabase DB01 -RpcClientAccessServer ↵
CONTOSO-CA02.contoso.com
```

Manage Database Redundancy

Exchange Server 2010 made leaps and bounds in the area of data redundancy over Exchange Server 2007. A Mailbox database can now exist on multiple Mailbox servers. One Mailbox server holds the active copy of the database and the other servers hold passive copies. When a change is made to the active copy of the database, the change is recorded in the transaction log. When the transaction log is filled up, it is closed and the log is replicated to the passive copies of the database. The passive copies replay this transaction log into their own copy of the database in order to keep the passive copies of the database up-to-date.

In Exchange Server 2010, databases are global objects and exist at the organization level. Therefore, each database has its own unique identity and it may be mounted by any server. Databases can be moved freely between Mailbox servers, even if the Mailbox server hosts additional databases or additional roles, such as the Hub Transport role or the Client Access role. Databases can be activated on another server in either an administrator-activated controlled manner (called a *switchover*) or in a failure scenario (called a *failover*).

WARNING There have been many discussions on using replicated copies of the database as your backup in Exchange Server 2010. One of the main points is that Exchange Server 2010 allows your database to be as big as 2TB! With such a large database, conventional backup and restore methods may not be viable. Although using replicated databases as your backup is definitely a possibility, it's not for everybody, so make sure that you understand the implications before determining whether you want to do it. And if you do it, make sure that you have at least three copies of the database replicated to other servers. For more information about using replicated copies for backups, see Chapter 10.

The next section of the chapter will show you how to configure, administer, and use redundant Mailbox databases.

Configure Redundant Databases

A database can have up to 16 copies spread across any Exchange Server 2010 Mailbox server in the domain, although only one copy is active. The remaining copies are passive and are kept up-to-date using the log shipping and replay technology described in the previous section.

To replicate a database across multiple servers, those servers must be in the same DAG. The DAG monitors the databases that its servers hold and contains the necessary information to determine which passive copy should be used if the active copy goes offline. The component called the Active Manager makes these determinations. Figure 7.10 illustrates the concept of DAGs at a high level. Note that databases can be spread across servers in a DAG in any manner that you see fit.

NOTE Each server in a DAG can hold up to 100 databases, whether they are active or passive. You can have up to 16 servers in a DAG, which means that you could potentially have 16 copies of a single database.

Create a Database Availability Group

A DAG consists of three primary components, all of which do not need to be explicitly defined when you create the DAG:

- DAG name
- IP address
- Witness location

Figure 7.10: A DAG contains servers that host database copies.

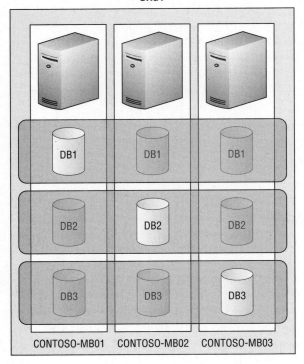

The DAG name and IP address are used internally by Exchange. If you do not specify a static IP address, the DAG will attempt to get an address through a Dynamic Host Configuration Protocol (DHCP) server. The DAG name must follow the standard rules of naming a computer and cannot exceed 15 characters. When you specify the IP address of the cluster, be sure to include IP addresses for each subnet if you have DAG nodes from different subnets.

> **NOTE** You can't start using a DAG immediately after it's created. Even though you specified the parameters for the DAG, the cluster isn't created until the first node is added to the DAG. So before you can use the DAG, you must add servers to it. This topic is covered later in this chapter in the section called "Add Servers to a DAG."

The witness location is where the file share witness is stored. To ensure that a cluster has an accurate understanding of which node is the active one, a quorum is needed. Since DAGs could potentially contain an even number of Mailbox servers and there is no shared disk resource as in traditional clusters, there is the possibility that more than one node could think that it should be active if there are network issues. Therefore, the witness resource makes this arbitration when there is an even number of servers. The witness resource is managed by Exchange and is added and removed from the DAG as needed when the number of DAG servers changes. You can specify the server that hosts the witness resource and the name of the share, but Exchange manages the resource itself. There is no harm in just letting Exchange handle this aspect unless you want to make a point of placing the witness on a server that doesn't host the Hub Transport role.

To create a DAG in the EMC:

1. Open the EMC and browse to the Organization Configuration ➤ Mailbox node in the Console tree.

2. In the Actions pane, click the New Database Availability Group option. This will launch the New Database Availability Group wizard.

3. At the New Database Availability Group screen, type the name of the DAG into the Database Availability Group Name field.

4. Click the New button to create the DAG and let Exchange handle the witness configuration.

5. At the Completion screen, click Finish.

To create a DAG with the EMS, you can use the `New-DatabaseAvailabilityGroup` cmdlet. The only thing that you are required to specify in the command is the name of the DAG. The following command creates the DAG with the default parameters:

```
New-DatabaseAvailabilityGroup -Name DAG01
```

If you want to specify the witness location, you can use the `WitnessServer` and `WitnessDirectory` parameters. You may be required to manually set the witness location if you don't have any Hub Transport servers without the Mailbox server role installed.

If you want to specify the IP addresses used by the DAG, you can include the `DatabaseAvailabilityGroupIPAddresses` parameter. For example, the following command creates a DAG that will have nodes on the 10.0.1.0/24 subnet and the 192.168.1.0/24 subnet:

```
New-DatabaseAvailabilityGroup DAG02 ↩
-DatabaseAvailabilityGroupIPAddresses ↩
10.0.1.100,192.168.1.100
```

Change the Witness Server

There may be cases where you want to customize the witness server and witness directory for a DAG. For example, if you want to place the witness on a server that doesn't run Exchange or doesn't host the Hub Transport role, you will need to specify the witness location yourself.

WARNING   If you are moving the witness to a server that does not have Exchange installed, you will need to add the Universal group called Exchange Trusted Subsystem to the local Administrators group on the server. This will ensure that the Exchange servers have the appropriate permissions to the witness share.

To change the witness using the EMC, use the following steps:

1. Open the EMC and browse to the Organization Configuration ➢ Mailbox node in the Console tree.

2. Click the Database Availability Group tab in the Work area. This will list the current DAGs that you have configured.

3. Select the DAG that you want to set the witness on and click the Properties option for the DAG in the Actions pane.

4. In the General tab of the DAG's properties dialog box, modify the Witness Server and Witness Directory fields to correspond to the server and location where you want to place the DAG (see Figure 7.11). File sharing must be enabled on the server that you are moving the witness to.

5. Click OK to move the witness and close the properties dialog box.

If you prefer to move the witness using the EMS, you can use the Set-DatabaseAvailabilityGroup cmdlet with the WitnessServer and WitnessDirectory parameters. The WitnessServer parameter specifies the name of the server that the witness is moved to. The `WitnessDirectory` parameter specifies the location of the witness folder on the server. The following command illustrates the syntax:

```
Set-DatabaseAvailabilityGroup DAG01 -WitnessServer ↵
contoso-dc01.contoso.com -WitnessDirectory C:\DAG01Witness
```

Figure 7.11: Change the DAG witness location in the EMC.

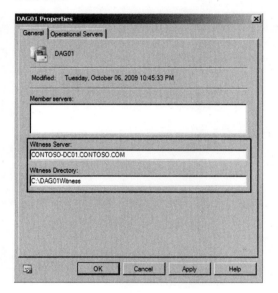

Add Servers to a DAG

After the DAG is created, you will need to add servers to it before Mailbox databases can be replicated. DAGs allow you to add Mailbox servers that hold additional roles as well, which is an advantage over Exchange Server 2007. Each Mailbox server that you add to a DAG must have two network cards with properly configured IP addresses on different subnets, one for client traffic and the other for cluster traffic.

To add a server to a DAG using the EMC, follow these steps:

1. Open the EMC and browse to the Organization Configuration ➤ Mailbox node in the Console tree.

2. Click the Database Availability Group tab in the Work area. Select the DAG that you want to add a server to.

3. In the Action menu for the DAG, click the Manage Database Availability Group Membership option, as shown in Figure 7.12. This launches the Manage Database Availability Group Membership wizard.

Figure 7.12: Adding a server to a DAG in the EMC

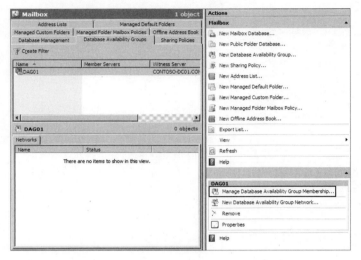

4. At the Manage Database Availability Group Membership screen, click the Add button to browse for a server to add to the DAG (see Figure 7.13).

5. After you add the server to the list, click the Manage button to add the server.

6. At the Completion screen, click the Finish button.

To add a server to a DAG using the EMS, you can run the Add-DatabaseAvailabilityGroupServer cmdlet. Specify the name of the DAG that you are adding the server to and specify the name of the server using the MailboxServer parameter. The following example adds a server to a DAG:

```
Add-DatabaseAvailabilityGroupServer DAG02 -MailboxServer ↵
CONTOSO-MB02
```

Figure 7.13: Adding a server to the DAG list

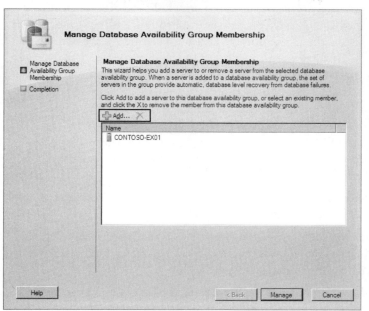

Replicate Databases to Additional Servers

When you want to replicate a database onto other Mailbox servers, those servers must be in the same DAG as the database. In addition, the database and transaction log paths for the database copy must be the same on each server. For example, if the database and logs are in D:\DB01 on one server, then they must be in D:\DB01 on all servers that have a copy of that database.

When you add a copy of the database to a server, the database must first be *seeded*, that is, copied to the target server. If the database is large, seeding can take a long time and you may not want to start it in the middle of the day. Because of this, you have the option of postponing the seeding process. You can also choose to seed from another passive copy of the database.

WARNING   If you postpone seeding, you will need to manually seed the database later. Steps for manual seeding are covered later in this chapter in the section "Manage Database Replication."

Another option that you need to consider before adding a database replica is the *activation preference number.* This number specifies the order in which passive databases are brought online if more than one copy passes the activation criteria imposed by Active Manager. For example, if there are three copies of the database and the active copy fails, then two passive copies are available. If it is determined by Active Manager that both copies are healthy and current and that their transaction log queue lengths are small enough, the database copy with the lowest activation preference number is activated.

You can modify the activation preference number after a database copy is added to a server in the DAG. Use the following steps in the EMC after you have added the server to the DAG:

1. Open the EMC and browse to the Organization Configuration ➤ Mailbox node in the Console tree.

2. Click the Database Management tab in the Work area. Select the database that you want to modify the activation preference number on from the list of available databases.

3. In the bottom half of the Work area, the list of database copies will be populated for the database that you selected. Select the copy for the server that you want to modify the activation preference number for and choose Properties from the Action menu. Make sure that you select the Properties option for the database copy and not the database itself.

4. In the properties dialog box for the database copy, click the General tab.

5. Modify the Activation Preference Number to make this database copy activate in the order that you choose.

6. Click OK to close the properties dialog box and commit the changes.

You can also modify the Active Preference Number using the Set-MailboxDatabaseCopy cmdlet with the ActivationPreference parameter, as shown here:

```
Set-MailboxDatabaseCopy "DB01\CONTOSO-MB01" ↵
-ActivationPreference 2
```

You can add a database replica inside a DAG with the EMC using these steps:

1. Open the EMC and browse to the Organization Configuration ➤ Mailbox node in the Console tree.

2. Click the Database Management tab in the Work area. Select the database that you want to replicate from the list of available databases.

3. In the Action menu for the database you selected, click the Add Mailbox Database Copy option, as shown in Figure 7.14. This launches the Add Mailbox Database Copy wizard.

Figure 7.14: Replicating a Mailbox database

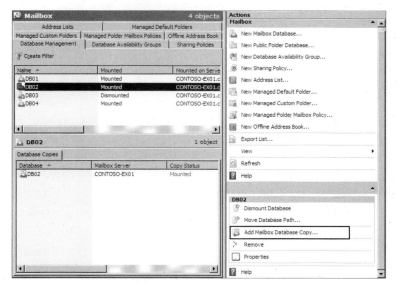

4. At the Add Mailbox Database Copy screen, click the Browse button to select a server that you want to add the database copy to. This server needs to be in the same DAG as the server that already has the active copy of the database.

5. Click the Add button to add the database copy to the server that you selected.

6. At the Completion screen, click the Finish button.

You can also add a database replica using the EMS. To do so, use the `Add-MailboxDatabaseCopy` cmdlet and specify the Mailbox server and activation preference using the parameters `MailboxServer` and `ActivationPreference`, respectively. You can also specify the `SeedingPostponed` parameter to postpone the seeding of the database file. The following example adds a database copy with an activation preference of 2:

```
Add-MailboxDatabaseCopy DB01 -MailboxServer CONTOSO-MB02 ↵
-ActivationPreference 2
```

Configure the Network Used by an Availability Group

DAGs can have multiple networks assigned to them. When you assign a network to a DAG, you associate subnets with it. Those subnets can be isolated for either client traffic or replication traffic. By using a DAG network, you can tune the type of traffic that is passed over the various IP addresses for the servers that are members of the DAG.

Create a DAG Network

When you create a DAG network, you must specify the subnet in the form of an IP address and bitmask. For example, if you specify `192.168.0.0/24`, the IP addresses `192.168.0.1–192.168.0.254` are included in that subnet. You can have multiple subnets in a single DAG network. You can create a DAG network in the EMC using the following steps:

1. Open the EMC and browse to the Organization Configuration ➢ Mailbox node in the Console tree.

2. Select the Database Availability Groups tab in the Work area. The list of DAGs is presented.

3. Select the DAG that you want to create the network for and choose the New Database Availability Group Network option from the DAG's Action menu, as shown in Figure 7.15.

4. In the New Database Availability Group Network wizard, type a name for the network in the Network Name field. Click the Add button to add a subnet to the subnet list, as shown in Figure 7.16. When you enter the subnet in the Add Subnet dialog box, you will need to use the format of IP Address/Bitmask. For example, the `192.168.0.1–192.168.0.254` subnet would be represented with `192.168.0.0/24`.

Figure 7.15: Adding a DAG network in the EMC

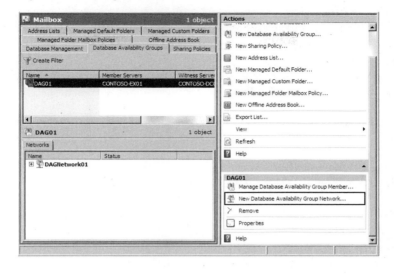

Figure 7.16: Adding a subnet to the DAG network

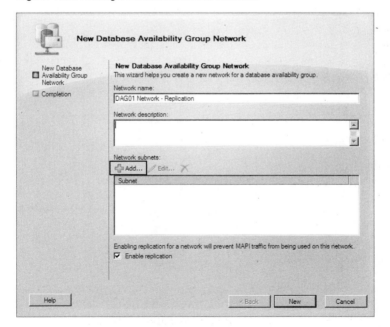

5. If you want to use this network for only database replication traffic, you can check the Enable Replication box. Click the New button to create the DAG network.

6. At the Completion screen, click the Finish button.

WARNING During creation, if you specify a subnet that is already assigned to another DAG network, that subnet will be moved to the DAG network that you are creating.

You can also create the DAG network with the New-DatabaseAvailabilityGroupNetwork cmdlet in the EMS. When you run this cmdlet, you will need to specify the parameters in Table 7.1.

Table 7.1: EMS Parameters Used When Creating a DAG Network

Parameter	Description
DatabaseAvailabilityGroup	The name of the DAG for which you are creating the DAG network.
Name	The name of the DAG network.
Subnets	The subnets in the network, using the IP Address/ Bitmask format.
ReplicationEnabled	If set to $True, the network is only used for replication. If set to $False, the network is only used for client traffic.

The following command creates a DAG network that is dedicated to replication:

```
New-DatabaseAvailabilityGroupNetwork ↵
"DAG01 Network - Replication" -DatabaseAvailabilityGroup ↵
DAG01-Subnets 192.168.0.0/24 -ReplicationEnabled:$True
```

Dedicate a DAG Network to Replication or MAPI Only

A DAG network can be enabled for either MAPI client traffic or data replication. If you are disabling replication on a DAG network, you should have at least one other DAG network available for replication to take place on. If not, the server will use the IP address that is published in DNS for database replication.

To configure a DAG network for replication or MAPI access only, use the EMC to complete the following steps:

1. Open the EMC and browse to the Organization Configuration ➤ Mailbox node in the Console tree.

2. Select the Database Availability Groups tab in the Work area. Select the DAG that contains the network you want to dedicate traffic to.

3. The bottom half of the Work area will list the DAG networks that exist for the DAG you selected. Click on the DAG network that you want to modify and choose the Properties option from the network's Action menu.

4. In the properties dialog box for the DAG network, check the option Enable Replication to ensure that this network is used only for replication (Figure 7.17). If you want the network available for client traffic only, uncheck the box.

5. Click OK to make the changes and close the properties dialog box.

Figure 7.17: Setting the type of traffic on a DAG network

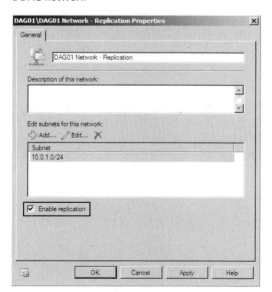

To configure the traffic type on the DAG network with the EMS, run the `Set-DatabaseAvailabilityGroupNetwork` cmdlet with the `ReplicationEnabled` parameter. Set the parameter to `$True` to enable replication only or set it to `$False` to enable MAPI traffic only.

When you reference the name of the DAG network, use the format *DAGName\DAGNetworkName*. For example, if the DAG network called `DAG01Network` is a part of the DAG named `DAG01`, you should use `DAG01\DAG01Network` in the command.

The following example sets the DAG network to MAPI client traffic only:

```
Set-DatabaseAvailabilityGroupNetwork ↵
"DAG01\DAG01Network -MAPI" -ReplicationEnabled $False
```

Manage Database Replication

Databases can be replicated between Mailbox servers in the same DAG. Managing these database replicas is a straightforward process. The information covered in this section will help ensure that your database copies remain healthy.

Manually Seed a Database Copy

Seeding the database is the act of performing the initial database copy to the target replicas. Once the database copy exists on the replica, it is kept up-to-date with the transaction logs as they are replicated over. Database seeding can take a long time to complete, particularly if you take advantage of the larger database size recommendations with Exchange Server 2010. Therefore, you may decide to seed the replica in advance of creating the database copy or afterward during non-peak hours. There are multiple ways you can manually seed a database copy.

Manual Seeding Through Exchange

When you manually seed the database inside Exchange, the database copy is being done with Exchange resources. If the database is already replicating to the target location, replication needs to be suspended. For steps on suspending database replication, see the section, "Pause Database Replication." If there is an existing database file on the replica, you will need to delete it manually or configure the database to be overwritten during the reseed.

One of the advantages of manually seeding the database is that you can choose which copy of the database provides the source replica. By default, when automatic database seeding occurs the active copy of the database is the source replica. However, Exchange Server 2010 allows you to choose which replica you want to use, even if it's a passive copy of the database.

WARNING After you have started seeding a database copy, don't close the EMC or the EMS! If you do, the seeding stops along with it.

You can reseed the database copy with the Update-MailboxDatabaseCopy cmdlet. The parameters that can be used with this command are laid out in Table 7.2.

Table 7.2: Parameters for Reseeding a Database in the EMS

Parameter	Description
DeleteExistingFiles	If set to $True, any existing database files will be removed before reseeding.
ManualResume	If set to $True, replication does not automatically resume after seeding is finished.
SourceServer	The name of the Mailbox server that you want to be used as the source replica for the reseed.

The following example deletes the existing files and uses a passive copy of the database for seeding. Before running this command, replication must be suspended:

```
Update-MailboxDatabaseCopy DB1\CONTOSO-MB03 -SourceServer ↵
CONTOSO-MB02 -DeleteExistingFiles:$True
```

Manual Seeding by Copying the File

In addition to seeding through Exchange, you have the ability to seed the database by hand by simply copying the database to the target replica. To perform this process, you have to dismount the database, which means that the database will be taken offline during the copy.

Managing Exchange Server Roles

PART II

You can use any method you wish to get the database copy over to the target replica. If you are going to be copying the database to the target replica through a file share, I recommend that you use robocopy.exe instead of just performing a drag-and-drop in Windows Explorer.

You can use the following steps to seed the database by hand:

1. Suspend the database copy if it is already replicating. See the next section, "Pause Database Replication," for steps on how to do this.

2. Dismount the active copy of the database. Mounting and dismounting databases is covered earlier in this chapter in the section "Mount a Mailbox Database."

3. On the server that you are reseeding the database to, log in and delete the database file and the log files on the server.

4. Copy the database file from the source server to the target server that hosts the passive copy.

5. Mount the Mailbox database on the source copy.

6. Resume replication of the database.

Pause Database Replication

At any time, you may want to temporarily stop the replication of a database copy. Suspending replication is required if you want to perform a reseed, and it's a recommended practice before performing other database maintenance activities, such as moving the location of database files. The following order is usually followed:

1. Stop database replication.

2. Perform maintenance on database.

3. Resume database replication.

Stop Database Replication

You can stop database replication in the EMC using the following steps:

1. Open the EMC and browse to the Organization Configuration ➤ Mailbox node in the Console tree.

2. Click the Database Management tab in the Work area. Select the database that you want to stop replication for.

3. In the list of database copies in the bottom pane of the Work area, select the database copy that you want to stop replication to.

4. In the Action menu for the database copy that you selected, click the Suspend Database Copy option, as shown in Figure 7.18.

Figure 7.18: Stopping a database copy in the EMC

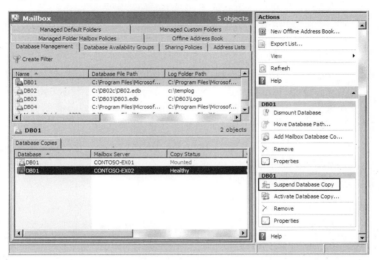

Managing Exchange Server Roles

PART II

5. The Administrative Suspend dialog box will appear, asking you if you are sure that you want to continue. You can option-ally type in a reason for why you are suspending the copy in the Comment box in the dialog box. You may want to enter a com-ment here in case another administrator notices that replication is suspended and tries to resume it. When the other administra-tor attempts to resume replication, they will be presented with the comment that you made in the confirmation dialog box and given the option of not continuing. When you are ready to stop the copy, click the Yes button.

You can also use the Suspend-MailboxDatabaseCopy cmdlet to stop database replication. The following example suspends the copying of the database DB1 to the server CONTOSO-MB03:

```
Suspend-MailboxDatabaseCopy DB1\CONTOSO-MB03
```

Resume Database Replication

After maintenance has been performed on the Mailbox database, you can resume replication to the target replica. To resume replication in the EMC, follow these steps:

1. Open the EMC and browse to the Organization Configuration ➢ Mailbox node in the Console tree.

2. Click the Database Management tab in the Work area. From the list of databases, select the database that you want to resume replication for.

3. The list of database copies is propagated in the bottom pane of the Work area. Find the database copy that you want to resume replication for. The Copy Status should read Suspended. Select this database copy.

4. From the Action menu of the database copy, select the Resume Database Copy option, as shown in Figure 7.19.

Figure 7.19: Resuming the replication of a database copy

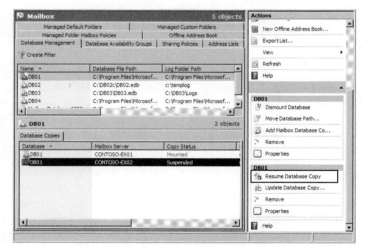

5. The Administrative Resume dialog box will appear, asking you if you are sure that you want to continue. This dialog box also displays the comment that the person who suspended the database copy typed in. If you want to continue, click the Yes button to resume replication.

The `Resume-MailboxDatabaseCopy` cmdlet in the EMS can also be used to resume database replication. The following example resumes replication of the database copy that we previously stopped:

```
Resume-MailboxDatabaseCopy DB1\CONTOSO-MB03
```

Modify the Replication Settings of a Database

There are some settings associated with a database copy that affect how the database handles logs and failover. For handling transaction logs, you should be aware of two primary settings:

Replay Lag Time   This setting determines how many minutes must pass before the replicated log is replayed into the passive copy of the database. This is disabled by default, but you can enable it if you are concerned about replaying a corrupted log into your database copy.

Truncation Lag Time   This setting specifies how many minutes to wait before deleting the transaction logs. The countdown of the truncation lag time starts after the transaction log has successfully replayed into the database.

You can also use the EMS to configure these setting by specifying the correct parameter on the `Set-MailboxDatabaseCopy` cmdlet. Table 7.3 displays these parameters and their options.

Table 7.3: EMS Parameters for Database Copy Settings

Parameter	Description	Possible Values
ReplayLagTime	The amount of time that passes before logs are replayed into the passive copy of the database.	A time-based value of up to 14 days in the format of Days.Hours:Minutes:Seconds. For example, 1 day would be 1.0:0:0.
TruncationLagTime	The amount of time that must pass before a log file can be deleted on a database copy.	A time-based value of up to 14 days. This value should be in the format of Days.Hours:Minutes:Seconds. For example, 12 hours and 34 minutes would be 0.12:34:00.

The following example adjusts the replay lag time of a database copy to 1 day and sets the truncation lag time to 1 week:

```
Set-MailboxDatabaseCopy DB1\CONTOSO-MB03 ↵
-ReplayLagTime 1.0:0:0 ↵
-TruncationLagTime 7.0:0:0
```

View the Current Status of Replication

If you want to retrieve statistics on your database copies, you can use the Get-MailboxDatabaseCopyStatus cmdlet. This cmdlet will present information about your database copies that you can use to determine what state they are in and what the overall health is.

When you run this command from the EMS, the following types of status information is gathered:

- The health of the copy status
- The name of the server that holds the active database copy
- The number of logs in the replay queue
- The last time backups were completed against the database

The following command will display the status of a database copy and all the information available in a list:

```
Get-MailboxDatabaseCopyStatus DB01\CONTOSO-MB02 | fl
```

You can also gather information about multiple database copies. The following command will display the database, the name of the active server, and the health of the database copies in a table:

```
Get-MailboxDatabase | Get-MailboxDatabaseCopyStatus | ft ↵
Name, Status, ActiveDatabaseCopy
```

Manage Database Availability

When you configure your DAGs and replication, you are preparing your system to be able to handle an outage. But what should you do when the inevitable happens? This section of the chapter will walk you through the procedure of performing a database switchover and show you how to check the status of your database copies during a failover.

Perform a Database Switchover

When a database switchover is performed, the active copy of the database is moved to another Mailbox server and there is no data loss expected. This is a process that is initiated by an administrator while the active copy of the database is still healthy.

When you perform a switchover, you have the option of overriding the database mount dial settings. The database mount dial settings define the data loss tolerance when a database copy is activated.

You can perform a switchover in the EMC using the following steps:

1. Open the EMC and browse to the Organization Configuration ➢ Mailbox node in the Console tree.

2. Click the Database Management tab. From the list of databases, select the database that you want to move to another server.

3. In the bottom pane of the Work area, the list of database copies is displayed. Click on the copy of the database that you want to switch over to.

4. From the Action menu for the database copy that you selected, choose the Activate Database Copy option to perform the switchover, as shown in Figure 7.20.

Figure 7.20: Performing a database switchover with the EMC

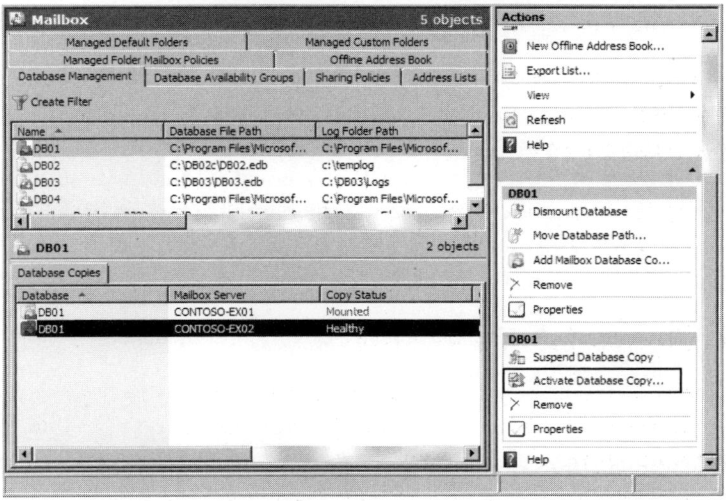

5. A dialog box will be displayed, asking you if you want to override the database mount dial settings on the target server. Since this is an administrator-initiated switchover, we don't expect any log loss, so leave the option at None and click OK.

6. When the database switchover is complete, the database copy status is reversed. When you refresh the EMC, you should see that the status of the database copy is Mounted on the server that you switched over to, as shown in Figure 7.21. Replication will automatically reverse itself and synchronize back to the node that used to be the active node.

Figure 7.21: Status of the database copies in the EMC after a switchover

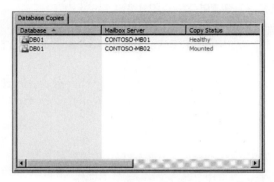

You can also use the `Move-ActiveMailboxDatabase` cmdlet in the EMS to move the active copy of the database to another Mailbox server in the DAG. When running this command, you need to specify the database that you want to move, the server that you want to activate it on, and whether or not you want to override the database mount dial settings.

The following example activates a database copy and does not change the database mount dial settings:

```
Move-ActiveMailboxDatabase "DB1" -ActivateOnServer ↵
CONTOSO-MB02 -MountDialOverride:None
```

Perform a Database Failover

When an active node in the DAG goes offline, the database copy that is next in the activation preference order will come online. This happens automatically and requires no intervention by an administrator. When a server hosting the active copy of the database fails, you will see the status of the active copy listed as ServiceDown. This is shown in Figure 7.22.

Figure 7.22: Status of database copies after a failover

8

Managing Public Folders

Public folders have been around since the earliest versions of Exchange. They provide an open forum for users to post content that others can also access. The concept caught on early and many organizations began using public folders for sharing all sorts of data, though much of the data would have been better served using a different method of sharing. In Exchange Server 2007, Microsoft began the de-emphasis of public folders—this was the first release of Exchange where public folder usage was completely optional.

Still, public folders are a big part of many organizations, and managing them is just as important as managing mailbox data. This chapter will take you through the essentials of managing public folders in Exchange Server 2010.

Perform Essential Public Folder Management

The basics of public folder management are easy to grasp. After all, a public folder is nothing more than a shared folder that many people can access through Outlook. This section goes into the essentials of public folder management and helps you understand the basics.

Manage Public Folder Content

There are two parts to managing public folders. One part entails managing the back-end configuration of public folders. This includes things like managing the databases, referrals, and replication. The other part of public folder management is less complex, and it encompasses managing the behavior of the folders. This section walks you through several key activities in managing the behavior of public folders.

Understand the Public Folder Management Console

Just like the Exchange Management Console (EMC), the Public Folder Management Console (PFMC) is built on the Microsoft Management Console (MMC) version 3.0. Both consoles contain the same components:

- Console tree
- Results pane
- Actions pane

These components are laid out in Figure 8.1.

Figure 8.1: Components of the Public Folder Management Console

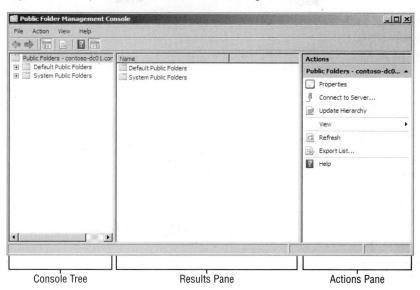

Console Tree   Results Pane   Actions Pane

Launch the Public Folder Management Console

You can launch the PFMC from the EMC using the following steps:

1. Open the EMC and browse to the Toolbox node in the Console tree.

2. A variety of tools are displayed in the Work area in the EMC. Browse down to the Public Folder Management Console icon and double-click on it (Figure 8.2).

3. The PFMC will launch as a separate window. You can safely close the EMC if you don't want to keep it open while using the PFMC.

By default, the PFMC will connect to the Exchange server that you are currently logged into. If you want to connect to a different Exchange server, you can use the following steps:

1. Select the top-level folder in the Console tree. This will be displayed in the format of `Public Folders - <server that you are currently connected to>`.

2. In the Actions pane, click the Connect To Server option.

3. In the Connect To Server dialog box, click the Browse button to find another Public Folder server that you want to connect to.

4. After selecting your server, click the Connect button. You also have the option of checking the Set As Default Server box to automatically connect to this server whenever you open the PFMC again in the future.

Figure 8.2: Launching the PFMC from the EMC toolbox

When you select a public folder from the Default Public Folders tree, the subfolders appear in the Results pane in the center of the console. When a public folder is selected, the actions that you can take on the public folder are displayed in the Actions pane on the right. You can also access these actions by right-clicking on the folder that you have selected. These actions will appear in the drop-down menu.

You can also open the PFMC without having to open the EMC first by using the following steps:

1. Click Start ➤ Run.

2. Type "**Public Folder Management Console.msc**" (with the quotes) and click OK, as shown in Figure 8.3.

Figure 8.3: Running the PFMC without going
through the EMC

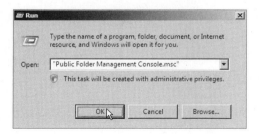

The PFMC's Console tree in the left pane displays a list of public
folders in a hierarchy. The Default Public Folders folder shows all of the
user-accessible folders. You can create new folders here that users can
access and post items to. The System Public Folders folder is reserved
for Exchange to use internally. The system folders are used for a variety of things, such as Offline Address Book usage by clients older than
Outlook 2007. The system folders should not be modified.

Modify the Information Shown in the Results Pane

By default, the Results pane only displays the name of the public folder
and the path of its parent folder. You can modify this to display more
information. Table 8.1 shows the optional information that you can add
to the list of results in the Results pane.

Table 8.1: Display Options for Folders in the PFMC

Item	Description
Age Limit In Days	The number of days that content remains in the public folder before it is automatically deleted
Hidden From Address List	Displays True if this public folder appears in the Address List; displays False otherwise
Local Replica Age Limit In Days	The number of days that content remains on this specific public folder replica
Mail-Enabled	Displays True if the public folder has an email address associated with it, displays False otherwise
Replicas	Lists the servers that have a copy of this public folder

To add this additional information to the view, follow these steps:

1. In the PFMC, click on the folder that you want to view from the Console tree.

2. Click the View option in the Actions pane and select Add/Remove Columns from the drop-down menu.

3. In the Add/Remove Columns dialog box, select the information that you want to add and click the Add button. You can also click Add All to add all the information to the result list in the PFMC.

4. Click OK to close the dialog box and return to the PFMC.

Like the EMC, the PFMC has the ability to log the PowerShell commands that it uses in the background. This functionality is enabled in the PFMC in the same way that it's enabled in the EMC. These steps are covered in Chapter 2, "Using the Exchange Management Console and the Exchange Management Shell."

Create a New Public Folder

Public folders can be created by any authorized user in your Exchange organization. You can use these tools to create public folders:

- Public Folder Management Console
- Exchange Management Shell
- Microsoft Outlook

Create a New Public Folder Using the Public Folder Management Console

To create a public folder in the PFMC, follow these steps:

1. Open the Public Folder Management Console and select the Default Public Folders node from the Console tree.

2. Using the Console tree, browse to the folder that you want to create the new public folder in, or remain at the Default Public Folders node to create a top-level folder.

3. In the Actions pane, select the New Public Folder option. This will launch the New Public Folder wizard.

4. At the New Public Folder initial screen, type the name of the folder in the Name field.

5. Click the New button to create the folder.

6. After the folder is successfully created, click the Finish button on the Completion screen.

Create a New Public Folder Using the Exchange Management Shell

To create a new public folder with the EMS, you can run the `New-PublicFolder` cmdlet. The only parameter that you are required to specify in the command is the name of the new public folder. However, if you only specify the name, the public folder is created in the root. You can specify the `Path` parameter to specify the parent folder for the new public folder. The following example creates a new folder called `IT Support` under the `Business Units` folder:

```
New-PublicFolder "IT Support" -Path "\Business Units"
```

When you use the EMS to create the public folder, the folder is created on the server that you are currently logged on to if it has a public folder store. If the current server does not have a public folder database, the cmdlet uses Active Directory site link costing to determine which Mailbox server is the closest one with a Public Folder database. If you want to specify which server the folder is created on, you can use the `Server` parameter as demonstrated in this command:

```
New-PublicFolder "IT Support" -Path "\Business Units" ↵
-Server CONTOSO-PF02
```

Create a New Public Folder Using Outlook

Public folders can be created using Outlook, as long as the user has the appropriate permissions. When creating folders in Outlook, users have the ability not only to modify the permissions, but also to determine the type of content that can be stored in the folder. Outlook is an extremely flexible public folder management tool for end users managing content. To create a public folder in Outlook, users can use the following steps:

1. Open Microsoft Outlook 2003 or newer and browse to the list of public folders in the Folder List, as shown in Figure 8.4.

2. Right-click on the parent folder that you want to create the new public folder under and select New Folder from the context menu.

3. In the Create New Folder dialog box, type the folder name in the Name field and click OK.

Managing Exchange Server Roles

PART II

Figure 8.4: The public folder list in Outlook

Allow a Public Folder to Receive Mail

A public folder can be mail-enabled, allowing it to have a unique email address at which it can receive mail. When a message is received by a mail-enabled public folder, the message is stored in the folder and accessible by everyone who has access to the folder.

When a public folder is mail-enabled, the public folder object is given a mail alias and a similar set of Active Directory attributes that other mail-enabled users and contacts have. This mail-enabled public folder object also appears in the address lists unless you explicitly hide it.

Mail-Enable a Public Folder Using the Public Folder Management Console

You can mail-enable public folders using the following steps in the PFMC:

1. Open the PFMC and browse to the parent folder of the public folder that you want to mail-enable.

2. The subfolders are displayed in the Results pane. Click on the subfolder that you are mail-enabling.

3. In the Actions pane, under the menu for that folder, click the Mail Enable option, as shown in Figure 8.5.

Figure 8.5: Mail-enabling a public folder in the PFMC

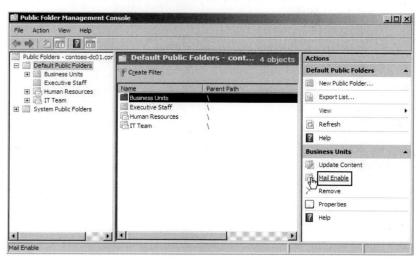

There is no prompt or dialog box. The folder is immediately mail-enabled with a mail alias that is generated by the server based on the name of the folder. The alias and email are the name of the public folder minus any illegal characters, such as spaces. For example, when mail-enabling the folder called Human Resources, the mail alias becomes HumanResources and the email address becomes HumanResources@contoso.com.

Mail-Enable or Disable a Public Folder Using the Exchange Management Shell

To mail-enable a public folder using the EMS, you can run the `Enable-MailPublicFolder` cmdlet. When you run this command, you only need to specify the path of the public folder. However, you can also use the `HiddenFromAddressListsEnabled` parameter to specify whether the public folder shows up in the address list. The following example mail-enables a public folder called Helpdesk and hides it from the address lists:

```
Enable-MailPublicFolder "\Helpdesk" ↵
-HiddenFromAddressListsEnabled $True
```

To disable the mail properties on a public folder, you can use the `Disable-MailPublicFolder` cmdlet. The following example disables mail on the Helpdesk folder without asking for confirmation:

```
Disable-MailPublicFolder "\Helpdesk" -Confirm:$False
```

Gather the Statistics of a Public Folder

You can obtain some basic statistics about your public folders, such as the number of items, the size of items, and the size of deleted items. When you gather this information, you must connect to a server that has a copy of the replica.

You can view this information in the PFMC by viewing the properties on an existing public folder:

1. Open the PFMC and select the Default Public Folders node in the Console tree.

2. Using the Console tree, browse to the parent folder that contains the public folder that you want to view the statistics for.

3. In the Results pane, click on the public folder that you want to view the statistics for.

4. In the Actions pane, click the Properties option under the Action menu that corresponds to the public folder.

5. In the properties dialog box for the public folder, click the Statistics tab to view the statistics.

If you are not connecting to the server that has a copy of the public folder, you will receive the message "Not available on this server," as shown in Figure 8.6. You will have to close the dialog box and connect to a server that contains a copy of the public folder data in order to obtain the statistics.

You can also gather additional statistics data using the EMS. The Get-PublicFolderStatistics and Get-PublicFolderItemStatistics cmdlets offer more information in addition to the data viewed in the PFMC. Get-PublicFolderStatistics can be used to output information about the public folder itself. On the other hand, Get-PublicFolderItemStatistics retrieves information about the items inside the public folder.

To output statistics about a public folder, you can run the following command. If you are not connected to a server that has a copy of this folder, you need to specify the Server parameter. Otherwise, it can be left off. The following example gets statistics about the Helpdesk folder on the CONTOSO-PF02 server:

```
Get-PublicFolderStatistics "\Helpdesk" -Server CONTOSO-PF02
```

If you want to gather statistics on every item in a public folder, you can use the Get-PublicFolderItemStatistics command. By default, this command will display the identity of each item in the public folder along with the timestamp of when it was created and the subject line. The following example gets statistics about all the items in the Helpdesk folder:

```
Get-PublicFolderItemStatistics "\Helpdesk"
```

Figure 8.6: Trying to obtain statistics on the wrong server

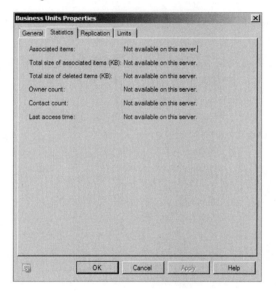

Managing Exchange Server Roles

PART II

Maintain Per-User Message Read State

Since public folders are accessed by many people, changes to the content in the folder can affect how others view the content as well. If a user deletes a message, other users will not see the message. One property of the items in a public folder that can be controlled is *per-user message read state*. When this is turned on, a different message read state is maintained for each user. When a user reads a message in the public folder, that message is marked as read-only by that user. When per-user message read state is turned off, the message is marked as read for everybody who views the folder.

To enable or disable the per-user message read state in the PFMC, use the following steps:

1. Open the PFMC and select the Default Public Folders node in the Console tree.

2. Select the parent folder that contains the public folder that you want to modify from the Console tree.

3. In the Results pane, select the public folder that you want to modify and click the Properties option in the Actions pane.

4. In the properties dialog box for the public folder, click the General tab.

5. To enable per-user message read state, select the Maintain Per-User Read And Unread Information For This Folder check box, as shown in Figure 8.7.

Figure 8.7: Enabling per-user message read state in the PFMC

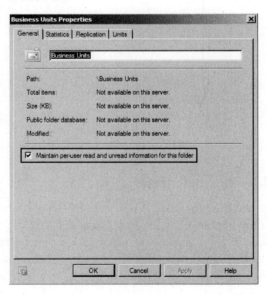

6. Click OK to make the changes and close the properties dialog box.

This option can also be enabled or disabled in the EMS, using the Set-PublicFolder cmdlet with the PerUserReadStateEnabled parameter set to either $True or $False. The following example turns off the per-user message read state on the Helpdesk folder:

```
Set-PublicFolder "\Helpdesk" -PerUserReadStateEnabled $False
```

Impose Size Limits and Warnings on a Folder

In a similar manner to mailboxes, public folders can have limits defined, which prevent a folder from getting too big. Here are the three options for limiting a public folder size:

- Issue a warning when a folder reaches a particular size.
- Prevent posting new content when a folder reaches a particular size.
- Define the maximum size allowed for a single item in the folder.

By default, each public folder inherits these values from the setting on the database. However, you can override this inheritance on a per-folder basis.

To change the limits on a per-folder basis using the PFMC, follow these steps:

1. Open the PFMC and select the Default Public Folders node in the Console tree.

2. Select the parent folder that contains the public folder that you want to modify from the Console tree.

3. In the Results pane, select the public folder that you want to modify and click the Properties option in the Actions pane.

4. In the properties dialog box for the public folder, click the Limits tab.

5. Uncheck the Use Database Quota Defaults option.

6. Place a checkmark next to the limits that you want to define. In the field next to the limit, enter the size restriction that you want to enforce in KB. For example, to limit posts to 1 MB in size, enter **1024** in the Maximum Item Size (KB) box, as shown in Figure 8.8.

7. After you configure the limits that you want to impose, click the OK button to make the changes and close the properties dialog box.

Figure 8.8: Specifying the maximum size of posts in KB

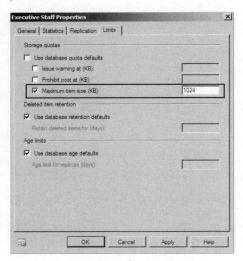

To define these limits using the EMS, you will use the Set-PublicFolder cmdlet. Table 8.2 displays the parameters to correspond to the limits in the PFMC.

Table 8.2: EMS Parameters for Defining Public Folder Limits

PFMC Option	EMS Parameter
Issue Warning At (KB)	IssueWarningQuota
Prohibit Post At (KB)	ProhibitPostQuota
Maximum Item Size (KB)	MaxItemSize

When you run the cmdlet, you will also need to set the UseDatabaseQuotaDefaults parameter to $False in order to override the limits set on the database. If you don't set this, the public folder's limit attributes will be set in Active Directory (AD), but the database limits will still be effective. For example, the following command will override the database defaults and set the maximum post size to 1 KB:

```
Set-PublicFolder "\Helpdesk" -MaxItemSize 1KB ↵
-UseDatabaseQuotaDefaults $False
```

Define Public Folder Permissions

You can classify public folder permissions into two categories: administrator permissions and client permissions. Administrators will use tools such as the Public Folder Management Console to manage public folders. When granting permissions to public folder content, administrators will typically need access that allows them to create top-level folders, manage the permissions on folders, and manage system folders. Content access for users typically consists of the ability to create new child public folders, post new content, and manage existing content.

When a new folder is created, the permissions on that folder are inherited from the parent folder. However, if you add permissions to an existing parent folder, only new child folders inherit the permissions. Existing child folders maintain the permissions that were inherited at the time the folder was created.

Grant Users Access to a Public Folder

Users accessing public folders through their client applications will primarily be concerned with creating new content and accessing or modifying existing content. Exchange has a set of predefined roles that users can be assigned on a public folder. Table 8.3 displays each of these predefined roles and the privileges that each has.

Table 8.3: Predefined Public Folder Client Roles

Role Name	Create Items	Create Subfolders	Read Items	Edit Items	Delete Items
Author	Yes	No	Yes	Only items the user owns	Only items the user owns
Contributor	Yes	No	No	No	No
Editor	Yes	No	Yes	Yes	Yes
None	No	No	No	No	No
Non-EditingAuthor	Yes	No	Yes	No	No
Owner	Yes	Yes	Yes	Yes	Yes
PublishingAuthor	Yes	Yes	Yes	Only items the user owns	Yes

Table 8.3: Predefined Public Folder Client Roles *(continued)*

Role Name	Create Items	Create Subfolders	Read Items	Edit Items	Delete Items
PublishingEditor	Yes	Yes	Yes	Yes	Yes
Reviewer	No	No	Yes	No	No

You cannot add client permissions to public folders through the Public Folder Management Console. Instead, permissions must be managed through the Exchange Management Shell.

To give a user rights to a public folder, use the Add-PublicFolderClientPermission cmdlet. In addition to identifying the public folder that you want to change permissions on, you will also need to use the User parameter to specify the user, and the AccessRights parameter to specify the role that you are assigning that user. The following command makes Nora Shea an Editor on the Helpdesk folder:

```
Add-PublicFolderClientPermission "\Helpdesk" -User ↵
"Nora Shea" -AccessRights Editor
```

One thing that the Add-PublicFolderClientPermission cmdlet does not allow you to do is add permissions recursively down the tree of public folders. The cmdlet only affects the folder that you specified. To get around this, you can create a one-liner to recursively read the list of public folders and then pipe them into the cmdlet. This one-liner would look like this:

```
Get-PublicFolder "\Helpdesk" -Recurse | ↵
Add-PublicFolderClientPermission -User "Nora Shea" ↵
-AccessRights Editor
```

A problem with this approach is that if the user already has permissions defined on one of the folders, the command line generates an error and does not add the new permission. So instead of using this method, you can use a PowerShell script called AddUsersToPFRecursive.ps1 that is included with Exchange 2010. This script is located in the \Scripts directory in your Exchange installation path. When you use this script, you must include the TopPublicFolder parameter to specify the public folder that you want to add permissions to. You will need to specify the user with the User parameter, and the privileges using the Permissions parameter. The following example demonstrates the syntax of this script:

```
.\AddUsersToPFRecursive.ps1 -TopPublicFolder "\Helpdesk" ↵
-User "Nora Shea" -Permissions Editor
```

Remove Access to a Public Folder

In addition to granting users access to public folders, you should know how to remove access. Since you can't work with client permissions on public folders in the Public Folder Management Console, you will have to use the EMS for removing permissions.

To remove existing rights from a public folder, you use the Remove-PublicFolderClientPermission cmdlet. When running this command, you must identify the public folder that you want to modify the permissions on and the user that you want to remove, using the User parameter. You will also need to give the command the AccessRights parameter and use it to specify the role that you are removing the user from, as shown in the following example.

```
Remove-PublicFolderClientPermission "\Helpdesk" -User ↵
"Nora Shea" -AccessRights Editor
```

This cmdlet also suffers from the same problem as the Add-PublicFolderClientPermission cmdlet—it does not remove permissions from the folder's subfolders. Because of this, there is another PowerShell script included with Exchange 2010 that solves this problem. You can use the RemoveUserFromPFRecursive.ps1 script to remove the user's access rights to all the subfolders as well. This script is located in the \Scripts directory of your Exchange Server 2010 installation path. To run this script, use the TopPublicFolder parameter to specify the folder that permissions are stripped from. You will also need to use the User parameter to identify the user who is losing their rights. The following example demonstrates this command:

```
.\RemoveUserFromPFRecursive -TopPublicFolder "\Helpdesk" ↵
-User "Nora Shea"
```

Manage Public Folder Administrators

Public folder administrators have a different set of privileges than clients. For clients, the access rights are different roles, which define what permissions clients have to view, add, and change content. Since administrators are focused more on managing the configuration of public folders, the list of access rights used is focused on the mechanics of public folders rather than the content. Table 8.4 describes the access rights available for administering public folders.

Table 8.4: Public Folder Administrative Access Rights

Access Right	Description
AdministerInformationStore	Modify properties of the folder in the information store.
AllExtendedRights	Change every setting on the folder.
ModifyPublicFolderACL	Add and remove client permissions on a folder.
ModifyPublicFolderAdminACL	Add and remove administrator permissions on a folder.
ModifyPublicFolderDeletedItemRetention	Change the settings for retaining deleted items.
ModifyPublicFolderExpiry	Change the settings for content expiration.
ModifyPublicFolderQuotas	Change the quotas for items in the folder and determine whether the default database quotas are overwritten.
ModifyPublicFolderReplicaList	Add and remove folder replicas.
None	No rights to modify folder settings.
ViewInformationStore	View properties of the folder in the information store.

Add Administrators to a Public Folder

You can add administrative rights to a public folder using the Add-Public FolderAdministrativePermission cmdlet in the EMS. This command will take the name of the folder, the name of the administrator using the User parameter, and the rights that you want assign using the AccessRights parameter. The access rights need to be entered as defined in Table 8.4.

For example, the following command delegates the Quota Admins group to have the ability to manage quotas on every public folder:

```
Add-PublicFolderAdministrativePermission "\" -User ↵
"Quota Admins" -AccessRights ModifyPublicFolderQuotas ↵
-InheritanceType All
```

Remove Administrators from a Public Folder

To remove administrative permissions from a public folder, you can use the Remove-PublicFolderAdministrativePermission cmdlet. You will need to specify the administrator with the User parameter and the rights that you want to remove with the AccessRights parameter. The following example demonstrates this command:

```
Remove-PublicFolderAdministrativePermission "\Helpdesk" ↵
-User "Nora Shea" -AccessRights ModifyPublicFolderQuotas
```

List the Permissions on a Folder

You can view the permissions on specific public folders and determine who has what kind of access rights. To get a complete list of these permissions, you need to view both the permissions assigned to administrators and the permissions assigned to clients. Both of these permission sets can be viewed in the EMS.

View Client Permissions

To list the permissions that clients have to a public folder, you can use the Get-PublicFolderClientPermission cmdlet. The only parameter required to run this command is the name of the public folder that you want to retrieve the permissions for. The following command lists each client who has permissions defined on the folder and lists what each client's permissions are:

```
Get-PublicFolderClientPermission "\Helpdesk"
```

You can further refine this command with the User parameter so it gives you information for a specific user. For example, if you want to know what permissions Nora Shea has on the Helpdesk folder, the following command will tell you and format the results into a table:

```
Get-PublicFolderClientPermission "\Helpdesk" -User ↵
"Nora Shea" | ft User, AccessRights
```

Managing Exchange Server Roles

PART II

View Administrator Permissions

To get a list of the administrator permissions on a public folder, you can use the `Get-PublicFolderAdministrativePermission` cmdlet. Similar to the cmdlet for listing client permissions, this cmdlet only requires the name of the public folder that you want to view the permissions for. The following command will list all the administrative permissions on a folder:

```
Get-PublicFolderAdministrativePermission "\Helpdesk"
```

One thing that you will notice if you run this command on a public folder is that the default set of permissions are applied to universal security groups that Exchange created in Active Directory when it was installed. These groups correspond to the role groups that Exchange uses. You will learn more about role groups and how Exchange 2010 enforces access control in Chapter 12, "Securing Exchange Server."

When using the `Get-PublicFolderAdministrativePermission` cmdlet, you can specify the `User` parameter. Use the `User` parameter along with the name of a user to view the administrative permissions that are assigned to that user, as shown here:

```
Get-PublicFolderAdministrativePermission "\Helpdesk" ↵
-User "Nora Shea"
```

WARNING When using this cmdlet to check user permissions, the permissions are listed only if the user is assigned rights *directly* to the folder. Group memberships are not evaluated. So if the user is a member of a group and the group has permissions defined on the folder, the cmdlet does not return these permissions. If you want to view the permissions that are assigned through a group member-ship, you will need to run the cmdlet with the name of the groups that the user is a member of instead of the user's name.

Configure Client Connectivity

There have been many changes in Exchange 2010 that redefined how clients, such as Microsoft Outlook, connect to Exchange. One of the bigger changes is MAPI on the Middle Tier (MoMT). MoMT moves the mailbox access point away from Mailbox servers and to the Client Access servers instead. So when Outlook clients connect to their mailbox, the connection is made to the Client Access server and the Client Access server brokers the interaction with the Mailbox server that contains the user's data. This is not the case with public folders, however. When a client connects to a public folder, the connection is made directly to the Mailbox server and is not brokered through the Client Access server.

The primary users of public folders are going to be the users in Outlook who use them to share data. When Outlook clients connect to public folders, they use a well-defined method for determining what Public Folder server to use and for ensuring that performance doesn't suffer by using a Public Folder server on the other side of the world. This section will help you understand what to do in order to optimize this experience for users in your organization.

Modify How Clients Choose a Public Folder Server

A user's mailbox database has a default public folder store associated with it. When a client accesses a public folder, it has to know which server has a copy of the public folder that it wants. So the client contacts the default public folder database that is associated with its mailbox database to get a referral for the server that it should get the public folder from.

If the default public folder database has a copy of the public folder that the client wants, the client uses that server. Otherwise, a list of referrals is generated by the server and given to the client. This referral process includes logic that ensures that the client accesses the Public Folder server that is closest to it. To determine which servers outside of the site are closest, the default Public Folder server queries Active Directory for site cost information. The servers that cost the least are placed near the top of the referral list.

Instead of depending on the site cost that is defined in AD for referrals, you can specify your own arbitrary referral costs for public folders.

Modify the Custom Referral List Using the Exchange Management Console

To configure custom referral costs in the EMC, use the following steps:

1. Open the EMC and browse to the Organization Configuration ➤ Mailbox node.

2. In the Work area, click the Database Management tab and select the public folder database for which you want to define a list of custom referral costs.

3. Choose Properties from the public folder's Action menu in the Actions pane.

4. In the properties dialog box for the folder, select the Public Folder Referral tab.

5. Choose the Use Custom List option. To add servers with custom referral costs, click the Add button.

6. The Server Referral Cost dialog box will open. Click the Browse button to choose a Public Folder server that you want to assign a custom cost to.

7. Type the cost that you want to use in the Cost field. This number must be between 1 and 100. Remember that a lower cost means that it is cheaper to contact that server, so that server is more likely to be used for referrals. Click OK to add the server to the list.

8. Continue adding additional servers to the custom cost list. If you exclude a server from the list, the cost is considered infinite, so it's effectively removed from getting a referral.

9. Click OK to make the changes and close the properties dialog box.

Modify the Custom Referral List Using the Exchange Management Shell

You can also modify this custom referral list using the Set-PublicFolderDatabase EMS cmdlet. When running the command, specify the public folder database that you are setting the custom referral list on. You will also need to use the CustomReferralServerList parameter, which details the list of servers and their custom referral costs. When indicating the server and its cost, you will use the format *ServerName:Cost*. For example, if you use CONTOSO-PF01:100, the referral cost of 100 would be used for referrals from that public folder database to the server CONTOSO-PF01. To add entries to the custom cost list, separate each entry with a comma. You will also need to set the UseCustomReferralServerList parameter to $True, to indicate that you are using a custom referral list. The following command demonstrates how to set the custom referral list using the EMS:

```
Set-PublicFolderDatabase "PFDB (CONTOSO-PF01) " ↵
-CustomReferralServerList CONTOSO-PF01:50,CONTOSO-PF02:100 ↵
-UseCustomReferralServerList $True
```

Change the Default Public Folder Database

As described in the previous section, clients connect to the default public folder database on their mailbox store in order to obtain referrals for public folders that are accessed. You can modify the default public folder database that clients use.

To change the default public folder database that clients connect to, use the following steps in the EMC:

1. Open the EMC and browse to the Organization Configuration ➤ Mailbox node in the Console tree.

2. Select the Database Management tab in the Work area.

3. Select the mailbox database that you want to modify the default public folder store for.

4. In the Actions pane, select the Properties option from the Action menu for the mailbox database that you have selected.

5. In the properties dialog box for the database, click the Client Settings tab.

6. Under the Default Public Folder Database field, click the Browse button to select a new default public folder database, as shown in Figure 8.9.

Figure 8.9: Modifying the default public folder store on a mailbox database

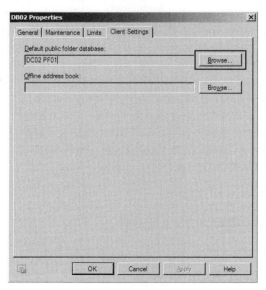

Managing Exchange Server Roles

PART II

7. A dialog box appears that lists the current public folder stores in the organization. Choose the store that you want to use and click OK.

8. When back in the properties dialog box, click OK to make the changes and close the dialog box.

You can also modify the default public folder database using the EMS. You can make this change through the `Set-MailboxDatabase` cmdlet. When you run the command, specify the `PublicFolderDatabase` parameter and enter the name of the public store that you want to use. The following example shows how to use this command:

```
Set-MailboxDatabase DB02 -PublicFolderDatabase PF02
```

Manage Public Folder Databases

In a similar manner to mailbox data, public folder data is stored in a database on a Mailbox server. In Exchange Server 2010, public folder databases are completely optional, so you are not required to have one on your server or even in your Exchange organization.

In Exchange Server 2007, there were limitations on how public folder databases could coexist on servers that used high availability. Because of this, many people hosted public folder databases alongside other server roles or they created dedicated Public Folder servers that hosted nothing but a public folder database. This often increased the number of servers required for Exchange, and subsequently increased management costs. However, in Exchange Server 2010, the new database replication model allows for a public folder database to coexist peacefully on a Mailbox server that is used for high availability.

Each server hosting the mailbox role can have a maximum of one public folder database. Like any other database, the public folder database consists of its own database file and set of transaction logs. For the most part, public folder databases can be managed in a similar fashion to mailbox databases. This section goes over various tasks that you will need to perform on public folder databases.

Configure Public Folder Databases

The configuration of public folder databases is similar to the configuration of mailbox databases. You will find that some of the steps outlined in this section are similar to configuring mailbox databases; the primary difference is that public folder databases cannot be replicated with a database availability group (DAG). DAGs are covered in detail in Chapter 7, "Managing Mailbox Databases," and Chapter 10, "Maintaining Reliability and Availability."

Create a New Public Folder Database

Public folder databases can be created on any Mailbox server, but each Mailbox server can contain only one public folder database. Like mailbox databases, public folder databases are composed of a database file and a set of log files. Before creating your database, you should decide in which drive and folder these files will be stored.

To create a new public folder database using the EMC, follow these steps:

1. Open the EMC and browse to the Organization Configuration ➢ Mailbox node in the Console tree.

2. In the Actions pane, from the mailbox's Action menu select the New Public Folder Database option.

3. In the New Public Folder Database wizard, enter the name for the public folder database in the Public Folder Database Name field.

4. Click the Browse button next to the Server Name field to select the server that you want to create the public folder database on. After selecting the server, click the Next button in the wizard.

5. At the Set Paths screen, you can define a custom location for the storage of the database and the log files. To keep the default locations, click Next.

6. At the Configuration Summary screen, verify that the information you entered is accurate and click New. The public folder database is created.

7. At the Completion screen, click Finish to close the wizard.

You can also create a new public folder database using the EMS. To do this, you will use the New-PublicFolderDatabase cmdlet. You are required to specify the name of the new database and the name of the server that it resides on, using the Server parameter. Note that you do not need to specify the path for the database file or the log files. If you leave this off, Exchange places these files in the default location in the

Exchange installation directory structure. The following example creates a new public folder database:

```
New-PublicFolderDatabase "PFDB (CONTOSO-PF01)" ↵
-Server CONTOSO-PF01
```

NOTE The New-PublicFolderDatabase cmdlet does not mount the database after it creates it. If you want to mount it afterward, run the Mount-Database cmdlet.

Impose Limits on all Public Folders in a Database

Earlier in this chapter, I talked about setting size limits and restrictions on individual public folders. When these limits are set on individual folders, they override limits that are set on the database. You can also modify the limits on the database itself, and each public folder in that database is affected unless the folder's settings are overridden. The default limits on a public folder database are outlined in Table 8.5.

Table 8.5: Default Public Folder Limits in the Database

Setting	Default Value
Issue Warning At (KB)	1991680 (1.9 GB)
Prohibit Post At (KB)	2097152 (2 GB)
Maximum Item Size (KB)	10240 (10 MB)

To modify the default limits for all public folders in a database, you can use the EMC:

1. Open the EMC and browse to the Organization Configuration ➢ Mailbox node in the Console tree.

2. Click on the Database Management tab in the Work area. The list of public folder databases is displayed in that tab.

3. Select the public folder database that you want to modify the limits for and click the Properties option in the Actions pane.

4. In the properties dialog box for the public folder database, select the Limits tab. The settings for the limits are defined in the Storage Limits section of the dialog box, as shown in Figure 8.10.

Figure 8.10: Setting the limits for all public folders in a database

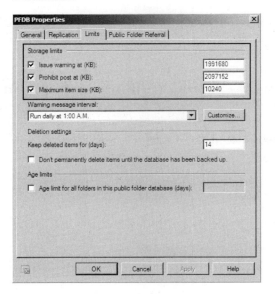

5. Modify the value in one of the three fields to reflect the limit that you want to impose. Remember that these limits are configured in KB. So if you want to set a 1 MB limit on items posted to the public folders, this value would be 1024.

6. Click OK to make the changes and close the properties dialog box.

TIP   You don't have to define any limits at all. If you want any of these values to be unlimited, you can just uncheck the box next to the setting. Caution should be exercised when allowing this. Make sure that your users understand that large posts under poor network conditions don't result in highly satisfied public folder users.

You can define these database-specific public folder limits in the EMS as well. Use the Set-PublicFolderDatabase cmdlet along with one of the parameters outlined in Table 8.6.

Managing Exchange Server Roles

PART II

Table 8.6: EMS Parameters for Setting Public Folder Limits at the Database Level

Setting	EMS Parameter
Issue Warning At (KB)	`IssueWarningQuota`
Prohibit Post At (KB)	`ProhibitPostQuota`
Maximum Item Size (KB)	`MaxItemSize`

To use the parameters, specify the size that you are setting the parameter to. You can specify the size in KB, MB, or GB. When you type the number in the command, specify what the unit is. For example, 1 MB can be represented by `1MB` or `1024KB`. If you do not want a limit on the setting, you can use `Unlimited` instead of the size limit. The following example allows items of any size but prohibits additional posts when the database size reaches 2 GB:

```
Set-PublicFolderDatabase "PFDB (CONTOSO-PF01)" ↵
-MaxItemSize Unlimited -ProhibitPostQuota 2GB
```

Maintain Public Folder Databases

There is not a lot of work required to maintain public folder databases. Public folders perform automatic maintenance that takes care of everything that needs to be cleaned up inside the database on a regular basis. Other than maintenance of the content stored inside the database, the other maintenance aspect that you need to be aware of is maintaining the database object and its files. This section discusses this in detail, including steps for moving a database to a different location as well as steps for completely removing a database from a server.

Manage the Database Maintenance Schedule

Online maintenance of a database occurs automatically on a predefined interval. During this period, Exchange cleans up several aspects of the databases, including things like purging old indexes, tombstones (items which, from the user's perspective, have been deleted but are still kept in the database for replication purposes), and expired folders. This is all configured out of the box, so you do not have to do anything to ensure that this maintenance is run on a regular basis. However, you can modify the timeframes that this maintenance work is performed during.

When modifying the maintenance window, ensure that you allow adequate time for the process to run. Because of efficiencies gained in the online maintenance process in Exchange 2010, this maintenance window can be smaller than in previous versions. Depending on the size of your database, you may only need to allocate a couple of hours for this process. If maintenance can't be completed in one sitting, the process will pick up where it left off during the next maintenance window.

You can modify the maintenance schedule on a public folder database in the EMC using the following steps:

1. Open the EMC and browse to the Organization Configuration ➤ Mailbox node in the Console tree.

2. Select the Database Management tab in the Work area.

3. From the list of public folder databases, select the public folder database that you want to modify the maintenance schedule for.

4. In the Actions pane, select the Properties option from the Action menu for the public folder database that you have selected.

5. In the properties dialog box for the public folder database, click the General tab.

6. In the Maintenance Schedule field, select the maintenance schedule that you want to use from the drop-down list. If you click the Customize button, you can create your own custom maintenance schedule instead of using a predefined one.

7. Click OK to make the changes and close the properties dialog box.

To set the maintenance schedule for public folder databases in the EMS, you use the `Set-PublicFolderDatabase` cmdlet with the `MaintenanceSchedule` parameter. In the `MaintenanceSchedule` parameter, you will specify the day and time that maintenance starts and ends. You can use the format *Day.H:MM* for this time value. For example, Friday at 3:00 a.m. would be `Fri.3:00 AM`. There must be a space between the time and the `AM/PM`. Also, when you specify the time range, the hyphen between the times should not have any spaces around it, as shown in this example. The following example sets the maintenance schedule on the public folder database to be Thursday from 8 p.m. to Friday at 4 a.m.

```
Set-PublicFolderDatabase "PFDB (CONTOSO-PF01)" ↵
-MaintenanceSchedule "Thu.8:00 PM-Fri.4:00 AM"
```

Managing Exchange Server Roles

PART II

Move Public Folder Database Files

You can move the database and log files of a public folder database to another location on your server. When you move the files, the database will need to be dismounted. This means that users that are connected to the database will be temporarily disconnected. Before moving the database, you will need to ensure that the new location for the files is large enough to hold them.

To move the public folder database in the EMC, follow these steps:

1. Open the EMC and browse to the Organization Configuration ➤ Mailbox node in the Console tree.

2. Click on the Database Management tab in the Work area. The list of public folder databases is displayed in the tab.

3. Select the public folder database that you want to move and click the Move Database Path option in the Actions pane.

4. In the Move Database Path wizard, type the location of the new database file in the Database File Path field. Ensure you put the name of the file at the end of this path—for example, `C:\PF01\PF01.edb`. Enter the new location for the logs in the Log Folder Path field.

5. Click the Move button to move the database and logs to the new location.

6. At the Completion screen, click the Finish button.

To move the public folder database through the EMS, you can use the `Move-DatabasePath` cmdlet. When you run this command, identify the database that you are moving and the new location for the database files and the log files. The `EdbFilePath` parameter is used to specify the database location. Make sure that you include the name of the database file at the end of the path—for example, `C:\NewPath\PFDB.edb`. For specifying the new location of the log files, you will use the `LogFolderPath` parameter. This parameter should specify the folder that the log files will be kept in, so make sure it's a valid folder path. The following command demonstrates how to move the public folder database files to a new location on the same server.

```
Move-DatabasePath PFDB -EdbFilePath "C:\DB\PFDB\PFDB.edb" ↵
-LogFolderPath "C:\DB\PFDB"
```

Delete a Public Folder Database

Before you can delete a public folder database, you must make sure that the database does not contain any data. Therefore, any public folder data in that database should be either deleted or moved to another server. To move the data to another server, see the section "Move Public Folders to a Different Server Using PowerShell Scripts" later in this chapter.

When you delete the database using the tools in Exchange, the database files remain on the disk. You should back these files up before deleting them unless you are sure that you will never need to recover the data.

WARNING   Exercise care if you are going to delete the last public folder database in the organization. Make sure that your users are not using the database for anything, such as Offline Address Book distribution or organizational forms.

PART II

Managing Exchange Server Roles

To delete a public folder database in the EMC, follow these steps:

1. Open the EMC and browse to the Organization Configuration ➤ Mailbox node.

2. In the Work area, select the Database Management tab. The list of databases that currently exist is displayed.

3. Select the public folder database that you want to remove from the list of databases.

4. In the Actions pane, select the Remove option from the Action menu for the public folder database that you have selected.

5. You will be prompted with a dialog box asking you if you are sure that you want to remove the database. Click the Yes button to continue.

6. The public folder database that you selected is removed. A dialog box will be displayed that instructs you to remove the database files for the public folder manually, as shown in Figure 8.11. Make note of the location of the old public folder database files and then click OK to close the dialog box.

7. Open a command prompt window by clicking Start ➤ All Programs ➤ Accessories ➤ Command Prompt.

8. Type the following command, replacing the *D:\Databases\PF01.edb* file path with the location of the old public folder database file. This will delete the old public folder database file.

```
del D:\Databases\PF01.edb
```

9. Type the following commands, replacing the *D:\Databases\PF01Logs* folder path with the location of the old public folder log files. The folder and the log files will be deleted.

```
del D:\Databases\PF01Logs /Q
rd D:\Databases\PF01Logs
```

Figure 8.11: The confirmation dialog box after removing a public folder database

You can remove a public folder database in the EMS using the Remove-PublicFolderDatabase cmdlet. The only parameter that you need to specify when running this command is the name of the public folder database that you are removing. As with the steps for removing the database in the EMC, you will need to manually remove the database and log files after you've deleted the database from Exchange. The following example shows how to use this command:

```
Remove-PublicFolderDatabase "PFDB" -Confirm:$False
```

You can also use the following PowerShell script to delete the public folder database and remove the database files for you. Specify the name of the public folder database as the input parameter into this script. For example, you would execute the script using the following command:

```
.\RemovePFDB.ps1 "PFDB"
```

RemovePFDB.ps1 Script

```
## File Name: RemovePFDB.ps1
## Description: Removes the specified public folder database
## and deletes its associated files.

## Check the input parameter
Param( [string] $PFDB = "" )
If ($PFDB -eq "")
{
    " "
    "You must specify a database to remove."
    " "
    "EXAMPLE:"
    "`t[PS] C:\> .\RemovePFDB.ps1 ""PFDB01"""
    " "
    exit;
}


## Get the properties of the database
$PFDBObj = Get-PublicFolderDatabase $PFDB
$PFDBEDB = $PFDBObj.EDBFilePath
$PFDBLogs = $PFDBObj.LogFolderPath

Remove-PublicFolderDatabase $PFDB -Confirm:$False
Remove-Item $PFDBEDB -Confirm:$False
Remove-Item $PFDBLogs -Recurse -Confirm:$False
```

Manage Public Folder Replication

Although databases can exist on servers with replicated mailbox databases, they do not use the same replication technology. Rather than using transaction log shipping and replay, public folder data uses a replication technique where data is transferred in messages that are sent between public folder stores that contain replicated folders. For public folders, replication occurs at the content level and not at the database level.

There are two types of replication in public folders: hierarchy replication and content replication. Every public folder database receives hierarchy replication from other Public Folder servers. The replicated hierarchy contains information about what folders the Exchange organization has and which servers have copies of those folders. On the other hand, only servers that are set up as replicas for a public folder participate in content replication. The idea is that every Public Folder server needs to know about the hierarchy in case a client connects to it. If the server does not have the public folder data, it needs to be able to direct the client to a server that does.

Configure Replication Parameters

You do have some control over how replication is performed across your organization. You can configure when and how often public folders replicate, as well as how replication bandwidth savings are used. The topics in this section will help you understand how to configure essential public folder replication parameters.

Change the Size of Replication Messages

Data is replicated between public folder databases via messages that are sent by the source where the data was changed. The size limit setting of the replication message determines how big a message can get when it contains multiple replicated changes. The default size limit is 300 KB. This means that when a replicated change is added that would cause the replication message to exceed 300 KB, the replicated change is sent in the next replication message.

For example, consider what would happen if you had four changes to replicate and their sizes were 100 KB, 150 KB, 75 KB, and 500 KB. The 100 KB change and the 150 KB change would be in the same replication message. However, the 75 KB change would make the message exceed 300 KB. Therefore, the 75 KB change would be sent in the next replication message. The 500 KB change causes the replication message to exceed 300 KB also, so the 500 KB change is sent in a separate message by itself. (A single replicated change can exceed the limit.)

To adjust the limit of the replication message size, follow these steps:

1. Open the EMC and browse to the Organization Configuration ➢ Mailbox node in the Console tree.

2. In the Work area, select the Database Management tab and choose the public folder database that you want to change the replication message size for.

3. In the Action menu for the selected public folder database, click the Properties option to launch the properties dialog box.

4. In the properties dialog box, click the Replication tab.

5. In the Replication Message Size Limit field, enter the size limit that you want to use, which is measured in kilobytes.

6. Click OK to make the change and close the properties dialog box.

You can also set the replication message limit in the EMS, using the Set-PublicFolderDatabase cmdlet. You will need to identify the database that you are changing and the new size of the replication message using the ReplicationMessageSize parameter. The following example demonstrates this command:

```
Set-PublicFolderDatabase PFB -ReplicationMessageSize 1024KB
```

Define the Replication Schedule

The replication schedule for public folders can be adjusted to suit your organization's needs. Replication occurs every 15 minutes by default, and this is defined on the public folder database. When you override this schedule, you can set a custom replication schedule on the database itself or on a per-folder basis.

Change the Replication Schedule on a Database

When you modify the replication schedule for the database, you affect all public folders that do not have custom replication schedules defined. You have two options for changing the replication schedule on the database:

- Change the days and times that replication occurs.

- Change the number of minutes between replication cycles when replication is performed continuously.

To modify these settings in the EMC, follow these steps:

1. Open the EMC and browse to the Organization Configuration ➢ Mailbox node in the Console tree.

2. In the Work area, select the Database Management tab and select the public folder database that you want to modify the replication schedule on.

3. In the Action menu for the public folder database, click the Properties option to open the properties dialog box for the database.

4. In the database's properties dialog box, select the Replication tab.

5. To modify the replication interval, select a new interval from the drop-down list in the Replication Interval section. You also have the option of clicking the Customize button to configure replication to occur only on certain days or during certain timeframes. For example, Figure 8.12 demonstrates setting replication to occur only on weekends between 8 p.m. and 6 a.m.

Figure 8.12: Setting a custom public folder replication schedule

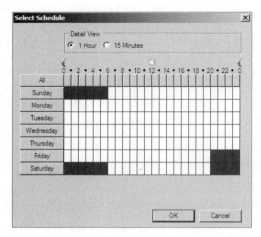

6. If you choose Always Run for the replication interval, you can modify how frequently the interval runs. In the field Replication Interval For "Always Run" (Minutes), enter the number of minutes that you want replication to wait before performing another replication cycle. The default time is 15 minutes.

7. After you have set the schedule that you want to use, click OK to close the properties dialog box and make your changes.

Define a Custom Replication Schedule on a Public Folder

To define a custom replication interval on a specific public folder, you will need to use the Public Folder Management Console. The following steps walk you through this process:

1. Open the PFMC and browse to the Default Public Folders node in the Console tree.

2. From the Console tree, select the parent folder of the public folder that you want to define a custom replication schedule on. When you select the parent folder, its child folders appear in the Results pane.

3. In the Results pane, select the public folder and click the Properties option in the folder's Action menu. This will launch the properties dialog box for the folder.

4. In the folder's properties dialog box, click the Replication tab.

5. Deselect the Use Public Folder Database Replication Schedule check box.

6. Below the check box is a drop-down list that defines the replication interval for that folder. Select the replication interval that you want to use from that drop-down list. You can also click the Customize button to customize the days and times that you want to schedule replication for.

7. Click OK to close the properties dialog box and make the changes to the public folder replication schedule.

Manage Replication

When managing replication, it's important to understand which public folders are replicated where and how to control this replication. This section shows you how to perform some key tasks in managing the replication of public folders.

Add a Replica Server

Public folder replication is defined on a per-folder basis. Therefore, public folder databases can contain replicas of different folders from multiple servers. A single public folder can be replicated across many servers. You can add replicas to an existing public folder using either the Public Folder Management Console or the Exchange Management Shell.

To add a replica with the Public Folder Management Console, follow these steps:

1. Open the PFMC and browse to the Default Public Folders node in the Console tree.

2. Using the Console tree, browse to the parent folder of the public folder that you want to create a replica of. When you click on the parent folder in the Console tree, all of its child folders are displayed in the Results pane.

3. In the Results pane, click on the public folder that you want to create the replica for. Select the Properties option from the Action menu or double-click the folder to open the properties dialog box.

4. In the properties dialog box, click the Replication tab. At the top of the tab, the replica databases are listed.

5. You can add a replica to the list by clicking the Add button, as shown in Figure 8.13.

Figure 8.13: Adding a replica to an existing public folder

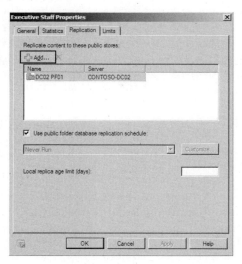

6. The Select Public Folder Database dialog box will be displayed and a list of existing public folder databases in the Exchange organization is displayed along with the server that those databases reside on. Select the database that you want to replicate the folder to and click OK to add it to the list of replicas.

7. Back in the properties dialog box, click OK to make the changes and close the dialog box.

To add a replica to an existing public folder using the EMS, you will use the `Set-PublicFolder` cmdlet with the `Replicas` parameter. The `Replicas` parameter lists each database that holds a replica of the public folder. When you add a replica to the set, you need to make sure that you also list the names of the existing replicas. If you run this command and leave one of the existing replicas out of the list, that replica is removed from the list and no longer receives replication of that folder. The following command shows you how to list the current replicas on the folder:

```
Get-PublicFolder "\Helpdesk" | ft Name, Replicas
```

The following command illustrates how multiple public folder replicas can be defined for a public folder using the EMS:

```
Set-PublicFolder "\Helpdesk" -Replicas ↵
"PFDB (CONTOSO-PF01)", "PFDB (CONTOSO-PF02)"
```

Move Public Folders to a Different Server Using PowerShell Scripts

There are common situations where you may need to move all public folders hosted on one server to another server. For example, this is a typical concern when you decommission a Mailbox server that has a public store. The following steps are involved if you wanted to move all the folders from PFDB01 on the server CONTOSO-PF01 to PFDB02 on the server CONTOSO-PF02:

1. Create the PFDB02 public folder database on CONTOSO-PF02.

2. Replicate the hierarchy to PFDB02.

3. Modify the default public folder database on Mailbox servers that are pointing clients to PFDB01.

4. Add PFDB02 to the replica list and remove PFDB01 from the list.

5. Wait for content replication to complete.

6. Remove PFDB01.

You can certainly perform these steps one at a time for each public folder on the old database. You can even use a series of EMS commands so you don't have to click through each public folder in the PFMC. However, Exchange Server 2010 provides you with PowerShell scripts that do the heavy lifting for you. Table 8.7 outlines the scripts available for moving public folders. All scripts are stored in the \Scripts folder under the path where the Exchange Server 2010 binaries are installed.

Table 8.7: PowerShell Scripts for Moving Public Folders

Script Name	Description
`MoveAllReplicas.ps1`	Moves all public folders from one server to another
`ReplaceReplicaOnPFRecursive.ps1`	Moves a public folder and all its child folders to another server

> **WARNING** The one thing that these scripts do not do for you is unset the old public folder database as the default public folder database on existing mailbox databases. You will need to do this manually on the mailbox databases.

To move all the public folders from one server to another using a PowerShell script, complete the following steps:

1. Open the Exchange Management Shell.

2. Use the following command to change your current directory to the scripts directory:

    ```
    cd "\Program Files\Microsoft\Exchange Server\v14\Scripts"
    ```

    If you did not install Exchange to the default location, you will need to change the current directory to the folder path that you installed Exchange into.

3. Run the `MoveAllReplicas.ps1` script, specifying the old server name and the new server name:

    ```
    .\MoveAllReplicas.ps1 -Server <OldServer> ↵
    -NewServer <NewServer>
    ```

4. Modify the default public folder store on the mailbox databases that were pointing to the old replica. You can use the following one-liner to change them to the new public folder store:

```
Get-MailboxDatabase | where { $_.PublicFolderDatabase ↵
-eq <OldServer> } | Set-MailboxDatabase ↵
-PublicFolderDatabase <NewServer>
```

5. After you are certain that content replication is complete, delete the old database using the steps in the section "Delete a Public Folder Database," earlier in this chapter. The easiest way to determine if content replication is complete is to look at the folders in the replicas and see if the public folder content is present.

Suspend and Resume Public Folder Content Replication

Having the ability to suspend replication across the Exchange organization gives you an "In case of emergency, break glass!" option if public folder replication is out of control. This may be helpful in situations where there is a lot of public folder data to replicate and bandwidth is at a premium.

> **NOTE**   Keep in mind that suspending replication of public folders only stops content replication. While replication is suspended, the hierarchy will continue to synchronize.

You must use the EMS to suspend replication of public folder content. Use the Suspend-PublicFolderReplication cmdlet to get the job done. This will suspend replication across the entire organization with one command:

```
Suspend-PublicFolderReplication -Confirm:$False
```

When you are ready to continue replication, the Resume-PublicFolderReplication will turn content replication back on:

```
Resume-PublicFolderReplication
```

Force Public Folder Replication

If you have public folders that are out of sync across replicas or if the hierarchy information is out of sync, you can manually trigger hierarchy replication or content replication. The methods for forcing hierarchy replication and content replication are different.

Force Public Folder Hierarchy Replication

To force hierarchy replication, you can use the Public Folder Management Console or the Exchange Management Shell.

To force public folder hierarchy replication in the PFMC, follow these steps:

1. Open the PFMC and click on the top node in the Console tree, which represents the server that you are currently connected to.

2. In the Actions pane, click the Update Hierarchy option, as shown in Figure 8.14.

Figure 8.14: Forcing public folder hierarchy replication through the PFMC

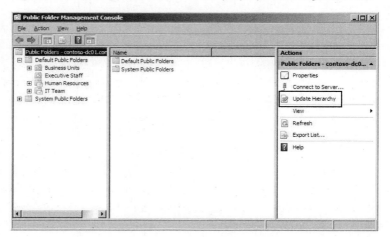

3. The public folder hierarchy is replicated. You will not receive a notification in the PFMC.

To update the hierarchy from the EMS, you can use the Update-PublicFolderHierarchy cmdlet. You must specify the Server parameter in the command. The server that you specify here will be the source server for the hierarchy update. The following command demonstrates hierarchy synchronization from a single server:

```
Update-PublicFolderHierarchy -Server CONTOSO-PF01
```

Force Public Folder Content Replication

You can force the replication of content from a specific public folder replica. To do this in the PFMC, use these steps:

1. Open the PFMC and browse to the Default Public Folders node in the Console tree.

2. From the Console tree, select the parent folder of the public folder that you want to force replication for. When you select the parent folder, the child folders will be listed in the Results pane.

3. Click on the public folder that you want to force replication for from the Results pane. In the Actions pane, click Update Content from the public folder's Action menu.

If content replication is successful, you will not receive a notification. You will only receive notification if there was an error with replication of the folder.

TIP If you receive an error stating that the server doesn't have a replica of the folder that you are trying to replicate, you can connect to a server that does contain a replica from the same PFMC session. To do this, follow the steps in the section "Launch the Public Folder Management Console," earlier in this chapter.

To force replication of a public folder's content in the EMS, you can use the Update-PublicFolder cmdlet. You will need to specify the identity of the public folder that you want to replicate and the server that should be used as the source of replication, using the Server parameter. The following example demonstrates the syntax of this command:

```
Update-PublicFolder "\Human Resources" -Server CONTOSO-PF01
```

PART III

Mitigating Risk

Mitigating Risk

PART III

9

Administering Mailbox Content

Mitigating Risk

PART III

S o far, this book has focused on managing the various settings and capabilities of Exchange Server 2010. In this chapter, we'll dive into the management of the message content itself. Exchange Server 2010 includes many enhancements in content management; some of the more compelling are as follows:

- Additional capabilities in Messaging Records Management
- Email archiving
- Email discovery and searching across mailboxes

These capabilities allow Exchange to more easily meet compliance requirements in addition to meeting the increasing demand of keeping more data for longer periods of time. These features, along with additional content management tasks, are covered in this chapter.

Meet Message Retention Compliance

In business today, information spreads very fast, thereby making it difficult to track and maintain records. The demand to maintain records of communication between people has increased in order to satisfy legal requirements. There have been many cases in recent years of large companies that could not comply with government email compliance mandates, and many of them paid large penalties, to the tune of millions of dollars.

These legal responsibilities are accompanied by several technical challenges. When users are required to keep email messages about specific topics, they need a place to put them. Keeping them in their mailbox eats precious space that contributes to the user's email quota. If messages are kept in personal folders (PST files), they are moved off the mail server and onto the user's local hard drive or onto a network share. This makes the mail data hard to collect and search for. You have to find the PSTs on various client computers and on your network, hope that they are not password protected, and search through them for what you are looking for. When you are required by law to produce proof in a legal matter, not having access to these messages can cost your organization dearly.

Exchange Server 2010 brings a lot to the table to ease these pains. This section discusses how to implement the mechanisms that will keep your organization legally sound.

Enforce Records Management

There are two ways to enforce records management in Exchange Server 2010. The old method, adopted from Exchange Server 2007, uses managed folders. Managed folders operated on the notion that users would drag messages into an administrator-defined folder that meets the records management requirement of the message. This method assumed that users would be "filers" and file their messages away into separate buckets.

However, some users can be classified as "pilers." Because of the robust search capabilities in Outlook, many people will keep large amounts of email in their inbox or in a single folder. To find the messages they need, they simply search for them based on keywords. The managed folders approach does not work well for these individuals, so Exchange Server 2010 introduces the option of retention tags. With retention tags, individual messages can be tagged with retention policies that enforce the records management requirement.

Use Managed Folders

Managed folders are created by administrators in the Exchange organization and applied to mailboxes using a managed folder policy. Each managed folder has managed content settings associated with it. The managed content settings define what happens to the items in the managed folder when they expire. The Managed Folder Assistant runs in the background on Mailbox servers and applies managed folder policies to mailboxes on a scheduled interval.

You need to complete three tasks to implement managed folders:

1. Create managed folders. (You only need to do this if you want custom managed folders. Managed default folders are created automatically.)
2. Create managed folder policies.
3. Apply managed folder policies to mailboxes.

Create Managed Folders

There are two types of managed folders that you can work with: managed default folders and managed custom folders. Managed default folders are the default folders inside a user's mailbox, such as the Inbox folder or the Sent Items folder. You can also create managed custom folders that you want to appear in user's mailboxes. These folders appear under the folder called Managed Folders at the root of the mailbox.

To create a new managed custom folder in the Exchange Management Console (EMC), use the following steps:

1. Open the EMC and browse to the Organization Configuration ➢ Mailbox node in the Console tree.

2. In the Actions pane, click the New Managed Custom Folder task to launch the configuration wizard.

3. On the New Managed Custom Folder screen, enter the name of the folder in the Name field. The field below it can be used to define a different name when the folder is viewed in Outlook. By default, this field is set to the same value that you type in the Name field.

4. If you want to apply a storage quota to the managed custom folder, click the option Storage Limit (KB) For This Folder And Its Subfolders. In the text box to the right, enter the limit of the folder in kilobytes. For example, a 10 MB quota would be entered as **10240**.

5. You can also set a comment for this folder that the user sees when the folder is opened. Enter this comment in the field Display The Following Comment When The Folder Is Viewed In Outlook. If you check the box Do Not Allow Users To Minimize This Comment In Outlook, then the comment is always visible to the user.

6. After filling out the fields as shown in Figure 9.1, click the New button to create the folder.

7. At the Completion screen, click Finish.

The managed custom folder is created, but it will not yet show up in anyone's mailbox. You must perform these tasks first:

1. Define what happens to items in this folder. (See the next section, "Control the Lifespan of Messages.")

2. Apply this managed folder to a managed folder policy and apply the policy to a mailbox (See "Configure Managed Folder Policies," later in this chapter.)

Control the Lifespan of Messages

Now that you have a managed folder, you need to set managed content settings to determine what happens to items in the folder. You can define how long items stay in the folder before something is done to them and what action is taken when the time period expires. You can also choose to forward a copy of any message placed in the folder to another mailbox, which is also known as *journaling* the item.

Figure 9.1: Creating a managed custom folder in the EMC

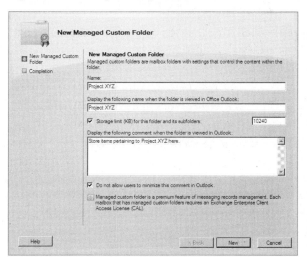

> **WARNING** Although you can have multiple managed content settings for each managed folder, you can have only one setting for each type of item. For example, if you already have managed content settings defined for Calendar items in the folder, you can't create another set of managed content settings for Calendar items.

To configure managed content settings for a folder using the EMC, use the following steps:

1. Open the EMC and browse to the Organization Configuration ➢ Mailbox node in the Console tree.

2. Select either the Managed Default Folders tab (if you are defining content settings on default mailbox folders) or the Managed Custom Folders tab (if you are defining content settings for a folder that you created).

3. In the list of managed folders, select the folder and click the New Managed Content Settings task in the Actions pane.

4. In the New Managed Content Settings wizard, type a name for content settings, such as **Delete After 1 Year**.

5. From the Message Type drop-down list, select the type of content that you want this setting to apply to. For example, you can apply the setting to specific items such as email only. Or you can apply the setting to every item type by choosing All Mailbox Content.

6. Check the Length Of Retention Period (Days) box and type the number of days that you want the items to be retained before an action is taken on them.

7. In the Retention Period Starts box, you can choose when the retention period starts. It can start either when the item is delivered or when it is moved into the folder. For example, if you want to create a setting to delete items after one year, you could set the retention period for 365 days.

8. In the field Action To Take At The End Of The Retention Period, choose what happens to the item when the period is over. If you choose to move it to a managed folder, click the Browse button to select that folder.

9. After you have filled out these fields as shown in Figure 9.2, click Next to continue.

Figure 9.2: Configuring the managed content settings for a folder

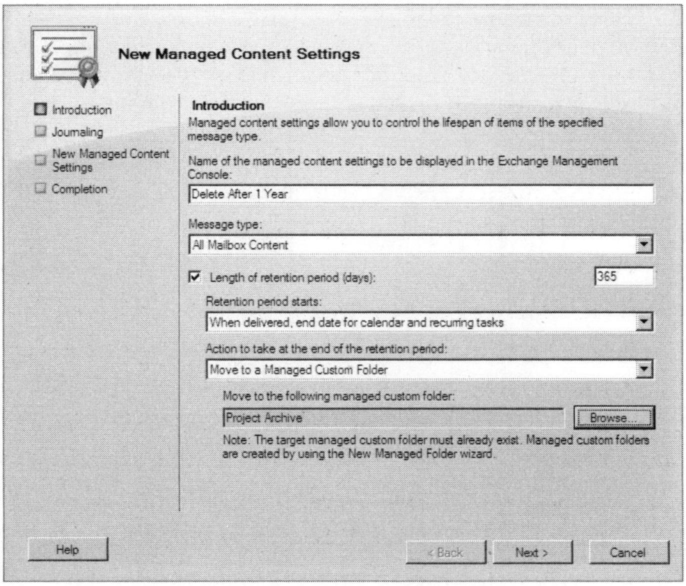

10. At the Journaling screen, you can choose to forward copies of the message to a mailbox when it's placed in the folder. Check the Forward Copies To option and click the Browse button to select the mailbox. You can also define a label for the message in the field Assign The Following Label To The Copy Of The Message. Doing so can make the messages easier to sort through. Click Next to continue.

11. These messages are forwarded when the Managed Folder Assistant runs and processes the managed items in the mailboxes.

12. In the Configuration Summary screen, click New to create the managed content settings for the folder.

13. At the Completion screen, click Finish to exit the wizard.

The settings for the managed folder are now configured and the folder is ready to be added to a managed folder policy.

Configure Managed Folder Policies

To apply managed folders to users, you need to add the managed folders to a managed folder policy. There are two parts to this process:

1. Configure the managed folder policy.

2. Assign the policy to one or more mailboxes.

You can have multiple managed folder policies with multiple managed folders in each. You can deploy different policies to different users, but each user can have only one managed folder policy applied to them. To create and assign a managed folder policy in the EMC, use the following steps:

1. Open the EMC and browse to the Organization Configuration ➤ Mailbox node in the Console tree.

2. Select the New Managed Folder Mailbox Policy task in the Actions pane.

3. In the New Managed Folder Mailbox Policy wizard, enter a name for this policy in the field Managed Folder Mailbox Policy Name.

4. Click the Add button to add a managed folder to this policy. The Select Managed Folder dialog box will be displayed. Select either a managed default folder or a managed custom folder and click OK.

5. After you have added all the managed folders that you want in this policy, as shown in Figure 9.3, click New to create the policy.

Figure 9.3: Creating a managed folder policy

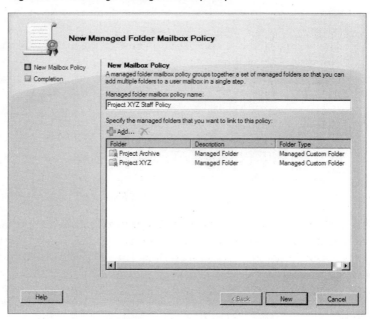

6. At the Completion screen, click Finish to close the wizard.

7. Back in the EMC, browse to the Recipient Configuration ➤ Mailbox node in the Console tree.

8. From the list of mailboxes displayed in the Results pane, select one or more mailboxes that you want to apply the policy to.

9. Click the Properties option for the selected mailboxes in the Actions pane.

10. In the properties dialog box, select the Mailbox Settings tab.

11. Select the Messaging Records Management option in the list of mailbox settings and click the Properties button above the list.

12. In the Messaging Records Management dialog box, select the Managed Folder Mailbox Policy check box. Click the Browse button to select the policy that you just created. When you have added the policy, as shown in Figure 9.4, click OK to close the Messaging Records Management dialog box.

Figure 9.4: Adding a managed folder policy
to a mailbox

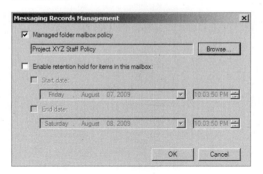

13. Click the OK button to close the Properties dialog and make the changes to the managed folder Mailbox Policy. You may receive a warning indicating that some versions of Outlook will not support managed folders. If you are sure that these mailboxes are using compatible versions of Outlook, click Yes to continue.

The policy is now created and assigned to your users. This policy will be applied when the Managed Folder Assistant runs.

Modify the Managed Folder Processing Schedule

By default, the Managed Folder Assistant runs every day from 1 a.m. to 9 a.m. During this time, the settings defined in the managed folder mailbox policy for each mailbox are enforced. The assistant runs once during this interval and stops. If it doesn't finish processing before this interval is over, it picks up where it left off at the next scheduled interval. You can adjust this schedule. You can also use the Exchange Management Shell to manually start the Managed Folder Assistant.

To adjust the Managed Folder Assistant schedule in the EMC, follow these steps:

1. Open the EMC and browse to the Server Configuration ➢ Mailbox node in the Console tree.

2. In the list of Mailbox servers, select the server that you want to modify the Managed Folder Assistant's schedule for and click the Properties option in the Actions pane.

3. In the server's properties dialog box, click the Messaging Records Management tab.

Mitigating Risk

PART III

4. Click the Customize button to create a custom schedule for the assistant to run during. You must allot at least one 15-minute interval between the time the assistant stops and starts again. Therefore, you cannot schedule it to run 24 hours per day for an entire week.

5. In the Select Schedule dialog box, click the boxes that correspond to the hours that you want the assistant to run. When the box is blue, that means the assistant is allowed to run during that hour. You can see this in Figure 9.5, which shows a modified schedule, every day from 1 a.m. to 5 a.m. After selecting the schedule, click OK to close the dialog box.

Figure 9.5: Selecting the schedule at which managed folders are processed

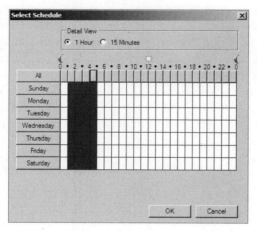

6. Back in the properties dialog box, click OK to close the dialog box and make the changes to the schedule.

You can manually launch the Managed Folder Assistant and it will run even if it's not within a scheduled time interval. You can do this by running the following two commands in the EMS:

```
Restart-Service MSExchangeMailboxAssistants
Start-ManagedFolderAssistant
```

The managed folder settings will be updated in your Outlook clients as soon as the mailboxes are processed. For small organizations, this could happen quickly, but it might take a while longer (potentially hours) for larger organizations with thousands of mailboxes. When the process finishes, an event with ID 9018 (or ID 9022 if you manually launched the process) will be written to the Application event log on the server. The event description will say that the Managed Folder Assistant completed, and it tells you how many mailboxes were processed.

Use Retention Tags

Retention tags are a new feature in Exchange Server 2010 that offers more flexibility for users than managed folders. With managed folders, users are required to file email away into specific folders. However, with retention tags, a user can apply retention settings directly to specific items. This eliminates the need for users to change their email management habits to conform to your organization's managed folders structure. Also, users can create their own folders and apply retention tags to those folders, effectively duplicating the same functionality as managed folders, but the process is controlled by the users rather than the administrators.

Retention tags are similar to managed folder content settings. You define the type of message the tag applies to, the retention period, the action that you want to take when the item expires, and the journaling options. Retention tags are linked to retention policies, which are similar to managed folder policies. A retention policy can be applied to mailboxes.

The following process is used for setting up retention tags for your users:

1. Create the retention tags.
2. Link the retention tags to retention policies.
3. Apply the retention policies to mailboxes.

Create Retention Tags

You can create a new retention tag using the New-RetentionPolicyTag cmdlet in the EMS. You will need to specify the name of the tag, the type of items that the tag applies to, the age limit, and the action to take when the item expires. You can also specify a journaling address so that the message is forwarded to another mailbox when it's tagged. Some of the important parameters are listed in Table 9.1.

Table 9.1: Parameters for Creating New Retention Tags

Parameter	Description
Name	The name of the retention tag.
Type	The folder that the retention tag applies to—for example, Calendar, Inbox, SentItems. You can also specify a value of Personal to allow the user to use the tag for custom folders and single items.
MessageClass	The class of item that the retention tag applies to. For example, this could be E-mail or CalItems (for calendar items).
AgeLimitForRetention	The number of days that an item is retained for before an action is taken.
RetentionAction	The action to take when the message expires. The possible values are MoveToDeletedItems, MoveToFolder, DeleteAndAllowRecovery, PermanentlyDelete, MarkAsPastRetentionLimit, and MoveToArchive.
RetentionEnabled	Set to $true to enable retention. This must be enabled before the retention limit applies to the tagged items.
AddressForJournaling	The address for where a copy of the tagged items will be sent.
JournalingEnabled	Set to $true to enable journaling of the tagged items.

Using these parameters, you can create meaningful retention tags for your content. The following example creates a tag that archives every message after 5 years (1,825 days):

```
New-RetentionPolicyTag "RPT-ArchiveAfter5Years" -Type All ↵
-MessageClass E-mail –AgeLimitForRetention 1825 ↵
-RetentionAction MoveToArchive -RetentionEnabled $True
```

Link Retention Tags to Retention Policies

Now that you have a retention tag created, you need to create a retention policy to link the tag to. You can use the New-RetentionPolicy cmdlet in the EMS to create the new policy. You can link the retention tags to the policy when you create it, or you can do it later. The following example creates a new retention policy and applies the tag we created previously:

```
New-RetentionPolicy "RP-FinancialTeam" ↵
-RetentionPolicyTagLinks "RPT-ArchiveAfter5Years"
```

You can also link a retention tag to an existing policy using the Set-RetentionPolicy cmdlet. You will need to specify the RetentionPolicyTagLinks parameter and list all the tags that apply to the policy, separated by commas.

WARNING   If you omit a retention tag that is already linked to the retention policy, the tag will be removed.

The following example illustrates how the retention tag is linked to an existing retention policy:

```
Set-RetentionPolicy "RP-FinancialTeam" ↵
-RetentionPolicyTagLinks "RPT-ArchiveAfter5Years", ↵
"RPT-Default"
```

Apply Retention Policies to Mailboxes

After the retention policy is created and retention tags are linked to it, you can apply the policy to mailboxes. To do this, use the Set-Mailbox cmdlet with the RetentionPolicy parameter:

```
Set-Mailbox "John Smith" -RetentionPolicy RP-FinancialTeam
```

You may receive a prompt indicating that retention policies are only supported by certain Outlook versions. If you are sure that the user using this mailbox meets this requirement, press Y and then Enter to continue. The policy will be applied on the next scheduled managed folder processing run.

Suspend Retention Policies on a Mailbox

If users are away for an extended period of time, such as on vacation, it might be a good idea to suspend any retention policies until they get back. If not, users might not get an opportunity to review any messages that the retention policy would cause to be deleted or moved. You can do this by placing a mailbox on retention hold.

Mitigating Risk

PART III

TIP Be careful not to confuse retention hold and litigation hold. In retention hold, the messages can be deleted permanently and not returned in discovery searches. But in litigation hold, everything is kept for as long as the mailbox is in litigation hold. Retention hold just suspends the retention policies so that items aren't deleted or moved while the user is away.

To place a mailbox on retention hold using the EMC, follow these steps:

1. Open the EMC and browse to the Recipient Configuration ➤ Mailbox node in the Console tree.

2. In the Results pane, select the mailbox that you want to place on retention hold.

3. In the Actions pane, click Properties for the mailbox that you have selected.

4. In the properties dialog box for the mailbox, select the Mailbox Settings tab.

5. In the list of mailbox settings, select Messaging Records Management and click the Properties button.

6. In the Messaging Records Management dialog box, select the Enable Retention Hold For Items In This Mailbox check box. If you know the time period that the user will be away, you can set a start and end date for the retention hold, as you can see in Figure 9.6.

   When the time expires, retention hold is automatically lifted from the mailbox. Click OK to close the Messaging Records Management dialog box.

7. Click OK to close the properties dialog box and apply the retention hold.

To place a mailbox on retention hold in the EMS, you can use the Set-Mailbox cmdlet with the EnableRetentionHold parameter, as shown here:

```
Set-Mailbox "John Smith" -RetentionHoldEnabled $true
```

When the user returns to work, you can take the mailbox out of retention hold by setting the RetentionHoldEnabled parameter to $false.

Figure 9.6: Setting a time period for retention hold

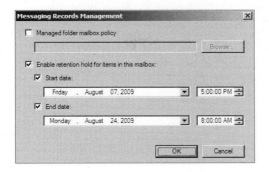

Convert from Managed Folders to Retention Tags

Both managed folders and retention tags exist in Exchange Server 2010. They both accomplish the same goal. If your environment consists only of Outlook versions that can support retention tags (such as Outlook 2010), you can solely use retention tags for managing content instead of managed folders. You can convert your existing managed folders into retention tags by using an existing managed folder as a template.

To create a retention tag that uses a managed folder as a template, you can run the `New-RetentionPolicyTag` cmdlet and specify the `ManagedFolderToUpgrade` parameter. The following example creates a new retention tag that mirrors an existing managed folder:

```
New-RetentionPolicyTag "RPT-ProjectABC" ↵
-ManagedFolderToUpgrade "Project ABC"
```

Archive Email

A new feature of Exchange Server 2010 is the ability for users to have online email archives. One of the challenges of Exchange over the years has been controlling the size of user mailboxes. Many users got into the habit of moving email out of their inbox and into personal folders (PST files). When mail is moved to Personal Storage Table (PST) files, it is removed from the mail server and the user regains some of the space allocated for their mail quota. The problem is that PST files reside on user workstations or sometimes even network shares, which makes the email inside the files unmanageable. It's up to the user to back up the PST files, and if a PST gets corrupted, all the data can be lost with no backup to restore from.

Mitigating Risk

PART III

The online archive in Exchange Server 2010 can replace PST files. Users can drag and drop email from their mailbox or from existing PSTs into their online archive, which has a bigger storage quota than the mailbox. Unlike PST files, the archive is accessible in Outlook Web Access as well as locally in Outlook 2010. Large amounts of data can reside in an archive folder because the archive is only available online. Users do not need to download many gigabytes of data into their Outlook client when working in cached mode with the online archive.

Create an Archive for a User

You can create an archive for new users up front when you create their mailboxes or you can add the archive to existing mailboxes at any time. Creating the archive mailbox is an easy process and users don't have to do anything to enable it. Outlook 2010 determines whether a user has an archive mailbox during the AutoDiscover query. When the archive mailbox is added for a user, it will simply appear in Outlook after a few minutes. The user can close Outlook and reopen it to expedite this process.

You can create an archive for a new user when you create the mailbox in the EMC. To do so, follow the steps outlined in Chapter 4, "Administering Recipients." When you get to the Archive Settings dialog box, select the Create An Archive Mailbox For This Account check box, as shown in Figure 9.7.

Figure 9.7: Enabling the archive on a new mailbox

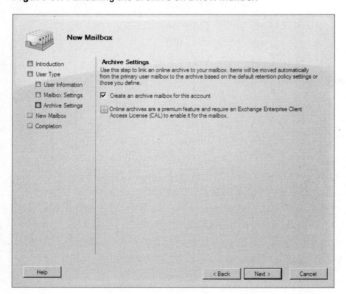

You can also use the EMS to create the archive when you create the mailbox. You will need to use the `Archive` parameter when you run the `New-Mailbox` cmdlet. The following example creates a new mailbox with an archive attached to it. This command does not specify the password of the new mailbox, so you will be prompted for a password when you run the command:

```
New-Mailbox "Doug Fidler" -UserPrincipalName ↵
doug@contoso.com -Archive
```

Enabling archiving for existing mailboxes is also a simple task. To enable an archive in the EMC, use the following steps:

1. Open the EMC and browse to the Recipient Configuration ➤ Mailbox node in the Console tree.

2. From the list of existing mailboxes, select the mailbox that you want to create an archive for.

3. In the Actions pane, click the Enable Archive action, as shown in Figure 9.8.

4. You may be prompted with an informational dialog box, explaining that you need an Enterprise Client Access License for the archive and asking you if you want to proceed. If you have the required license, click the Yes button and the archive is created.

Figure 9.8: Creating an archive for an existing mailbox

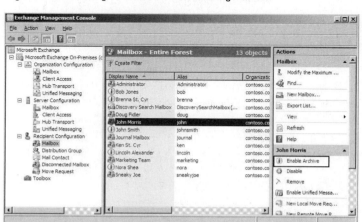

Mitigating Risk

PART III

To enable an archive for an existing user in the EMS, use the `Enable-Mailbox` cmdlet with the `Archive` parameter. For example, the following command creates an archive for a mailbox that already exists:

```
Enable-Mailbox "Nora Shea" -Archive
```

Modify the Archive Quota

Like primary user mailboxes, archive mailboxes have quotas that apply to them. However, when an archive mailbox reaches its quota, the user's ability to send and receive email is not restricted.

There is a warning quota and a hard quota. When an archive reaches the warning quota, an event is logged in the server's Application event log. When the hard quota is reached, items can no longer be placed in the archive. You can modify the warning quota in the EMC or the EMS, but the hard quota must be modified in the EMS.

To modify the archive warning quota, follow these steps in the EMC:

1. Open the EMC and browse to the Recipient Configuration ➢ Mailbox node in the Console tree.

2. In the Results pane, select the mailbox that you want to adjust the archive quota for.

3. In the Actions pane, click the Properties task under the Action menu of the mailbox that you selected. This displays the properties dialog box for the mailbox.

4. In the properties dialog box, select the Mailbox Settings tab.

5. In the list of mailbox settings, select Archive Quota and click the Properties button above the list.

6. In the Archive Quota dialog box, select the Issue Warning At (MB) check box and enter a size limit in the text field, as shown in Figure 9.9.

Figure 9.9: Placing a warning quota on the archive

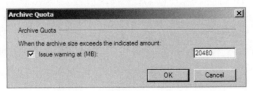

You can modify both the warning quota and the hard quota in the EMS. Use the `Set-Mailbox` cmdlet and specify the `ArchiveWarningQuota` parameter (for the warning quota) or the `ArchiveQuota` parameter (for the hard quota). The following example demonstrates this command:

```
Set-Mailbox "John Smith" -ArchiveWarningQuota 20GB ↵
-ArchiveQuota 25GB
```

Retrieve Statistical Data on an Archive

Similar to primary mailboxes, archive mailboxes have statistical data that you can gather. This data allows you to see various aspects of the archive, such as the number of items in the archive and the size of the items.

To view the statistics of an archive, you can use the `Get-MailboxStatistics` cmdlet in the EMS and specify the `Archive` parameter. For example, the following command retrieves the archive statistics for a mailbox:

```
Get-MailboxStatistics "John Smith" -Archive
```

Import PSTs into an Archive

Users can pull data out of their mailbox or their PST files and drop it directly into the archive. The archive appears in the user's Outlook view at the same level as a PST file would. This is illustrated in Figure 9.10.

Users can simply drag folders or items from the PST file and drop them into a folder in the archive. This is a manual process that is completed by the user. There is no automated way to search out PST files and import them into the archive.

Keep a Record of Email Communications

Some organizations are required to keep an account of every message sent and received in the organization or by specific users. This is particularly true in the financial industry, as several laws and regulations govern how electronic communications should be handled and retained. Exchange offers multiple ways to help organizations meet these regulations. One of these ways is called journaling. Journaling silently copies messages to an alternate mailbox, which is designated as the journal mailbox.

Mitigating Risk

PART III

Figure 9.10: The online archive in Outlook

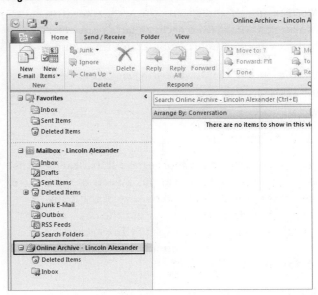

Journaling does come with some challenges. Since large volumes of information are sent across messaging systems, journal mailboxes can quickly get very large. Because of this, many organizations will not journal their entire user base. Some organizations might also use a third-party archiving system to manage the size of journal mailboxes by removing messages from journal mailboxes and keeping them elsewhere.

In this section, you'll learn how to configure journaling in your organization.

Configure Journaling for an Entire Mailbox Database

In Exchange, you can configure journaling on a mailbox database. Every message sent or received by every user on that database will be sent to the Journaling mailbox. When you turn on journaling at the database level, this is known as standard journaling. To configure standard journaling on a database in the EMC, use the following steps:

1. Open the EMC and browse to the Organization Configuration ➤ Mailbox node in the Console tree.

2. In the Work area, click the Database Management tab.

3. From the list of databases, select the mailbox database that you want to enable journaling on.

4. In the Actions pane, click the Properties task that corresponds to the database that you have selected. This opens the properties dialog box for the database.

5. In the properties dialog box, click the Maintenance tab.

6. Check the Journal Recipient box.

7. Click the Browse button to select the mailbox that journal reports are sent to. In the Select Recipient dialog box, select the journal mailbox and click OK.

8. In the properties dialog box for the database, click OK to apply the journaling changes and close the dialog box. Figure 9.11 shows the mailbox database properties with a journal recipient designated.

Figure 9.11: Configuring a journal recipient for a mailbox database

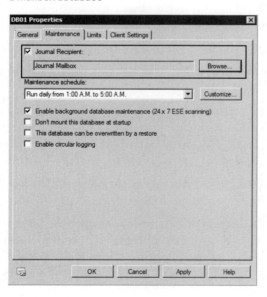

You can also enable standard journaling with the EMS using the Set-MailboxDatabase cmdlet. Specify the JournalRecipient parameter and include the address of the journal mailbox. The following command demonstrates this usage:

```
Set-MailboxDatabase "DB01" -JournalRecipient ↵
journal@contoso.com
```

Mitigating Risk

PART III

If you want to turn off journaling on a mailbox database, you use the same command, except specify $null instead of a journal mailbox address, as shown here:

```
Set-MailboxDatabase "DB01" -JournalRecipient $null
```

Configure Journaling for Specific Users

You also have the ability to journal messages sent and received by specific users only. This process uses a feature called journal rules. Journal rules are applied by Transport servers as they process messages that pass through them. Journal rules define what messages are journaled for which users. You have the option of journaling all messages, messages sent inside the organization, or messages sent outside the organization.

You can configure a journal rule using the following steps in the EMC:

1. Open the EMC and browse to the Organization Configuration ➢ Hub Transport node in the Console tree.

2. In the Actions pane on the right, select the New Journal Rule task.

3. In the New Journal Rule wizard, type a name for the rule in the Rule Name field.

4. In the field Send Journal Reports To E-mail Address, click the Browse button and select the mailbox that you want to use as the journal mailbox. You can select an individual mailbox or a distribution group.

5. In the Scope section, select whether all messages will be journaled or only internal or external messages.

6. In the Journal Messages For Recipient field, click the Browse button and select the mailbox of the user that you want to journal. You can journal multiple mailboxes in this rule if you select a distribution group instead of a single mailbox.

7. Ensure that Enable Rule is checked and click the New button to create the journal rule. Figure 9.12 shows how a journal rule may be configured.

8. At the Completion screen, click Finish.

You can also use the EMS to configure journaling for specific users. To do so, you use the New-JournalRule cmdlet. Table 9.2 describes the parameters used in this command.

Figure 9.12: Creating a new journal rule

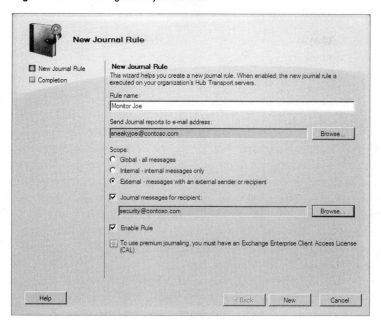

Table 9.2: Parameters Used When Creating a New Journal Rule

Parameter	Description
Name	The name of the rule.
JournalEmailAddress	The email address of the person or distribution group that you are journaling.
Recipient	The address of the mailbox that the journaled messages are sent to.
Scope	Determines which types of messages are journaled. This value can be either Global (all messages), Internal (messages inside the organization), or External (messages outside the organization).
Enabled	Set to $true to enable the journal rule.

Mitigating Risk

PART III

The following example configures the same journaling that we set in the EMC, as shown in Figure 9.12:

```
New-JournalRule "Monitor Joe" -JournalEmailAddress ↵
sneakyjoe@contoso.com -Recipient security@contoso.com ↵
-Scope External -Enabled $true
```

Secure the Journal Mailbox

When you enable journaling, you need to specify the mailbox that messages are sent to. This mailbox must be adequately protected. Sensitive information is stored in the journal mailbox that only certain people should have access to. Also, the journal mailbox should only accept messages from the Journal Agent. The Journal Agent is what applies the journaling rules and sends journal reports to the journal mailbox. By restricting who can send messages to the mailbox, you ensure that no false data is injected into the mailbox.

To provide these protective capabilities to an existing journal mailbox, you use the Set-Mailbox cmdlet in the EMS. To secure a journal mailbox, use the following EMS command:

```
Set-Mailbox "Journal Mailbox" -AcceptMessagesOnlyFrom ↵
"Microsoft Exchange" -RequireSenderAuthenticationEnabled ↵
$true
```

Protect and Disclose Information

When an organization is in the midst of a legal battle, it's vital that they be able to capture and produce important information quickly. Exchange helps in this area by providing new ways to ensure that messages cannot be modified or deleted. Exchange also provides a new discovery capability, which allows multiple mailboxes to be searched for information. This section discusses how to implement and use these features.

Perform Search and Discovery of Email

Exchange Server 2010 has introduced the concept of email discovery. With email discovery, multiple mailboxes can be searched for items that contain keywords. Discovery searches are restricted to people who have explicit permissions. When used in conjunction with litigation holds (discussed later in this section), discovery can uncover messages that users deleted and restore the original versions of messages users have modified.

Discovery searches are performed using the Exchange Control Panel (ECP), which is a web service that is accessible through Client Access servers in a similar manner as Outlook Web App (OWA). In this section, you'll learn how to use discovery searches.

Create a New Discovery Search

When you create a discovery search, you define the parameters that are used for searching across mailboxes. You can specify multiple keywords as well as parameters such as OR and AND. After you create a discovery search, it is available for other people with discovery permissions to view, modify, and rerun. Use the following steps to create a discovery search:

1. Open a web browser and navigate to the ECP URL on one of your Client Access servers. The ECP is hosted on Client Access servers in a similar manner to how OWA is hosted. A Client Access server that can be used for OWA can also likely be used for ECP as well. For example, the ECP URL on an internal Client Access server in Contoso may be https://contoso-cas1/ecp. If there is an Internet-facing server, the URL could be https://mail.contoso.com/ecp.

2. Log into the web interface with an account that has access to create and execute discovery searches. To give someone such access, follow the steps in the section "Allow People to Search Mailboxes," later in this chapter.

3. After you are logged into the ECP, ensure that My Organization is selected in the drop-down list in the upper left, as shown in Figure 9.13. If you don't see this drop-down list, that means you don't have permission to perform discovery searches.

Figure 9.13: Ensure that My Organization is selected in the ECP.

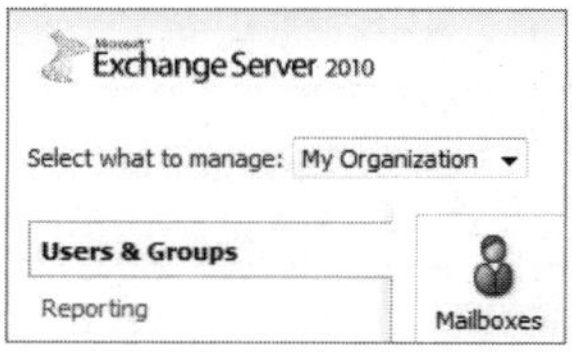

Select what to manage: My Organization ▼

Users & Groups

Reporting

Mailboxes

Mitigating Risk

PART III

4. In the list of categories on the left side of the ECP, select Reporting.

5. In the list of tabs along the top of the Reporting interface, select the Mailbox Searches tab, as shown in Figure 9.14.

Figure 9.14: Select the Mailbox Searches tab.

6. This is your primary interface for creating and executing discovery searches. To create a new search, click the New button in the Multi-Mailbox Search tool.

   The New Mailbox Search dialog box opens. If you get a certificate error, you may still be using an untrusted self-signed certificate. Click the option Continue To This Website.

7. In the New Mailbox Search dialog box, under the Keywords category, enter the keywords that you want to search for, as shown in Figure 9.15.

8. To search for messages to or from specific users, click the category Messages To And From Specific E-Mail Addresses.

9. Click the Date Range category to select the range of dates that you want to search in.

10. Select the category Mailboxes To Search. You can choose the option Search All Mailboxes, or you can add specific mailboxes to the list by clicking the Add button.

11. Click the Search Name And Storage Location category. In the Search Name field, type a name for this search. When naming your search, remember that other users with discovery search permission can also execute this search, so make it as descriptive as you need it to be.

12. In the field Select A Mailbox In Which To Store The Search Results, click the Browse button and choose the discovery mailbox that the results will be stored in.

Figure 9.15: Adding keywords to search for

13. You can also check the box Send Me An E-Mail When The Search Is Done. Searches may take a long time to complete if many mailboxes are involved. If you select this box, you will receive an email notification when the search is complete.

14. When you have finished filling out the search options, click the Save button, as shown in Figure 9.16.

Figure 9.16: Saving a discovery search

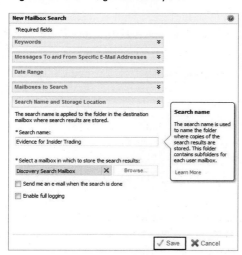

Rerun a Discovery Search

After you create a discovery search, the search is executed and the results are stored in the discovery mailbox that you designated. You can rerun this search at any time to refresh the results. When you rerun the search, the items that are already in the discovery mailbox are deleted and the new search results are populated instead.

To rerun a discovery search, use the following steps:

1. Open a web browser and navigate to the ECP URL on a Client Access server. This URL is typically the URL for the server with /ecp appended—for example, `https://contoso-cas1/ecp` or `https://mail.contoso.com/ecp`.

2. After logging into the web application, you will be taken to the ECP page for your organization. Ensure that My Organization is selected from the drop-down list in the upper left. If this list isn't present, that means you don't have permissions to perform discovery searches.

3. In the category list on the left side of the ECP, select Reporting.

4. In the list of tabs in the Reporting category, select the Mailbox Searches tab. This tab is only available if you have permissions to perform discovery searches.

5. Every search is listed in the Multi-Mailbox Search tool. If you click on a search, you can view information about the search, including the last time that the search was run, as shown in Figure 9.17.

6. To rerun the search, select the search that you want to rerun and click the Restart Search icon, which is highlighted in Figure 9.18.

Figure 9.17: Viewing information about an existing search

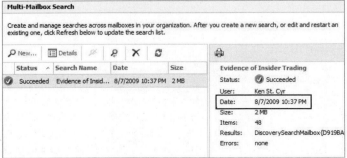

7. You may be prompted with a warning that says the existing search results will be removed from the discovery mailbox. This is expected if the mailbox holds results from a previous search. Click the Yes button to continue.

Figure 9.18: Rerunning a search

View the Results of a Discovery Search

When a discovery search is executed, the emails that are included in the search result list are copied to a discovery mailbox that you specified when you set up the search. The discovery mailbox is a resource mailbox, which has no specific owner. Only people who have permissions to the discovery mailbox can view the results of the search.

You can view the results of the discovery search by clicking the Open link in the properties pane next to the discovery search. This is illustrated in Figure 9.19.

Figure 9.19: Opening the discovery mailbox containing the search results

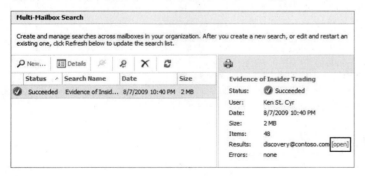

When you click the Open link, the discovery mailbox will be opened in OWA for you to view just like any other regular mailbox. The search results are stored in the mailbox under a folder with the same name as the search you created. If you open this folder, you will notice that each mailbox that had messages discovered by the search is listed as a separate

Mitigating Risk

PART III

folder. Inside these mailbox folders, the folder hierarchies are maintained, as shown in Figure 9.20. Preserving the folder hierarchy is sometimes useful in a court case.

Figure 9.20: The folder hierarchy of the discovery search results

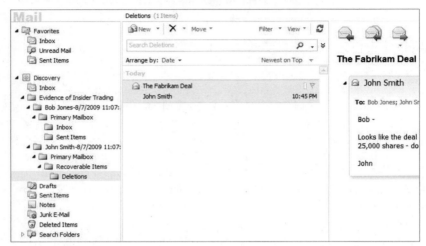

One thing you will notice in the example is a folder called Recoverable Items. This folder contains the messages that the user deleted.

TIP The discovery search doesn't just search against the mail in a user's mailbox; it also searches against the user's archive. When messages are in PST files, they are not searched, but if you require users to move their data from PSTs to their online archive, you then will have this data to search across as well.

Create a Discovery Mailbox

By default, one discovery mailbox is created when Exchange is installed. You can create additional discovery mailboxes that store results for different searches. You can then give different people permissions to those specific discovery mailboxes. For example, a lawyer may want to create a search and store the results in a mailbox that a paralegal has access to. In this case, the lawyer can maintain access to create and run the searches, while the paralegal can only view the results.

To create a discovery mailbox, you must use the EMS. Run the New-Mailbox cmdlet with the Discovery parameter. The following command creates a new discovery mailbox:

```
New-Mailbox "Discovery Mailbox - Insider Trading" ↵
-UserPrincipalName discovery1@contoso.com -Discovery
```

Allow People to Search Mailboxes

You can give users access to create and execute searches using the ECP or the EMS. To give a user the ability to search mailboxes, you must delegate that user to the Discovery Management role. If you want users to be able to view the results of the search, they need full access to the discovery mailbox in which the search results are stored.

Delegate Discovery Management in the ECP

To delegate the Discovery Management role in the ECP, use the following steps:

1. Open a web browser and navigate to the ECP URL on a Client Access server. This URL is typically the URL for the server with /ecp appended—for example, https://contoso-cas1/ecp or https://mail.contoso.com/ecp.

2. After logging into the web application, you will be taken to the ECP page for your organization. Ensure that My Organization is selected from the drop-down list in the upper left. If this list isn't present, that means you don't have permission to delegate the Discovery Management role to other users.

3. In the category list on the left side of the ECP, select Users & Groups.

4. In the list of tabs in the Users & Groups category, select the Administrator Roles tab. These tabs are only available if you have the permission to delegate roles.

5. In the list of Role Groups, select the Discovery Management role group and click the Details button, as shown in Figure 9.21.

6. In the Role Group dialog box, click the Add button under the Members section. In the Select Members dialog box, double-click the users to whom you want to give Discovery Management permissions and click OK. After you have added people to the list, click the Save button. This is shown in Figure 9.22.

Figure 9.21: Modifying the Discovery Management role group

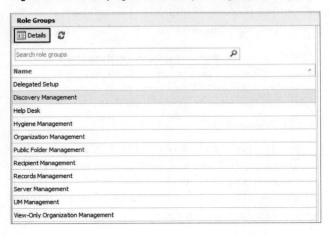

Figure 9.22: Adding people to the Discovery Management role

Delegate Discovery Management in the EMS

You can also give users the right to perform discovery searches by using the `Add-RoleGroupMember` cmdlet in the EMS. You will need to specify the user that you are adding to the role. The following example illustrates this command:

```
Add-RoleGroupMember "Discovery Management" -Member ↵
"Nora Shea"
```

If you want to see who else has discovery management permissions, run the following EMS command:

```
Get-RoleGroupMember "Discovery Management"
```

Add Disclaimers and Ensure Message Integrity

Exchange Server 2010 provides many features that help your organization protect its information. Two of these features are automatic disclaimers and litigation hold. Disclaimers are not guaranteed to protect you in a lawsuit, but they may help in making you exempt from liabilities. Litigation hold helps to preserve data and ensure that it hasn't been tampered with by users. This section walks you through the process of setting up disclaimers and putting mailboxes on litigation hold.

Add Automatic Disclaimers to Messages

A disclaimer is a statement that you can add at the end of email messages that recipients can view. These are usually legal statements that are required to be on messages for compliance reasons. Many organizations attach disclaimers to messages going outside the organization. The following is a sample of a disclaimer:

This message is intended only for the parties that are addressed as recipients. This message may contain confidential information that is legally protected. Any unauthorized use, distribution, or modification is strictly prohibited.

Disclaimers are stamped on messages by Transport servers. To set up a disclaimer, you must create a new transport rule. Transport rules are covered in detail later in this chapter in the section called "Perform Basic Message Policy Configuration."

Use the following steps to append a disclaimer to all messages in your organization:

1. Open the EMC and browse to the Organization Configuration ➢ Hub Transport node in the Console tree.

2. In the Actions pane, click the New Transport Rule task. This will launch the New Transport Rule wizard.

3. In the Introduction screen, type a name such as **Disclaimer** in the Name field. Click Next to continue.

4. This disclaimer will apply to all messages, so in the Conditions screen, do not select anything. Click Next and you will then be prompted with a dialog box informing you that this disclaimer will apply to all messages sent. Click Yes to continue.

5. On the Actions screen, select the action Append Disclaimer Text And Fallback To Action If Unable To Apply.

6. In the rule description text box below the selected action, click the blue, underlined text that reads disclaimer text. The Specify Disclaimer Text dialog box appears, allowing you to type your disclaimer.

7. After you have typed your disclaimer, click OK to return to the wizard. The Actions dialog box should now be configured in a way that is similar to Figure 9.23.

   Click the Next button to continue.

8. At the Exceptions screen, ensure that no exceptions are selected and click Next.

9. On the Create Rule screen, click New to create the rule.

10. On the Completion screen, click Finish to complete the process and close the wizard.

Place a Litigation Hold on a Mailbox

In Exchange Server 2010, you have the ability to place a litigation hold on a mailbox. While a mailbox is in litigation hold, all deleted and edited items are preserved and will be included in discovery searches, which were covered earlier in this chapter. Litigation hold is likely to be used by organizations during a lawsuit or an investigation. The mailboxes of people involved can be placed on hold, preserving all the data.

Figure 9.23: Configuring the disclaimer message

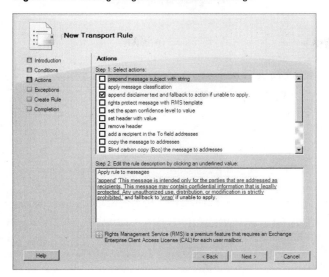

When a mailbox is on hold, the deleted and edited items are placed in hidden folders. There is no apparent impact on the users, and the users on hold will not even be aware of it unless they are notified.

To place a mailbox in litigation hold, you can use the `Set-Mailbox` cmdlet in the EMS. Set the `LitigationHoldEnabled` parameter to `$true` to turn litigation hold on. The following example shows how to place a mailbox on litigation hold:

```
Set-Mailbox "John Smith" -LitigationHoldEnabled
```

Monitor and Restrict Communication

Every organization has legal or ethical obligations that require the enforcement of rules around electronic communications. Many of these situations can be damaging to organizations and pose legal risks that can cost the organization a lot of money. Sometimes it's necessary to implement some form of monitoring or restriction to limit the damage to the company and to protect the people involved. In this portion of the chapter, I will show you how to use basic message policies in Exchange and walk you through some common scenarios where you may want to monitor and restrict communications.

Mitigating Risk

PART III

Perform Basic Message Policy Configuration

Exchange Server 2010 is very flexible in how policies can be applied to messages and what actions can be taken based on those policies. The underlying engine for enforcing policies on messages at a basic level is the transport rule. In this section, I'll help you understand what transport rules are and show you how to configure basic rules based on predefined criteria inside Exchange.

Understand Transport Rules

When a message is sent by a user in Exchange, it always passes through a Transport server. This occurs even when the mailboxes are on the same server or even in the same database. This design helps ensure that all messages flowing through an organization run through a common process before being delivered.

When a Transport server processes a message, it can apply transport rules to the message. Transport rules allow specific policies to be applied to messages, and an action can be taken based on those policies. For example, you could create a transport rule that notifies Bob's manager when Bob sends an email to Joe. You can even have more complex transport rules that do things such as filter information based on certain keywords contained in the message.

You can create transport rules for both Hub Transport and Edge Transport servers. In Exchange Server 2010, transport rules created for Hub Transport servers exist at the organization level. These rules are replicated to every Hub Transport server, and each server applies them to messages that flow through its transport pipeline. This ensures that you don't have to configure transport rules separately on each Hub Transport server.

When you create a transport rule on an Edge Transport server, the rule is stored in the server's Active Directory Lightweight Directory Service store and only applies to that server. Edge servers do not replicate transport rules.

Configure Transport Rules

Transport rules are flexible and you can create rules to meet a variety of conditions. To illustrate how to create and customize a transport rule, I'm going to walk you through the process of creating a rule that notifies Bob Jones's manager, John Morris, when Bob sends an email to anyone in a competitor organization name Fabrikam Motors.

1. Open the EMC and browse to the Organization Configuration ≻ Hub Transport node in the Console tree.

2. In the Actions pane, click the New Transport Rule action. This launches the New Transport Rule wizard.

3. In the Introduction screen, type a name for the Transport Rule in the Name field. Click Next to continue.

4. In the Conditions dialog box, select the conditions that cause this rule to be applied. In this example, I will select the From People condition and the When A Specific Recipient's Address Contains Specific Words condition.

   When you select these conditions, they are added to the text box in the bottom half of the dialog box. You can click on the blue, underlined text in this box to specify the conditions that the rule must match. For example, click on the term "people" to select the people who will trigger this rule. Figure 9.24 illustrates how I have configured the conditions for our example scenario.

   After you have set the conditions, click the Next button.

Figure 9.24: Configuring the conditions for a transport rule

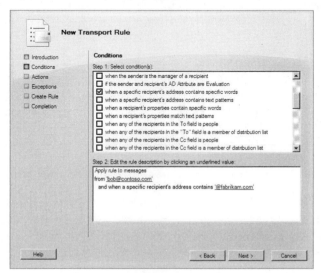

5. On the Actions screen, you will determine what actions are taken on the message. When you select an action from the list, the action is added into the rule description text box below it.

In this scenario, I added the action Add The Sender's Manager As A Specific Recipient Type and adjusted the recipient type to BCC in the rule description field, as shown in Figure 9.25.

Figure 9.25: Configuring the actions taken on a message by a transport rule

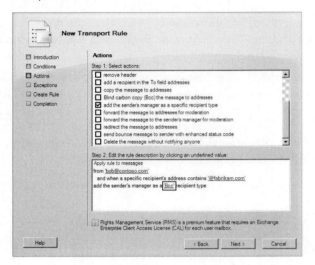

NOTE In this example, the transport rule determines who Bob's manager is based on his account in Active Directory. I could have also defined John Morris as a specific BCC'd recipient on the message if I'd wanted to.

Click the Next button to continue after setting up your actions.

6. On the Exceptions screen, you can define an exception for this rule. For example, there may be cases when you don't want this rule to apply. This example will not use any exceptions. Click Next to continue.

7. At the Create Rule screen, click New to create the rule.

8. On the Completion screen, click Finish to complete the process and close the wizard.

Disable Transport Rules

You can temporarily suspend the application of a transport rule by disabling it. Disabling the rule keeps the rule in place but ensures that it's not applied to any users. To disable a transport rule in EMC, follow these steps:

1. Open the EMC and browse to the Organization Configuration ➢ Hub Transport node in the Console tree.

2. In the Work area, select the Transport Rules tab. A list of current transport rules is displayed.

3. Select the transport rule that you want to disable.

4. In the Actions pane, click the Disable Rule task under the Action menu for the rule that you selected. This is shown in Figure 9.26.

5. You will get a warning dialog box, asking you if you are sure that you want to disable the rule. Click Yes to continue.

Figure 9.26: Disabling a transport rule

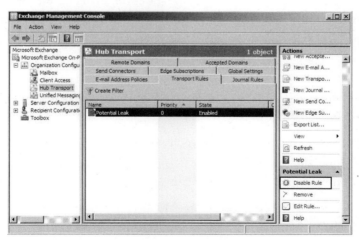

You can also disable a transport rule using the `Disable-TransportRule` cmdlet in the EMS. The following example demonstrates this command:

```
Disable-TransportRule "Potential Leak" -Confirm:$false
```

Apply Common Monitoring and Restriction Scenarios

This section of the chapter walks you through a few fictitious scenarios where monitoring or restricting email would be a good idea. You'll learn how to do the following:

- Prevent two parties from sending email to each other.

- Require approval by a third party when messages are sent about a specific topic.

- Monitor email between two people without their knowledge.

Restrict Communications with an Ethical Wall

In Exchange Server 2010, you can restrict communications between parties using an *ethical wall*. An ethical wall is a transport rule that drops messages from one party to another. Some organizations may implement ethical walls to prevent any potential conflicts of interest. For example, some large contracting organizations may have multiple programs that compete for the same contract. You could use an ethical wall to prevent these programs from exchanging messages.

To establish an ethical wall, you can use a transport rule that drops messages. The high-level steps for configuring an ethical wall are as follows:

1. Create two distribution groups and place both parties in different groups.

2. Create a transport rule to drop messages and return a Non-Delivery Report (NDR) when a message is sent from the members of one group to another.

To create an ethical wall between two parties using the EMC:

1. Open the EMC and browse to the Organization Configuration ➢ Hub Transport node in the Console tree.

2. In the Actions pane, click the New Transport Rule action. This launches the New Transport Rule wizard.

3. On the Introduction screen, type a name for the transport rule, such as **Ethical Wall between Program A and Program B**, in the Name field. Ensure that the Enable Rule box is checked and click Next.

4. On the Conditions screen, select the condition Between Members Of Distribution List And Distribution List. In the rule description

text box, click on the words Distribution List and select the two distribution groups that should not communicate with each other. This completed configuration is shown in Figure 9.27.

Figure 9.27: Configuring ethical wall conditions

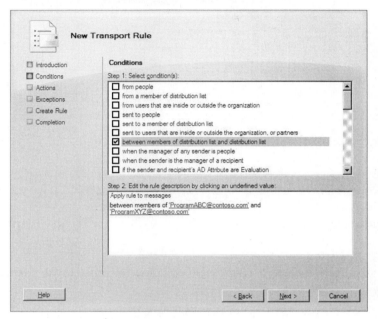

Click the Next button to continue.

5. In the Actions dialog box, select the action Send Rejection Message To Sender With Enhanced Status Code. In the rule description text box, modify the Rejection Message text to the message that you want the sender to receive when mail is sent to the other party.

   Also, change the Enhanced Status Code to 5.7.1, which is a standard message rejection code. The configuration of the actions is shown in Figure 9.28.

   Click Next to continue.

6. On the Exceptions screen, leave everything unchecked and click Next.

Figure 9.28: Specifying the ethical wall actions

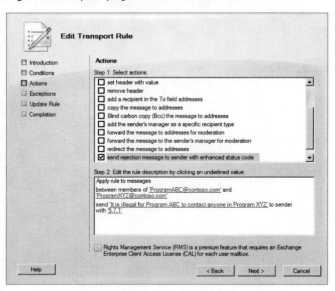

7. On the Create Rule screen, click New to create the ethical wall.

8. At the Completion screen, click Finish to complete the process and close the wizard.

Enforce Email Approval Based on Keyword

A scenario that you may encounter is the potential leakage of important information about a topic. In this scenario, there have been leaks to the public about Contoso's new product called "Arius." Contoso doesn't want to restrict all communication about Arius, but it does want to ensure that any explicitly malicious communication is caught. In this scenario I will show you how to create a rule that forwards messages that are sent outside the company about Arius to the marketing team for approval. To configure this email inspection rule in the EMC, use the following steps:

1. Open the EMC and browse to the Organization Configuration ➢ Hub Transport node in the Console tree.

2. In the Actions pane, click the New Transport Rule task. This launches the New Transport Rule wizard.

3. On the Introduction screen, type a name for the transport rule, such as **Arius Approval,** in the Name field. Ensure that the Enable Rule box is checked and click Next.

4. On the Conditions screen, select the condition When The Subject Field Or The Body Of The Message Contains Text Patterns. In the rule description text box, click on the words Text Patterns and type the keywords that you want to trigger this rule. In this scenario, I will only use the keyword arius.

   Also select the condition Sent To Users That Are Inside Or Outside The Organization, Or Partners. In the rule description, set this rule to trigger when messages are sent outside the organization. This completed configuration is shown in Figure 9.29.

Figure 9.29: Configuring the conditions for email inspection

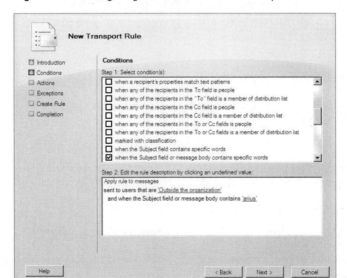

Click Next to continue.

5. On the Actions screen, select the action Forward The Message To Addresses For Moderation. In the rule description text box, click the Addresses text and select the mailbox that you want to use for approving these messages. In this scenario, the marketing@contoso .com mailbox will approve all external communications about Arius.

   The configuration of the actions is shown in Figure 9.30.

Mitigating Risk

PART III

Figure 9.30: Specifying the approver for moderated messages

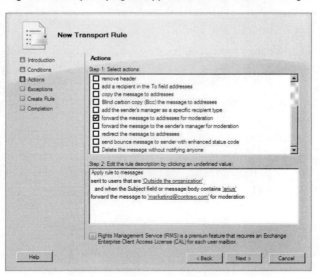

Click Next to continue.

6. On the Exception screen, leave everything unchecked and click Next.

7. On the Create Rule screen, click New to create the ethical wall.

8. At the Completion screen, click Finish to complete the process and close the wizard.

Quietly Monitor Communications Between Certain Parties

In this final scenario, Contoso suspects that one of their employees, John Morris, is collaborating with Bob Jones in accounting, in order to launder money for an underground crime ring. One acceptable way of monitoring communications between John and Bob is through journaling. However, journaling will obtain everything sent and received by those two people instead of just the messages that they sent to each other. Therefore, we will use a transport rule to monitor the email conversations between Bob and John without them knowing.

1. Open the EMC and browse to the Organization Configuration ➢ Hub Transport node in the Console tree.

2. In the Actions pane, click the New Transport Rule task. This launches the New Transport Rule wizard.

3. On the Introduction screen, type a name for the transport rule, such as **Monitor Bob and John,** in the Name field. Ensure that the Enable Rule box is checked and click Next.

4. At the Conditions screen, select the conditions From People and Sent To People. In the rule description text box, click the word People and select John and Bob's addresses. Click Next to continue.

5. On the Actions screen, select the action Blind Carbon Copy (Bcc) The Message To Addresses. In the rule description text box, click the Addresses text and select the mailbox that you want to use for monitoring these messages. This configuration is shown in Figure 9.31.

Figure 9.31: Configuring the transport rule to monitor email communications

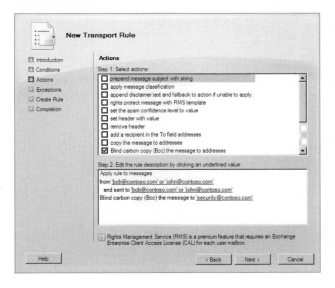

Click Next to continue.

6. On the Exception screen, leave everything unchecked and click Next.

7. On the Create Rule screen, click New to create the ethical wall.

8. At the Completion screen, click Finish to complete the process and close the wizard.

10

Maintaining Reliability and Availability

IN THIS CHAPTER, YOU WILL LEARN TO:

Mitigating Risk

PART III

t could be well said that perhaps the most important job for any Exchange administrator is to keep the mail system up and running. Sometimes, a downed messaging infrastructure could cause more harm than just a few unsatisfied end-users. Many organizations consider email to be a mission critical service. In these organizations, if email goes down, the mission can't be accomplished. There are many organizations where an email outage can hurt financially, and the financial loss isn't always caused by lost revenue. Some IT organizations have Service Level Agreements (SLAs) that dictate the acceptable length and frequency of unanticipated outages. In many cases, when an SLA isn't met, there is a financial penalty to be paid. The truth is that keeping Exchange highly available isn't always easy. There are many parts that make up Exchange, and in many cases, each of those parts needs a different method of high availability.

In this chapter, we're going to explore the availability and reliability aspects of Exchange. We'll start out by looking at the availability options for different Exchange server roles. Here, you'll learn how to maximize your up-time for your servers. Then, we'll look more at backup and recovery. I'll show you how to form a simple backup strategy and execute it with the built-in tools. I'll also walk you through the process of recovering data in different situations.

Utilize the Availability Options for Servers Based on Role

As discussed in Chapter 1, "Deploying Exchange Servers," Exchange Server 2010 separates functionality into different roles. Because each role performs a different primary task, the methods used to make them redundant are different. Table 10.1 outlines the primary redundancy methods used for each role.

Table 10.1: Redundancy Methods for Each Exchange Role

Role	Primary Function	Redundancy Method
Client Access	Provides end-user connectivity into Exchange	Install Microsoft Network Load Balancing (NLB) across multiple Client Access servers.

Table 10.1: Redundancy Methods for Each Exchange Role *(continued)*

Role	Primary Function	Redundancy Method
Transport	Sends and receives email to and from external systems and other Transport servers	Add multiple Transport servers and configure DNS and the connectors to use more than one server. NLB is also an option, though it may be unnecessary in many cases.
Mailbox	Hosts the data stored by Exchange in various databases	Implement database availability groups (DAGs) to replicate passive copies of the databases across multiple Mailbox servers.

In this section, we will look at the availability options for each of these roles and walk you through the process of implementing these methods.

Load-Balance Client Access Servers

The methodology used for load-balancing Client Access servers and making them redundant is to use the Microsoft NLB service. After installing and configuring the NLB service on your Client Access servers, you create a new client access array. Each node in the client access array runs the NLB service, and a virtual identity is used to present all the servers as a single server to clients. You can have up to 32 Client Access servers in the array.

For example, in your site you may have three Client Access servers called CONTOSO-CAS01, CONTOSO-CAS02, and CONTOSO-CAS03. If these three servers are in a client access array, the virtual name may be CLIENTACCESS.CONTOSO.COM. Instead of connecting individually to CONTOSO-CAS01, CONTOSO-CAS02, or CONTOSO-CAS03, the clients would connect to CLIENTACCESS.CONTOSO.COM and the NLB service would determine which of the three Client Access servers service the connection.

When creating a client access array, use these steps:

1. Install NLB.

2. Create the NLB cluster.

3. Configure the client access array in Exchange.

Mitigating Risk

PART III

WARNING   You can install a client access array on a server that shares the Client Access and Hub Transport roles. However, I don't recommend that you load-balance the Hub Transport ports when doing so. If your Client Access server (CAS) is also hosting the Mailbox role and is a member of a DAG, you cannot join the CAS to a client access array.

Install the Network Load Balancing Feature

The first step to creating a client access array is to install the NLB service on the Client Access servers that you want in the array. To install NLB, use the following steps:

1. Log in at a Client Access server that will be in the client access array.

2. Open a command prompt by choosing Start ➤ All Programs ➤ Accessories ➤ Command Prompt.

3. Run the following command:

   ```
   ServerManagerCmd -I NLB
   ```

4. Repeat steps 1–3 on each of the Client Access servers that will be a member of the client access array.

Create the NLB Cluster

After NLB is installed, you can create the NLB cluster and add the Client Access servers to it. Before creating the cluster, decide on the hostname and the virtual IP address that will be used. You also need to determine what cluster operation mode you will use.

You have two options for the cluster operation mode: unicast or multi-cast. The difference is that unicast mode replaces the Media Access Control (MAC) address of the network with the cluster's MAC address, whereas multicast mode adds an additional multicast MAC address to the card. If you choose unicast mode, ensure that there are at least two network cards so that the Client Access servers in the NLB can still communicate with each other. If you use multicast mode, ensure that your network infrastructure allows multicast.

Create the Cluster with the First Node

Use the following steps to create the NLB cluster and add the first node. In this example, I'm using a single network card in the Client Access servers, so I will use multicast mode for the cluster.

1. Log in at one of the Client Access servers that will be in the client access array.

2. Launch the Network Load Balancing Manager tool by choosing Start ➢ All Programs ➢ Administrative Tools ➢ Network Load Balancing Manager.

3. In the NLB Manager tool, choose Cluster ➢ New, as shown in Figure 10.1. This will launch the New Cluster wizard.

Figure 10.1: Launching the New Cluster wizard in the NLB Manager

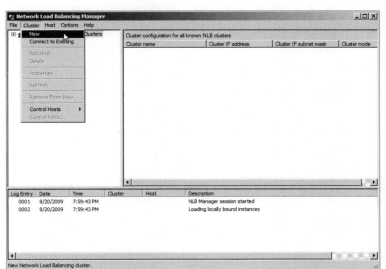

4. On the Connect screen of the New Cluster wizard, type the name of one of the Client Access servers that will be in the client access array. For the sake of simplicity, you can just type in the name of the Client Access server that you are currently connected to. Click the Connect button.

The list of interfaces will be populated with the network interfaces that are currently installed on the server. Select the interface that will host the clustered services. If you have multiple network adapters, use the adapter that you want to send and receive Client Access traffic with. Click Next to continue.

5. On the Host Parameters screen, select the priority for the host. The host with the lowest priority processes the cluster network traffic that is not covered by a port rule in the cluster configuration. Ensure that Default State is set to Started and click Next.

6. On the Cluster IP Addresses screen, click the Add button to add the virtual IP address of the cluster. In the Add IP Address dialog box, type the IP address and the subnet mask and click OK (Figure 10.2).

Figure 10.2: Adding the virtual IP address used by the NLB cluster

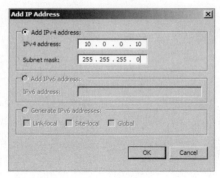

When back in the New Cluster wizard, click Next to continue.

7. On the Cluster Parameters screen, type the fully qualified domain name of the cluster in the Full Internet Name field. For example, this could be **casarray.contoso.com**.

    In the Cluster Operation Mode portion of the screen, select Multicast and click Next.

8. On the Port Rules screen, select the port rule with the Start port of 0 and the End port of 65535 and click the Edit button.

9. In the Add/Edit Port Rule dialog box, change the Port Range From value to **1024** and click OK. This modifies the load-balanced port range to include the dynamic ports that can be assigned by the RPC endpoint mapper.

10. While still on the Port Rules screen, click the Add button to add another port rule. In the Add/Edit Port Rule dialog box, set both the From and To values to **135**. Also, select TCP as the protocol. This ensures that the RPC endpoint mapper port is load balanced as well. This configuration is shown in Figure 10.3.

Figure 10.3: Adding port rules to the NLB cluster

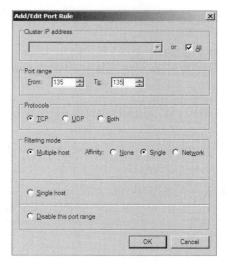

Click the OK button to add the port rule.

11. Repeat step 10 for additional ports that you want to be accessed using the NLB cluster. For example, adding ports 80 and 443 would ensure that the web services running on the CAS are load balanced. You can add the ports for POP and IMAP connections as well, if you want to load-balance those services.

12. After you have added all the ports that you want to load-balance, click the Finish button to create the NLB cluster with the first node added.

Mitigating Risk

PART III

> **WARNING**   The server may be temporarily disconnected from the network while the Network Load Balance settings are being applied. Connectivity should return within a few seconds.

Add Additional Nodes to the Cluster

Now that the NLB cluster exists, you can add additional Client Access server nodes to the cluster. Use the following steps to add more nodes:

1. Launch the NLB Manager tool by choosing Start ➢ All Programs ➢ Administrative Tools ➢ Network Load Balancing Manager.

2. In NLB Manager, choose Cluster ➢ Connect To Existing.

3. In the Connect To Existing dialog box, type the name of one of the nodes that is already in the cluster.

   The list of clusters will be displayed. Select the NLB cluster that you create for the client access array and click the Finish button.

4. When back in NLB Manager, select the cluster in the tree in the right pane. Right-click on the cluster and select Add Host To Cluster from the menu (Figure 10.4).

Figure 10.4: Adding an additional Client Access server to the NLB cluster

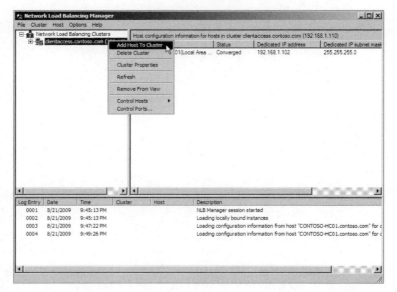

5. On the Connect screen of the Add Host To Cluster wizard, type the name of one of the Client Access servers that you are adding. Click the Connect button.

   The list of interfaces will be populated with the network interfaces that are currently installed on the server. Select the interface that will host the clustered services. If you have multiple network adapters, use the adapter that you want to send and receive client access traffic with. Click Next to continue.

6. On the Host Parameters screen, select the priority for the host. The host with the lowest priority processes the cluster network traffic that is not covered by a port rule in the cluster configuration. Ensure that Default State is set to Started and click Next.

7. On the Port Rules screen, review the port rules that are currently configured in the NLB cluster. These port rules should be the same rules that you created when you created the cluster in the previous section. Click Finish to close the wizard.

   You will be returned to NLB Manager, but it may take a moment before the new node is added to the cluster. When the nodes are added successfully to the NLB cluster, the icons turn green and the status will be set to Converged on both nodes, as shown in Figure 10.5.

Figure 10.5: The status of the cluster nodes is good.

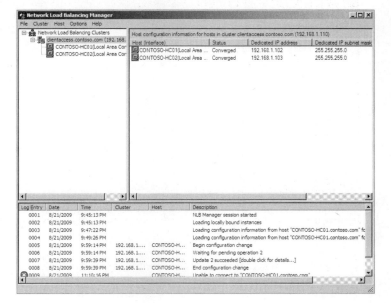

Mitigating Risk

PART III

Configure the Client Access Array in Exchange

After the NLB cluster is up and running, you will need to create the client access array object for Exchange. When you create the object, you can assign it to an Active Directory site. All of the Client Access servers in the site will be listed as members of the array. Each new mailbox database that you create will be tied to this array using the RpcClientAccessServer attribute on the mailbox database. When users in that database connect to their mailbox, they will use the Client Access server specified in that attribute.

To create the client access array, run the New-ClientAccessArray cmdlet in the EMS and specify the parameters listed in Table 10.2.

Table 10.2: EMS Parameters for Creating the Client Access Array

Parameter	Description
FQDN	The fully qualified domain name of the NLB cluster; example: clientaccess.contoso.com
Site	The name of the Active Directory site that the client access array is in

The following example command creates a client access array object in Exchange and assigns it to the Baltimore site:

```
New-ClientAccessArray -FQDN clientaccess.contoso.com -Site ↵
Baltimore
```

If you have mailbox databases that existed before the client access array was created, they are probably pointing to the existing Client Access server directly before the NLB cluster was created. You will need to ensure that the RpcClientAccessServer attribute on those mailbox databases is up-to-date if you want users to access their mailboxes using the client access array. Run the following EMS command for each mailbox database in the site that was created before the client access array was created:

```
Set-MailboxDatabase [DBName] -RpcClientAccessServer ↵
[CASArrayFQDN]
```

For example, the following command changes the mailbox database DB02 to point to the client access array that we just created:

```
Set-MailboxDatabase DB02 -RpcClientAccessServer ↵
clientaccess.contoso.com
```

Increase Mailbox Database Availability

One of the primary areas of focus for keeping a high degree of availability is the data that each user stores in their mailbox. Maximizing mailbox database availability is one of the most difficult challenges in managing Exchange. The capabilities around database availability have changed from one Exchange version to the next, with each method becoming increasingly more effective. This section helps you understand how to maintain high levels of availability for your mailbox databases in Exchange Server 2010.

Understand Database Availability Options

The options for database availability have changed in Exchange Server 2010. In previous versions of Exchange, you had the ability to cluster mailbox servers in order to keep mailbox databases highly available. In Exchange Server 2007, continuous replication was introduced, which provided database availability by copying the transaction logs from an active database to a passive copy of the same database.

Exchange 2010 further expands on the continuous replication technology and provides a single database availability solution that fits every common scenario. This technology is referred to as a database availability group (DAG).

Understand the Basics of DAGs

A DAG is a collection of Mailbox servers (up to 16 servers) that can share copies of the same mailbox databases. One server in the DAG holds the active copy of the database, and one or more other servers can contain passive copies of the same database. The databases are kept synchronized using the continuous replication log shipping method that was used in Exchange Server 2007. There are many advantages to the DAG approach:

- Databases can be hosted on any of the Mailbox servers in the DAG.
- Mailbox servers in a DAG can also perform other Exchange roles.
- Recovery from a database failure is automatic.
- Mailbox servers in a DAG can live in different sites.
- DAGs use Windows Failover Clustering in the back end, but all configuration and administration is performed through the Exchange tools.
- Failover occurs within 30 seconds.

Mitigating Risk

PART III

Figure 10.6 shows how a DAG configuration might look.

Figure 10.6: An example of a DAG configuration

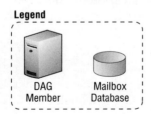

MB01	DB01 (Active)	DB02	DB03	DB04	
MB02	DB01		DB03 (Active)		DB05
MB03	DB01	DB02 (Active)			DB05

Legend

DAG Member   Mailbox Database

In this example, there are three Mailbox servers and five databases that are replicated between the mailbox servers in the DAG. Only one server has an active copy of the database. As you can see in the figure, the database can be selectively replicated to other servers. Each server is not required to host a replica of every database. This offers great flexibility in designing your database availability solution.

Determine How Databases Fail Over

When the active copy of a replicated database fails, how does Exchange determine which passive copy gets activated? This process is determined by a component called the Active Manager. The Active Manager has two roles:

- The Primary Active Manager (PAM) is hosted on one of the servers in the DAG. The PAM determines which of the databases should be active.

- The Standby Active Manager (SAM) is hosted on the remaining Mailbox servers in the DAG. The SAM keeps tabs on the databases running on the Mailbox server and notifies the PAM when a database fails. The SAM also informs Hub Transport servers and Client Access servers about which server hosts the active copy of a database.

When a database failure occurs, the Active Manager looks at the health of the passive copies of the databases to determine which copies should be targeted for failover. In making its determination, the Active Manager looks at the database copy status, the health of the content index, and the length of the log copy queue and the log replay queue.

If multiple passive copies of the database meet the Active Manager's criteria list, the database with the lowest Activation Preference setting is activated. The activation preference order is determined by you when you add database copies to other Mailbox servers in a DAG.

Implement Database Availability Groups

To implement DAGs, use the following steps:

1. Configure the network adapters on the mailbox servers that will be in the DAG.

   Every mailbox server in the DAG must have two adapters installed. One adapter will be for clients to access the data in the mailbox stores (MAPI traffic), and the other adapter will be used for data replication between DAG members. These two adapters must be on different subnets and the subnets must map to networks that are assigned to the DAG.

2. Create the DAG. For the proper steps, refer to the section "Creating a Database Availability Group" in Chapter 7, "Managing Mailbox Databases."

3. Add members to the DAG. Up to 16 members can be added. When a member is in the DAG, it can host copies of databases from any other member in the DAG.

To add a DAG member, refer to the section "Adding Services to a DAG" in Chapter 7.

4. Create some mailbox databases. If you don't already have a mailbox database on one of your Mailbox servers in the DAG, go ahead and create some.

   For steps on creating a mailbox database, refer to the section "Creating a New Mailbox Database" in Chapter 7.

5. Add a copy of a mailbox database in a DAG to another server in the DAG. Now that you have multiple servers in your DAG and at least one database, you can enable that database to be copied to other servers.

   To enable database copies, follow the steps outlined in the section "Replicating Databases to Additional Servers" in Chapter 7.

Implement Redundant Transport Servers

When implementing redundancy for Transport servers, it's important to consider each job that the server performs. Here are the primary components of Transport servers that you will want to make redundant:

- Internal message routing
- External message processing

Implement Redundancy for Internal Message Routing

When a user sends a message in Exchange, the message is submitted by the Mailbox server to a Hub Transport server that is in the same Active Directory site. The Hub Transport server is then responsible for sending that message to another Transport server that is considered to be the next hop in order for the message to reach its destination. So when considering redundancy for internal message routing, you need to ensure that you have redundant Transport servers for Mailbox servers to submit mail to. You also need to ensure that you have redundant servers to receive the messages that are sent from site to site by the Hub Transport servers that are routing the messages inside Exchange.

The need for this level of redundancy is evident when you look at the example routing topology in Figure 10.7.

Figure 10.7: Why multiple transport servers are preferred

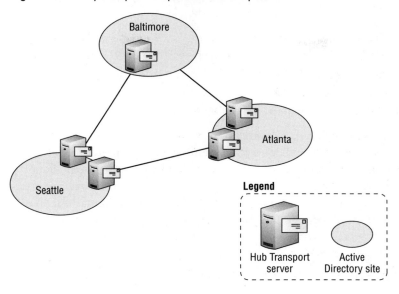

The Baltimore site only has one Hub Transport server. If a message is sent from a user in Seattle to a user in Baltimore and if the Baltimore Hub Transport server is offline, the message will remain queued at one of the Seattle Hub Transport servers. However, if a user in Baltimore sends a message to a user in Seattle and one of the Hub Transport servers in Seattle goes down, the message will be sent to the other Hub Transport server that is still functioning. Users in Seattle can still send and receive email until the problem is resolved and the second Hub Transport server is brought back online. Leaving only one Hub Transport server in an Active Directory site introduces a single point of failure for mail routing to that site.

Accomplishing this level of redundancy for internal message routing is easy. You simply install multiple Hub Transport servers in each Active Directory site that contains Mailbox servers. No special configuration is necessary to have internal message routing redundancy.

Implement Redundancy for External Message Routing

Ensuring that external message routing is redundant requires a little more work than internal routing redundancy. Whether you are using

Mitigating Risk

PART III

Hub Transport servers for external messages or Edge Transport servers, implementing redundancy is the same. There are two facets to consider:

- Redundancy for sending mail outside the organization
- Redundancy for receiving mail directly from the Internet

Add Redundancy for Sending External Messages

To send mail outside an organization, you need to have a send connector configured. The send connector (discussed in Chapter 6, "Managing Message Routing") determines how mail destined for different email domains is processed. Each send connector has a list of source servers, which are the Transport servers that can be used to send mail for the email domain name specified on the send connector. If there is only one Transport server defined on a send connector and the Transport server goes offline, messages destined to that domain namespace will not be sent. Therefore, it's important to use multiple Transport servers in a send connector.

To add Transport servers to an existing send connector, use the following steps:

1. Open the EMC and browse to the Organization Configuration ➤ Hub Transport node in the Console tree.

2. Click the Send Connectors tab in the Work area.

   The configured send connectors for the Exchange organization are displayed in the list.

3. Select the send connector that you want to add redundant Transport servers to. Click the Properties task in the Actions pane on the right.

4. In the properties dialog box for the send connector, click the Source Server tab.

   The current Transport servers configured to send mail for the connector are listed on this tab.

5. Click the Add button to add an additional Transport server.

6. In the search dialog box that appears, select the Transport server that you want to add and click OK.

Add any additional Transport servers that you want to include by repeating this step.

7. When back in the properties dialog box, click OK to makes the changes and close the dialog box.

Add Redundancy for Receiving Internet Mail

When a Transport server is Internet facing, the Mail Exchanger (MX) records for the domain's DNS name are configured to point Internet mail servers to the Transport server. For example, if joe@contoso.com is receiving a message from tim@fabrikam.com over the Internet, the fabrikam.com Mail server queries the contoso.com DNS domain for MX records to determine which server should receive the incoming message. Therefore, it's important to ensure that there are multiple servers that can receive mail based on that MX record lookup.

There are two methods for making MX records redundant:

- Create more than one MX record for a DNS domain. Point each MX record to an Internet-facing Transport server.

- Create a single MX record, but point it to multiple host records. Each host record maps to the IP address of the Transport servers that are Internet-facing.

When the first approach is used, a DNS query returns all the MX records. It is then up to the mail system that is sending the message to select the MX record to use according to its internal algorithm. There is no guarantee that a different server will be used each time, as the external server gets to choose what to use.

However, with the second approach, only a single MX record is returned. This MX record is the host record that uses multiple IPs. When the sending server receives the MX record, it performs a host record lookup and receives the list of IP addresses behind that host record. The order of the IP list is controlled by the DNS server, which uses a round-robin ordering or a random ordering. The sending server chooses the first IP address in the list and sends the message to that IP address. This method puts the control in the hands of the DNS server and not the email system. Figure 10.8 and Figure 10.9 show how the DNS response is different in these two methods.

Mitigating Risk

PART III

Figure 10.8: The DNS response when using multiple MX records

```
Administrator: Command Prompt                                              _ □ ×
C:\>nslookup -type=mx contoso.com
Server:  localhost
Address:  127.0.0.1

contoso.com      MX preference = 10, mail exchanger = transport1.contoso.com
contoso.com      MX preference = 10, mail exchanger = transport2.contoso.com
contoso.com      MX preference = 10, mail exchanger = transport3.contoso.com
transport1.contoso.com   internet address = 10.0.0.100
transport2.contoso.com   internet address = 10.0.0.101
transport3.contoso.com   internet address = 10.0.0.102

C:\>
```

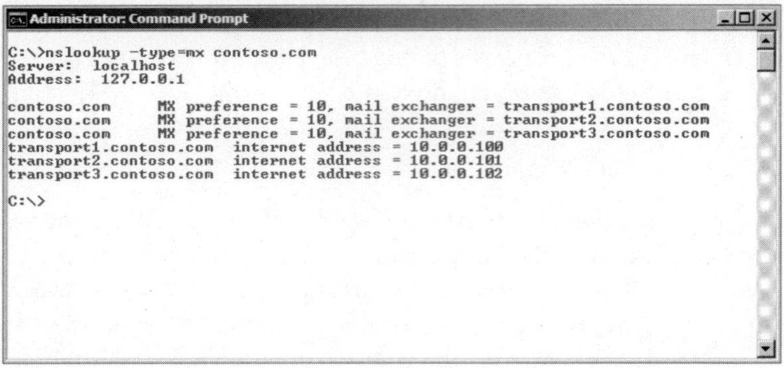

Figure 10.9: The DNS response when using multiple host records

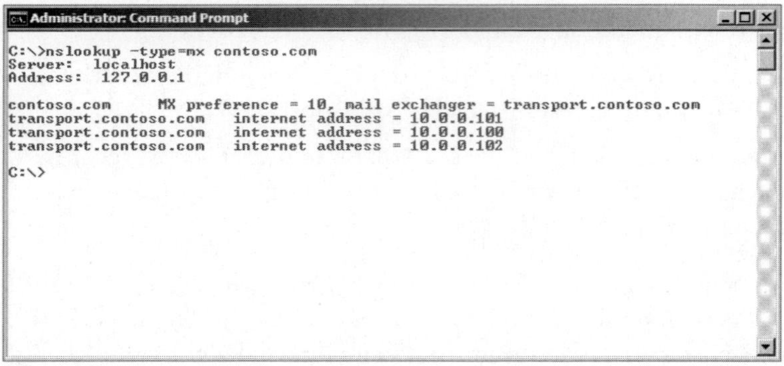

```
Administrator: Command Prompt                                              _ □ ×
C:\>nslookup -type=mx contoso.com
Server:  localhost
Address:  127.0.0.1

contoso.com      MX preference = 10, mail exchanger = transport.contoso.com
transport.contoso.com    internet address = 10.0.0.101
transport.contoso.com    internet address = 10.0.0.100
transport.contoso.com    internet address = 10.0.0.102

C:\>
```

For steps on creating MX records, refer to section "Configuring the DNS Records for Receiving Email" in Chapter 6.

In addition to configuring multiple MX records, you will want to ensure that you have a receive connector on each of your Internet-facing Transport servers. The receive connector allows the Transport server to listen for incoming mail on the port that is configured. Edge Transport servers configure receive connectors to receive Internet email automatically when the Edge role is installed. However, if you have Internet-facing Hub Transport servers, you need to modify the permissions on the default receive connector on each Hub Transport server that is Internet-facing so that it can receive messages from the Internet.

To configure receive connectors on each Internet-facing Hub Transport server to receive Internet email, follow the steps in the section "Configuring a Hub Transport Server to Receive Internet Email" in Chapter 6.

Back Up Exchange

At the heart of Exchange lies the ability to retain and allow access to vast amounts of data. Emails get populated in user's mailboxes from both internal and external sources. Often, once an email is received from someone, the only copy exists in the recipient's mailbox. Inadvertently losing this data and not being able to recover it can cause many problems.

It's difficult to overstress the benefits of keeping backups of data for Exchange. Traditionally, it was important to keep backups not only for data recovery purposes, but also for the purpose of truncating transaction logs. If you went multiple days without a backup, you risked the possibility of transaction logs filling up the disk volume, which forced Exchange to shut down the access to those databases.

However, backup technology has evolved over the years and Exchange has kept pace with the changes in backup technology. With technology like volume snapshots, it no longer takes hours upon hours to back up databases in Exchange. In some instances in Exchange Server 2010, it may be wise to eliminate backups altogether and instead rely on data replication to meet your recovery goals.

This section will help you develop an effective backup strategy and show you how you can use Windows Server Backup to meet your data recovery goals.

Develop an Effective Backup Strategy

At the cornerstone of meeting your data recovery goals is the development of an effective backup strategy. Without a backup strategy in place, you won't understand what your backup requirements are or whether the backup tool you use fits those requirements. It's also important to lay out your recovery plans. When a disaster strikes and you have a limited time to react, it's important to be able to pull out your recovery plan and follow it with the assurance that it works.

To determine what your backup requirements are, you must first understand why you are backing up the data. Then you can determine what your goals are for recovery. And finally, you can decide how often you want to perform backups.

Mitigating Risk

PART III

Understand the Reasons for Backups

There are many reasons that an organization would want to perform backups, such as the following:

- To have the ability to restore an entire server from scratch
- To have the capability of restoring a failed or damaged database
- To maintain a copy of the mailboxes of people who recently left the organization
- To recover messages that a user has deleted

You will need to determine which of these scenarios apply to your goals for recovery. For example, you may not want the capability to restore an entire server from backup if you are using DAGs for database availability. In this case, it might not be a big deal to install a new Mailbox server with a different name and enable a database copy on the server.

Determine Recoverability Goals

After you have an understanding of why you want to perform backups, you can start determining your goals for recovery. You will want to consider each scenario for which that the backup is maintained and determine how long you want to retain the data and how quickly you want to be able to restore the data. You will use these metrics to determine what your backup architecture will be. For example, you may decide to keep backups on site instead of shipping them offsite in order to meet your data recovery time objective.

Each scenario may have different recovery objectives. Table 10.3 demonstrates how recoverability goals can be different for each scenario.

Table 10.3: How Recoverability Goals Differ Between Scenarios

Scenario	Data Retention Goal	Data Restoration Goal
Database becomes corrupt	Restored database must not be older than 1 day	Must have dial-tone service up within 1 hour and the database must be restored within 8 hours
Mailbox accidently deleted by administrator	Restored data must be less than 3 days old	Mailbox must be restored within 1 hour
User needs to recover a message that was deleted 30 days ago	Must be able to restore messages for up to 60 days	Message must be restored within 1 business day

The key is to determine the minimum and maximum lengths of time that backed up data must be kept and select a backup methodology that allows you to restore the data within your target restoration goal.

Decide on a Backup Schedule

When you know how frequently you must back up the data, you can more easily determine what your backup schedule should be. In keeping with the example described in Table 10.3, you can see that restored databases must not be older than one day. This means that databases need to be backed up daily.

Also from Table 10.3, you can see that the scenario requires you to be able to restore messages for up to 60 days. Therefore, you know that you must be able to keep 60 days of backups in order to meet this goal.

Consider Backup Alternatives in Exchange

It is worth mentioning the new school of thought about backups in Exchange Server 2010. The idea is that in some situations, backups may not need to be kept at all. In fact, Microsoft decided to use this approach when deploying Exchange Server 2010 internally and completely eliminated the cost of maintaining data backups.

The idea of using replication as an alternative to backups is met with mixed emotions by different people. In many organizations, backups are performed in a certain manner because that's the way they've always done it. In many ways, this consideration is less of a technical consideration and more of a psychological one. An environment where replication is used for backups is not the right solution for everyone. However, the following capabilities in Exchange Server 2010 fill in the gaps that backups have traditionally been used to fill.

Server Failure Add mailbox servers to a DAG and replicate copies of the databases to other servers.

Disk Failure Place each database and transaction log folder on the same physical disk. Add the mailbox server to a DAG and ensure that at least three copies of the database exist in the DAG.

Database Corruption Enable transaction log replay lag on the database copies in the DAG. This allows you to recover the database without the transaction log that caused the corruption.

Single Message Recovery Exchange now has single-item recovery built in. You just need to enable it and specify how long you want to keep deleted messages for.

Mitigating Risk

PART III

Mailbox Recovery Exchange maintains a copy of deleted mailboxes for 30 days by default. This time is adjustable if you need to retain deleted mailboxes for longer periods of time.

Site Failure Instead of using off-site backups, consider stretching your DAG across sites for site resiliency.

If you decide to implement database replication as a replacement for traditional backups, you should keep the following recommendations in mind:

- Make sure that you have at least three copies of your databases replicated inside a DAG.

- Implement lagged database copies if you frequently experience logical corruption of your mailboxes due to third-party applications.

- Enable circular logging on your databases to ensure that transaction logs are truncated.

- Make sure that you implement your architecture in a way that allows you to sleep peacefully at night. If you're constantly worried that you may lose all three copies of the database, implement additional database copies and maybe even place one or two of the copies in a different site.

Perform Backups with the Windows Server Backup Tool

When the Windows Server Backup Tool came out in Windows Server 2008, support for native Exchange backups was removed. This capability is now back. Exchange Server 2010 installs a service called Microsoft Exchange Server Extension for Windows Server Backup. This service provides Windows Server Backup with the ability to make Volume Shadow Copy backups that are Exchange-aware. Having this capability out of the box in Windows Server 2008 is a good thing, but there are limitations to using Windows Server Backup for Exchange backups:

- Only full volumes can be backed up. You cannot make a backup of the Exchange database and transaction log files independently. Instead, the Exchange data is backed up when you back up the volume that the data lives on. Because of this, both the transaction logs and the database file for a given mailbox server database need to be available in the same backup set in order to restore the data.

- Backups cannot be taken remotely. Backups must be initiated on the server either manually or via a scheduled task.

- In order for transaction logs to be truncated, only full backups must be taken.

- Single databases cannot be restored. When you perform a restore, all the databases that were backed up in the backup job are restored.

- You can only back up active copies of the databases. Passive copies cannot be backed up with Windows Server Backup.

Install Windows Server Backup

Windows Server Backup exists as an installable feature in Windows Server 2008. To install Windows Server Backup and the command-line backup tools, run the following command from a command prompt:

```
ServerManagerCmd -i Backup-Features
```

Perform a One-Time Manual Backup

To perform a one-time backup manually with Windows Server Backup, use the following steps. These steps may vary slightly if you are using Windows Server 2008 to perform the backup.

1. Open Windows Server Backup by choosing Start ➤ All Programs ➤ Administrative Tools ➤ Windows Server Backup.

2. In the Actions pane on the right, select the task Backup Once. This launches the Backup Once wizard.

3. On the Backup Options screen of the wizard, select Different Options and click the Next button.

4. On the Select Backup Configuration screen, select Full Server to back up the entire server or select Custom to choose which volumes you want to back up.

   In this example, we're only going to back up the volumes that contain Exchange databases. So choose Custom and click Next.

5. On the Select Items For Backup screen, click the Add Items button to add a volume to the backup list. This opens the Select Items dialog box.

In the Select Items dialog box, check the box next to the volumes that contain the databases that you want to back up. After you have chosen your volumes, click OK to close the dialog box. Then click the Advanced Settings button.

6. In the Advanced Settings dialog box, select the VSS Settings tab. Choose the option VSS Full Backup and click OK. Only full VSS backups are supported when you are using the Windows Server Backup tool to back up Exchange data.

   Back in the Backup Once wizard, click Next.

7. On the Specify Destination Type screen, select Local Drives to store the backup on a local disk or select Remote Shared Folder to store the backup on a network share.

   In this example, we are going to store the backup on a local disk. Select Local Drives and click Next.

8. On the Select Backup Destination screen, select the volume that you want to store the backup on from the Backup Destination drop-down list. Only volumes that have enough free space are displayed in the list.

   Click Next to continue.

9. At the Confirmation screen, verify that the backup settings are accurate and click the Backup button to begin the backup.

   While the backup is running, you can safely close the Backup Once wizard by clicking the Close button. This does not stop the backup.

10. When the backup is complete, click Close to close the Backup Once wizard if you haven't done so already.

Perform Automated Backups

In addition to performing manual backups, you can set up scheduled backups that occur in an automated fashion through Windows Server Backup. To set up scheduled automated backups, use the following steps. These steps may vary slightly if you are backing up a server that is using Windows Server 2008 R2.

1. Open Windows Server Backup by choosing Start ➤ All Programs ➤ Administrative Tools ➤ Windows Server Backup.

2. In the Actions pane on the right, select the task Backup Schedule. This launches the Backup Schedule wizard.

3. On the Getting Started screen of the wizard, click Next.

4. In the Select Backup Configuration dialog box, select Full Server to back up the entire server or select Custom to choose which volumes you want to back up.

    In this example, we're only going to back up the volumes that contain Exchange databases. So choose Custom and click Next.

5. On the Select Backup Items screen, the list of volumes on the server is presented. Check the box next to the volumes that contain the databases that you want to back up. Then click Next to continue.

6. On the Specify Backup Time screen, select Once A Day to back up Exchange only one time each day. From the Select Time Of Day drop-down list, select the time that you want to start the backups.

    You also have the option of selecting More Than Once A Day if you want to back up Exchange multiple times throughout the day.

    After you have selected your backup schedule, click Next.

7. On the Select Destination Disk screen, place a check mark next to the disks that you want to store your backups on. If you want to use disks that are local to the server, click the Show All Available Disks button. By default, only external disks are shown. Click Next to continue.

    Note that the disk you selected will be formatted and dedicated for storing backups. If you see a dialog box that warns you about this, click the Yes button to continue. You will lose the data on this disk if you click Yes, so ensure that you really want to dedicate the disk for backups.

8. At the Label Destination Disk screen, view the labels that are designated for your backup disks. You can physically write this name on the disk or record it on paper to ensure that you know what disk corresponds to which label. Click Next to continue.

9. At the Confirmation screen, verify that the backup settings are accurate and click the Finish button to complete the process and prepare your disks.

Mitigating Risk

PART III

10. At the Summary screen, view the results of the scheduled backup and click Close to close the Backup Schedule wizard. If you previously had a mounted volume and used that disk as your backup location, the volume will no longer be available.

Recover Data

Many scenarios exist where you might need to recover data in Exchange. Knowing how to perform data recovery and practicing your recovery process regularly are key factors to a successful data recovery plan. Different types of recovery require different strategies; therefore, it's essential to ensure that you clearly know how to react in each situation in which recovery may be needed. Some of the common scopes of data recovery are

- Entire mailbox databases
- Individual user mailboxes
- Single items in a mailbox

This section will show you how to perform a recovery of data in each of these scopes.

Recover Databases with the Windows Server Backup Tool

Windows Server Backup isn't the only backup tool that can be used in Exchange, but Exchange Server 2010 brings back the ability to use the built-in backup product. If you used the Windows Server Backup tool to back up your Exchange databases, you can restore the database from your backup either to the original location of the database or to an alternate location. This section shows you how to recover a database from the backup created with the Windows Server Backup tool.

Restore the Database from Backup

When you used Windows Server Backup to create a backup, you had to back up the entire volume and the Exchange databases are backed up with it. When you restore a backup in Windows Server Backup, however, you can choose to only restore the Exchange databases. When you perform the restore, all the databases on the volume are restored. You do not have the option of choosing which databases to restore.

To restore all the databases that were backed up on a particular volume, use the following steps:

1. Open Windows Server Backup by selecting Start ➢ All Programs ➢ Administrative Tools ➢ Windows Server Backup.

2. In the Actions pane on the right, select the Recover task. This launches the Recovery wizard.

3. At the Getting Started screen of the wizard, select This Server to restore a backup of the current server from a local volume.

   Click Next to continue.

4. On the Select Backup Date screen, select from the calendar control the date of the backup that you are restoring. The dates that have backups are displayed in bold text.

   After selecting the date, select the time of the backup from the Time field. Click Next after you've chosen the backup that you want to restore (see Figure 10.10).

Figure 10.10: Selecting the backup to restore

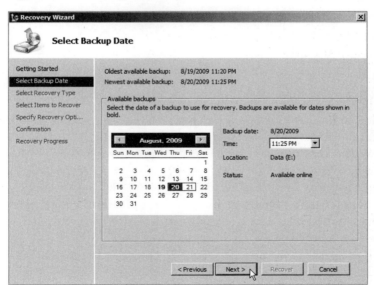

5. On the Select Recovery Type screen, choose Applications and click Next.

6. On the Select Application screen, choose the Exchange application and click Next.

7. At the Specify Recovery Options screen, choose Recover To Original Location to restore the backup to the original location of the databases.

   You might also choose the Recover To Another Location option if you want to restore only one of the databases on the volume. You can then specify the folder that you want to restore the databases to and manually copy the restored database files to the original location of the database.

   In this example, we're restoring the database to its original location. Choose the Recover To Original Location option and click Next.

8. On the Confirmation screen, click the Recover button to begin recovery.

9. The Recovery Progress dialog box is displayed while the recovery is being performed. You can safely close this dialog box and the recovery will continue.

   If you choose to the keep the dialog box open, you can click the Close button after the recovery completes to close the Recovery wizard.

Mount a Database Restored to an Alternate Location

There are a couple of differences between restoring data to its original location and restoring data to an alternate location.

When you perform a restore in Windows Server Backup, all the databases in the backed up volume are restored; therefore, you can't restore a single database to its original location in Windows Server Backup. If you want to restore a single database, you must first restore the databases on the volume to an alternate location and then overwrite the database files with the restored copy.

If the database is restored to its original location, the database is automatically mounted and made current by replaying any transaction logs that are still in the location. However, if you restored the database to an alternate location, the database must be brought into a clean shutdown state before it can be mounted.

To bring the database into a clean shutdown state:

1. Take note of the database base name. You can find out the base name of the database by browsing to the folder that contains the restored backup and examining the first three characters of the log files. For example, if there is a log file named E0200000003.log, then the base name of the database is E02.

2. Open a command prompt by selecting Start ➢ All Programs ➢ Accessories ➢ Command Prompt.

3. Change directories to the folder that contains the restored backup. For example, if the backup was restored to C:\RestoredData, run the following command:

    ```
    cd c:\RestoredData
    ```

4. Run the following ESEUTIL command, substituting *BaseName* for the three-digit base name discovered in step 1:

    ```
    Eseutil /r BaseName
    ```

    For example, the command to restore our database from step 2 is

    ```
    Eseutil /r E02
    ```

After the database is brought to a clean shutdown state, you can redirect the original database to use the restored files. To do this, use the Move-DatabasePath cmdlet in the EMS along with the ConfigurationOnly parameter. The following example command remaps the database and transaction log files for the database DB03 to the location of the restored files (C:\RestoredData\ and C:\RestoredData\DB03.edb):

```
Move-DatabasePath DB03 -EdbFilePath ↵
C:\RestoredData\DB03.edb -LogFolderPath C:\RestoredData ↵
-ConfigurationOnly
```

You can then mount the database using the Mount-Database cmdlet. The following EMS command mounts the database that we just restored, named DB03:

```
Mount-Database DB03
```

Recover Mailboxes

Exchange Server 2010 gives you a few options for recovering a mailbox. This section shows you how to configure and use some of the mailbox recovery options. The options discussed are as follows:

Recovering a Mailbox Using the Deleted Mailbox Retention Capability   This works well for recovering mailboxes that were recently deleted (such as within the last 30 days).

Recovering a Mailbox Using a Recovery Database   You can use this option if you have a valid backup or copy of the database that you want to restore the mailbox from.

Recovering a Mailbox Using a Lagged Database Copy   This option is good if you are concerned about mailboxes being logically corrupted from a third-party application or a virus.

Use Deleted Mailbox Retention

By default, when a mailbox is removed from Exchange, the mailbox is not actually deleted. The mailbox is disjoined from the Active Directory account that it was paired with and remains in Exchange as a disconnected mailbox for a specified amount of time. After a time period expires (30 days by default), the mailbox is removed completely from Exchange. However, within this time period, you can reconnect a mailbox to another Active Directory account or to the same account that it used to be attached to (if the account still exists). This is useful for situations where mailboxes were accidentally deleted.

Adjust the Deleted Mailbox Retention Time

You can adjust the default mailbox retention time using the EMC. The following steps show you how:

1. Open the EMC and browse to the Organization Configuration ➤ Mailbox node in the Console tree.

2. Click the Database Management tab in the Work area to open a list of databases that exist in the organization.

3. Select the database from the list and click the Properties action in the Actions pane for the database that you selected.

4. In the Database Properties dialog box, select the Limits tab.

5. In the Keep Deleted Mailboxes For (Days) field, enter the number of days that you want to keep deleted mailboxes. The default setting is 30 days.

6. Click OK to save the changes and close the properties dialog box.

You can also modify the default mailbox retention time using the EMS by running the Set-MailboxDatabase cmdlet with the MailboxRetention parameter, specifying the number of days that you want to keep mailboxes for. This setting affects every mailbox on the database. The following example changes the mailbox retention time on the database named DB01 from 30 days to 60 days:

```
Set-MailboxDatabase DB01 -MailboxRetention 60.00:00:00
```

Reconnect a Disconnected Mailbox Using the Exchange Management Shell

A disconnected mailbox can be reconnected to an Active Directory account using the Connect-Mailbox cmdlet in the EMS. Before you can use the Connect-Mailbox cmdlet, you need a way to identify the disconnected mailbox, since it is no longer tied to a user account. You can use either the Display Name of the mailbox, the legacy Distinguished Name (LegacyDN), or the Globally Unique Identifier (GUID). You can use the following command to list each disconnected mailbox and its associated display name, GUID, and legacy DN. We'll also include the date that the mailbox was disconnected so it will be a little easier to narrow down the disconnected mailbox that you are looking for. In the example, the mailbox is on the server named CONTOSO-EX01.

```
Get-MailboxStatistics -Server CONTOSO-EX01 | ↵
where {$_.DisconnectDate -ne $null} | ↵
fl DisplayName, MailboxGUID, LegacyDN, DisconnectDate
```

This command is a little more complex than some of the others that we've used in this book, so I'll break it down to help you understand what is happening here. The first part of the command (Get-MailboxStatistics -Server CONTOSO-EX01) is getting the statistics for each mailbox on the server CONTOSO-EX01. The output from this command is being piped into the next command (where {$_.DisconnectDate -ne $null}). This part of the command is looking at each mailbox from the first part of the command and seeing if the DisconnectDate attribute on the mailbox is not equal to $null. If it is not equal to $null, that means there is a valid date in the DisconnectDate attribute. And if there is a valid date, the mailbox is a disconnected mailbox. Then each of the disconnected mailboxes is passed into the third part of this command (fl DisplayName, MailboxGUID, LegacyDN, DisconnectDate). This is just a Format-List command that lists each mailbox and the four attributes that we asked for in the command.

After you have an identifier, you can run the Connect-Mailbox cmdlet with the following syntax. As discussed previously, the MailboxID can be the display name, GUID, or legacy DN of the disconnected mailbox. Since you are essentially mail-enabling a user account, you will need to give the mailbox an alias, which can just be the same as the UserName.

```
Connect-Mailbox [MailboxID] -Database [DatabaseName] ↩
-User [UserName] -Alias [MailboxAlias]
```

For example, the following command will reconnect Abe's mailbox using the GUID:

```
Connect-Mailbox e3edfb68-88ea-4b38-93cc-35a2196ed3e9 ↩
-Database DB01 -User abe -Alias abe
```

Reconnect a Disconnected Mailbox Using the Exchange Management Console

You can also reconnect a disconnected mailbox with the EMC. When using the EMC, you do not need to use the mailbox GUID as you did in the EMS. The EMC uses the mailbox GUID for you in the background, so you only need to select the disconnected mailbox and tell the wizard what account you want to connect it to. Use the following steps to reconnect a user mailbox that was inadvertently deleted:

1. Open the EMC and browse to the Recipient Configuration ➤ Disconnected Mailbox node in the Console tree.

2. The Results pane lists the disconnected mailboxes that have not yet been removed from the database. Select the mailbox that you want to reconnect and click the Connect option in the Actions pane.

   The Connect Mailbox wizard launches.

3. At the Introduction screen, select User Mailbox and click Next.

4. On the Mailbox Settings screen, select the Active Directory account that you want to connect the mailbox to. If you click Matching User and select the Browse button, Exchange will attempt to find users whose properties match the mailbox.

If Exchange can't locate a user that matches the mailbox properties, you can select Existing User instead. When you select Existing User, a list of all enabled users in Active Directory without mailboxes will be returned.

Type an alias for the account in the Alias field and click Next.

5. On the Connect Mailbox screen, verify that the settings are correct and click the Connect button to connect the mailbox.

6. At the Completion screen, view the results and click Finish to close the wizard.

Use a Recovery Database

A recovery database (RDB) allows you to restore and mount a copy of a mailbox database and extract data from it. The RDB has some unique characteristics that make it well suited for recovery, because it ensures that the data in the database cannot be modified. Here are some of these characteristics:

- Mailbox databases can be mounted into an RDB, but the data cannot be accessed with methods used by traditional email applications. Users cannot use tools like Outlook to read from an RDB.

- Even though it's a mounted database, mail cannot flow to or from the database.

- No policies are applied to a database that is mounted in an RDB.

When using an RDB, the mail must be extracted from or merged into an existing mailbox. The process for recovering a mailbox from a database using an RDB is as follows:

1. Create the recovery database.

2. Restore the mailbox database files from the backup.

3. Point the RDB to the restored mailbox database and mount it.

4. Restore the mailbox.

Create a Recovery Database Using the Exchange Management Shell

You can create an RDB using the New-MailboxDatabase cmdlet in the EMS. The parameters used are the same parameters used for creating a mailbox database, as discussed in Chapter 7. The difference, however, is that you will need to specify the Recovery parameter to mark the database as a recovery database. The following command creates a recovery database called RDB01:

```
New-MailboxDatabase RDB01 -Server CONTOSO-EX01 -Recovery
```

Restore the Mailbox Database from Backup

When you restore the mailbox database from a backup, you can use the steps detailed in the section called "Back Up Exchange" earlier in this chapter. These procedures only apply to backups taken with the Windows Server Backup tool. If you use a third-party backup solution for Exchange, you will need to follow their steps for restoring the database.

Repair and Mount the Restored Database

Before the restored database can be mounted, you first must repair the database with ESEUTIL. Run the following command to repair the database:

```
Eseutil /p [PathToEDBFile]
```

For example, to repair the database restored to C:\Recovered, you might use this command:

```
Eseutil /p c:\recovered\e03.edb
```

After the database is repaired, you need to point the recovery database to the location of your restored files or copy the restored files into the location that the recovery database is currently using to store its data. To change the location of the RDB transaction logs and database file, use the Move-DatabasePath cmdlet with the ConfigurationOnly parameter. The following EMS command modifies the RDB to point to the recovered files:

```
Move-DatabasePath [RDBName] -EdbFilePath [RestoredEDBFile] ↵
-LogFolderPath [RestoredLogFolder] -ConfigurationOnly
```

For example, to modify the recovery database RDB01 to point to the files at C:\Recovered, you would use the following command:

```
Move-DatabasePath RDB01 -EdbFilePath c:\Recovered\e03.edb ↵
-LogFolderPath c:\Recovered -ConfigurationOnly
```

You can now mount the recovered database using the `Mount-Database` cmdlet, as shown here:

```
Mount-Database RDB01
```

Restore the Mailbox

Now that the recovery database is mounted with the recovered backup, you can restore the mailbox. To restore the mailbox, you use the `Restore-Mailbox` cmdlet in the EMS. When running the `Restore-Mailbox` command, you can either restore the data to the original mailbox or restore it to a different mailbox.

To restore the data to the original mailbox, run the following command:

```
Restore-Mailbox [Name] -RecoveryDatabase [RDBName]
```

For example, to restore Abe Berlas's mailbox, you would run this command:

```
Restore-Mailbox "Abe Berlas" -RecoveryDatabase RDB01
```

If you want to restore the data to a different mailbox than the original one, you need to specify the target mailbox, the source mailbox, and the folder that you want to put the data in. You must run `Restore-Mailbox` with the following parameters:

```
Restore-Mailbox [TargetMailbox] -RecoveryDatabase [RDBName] ↵
-RecoveryMailbox [SourceMailbox] -TargetFolder [FolderName]
```

The following command will restore Abe Berlas's mailbox from the backup into Jay Humphrey's mailbox inside the folder named Abe's Mail:

```
Restore-Mailbox "Jay Humphrey" -RecoveryDatabase RDB01 ↵
-RecoveryMailbox "Abe Berlas" -TargetFolder "Abe's Mail"
```

Use Lagged Database Copies

A lagged database copy allows you to replicate transaction logs to a passive database and wait a specified amount of time before replaying them into the database copy. This gives you some buffer in case you want a safeguard against potentially replaying a log that could cause a logical corruption. This scenario is unlikely in most cases, but there have been

Mitigating Risk

PART III

third-party applications known to cause logical corruption of data in mailboxes. If this is the case, you will probably incur some data loss when recovering from a lagged copy, since you will be deleting transaction logs that may still have valid transactions in them.

Configure a Lagged Database Copy Using the Exchange Management Shell

To enable lagged replay for an existing database copy, use the `Set-MailboxDatabaseCopy` cmdlet with the `ReplayLagTime` parameter. The following command enables a replay lag of 7 days on a database copy. (The max replay lag time is 14 days.)

```
Set-MailboxDatabaseCopy CONTOSO-MB02\DB01 -ReplayLagTime ↵
7.0:00:00
```

Recover from a Lagged Copy

To recover from a lagged database copy, perform these high-level steps:

1. Suspend replication to the lagged copy. You can suspend replication by following the steps in the section "Pausing Database Replication" in Chapter 7.

2. Take a Volume Shadow Copy Service (VSS) snapshot of the volume to ensure that you have a point-in-time copy of the lagged database copy. You can use the steps in the earlier section "Perform Backups with the Windows Server Backup Tool."

3. Determine the day and time that you want to restore the database to. Delete all the transaction logs that occurred after that time.

4. Repair the database using `ESEUTIL`. Use the steps in the earlier section "Mount a Database Restored to an Alternate Location."

5. Recover the data from the database using the recovery database method, as outlined in the earlier section "Use a Recovery Database."

6. Restore the VSS snapshot of the volume. You can follow the steps in the earlier section "Recover Databases with the Windows Server Backup Tool." When selecting the recovery type in the Recovery wizard, select the option to restore volumes instead of applications.

7. Resume replication to the lagged copy. These steps are found in Chapter 7, in the "Resuming Database Replication" section.

Recover Deleted Messages

One of the challenges over the years has been providing the ability to restore a single item after a user has deleted it. Many organizations turned to using third-party tools or kept backups for months on end, just to have this ability. Exchange Server 2010 now includes the ability to recover deleted messages after users purge them from their mailbox completely. This section helps you understand how this works and shows you how to configure and use single-item recovery.

Understand Single-Item Recovery

When a user deletes a message from their mailbox, it goes to the Deleted Items folder, where the message sits until the Deleted Items folder is emptied. After the folder is emptied, the message goes to the dumpster, which removes it from the view of the user's mailbox in Outlook. Users still have the ability to recover deleted items in Outlook using the Recover Deleted Items option. In previous versions of Exchange, once a user removed the message from the Recover Deleted Items tool or if the age of the message surpassed the deleted item's age limit, it was gone forever.

In Exchange Server 2010, a new step is added into the dumpster. After a user removes the message using the Recover Deleted Items tool in Outlook (by the way, the Recover Deleted Items tool is now available in Outlook Web App as well), the message is moved to a special Purges folder inside the dumpster. The Purges folder and the messages in it are hidden from the user. However, administrators who are delegated the right to perform discovery searches (covered in Chapter 9, "Administering Mailbox Content") can search through the Purges folder and recover items for individual users. This model allows administrators to recover deleted items for users without requiring permissions to restore and mount databases.

Configure Single-Item Recovery

By default, single-item recovery is configured to hold items for 14 days. However, you can modify this default value and hold items for longer.

TIP   The longer items are held, the more space they take up. Therefore, you don't want to enable single-item recovery for an extremely long period of time unless you've planned the storage capacity for it and adjusted the dumpster quotas appropriately.

Mitigating Risk

PART III

Enable Single Item Recovery on a Mailbox Using the Exchange Management Shell

You can enable single-item recovery for a mailbox by running the following command in the EMS:

```
Set-Mailbox MailboxName -SingleItemRecoveryEnabled $true
```

For example, to enable single-item recovery for Jay Humphrey's mailbox, you would use the following command:

```
Set-Mailbox "Jay Humphrey" -SingleItemRecoveryEnabled $true
```

Configure the Retention Period for Single-Item Recovery Using the Exchange Management Shell

To configure how long items are kept when single-item recovery is enabled, use the following EMS command:

```
Set-Mailbox MailboxName -RetainDeletedItemsFor NumberOfDays
```

For example, to enable single-item recovery to hold 60 days of messages, run this command:

```
Set-Mailbox "Jay Humphrey" -RetainDeletedItemsFor 60
```

Recover a Deleted Message

To recover a message using the single-item recovery feature, an administrator uses the discovery search tool to find the item. After the item is found, it is exported from the discovery search mailbox into the user's mailbox.

NOTE   To perform this recovery, you need to have the 64-bit version of Outlook 2010 installed on the computer with the Exchange ManagementTools and you must hold the role called Mailbox Import Export. For steps on adding a role to an account, see Chapter 12, "Securing Exchange Server."

These are the steps:

1. Perform a discovery search for the item that you need to restore. When performing the search, you can use keywords or a date range to narrow down the results of the search.

To perform a discovery search, follow the steps in the section "Create a New Discovery Search" in Chapter 9.

2. After the search is finished, open the discovery search mailbox using the steps in the section "Viewing the Results of a Discovery Search" in Chapter 9.

3. Find the item you're looking for in the discovery search mailbox.

4. Create a new folder in the discovery search mailbox. You can name this folder anything you'd like.

   This folder will be used to temporarily hold the item from the Recoverable Items folder in the discovery search mailbox. For example, you might call this folder Abe's Recovered Mail. Then drag the item from the Recoverable Items folder into the new folder that you just created.

5. Open the EMS and run the `Export-Mailbox` cmdlet on the discovery search mailbox.

   The following command exports the items from the Abe's Recovered Mail folder in the discovery search mailbox to the Recovered Mail folder inside Abe's mailbox:

```
Export-Mailbox "Discovery Search Mailbox" ↵
-IncludeFolders "Abe's Recovered Mail" ↵
-TargetMailbox abe -TargetFolder "Recovered Mail"
```

Abe's message is now restored in his mailbox in the folder called Recovered Mail.

Mitigating Risk

PART III

11

Monitoring Health and Performance

IN THIS CHAPTER, YOU WILL LEARN TO:

Mitigating Risk

PART III

W hen your Exchange servers are healthy and performing well, there
is a much smaller chance of problems surfacing that you didn't
anticipate. This chapter is about being proactive. That is, actively seek-
ing out potential issues before they happen. In order to be proactive,
we'll look primarily in two areas. The first area is ensuring that your
Exchange servers are healthy. I'll show you how to make sure that mail
is flowing freely throughout your transport servers. I'll also show you
how to proactively verify your health by monitoring your logs and other
factors. We'll also take a look at the Exchange Best Practices Analyzer,
and use that helpful tool to make sure that your Exchange implementation is in line with best practices.

The second area that we'll look at is the performance of Exchange.
There are many methods and tools that can be used to evaluate the performance of your Exchange servers. I'll show you how to use the most
common tools and methods that you'll want to use in your environment
as a minimum.

Keep Exchange Healthy

The Exchange administrator has no bigger task than to ensure that the
system stays up and running. Unfortunately, many administrators are
forced to live in reactive mode, constantly putting out the biggest fire.
Instead, administrators should strive to be consistently in proactive
mode. When you are in a state of proactivity, you don't need to "react"
to events, but instead you "respond" to them. In other words, living in
proactive mode means that you'll smell the smoke before the fire starts.
You'll detect little issues and quirks ahead of time so you can correct
them before they become big problems.

There are a few key areas that you need to become proactive in if you
want to be effective in keeping your Exchange implementation healthy:

- Keeping messages moving in and out of the Exchange
  organization

- Ensuring that your Exchange servers aren't standing on their last leg

- Using best practices in your implementation

This section shows you what you can do to proactively monitor the
health of Exchange in these areas.

Ensure That Mail Flows Freely

Ensuring that mail can be routed successfully throughout your environment is an important area to look at when you are monitoring Exchange health. A routing problem may not be easy to detect until it has compounded for a while. This is one of those areas where you can't depend on your users to notify you if there's a problem. If mail delivery is delayed, users may not even call the help desk because they may just blame it on the "slow network." And when messages are routed outside the organization, there are so many factors outside your control that you may not even realize the problem is with your servers.

Now more than ever, it's important to pay careful attention to your routing topology because Exchange relies heavily on an external dependency—Active Directory. Exchange administrators may not be aware of site topology changes in Active Directory (AD), and this can greatly affect how mail is routed.

Check Message Queues

When messages can't be routed to the next hop toward their destination, they will be held in one of the queues on the transport server that can't route the message. If users are sending mail and the messages are taking a long time to reach their recipients, there may be an excessive amount of messages in a queue. Therefore, it's important to monitor your queues and ensure that no issues exist that might prevent message delivery.

The two primary tools for checking message queues in Exchange Server 2010 are the Queue Viewer and the Exchange Management Shell (EMS). The Queue Viewer is accessible through the Toolbox portion of the Exchange Management Console (EMC). To open the Queue Viewer, follow these steps:

1. Open the EMC and browse to the Toolbox node in the Console tree. The Work area will list several tools that are included in Exchange Server 2010.

2. In the Mail Flow Tools section, double-click the Queue Viewer tool, as shown in Figure 11.1.

When the Queue Viewer is opened, the Submission queue is shown by default. Other queues that currently have messages in them will also appear. You can double-click on the queue to open it and view the details of the messages that are inside. Figure 11.2 shows a message stuck in the Unreachable queue because it couldn't find a Simple Mail Transfer Protocol (SMTP) connector to route the message over.

Figure 11.1: Opening the Queue Viewer tool from the EMC

Figure 11.2: A message trapped in the Unreachable queue

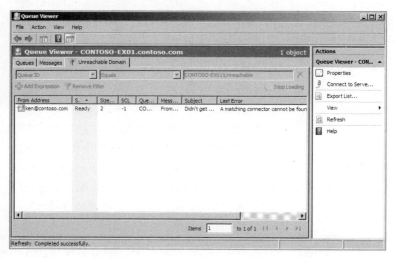

There are a few different things you can do to messages that are stuck in a queue. Table 11.1 lists your options.

Table 11.1: Actions You Can Take on Queued Messages

Action	Description	Usage Notes
Suspend the message	Stops the message from being delivered and moved out of the queue	Does not apply to the Submission queue or the Poison Message queue.
Remove the message	Removes the message from the queue	You have the option of sending a nondelivery report to the sender or just silently dropping the message from the queue. This does not apply to the Submission queue.
Export the message	Makes a copy of the queued message without removing the message from the queue	Cannot be done in the Queue Viewer. Exporting messages can only be performed with the EMS.
Resubmit the message	Moves the message out of the queue and resubmits it to the Submission queue	Causes the message to go through categorization again.

Suspend and Remove Messages from Queues

You can suspend and remove messages using the Queue Viewer. Use the following steps:

1. In the Queue Viewer, select the Messages tab in the main pane. The messages that are currently in the queue are listed.

2. Click on the message that you want to suspend or remove.

   The Actions pane on the right will present the options that you have (Figure 11.3). Remember that you cannot perform these options on messages that are in the Submission queue.

3. Click Suspend to suspend the message. Click Remove (With NDR) to remove the message and send a nondelivery report to the sender. Click Remove (Without Sending NDR) to drop the message from the queue without notifying the sender. The sender may assume that the message was delivered.

4. If you choose to remove a message, you are prompted for confirmation. Click the Yes button in the confirmation dialog box to continue.

Mitigating Risk

PART III

Figure 11.3: Suspending or removing a message from a queue

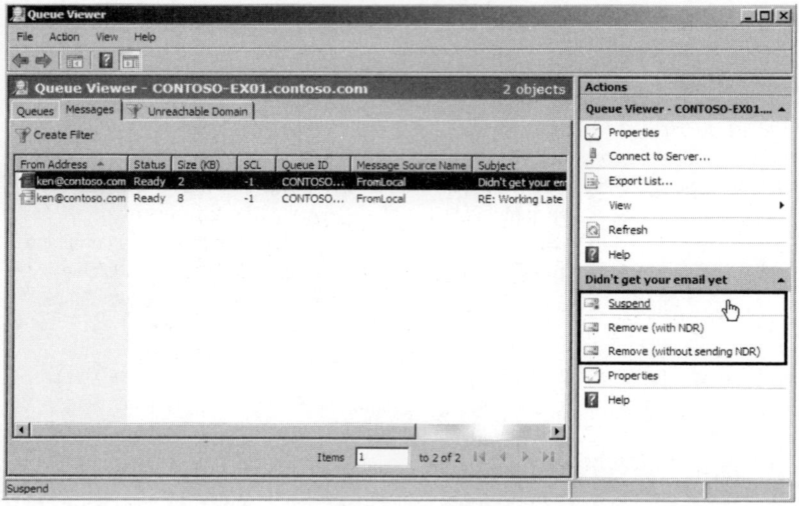

Export a Message from the Queue Using the Exchange Management Shell

If you want to export a message from a queue, you must use the Exchange Management Shell. Run the Export-Message cmdlet to export the message. You will need to specify the message identity and the file path to where you want to export the message. To get the message identity, you can view the properties of the queued message in the Queue Viewer or you can run the Get-Message cmdlet. The following example retrieves the message identity for the messages that are in the Unreachable queue:

```
Get-Message -Queue CONTOSO-EX01\Unreachable | ft Identity, ↵
FromAddress, Status
```

For further instructions on using the Export-Message cmdlet, refer to Chapter 6, "Managing Message Routing."

Resubmit a Queued Message Using the Exchange Management Shell

When you resubmit a message, you must resubmit all the messages in the queue. To resubmit messages, you use the Retry-Queue cmdlet in the EMS and specify the Resubmit parameter. The following example resubmits all of the messages in the Unreachable queue:

```
Retry-Queue CONTOSO-EX01\Unreachable -Resubmit $True
```

Use Protocol Logging to Diagnose Transport Problems

Protocol logging provides a method for you to determine what's happening behind the scenes in an SMTP exchange between servers. By turning on protocol logging, you can determine what the servers are saying to each other. Protocol logging can be enabled for send connectors or receive connectors. Send connectors and receive connectors maintain separate protocol logs.

To use protocol logging, follow these steps:

1. Turn protocol logging on at the connector that you want to log.

2. Determine or change the location of the protocol logs.

3. Examine the logs and understand what they are saying.

Enable Protocol Logging on Receive Connectors

To use the EMC to turn on protocol logging for receive connectors on a Hub Transport server, follow these steps:

1. Open the EMC and browse to the Server Configuration ➤ Hub Transport node in the Console tree.

2. Select the Hub Transport server that contains the receive connector from the list in the Results pane.

3. In the list of receive connectors, select the connector that you want to enable protocol logging on and click the Properties action in the Actions pane.

4. In the properties dialog box for the connector, select the General tab.

5. Next to the Protocol Logging Level option, select Verbose from the drop-down list, as shown in Figure 11.4.

6. Click OK to make the changes and close the properties dialog box.

You can also enable protocol logging on a receive connector through the EMS. Use the following command to enable protocol logging:

```
Set-ReceiveConnector ReceiveConnectorName ↵
 -ProtocolLoggingLevel Verbose
```

Enable Protocol Logging on Send Connectors

To enable protocol logging on send connectors in the EMC, follow these steps:

1. Open the EMC and browse to the Organization Configuration ➤ Hub Transport node in the Console tree.

Mitigating Risk

PART III

2. Select the Send Connectors tab in the Work area.

3. In the list of send connectors, select the connector that you want to enable protocol logging on.

4. In the Actions pane on the right, click the Properties action to open the properties dialog box for the connector.

5. In the properties dialog box, select the General tab.

6. To the right of the Protocol Logging Level field, select Verbose from the drop-down list.

7. Click OK to make the change and close the properties dialog box.

Figure 11.4: Enabling protocol logging on a receive connector

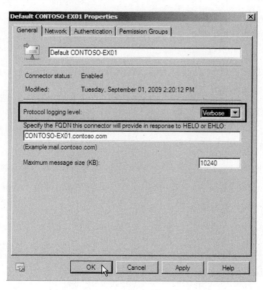

You can also enable the protocol logs for send connectors using the following EMS command:

```
Set-SendConnector SendConnectorName -ProtocolLoggingLevel ↵
Verbose
```

Configure the Location of the Protocol Logs

When you enable protocol logging, information is written to the protocol logs. On each server there is one instance of these logs for send connectors and one instance for receive connectors. To determine where those logs are or to change the location of those logs, you can use the following steps in the EMC:

1. Open the EMC and browse to the Server Configuration ➤ Hub Transport node in the Console tree.

2. In the list of Hub Transport servers in the Results pane, select the server that you want to modify the location of the protocol logs on.

3. In the Actions pane on the right, select the Properties task to display the properties dialog box for the server you have selected.

4. In the properties dialog box, click the Log Settings tab.

5. View or modify the folder path in the Send Protocol Log Path field or the Receive Protocol Log Path field (Figure 11.5).

6. If you changed any of the protocol log paths, click OK to make the changes and close the properties dialog box.

Figure 11.5: Viewing or modifying the folder path of the protocol logs

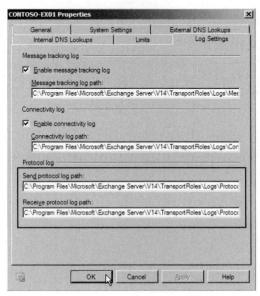

Read the Protocol Logs

After the protocol logs are configured, you can open the logs and start reading through them. Browse to the folder that the logs are stored in using the path that you discovered previously. You can simply double-click on the log to open it using Notepad.exe.

The protocol log records several parameters that you can use to determine why a message isn't being sent from or received by a particular server. The notable fields used by the protocol logs are detailed in Table 11.2.

Table 11.2: Fields Used by the Protocol Logs

Field Name	Description
date-time	The date and time that the event occurred.
connector-id	The name of the connector that the event occurred on.
session-id	The unique ID associated with the SMTP session. You can use this to distinguish SMTP sessions from one another.
sequence-number	A number that is associated with each event in the current SMTP session. This is used to determine which order things happened in.
local-endpoint	The IP address and port used on your Exchange server.
remote-endpoint	The IP address and port used by the external Mail server.
Event	Indicates what was happening in the exchange. The session can be connected (+) or disconnected (-). After a session is connected, commands can be sent (>) or received (<). The log also indicates informational (*) messages.

Using the information in the protocol logs, you can determine what exactly is happening during the SMTP session and take action accordingly. Figure 11.6 shows the send connector protocol logs from a message that was rejected by a server.

Track Message Flow

The ability to track message flow inside an Exchange organization is useful when you want to determine what has happened to a message after the user sent it. You can track message flow throughout an Exchange organization using the message tracking logs. The message tracking logs keep track of messages that are sent between transport servers and to and from mailbox servers. These logs can be enabled on Mailbox, Hub Transport, and Edge Transport servers. Message tracking logs are enabled by default, so unless you explicitly turned them off, you can just start analyzing them.

Figure 11.6: A sample protocol log from a send connector

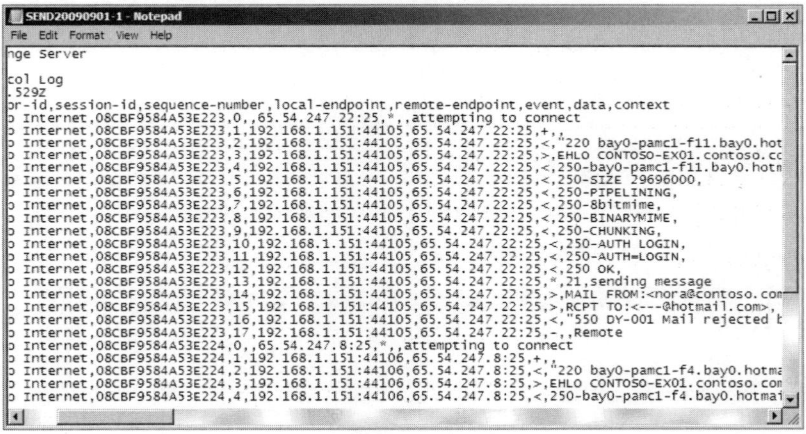

You have a few options for viewing message logs:

- Viewing the log files directly
- Using the Tracking Log Explorer
- Using the Exchange Management Shell

View the Log Files Directly

Directly viewing the log files with a tool such as Notepad.exe might not be the most efficient method of viewing the logs, but it's available to you as an option. Determine where the logs are kept on the Transport server by running the following EMS command:

```
Get-TransportServer ServerName | fl MessageTrackingLogPath
```

To determine where the logs are on a Mailbox server, use this EMS command:

```
Get-MailboxServer ServerName | fl MessageTrackingLogPath
```

Mitigating Risk

PART III

After you get the path of the logs, you can browse to the folder on your server. Log files on transport servers are given the name MSGTRK*yyyymmdd*-#.log and mailbox server message tracking log files are named MSGTRKM*yyyymmdd*-#.log. The identifier *yyyymmdd* corresponds to the year, month, and day that the log file was created. Each log file is given a number that increments for each log file created on that day. By default, after log files reach 10 MB, a new log file is created with an incremented number. If your server has the Hub Transport role and Mailbox role combined, you will see both the MSGTRK log and the MSGTRKM log in the folder. However, the tracking log files for the Transport server and Mailbox server are kept separate even
if it's the same server.

If you open one of the message tracking log files in Notepad.exe, you will see a comma-separated file similar to the one shown in Figure 11.7.

Figure 11.7: Message tracking log file

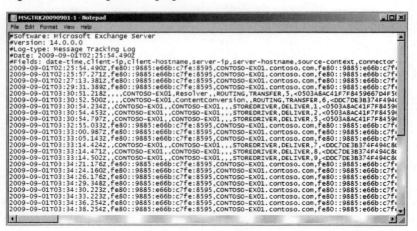

There are multiple fields in this file that indicate useful information such as the time that the message was sent or received, the servers that were involved in transporting the message, and the sender, recipient, and subject of the message. Although this information is available in the raw log files, using the Tracking Log Explorer to analyze the information may be a better choice.

Use the Tracking Log Explorer

The Tracking Log Explorer is part of the Exchange Troubleshooting Assistant, which is used in diagnosing multiple issues with Exchange.

You can use the Tracking Log Explorer to search through the message tracking logs and determine what exactly has happened to a message. As shown in Figure 11.8, there are multiple parameters you can perform the search with. If you don't specify the sender or the server, the search is performed against the Exchange server that you are currently logged in at.

Figure 11.8: Available search parameters in the Tracking Log Explorer

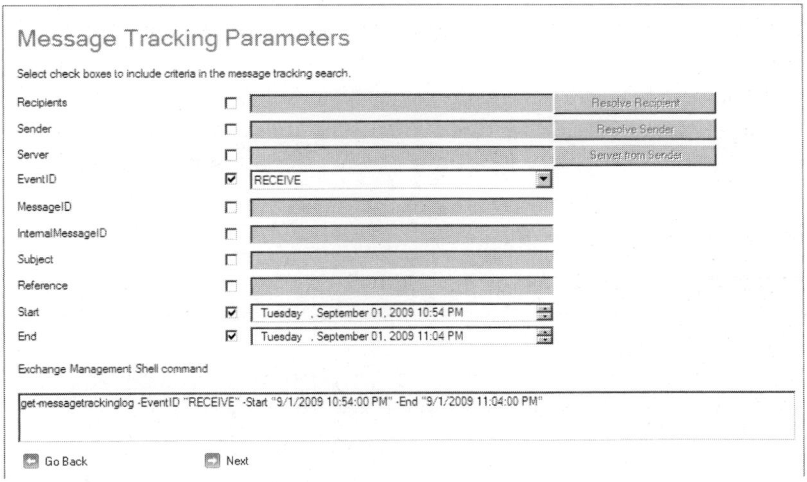

A field at the bottom of the parameters dialog box specifies the EMS parameter that is used in the search. You can copy and paste this command into the Exchange Management Shell to duplicate the results that the Tracking Log Explorer got.

The following steps demonstrate how to use the Tracking Log Explorer to track a message:

1. Open the EMC and browse to the Toolbox node in the Console tree.

2. In the Work area, double-click on the Tracking Log Explorer tool from the list of tools in the Mail Flow Tools section of the EMC.

   The Exchange Troubleshooting Assistant launches and goes straight to the Tracking Log Explorer. If this is your first time using the Tracking Log Explorer, you may see a welcome screen that you can safely bypass.

3. In the Message Tracking Parameters dialog box, select the parameters that you want to use to perform the search. You can use the

Sender, Recipients, or Subject fields to find the message that you
want to track.

4. Click Next to search for the message in the message tracking logs.

The Message Tracking Results dialog box will display all the
events that were found matching your search criteria. If you look
at the results shown in Figure 11.9, you can see that the particular message that was searched on was submitted by the Mailbox
server, received by the Transport server, and delivered to the
recipient's mailbox.

Figure 11.9: Viewing the results of a tracked message

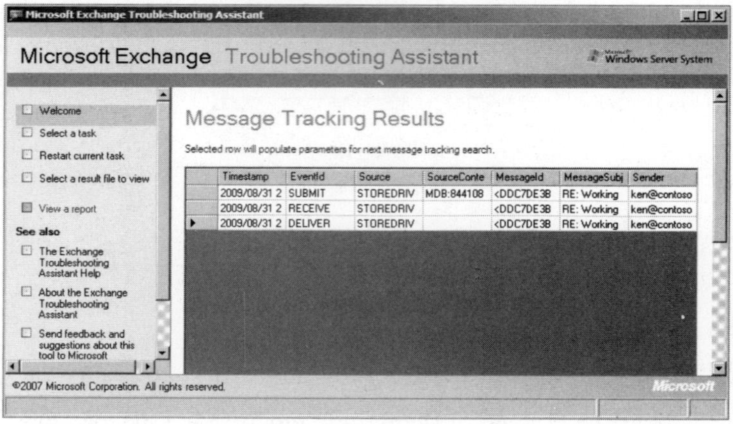

Track Messages in the EMS

You can use the Get-MessageTrackingLog cmdlet to perform various message tracking searches in the EMS. The easiest way to use the EMS for
searching through message tracking logs is to build the search using the
Tracking Log Explorer and then copy and modify the EMS command
that the tool creates for you.

For example, the EMS command that was used by the Tracking Log
Explorer in the previous example can be run directly in the EMS:

```
Get-MessageTrackingLog -Server CONTOSO-EX01 ↵
-MessageSubject "RE: Working Late"
```

Verify Exchange Server Health

A large part of being proactive in managing your Exchange environment is knowing where your servers stand in terms of health. This section discusses various things that you need to keep an eye on to help ensure that your servers are healthy.

Monitor the Event Logs

Event logs in Windows are used by several components and applications as a place to record critical alerts and notifications that may be of interest to system administrators. Exchange Server 2010 also uses the Windows event logs to record important events. Exchange records most of its events to the Application log, but you may also see some events recorded elsewhere. However, the majority of the events that you need to be concerned about for Exchange will appear in the Application log.

As a part of your responsibilities as an Exchange Server 2010 administrator, it's vital to check the event logs on each Exchange server and make sure that you don't see any undetected problems or other events that could become big issues in the future. You will primarily want to keep an eye out for any Warning or Error events, as they indicate problems that the server is currently having or could have.

View Relevant Events

To view the Application event log, follow these steps:

1. Click Start ➤ Administrative Tools ➤ Event Viewer.

   This launches the Event Viewer application that is built into Windows.

2. In the Event Viewer Console tree, browse to the Windows Logs ➤ Application node.

   The event logs for Exchange (and other processes) are displayed in the Results pane. You can search through the log line by line or you can create a filter.

3. If you want to filter out everything except for the Exchange logs, click the Filter Current Log task in the Actions pane on the right.

4. In the Filter Current Log dialog box, select the Critical, Error, and Warning check boxes. These events will indicate that something is wrong with Exchange or that something may soon break.

Mitigating Risk

PART III

5. While still in the Filter Current Log dialog box, click on the drop-down list for the Event Sources field and select the relevant events that begin with MSExchange from the list, as shown in Figure 11.10. Click OK when finished.

Figure 11.10: Filtering out everything except for the Exchange logs in Event Viewer

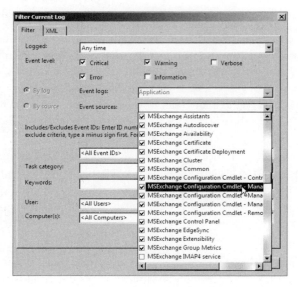

6. Back in the Event Viewer dialog box, you can now view only the events relevant to Exchange.

Specify the Level of Logging Detail

If you find that you need more detail than what is provided in the Application logs, you can turn the dial up on what Exchange logs in the Application log. To increase logging, use the `Set-EventLogLevel` cmdlet in the EMS. You will need to specify the category of logs that you want to increase and how much you want to increase it.

In the following example, we will check and change the log level for the MSExchangeRPC log:

1. To determine what component to enable higher logging on and to determine the current logging level, run the following command:

```
Get-EventLogLevel
```

2. The `Get-EventLogLevel` command displays information about each component. Use the built-in PowerShell filtering capabilities to narrow down this list to display only event log categories that have the characters rpc in the identity:

```
Get-EventLogLevel *rpc*
```

3. To specify a logging level of High for the MSExchangeRPC log, use the following command:

```
Set-EventLogLevel "MSExchangeSA\RPC Calls" -Level High
```

Monitor Disk Space on Database and Log Drives

The amount of free disk space is an important thing to monitor, particularly on your volumes that contain the database files or the transaction log files. On Mailbox servers, when the volume that contains the database gets full the database will be dismounted, which prevents users from accessing their mailboxes on that database. Dismounting the database is how Exchange protects the integrity of the data, as it cannot write additional data to the database if there is no space to do so. The database is dismounted when there is 2 MB of disk space left on the volume.

When the database is dismounted due to the disk being full, Exchange will log an event in the Application log with event ID 1003, as shown in Figure 11.11.

Figure 11.11: Event ID 1003 is logged when the database volume is out of free space.

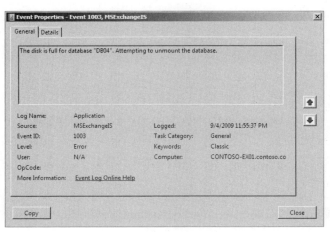

Before the database can be mounted again, you must free up some space on the volume. There are multiple ways to reclaim space:

- Back up the server and allow the transaction logs to truncate.

- Back up the server and permanently delete any mailboxes that may be stored in deleted mailbox retention.

- Perform an offline defragmentation of the database using the ESEUTIL /D command. This may take some time to complete.

- If you're using a SAN-based volume, you can grow the size of the LUN that is presented to the Exchange server.

- Back up any extraneous data or personal files and delete them or move them to a more appropriate server.

- Move any transaction logs that have already been committed to another volume.

On Transport servers, when the disk that contains the message queue database and logs nears capacity, Exchange applies back pressure, which instructs Exchange to stop accepting new connections and potentially stops all message flow. By default, the Transport servers require at least 500 MB of disk space free on the volumes that contain the queue database and logs, so you should monitor the free disk space on those locations.

If you get into the situation of being low on disk space on your Transport server and back pressure is being applied, alleviate the problem using one of the following methods:

- Free up disk space on the Transport server by removing extraneous data.

- Move the queue database and logs to a separate volume with more space available.

- Modify the threshold numbers used to determine when to apply back pressure.

When back pressure is applied or relinquished, the Transport servers will log events in the Application log with event IDs of 15004 and 15005. You can monitor the Application log for these events on your Transport servers to indicate that back pressure is being applied.

Ensure That Services Are Running

The various components of Exchange run as services in Windows. Not all of the services need to be running in order for Exchange to be functional, however. Certain services may only need to be started if Exchange is using a feature that relies on services, such as POP or IMAP. In fact, one of the best practices in hardening servers is to disable services that you are not required to run.

There are core services that need to be running in Exchange in order for an Exchange server in a particular role to function correctly. You should monitor these services to ensure that they are running. Many problems are attributable to a service that has stopped running for one reason or another. If you know when a critical service stops, you can respond rapidly to get the problem resolved.

Table 11.3 lists the services that Exchange Server 2010 uses and identifies which services are critical for each role.

Table 11.3: Critical Services That Need to Remain Running for Each Role

Service	Mailbox	Client Access	Hub Transport	Edge Transport
IIS Admin Service	Yes	Yes	Yes	No
Microsoft Exchange Active Directory Topology	Yes	Yes	Yes	No
Microsoft Exchange ADAM	No	No	No	Yes
Microsoft Exchange Credential Service	No	No	No	Yes
Microsoft Exchange EdgeSync	No	No	Yes	No
Microsoft Exchange Information Store	Yes	No	No	No
Microsoft Exchange Mailbox Assistants	Yes	No	No	No
Microsoft Exchange Address Book	No	Yes	No	No
Microsoft Exchange Forms-Based Authentication Service	No	Yes	No	No
Microsoft Exchange File Distribution	No	Yes	No	No
Microsoft Exchange Mail Submission	Yes	No	No	No

Table 11.3: Critical Services That Need to Remain Running for Each Role *(continued)*

Service	Mailbox	Client Access	Hub Transport	Edge Transport
Microsoft Exchange Mailbox Replication	Yes	Yes	No	No
Microsoft Exchange Protected Service Host	No	Yes	No	No
Microsoft Exchange RPC Client Access	Yes	Yes	No	No
Microsoft Exchange System Attendant	Yes	No	No	No
Microsoft Exchange Search Indexer	Yes	No	No	No
Microsoft Exchange Service Host	Yes	Yes	Yes	Yes
Microsoft Exchange Throttling	Yes	No	No	No
Microsoft Exchange Transport	No	No	Yes	Yes
Microsoft Exchange Transport Log Search	Yes	No	Yes	No
World Wide Web Publishing Service	Yes	Yes	Yes	No
Windows Remote Management	Yes	Yes	Yes	No

To determine if the required services for each role are running, you can execute the Test-ServiceHealth cmdlet in the EMS. You do not need to include any parameters.

The Test-ServiceHealth cmdlet will return the list of roles that are running on the Exchange server along with a list of the services for those roles. The cmdlet identifies the services that are running as well as the services that are not running but should be.

The following output demonstrates what is returned by the command when the Mail Submission service is stopped on a Mailbox server:

```
Role                     : Mailbox Server Role
RequiredServicesRunning : False
ServicesRunning          : {IISAdmin, MSExchangeADTopology,
                           MSExchangeIS, MSExchangeMailbox
```

```
                         Assistants, MSExchangeRepl, MSEx
                         changeRPC, MSExchangeSA, MSExchange
                         Search, MSExchangeServiceHost, MS
                         ExchangeThrottling, MSExchange
                         TransportLogSearch, W3Svc, WinRM}
ServicesNotRunning     : {MSExchangeMailSubmission}
```

Use the Test Cmdlets in the Exchange Management Shell

Exchange Server 2010 provides several cmdlets in the Exchange Management Shell that are focused on testing the functionality and configuration of Exchange. The list of test cmdlets has grown in comparison to those available with Exchange Server 2007, and there are several useful ones that can make your job as an Exchange administrator a lot easier. Table 11.4 describes the available test cmdlets. You may have seen some of these cmdlets used throughout this book when working with certain aspects of Exchange.

Table 11.4: The Test-* Cmdlets in Exchange Server 2010

Cmdlet	Description
Test-ActiveSyncConnectivity	Tests mobile device connectivity through ActiveSync. The cmdlet attempts to synchronize the mobile device that you specify in the command.
Test-EcpConnectivity	Tests access to the Exchange Control Panel on a Client Access server that you specify.
Test-EdgeSynchronization	Tests the synchronization of Edge Transport servers.
Test-FederationTrust	Tests the configuration of the federation trust with the Microsoft Federation Gateway.
Test-FederationTrustCertificate	Tests the certificate used for your federation trust.
Test-ImapConnectivity	Tests the connectivity of one or more IMAP clients.
Test-IPAllowListProvider	Tests that the configured IP allow list provider is available and checks an IP address against it.

Table 11.4: The Test-* Cmdlets in Exchange Server 2010 *(continued)*

Cmdlet	Description
Test-IPBlockListProvider	Tests that the configured IP block list provider is available and checks an IP address against it.
Test-IRMConfiguration	Tests the configuration of Rights Management in Exchange.
Test-Mailflow	Tests whether mail can be sent to and from mailbox servers in the Exchange organization.
Test-MapiConnectivity	Tests that a mailbox can be logged into. If run against a database, it tests that the system mailbox for the database can be logged into.
Test-Message	Submits a test message to the specified recipients. This can be used to test transport rules and have a report generated about the tests.
Test-MRSHealth	Tests to ensure that the Mailbox Replication Service is running properly.
Test-OutlookConnectivity	Thoroughly tests the connectivity of Outlook by testing profile creation, AutoDiscover, and mailbox access.
Test-OutlookWebServices	Tests that AutoDiscover is returning the correct configuration information for a user and tests each of the service endpoints returned by AutoDiscover.
Test-OwaConnectivity	Tests that Outlook Web App can be contacted and successfully logged into.
Test-PopConnectivity	Tests the connectivity of one or more POP clients.
Test-PowerShellConnectivity	Tests that PowerShell can be used remotely and can successfully issue commands.
Test-ReplicationHealth	Tests multiple aspects of replication for a server in a DAG.

Table 11.4: The Test-* Cmdlets in Exchange Server 2010 *(continued)*

Cmdlet	Description
`Test-SenderId`	Tests sender ID checking against an IP address and domain that you specify.
`Test-ServiceHealth`	Tests that the services for each Exchange role installed are running.
`Test-SystemHealth`	Tests the overall health of the Exchange server through multiple tests.
`Test-WebServicesConnectivity`	Tests the functionality of Exchange Web Services through the use of Outlook Anywhere.

TIP   The test cmdlets don't need to always be run on demand. You can choose a few of them that you want to run on a regular basis and create scheduled tasks out of them. For information on creating scheduled tasks from PowerShell scripts, refer to Chapter 2, "Using the Exchange Management Console and the Exchange Management Shell."

When running some of these test cmdlets, you may be required to have a specific test account created beforehand. To create this account, use the following steps:

1. Open the EMS and browse to the Scripts folder in the location where Exchange is installed. By default, this location is `C:\Program Files\Microsoft\Exchange Server\v14\Scripts`.

2. Run the PS1 script called `New-TestCasConnectivityUser.ps1`.

3. When prompted for a password, type a temporary password and press Enter. This password is just used for the creation of the test account and you will therefore not need to remember this password.

4. When prompted to continue creating the test user, press Enter.

   The test user is automatically created. When the test account is finished, the script will end and you will be returned to the EMS command prompt.

Use the Exchange Best Practices Analyzer

The Exchange Best Practices Analyzer (ExBPA) is a powerful tool in the Exchange administrator's toolbox that should be run on a regular basis. The ExBPA can perform a variety of tests that help ensure the health of your Exchange organization. In this section, I will show you how to run a health check.

The ExBPA health check component performs a variety of tests against your Exchange servers and presents the results in an easy-to-read report. When reviewing the report, you will be presented with the critical issues encountered and given the opportunity to read more about why the issue was detected and how to correct it.

To perform a health check with the ExBPA, use the following steps:

1. Open the Exchange Best Practices Analyzer. You can do this by opening the EMC and browsing to the Toolbox node in the Console tree. Under the Configuration Management Tools portion of the Toolbox, double-click on Best Practices Analyzer.

2. If this is the first time you are running the BPA, you will be presented with a welcome screen. Decide whether you want to join the Microsoft Customer Experience Improvement Program and then click Go To The Welcome Screen.

3. At the Welcome screen, select the option Select Options For A New Scan.

4. On the Connect To Active Directory screen, type the name of the domain controller you want to connect to and click Connect To The Active Directory Server.

5. If you want to use different credentials than what you are currently logged in as for communication with Active Directory, click Show Advanced Login Options and enter the credentials that you want to use.

   Your connectivity and access permissions are verified before continuing.

6. On the Start A New Best Practices Scan screen, enter a name for the scan and select Health Check from the list of scans to perform.

7. If you only want to scan specific Exchange servers, you can select those servers from the Specify The Scope For This Scan list.

8. After you configured your options, click Start Scanning, as shown in Figure 11.12.

Figure 11.12: Configuring the BPA to perform a health check

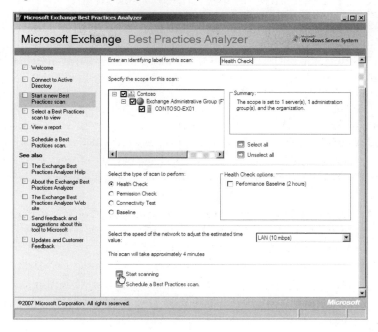

On the Scanning In Progress screen, the scan is performed. The amount of time that the scan takes to complete will vary depending on how many servers you are scanning and the speed of your network.

9. After the scan completes, you will be taken to the Scanning Complete screen. Select the option View A Report Of This Best Practices Scan.

10. View the results of the scan and take any necessary action on reported issues by selecting the option Tell Me More About This Setting, as you can see in Figure 11.13.

Track Exchange Performance

Ensuring that Exchange servers are highly performing machines is a vital area to focus on. This was more apparent in previous versions of Exchange where performance bottlenecks were more obvious. With the

Mitigating Risk

many improvements in the architecture of Exchange and with the move to a 64 bit–only operating system, the performance demands of the system are becoming easier to meet. But before you can meet your performance requirements, you need to have an idea of how your Exchange servers are performing. This section will show you how to gather this information and gauge the level of performance that you need for Exchange.

Figure 11.13: Viewing the results of your health check

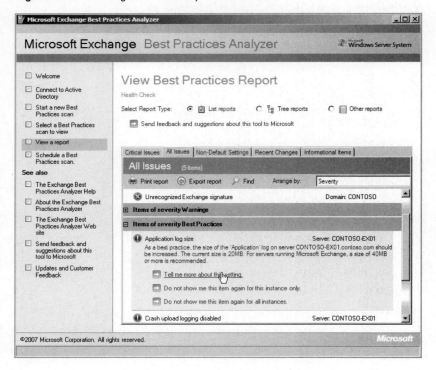

In this section, we'll first look at the tools that you can use for checking the performance of Exchange. Then I'll show you how to stress-test your servers and test the performance limitations of your configuration.

Use the Performance Tools Available

When analyzing the performance of Exchange, some of the best tools that you have at your disposal are the free ones that come with Exchange and Windows. The two tools that we'll look at in particular are the Performance Troubleshooter and the Performance Monitor tool.

Run the Performance Troubleshooter

The Performance Troubleshooter is a part of the Exchange Troubleshooting Assistant tool. With the Performance Troubleshooter, you can analyze and troubleshoot performance problems in Exchange as they are happening.

To use the Performance Troubleshooter, perform the following steps:

1. Open the EMC and browse to the Toolbox node in the Console tree.

2. Double-click on the Performance Troubleshooter tool in the list of tools in the Work area.

   The Microsoft Exchange Troubleshooting Assistant launches and takes you directly to the Performance Troubleshooter.

3. At the Welcome screen of the Performance Troubleshooter, type a name for the performance analysis that you are running. Select the option Troubleshoot New Performance Issue and then click Next.

4. On the Exchange Performance Troubleshooter screen you'll see the What Symptoms Are You Seeing? field. Select the appropriate symptom that you are troubleshooting from the drop-down list. Click Next to continue.

5. At the next screen, type the name of the Exchange server in the Server Name field and ensure that the domain controller in the Global Catalog Server Name field is the one that you want to use. Then click Next.

6. On the Configure Data Collection screen, determine whether you want to start the collection now or adjust it to run at a later time. If performing the data collection now, select Start Collection Now and click Next.

   You can also change the location where performance data is stored by changing the directory in the Root Data Directory field.

   The Performance Troubleshooter performs the data collection and compiles the performance report. These tasks may take some time to finish.

7. After the analysis is complete, you will be presented with the performance report in the View Results screen. You can view the results of the report and make the appropriate changes. If you click the Performance Issues tab (as shown in Figure 11.14), you can go through what the tool identified as potential performance problems and correct or ignore them.

Mitigating Risk

PART III

Figure 11.14: Viewing the results of the performance report

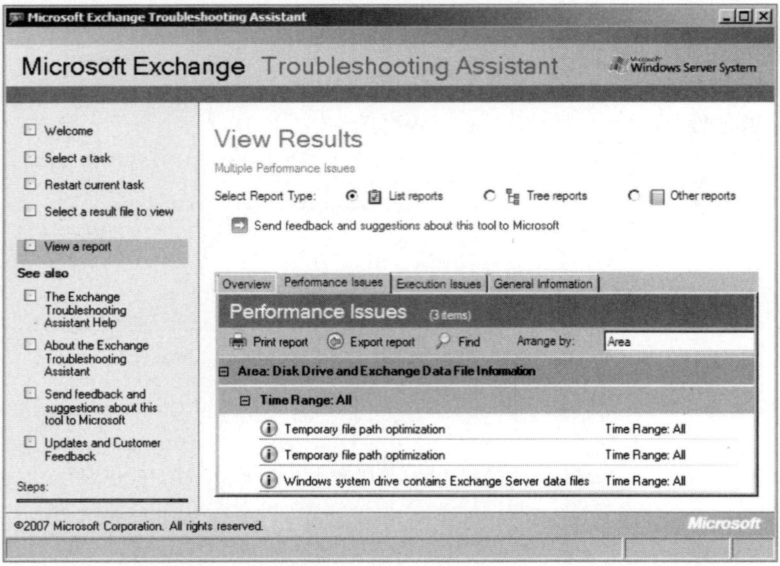

Analyze Performance with the Performance Monitor

The Performance Monitor tool allows you to specify one or more performance counters to collect data on and track. The tool is used for collection and reporting of the real-time or precollected performance statistics. You can add and remove counters from the monitor and generate and save reports based on those counters.

View Real-Time Performance Statistics

You can view performance statistics in real time by using the following steps:

1. Open the EMC and browse to the Toolbox node in the Console tree.

2. In the Work area, select Performance Monitor from the list of tools and double-click on it to launch it.

3. In the Exchange Server Performance Monitor tool, select the System Monitor node from the tree in the left pane.

   The System Monitor is used for viewing real-time statistics based on the performance counters that are currently loaded. The list near the bottom of the graph contains the currently loaded counters.

4. Check and uncheck counters to display them or remove them from the graph (see Figure 11.15).

Figure 11.15: Reviewing the performance counters in real time

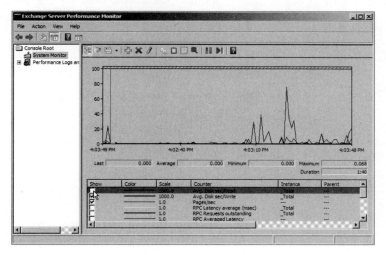

5. To add counters to the list, click the plus sign above the graph or press Ctrl+I.

The Add Counters dialog box will be displayed.

6. In the Available Counters section, scroll through the list of counters that are available and click the Add button to add counters to the tool. This is shown in Figure 11.16.

7. Click OK to close the Add Counters dialog box and go back to the System Monitor.

Capture and Save Performance Statistics for Analysis

You can create data collections that allow you to monitor the system for a period of time and save the results. These results can then be used later for analysis of the performance statistics. Use the following steps to collect the performance statistics:

1. Open the EMC and browse to the Toolbox node in the Console tree.

2. In the Work area, select Performance Monitor from the list of tools and double-click on it to launch it.

Mitigating Risk

PART III

Figure 11.16: Adding performance counters to the tool

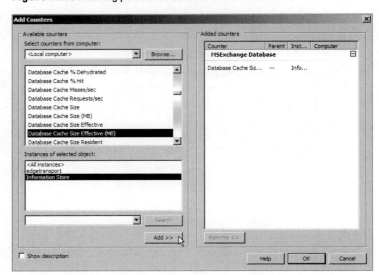

3. In the Exchange Server Performance Monitor tool, browse to the Performance Logs And Alerts ➢ Data Collector Sets ➢ User Defined node in the tree in the left pane.

4. Right-click on the User Defined node in the tree and select New ➢ Data Collector Set from the drop-down menu.

   This launches the Create New Data Collector Set wizard.

5. On the first screen of the wizard, type a name for the data collector set. This is an arbitrary name that you will use to uniquely identify this set of data from other sets that you create.

6. Choose the Create Manually option to create an advanced data set composed of the metrics that you want to capture. Click Next to continue.

7. In the screen What Type Of Data Do You Want To Include?, select the Performance Counter check box and click Next.

8. At the next screen, Which Performance Counters Would You Like To Log?, click the Add button to add your counters to the list.

   This launches the Add Counters dialog box.

9. In the Available Counters section, scroll through the list of counters that are available and click the Add button to add counters to the collection. Click OK when you've added all the counters that you are going to use.

10. When back in the wizard, adjust the interval that you want to collect the data in. Click Next to continue.

    The default interval is set to collect data every 15 seconds.

11. On the screen Where Would You Like The Data To Be Saved?, specify the folder that the data will be saved in, and then click Next.

12. At the Create The Data Collector Set screen, you can specify a custom account that the data will be collected under.

13. Select the option Save And Close and then click the Finish button to complete the creation of the data collector set.

    Back in the Exchange Server Performance Monitor tool, the new data collector set that you just created will be shown under the User Defined node.

14. Right-click on the data collector set and choose Start from the drop-down menu to start collecting the data.

15. When you are finished collecting the data, you can right-click on the data collector set and choose Stop.

Test the Performance Limitations in a Lab

When sizing your Exchange servers, most of the effort you are putting into the calculations for server hardware and user load are theoretical until you apply some real load to the system. It's always a good idea to stress-test your server configuration before placing it in your production environment. This section shows you how to stress-test the Mailbox servers and the client workload in your environment.

Stress-Test the Databases

When sizing Mailbox servers, one of the most important things is ensuring that your databases and storage can handle your anticipated user load. You will want to perform this testing before you deploy your servers in production to ensure that they are adequately sized.

Mitigating Risk

PART III

The Exchange Jetstress tool is designed to perform this type of testing on Exchange databases. Jetstress is not installed with Exchange. You will need to download the tool from the Exchange Server 2010 TechCenter and install it separately. This section will walk you through installing and using Jetstress before deploying your servers in production.

Install Jetstress

You can install Jetstress on your existing Exchange servers, but the preferred method is to install it and test your system before you install Exchange. Therefore, part of the installation procedures includes copying database files from your Exchange installation media. Use the following steps to install Jetstress:

1. Download Jetstress from the Exchange Server 2010 TechCenter at the following URL:

   `http://technet.microsoft.com/en-us/exchange/2010`

2. Double-click on the `Jetstress.msi` file that you downloaded. This will launch the Jetstress installation wizard.

3. In the Welcome screen of the installation wizard, click Next.

4. At the End-User License Agreement screen, click the option I Accept The Terms In The License Agreement and click Next.

5. On the Select Installation Folder screen, ensure that you are satisfied with the default location of the Jetstress files. If you anticipate that another person will be logging into the server with a different account and using Jetstress, then click the Everyone option and click Next.

6. At the Confirm Installation screen, click Next to start the installation.

7. After Jetstress is installed, you will see the Installation Complete screen. Click Close to close the wizard.

8. Copy the following files from your Exchange installation media or folder to the location where Jetstress was installed:

   - `ESE.DLL`
   - `ESEPERF.DLL`
   - `ESEPERF.INI`
   - `ESEPERF.HXX`

You can do this by opening a command prompt and running the following commands, assuming that you kept the default location of Jetstress and assuming that your Exchange media is in drive D:

```
copy d:\Setup\ServerRoles\Common\perf\amd64\eseperf.dll ↵
"c:\Program Files\Exchange JetStress"

copy d:\Setup\ServerRoles\Common\perf\amd64\eseperf.hxx ↵
"c:\Program Files\Exchange JetStress"

copy d:\Setup\ServerRoles\Common\perf\amd64\eseperf.ini ↵
"c:\Program Files\Exchange JetStress"

copy d:\Setup\ServerRoles\Common\ese.dll ↵
"c:\Program Files\Exchange JetStress"
```

Run Jetstress

You can use the following steps to perform a basic disk throughput test using the storage configuration on your Mailbox server. In this example, we're going to test the performance of disk subsystem throughput:

1. Launch Jetstress by clicking Start ➢ All Programs ➢ Microsoft Exchange ➢ Exchange Jetstress.

2. At the Jetstress Welcome screen, click Start New Test.

3. Jetstress will run some checks to make sure that it is installed properly. After the Jetstress checks run, on the Checking Test System screen, click the Next button.

4. On the Open Configuration screen, select Create A New Test Configuration and enter the location of the XML file that you want to store your test configuration in. Click Next to continue.

5. On the Define Test Scenario screen, you can choose to either test the disk subsystem in terms of the performance of the database, or you can test a specific planned mailbox I/O profile.

   The latter option will simulate I/O in the pattern that you antici-pate from your users and tell you if your server can handle it.

6. Select the Test Disk Subsystem Throughput option and click Next.

7. At the Select Capacity And Throughput screen, enter the capacity of the storage that you want to simulate.

Mitigating Risk

PART III

For example, if you anticipate that your database will grow to 500 GB and if you test 50% capacity, Jetstress will test the database at 250 GB.

You can also adjust the percentage of the Input/Output Per Second (IOPS) throughput. It is recommended that you leave these values at the default setting of 100 and click Next.

8. On the Select Test Type screen, select the type of test you want to perform and click Next.

   In this example, we're going to perform a performance test.

9. On the Define Test Run screen, type the location that you want to store the test results in. Also adjust the length of time that you want to run the test for. When you set this to a number higher than 6 hours, a stress test is run. Click Next.

10. At the Define Database Configuration screen, enter the number of databases that you want to test with. Also select the number of copies of each database.

11. In the table that lists the databases, you will need to enter the location of the database file and transaction log files for each database. After you enter this information, click Next.

12. On the Select Database Source screen, select whether you want to create new databases or attach the test to existing databases. Click Next to continue.

13. On the Review & Execute Test screen, review the options that you've picked for the Jetstress test and click Execute Test.

Simulate Client Workload

You can simulate client workload using the Exchange Load Generator (LoadGen) application. The Load Generator is not installed by default, so you will need to download it from the Exchange Server 2010 TechCenter and install it separately from Exchange.

With the Load Generator, you can benchmark and validate your Exchange configuration before it is deployed in production and users start using it. A variety of client simulation options give you a good idea of how your servers will perform against your anticipated load.

Install LoadGen

You can use the following steps to install the Load Generator tool on your Exchange servers before putting them into production:

1. Download LoadGen from the Exchange Server 2010 TechCenter at the following URL:

   http://technet.microsoft.com/en-us/exchange/2010

2. Double-click on the downloaded file LoadGen.msi to start the installation wizard.

3. On the Welcome screen of the installation wizard, click Next.

4. On the End-User License Agreement screen, click the option I Accept The Terms In The License Agreement and click Next.

5. At the Select Installation Folder screen, enter the location of where you want to install LoadGen and click the Next button.

6. On the Confirm Installation screen, click Next to begin the installation.

7. After LoadGen installs, you will see the Installation Complete screen. Click Close to close the installation wizard.

8. When prompted to reboot, click Yes and allow the Exchange server to reboot.

Use LoadGen

Use the following steps to launch the Load Generator and perform some basic user simulation testing:

1. Launch the LoadGen tool by clicking Start ➤ All Programs ➤ Microsoft Exchange ➤ Exchange Load Generator 2010.

2. At the Welcome screen of the Load Generator tool, click Start A New Test.

3. On the Start A New Test screen, click the option Create A New Test Configuration and click Continue.

   If you have an existing test configuration that you want to use, you can choose the Use The Following Saved Configuration File option and browse for the existing configuration that you want to use instead.

4. On the Specify Test Settings screen, you can adjust the settings that you want the test to simulate the load with. You can accept the default settings for the simulation time period or you can adjust them as necessary.

5. In the section Enter The Domain And Credential Settings, enter the name and password that you want to use for connecting to Active Directory (Directory Access Password) and the password you want to use for logging into the test accounts (Master Account Master Password). Then click Continue With Recipient Management.

   An example of the configuration of the test settings is shown in Figure 11.17.

Figure 11.17: Configuration of the test parameters in the Load Generator tool

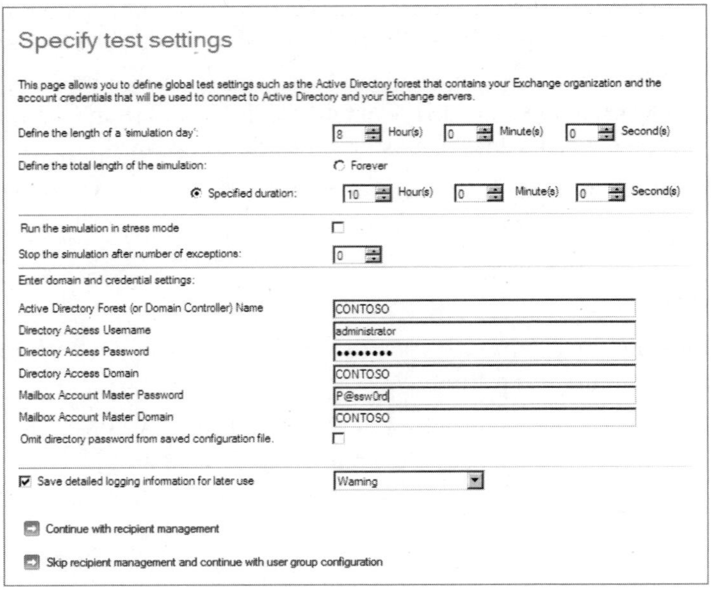

6. On the User Settings screen, enter the number of users that you want to test with each database and click Continue.

7. On the Advanced Recipient Settings screen, define the distribution list settings, contact settings, and external recipient settings that you want to use in the test. Click Continue after you are finished.

On the next screen, the test recipients will be created on the databases that you specified. This may take a few minutes to complete depending on how many recipients you decided to test with.

8. On the Specify Test User Groups screen, specify the load parameters that you want to simulate in the test. Click the plus sign to add a user group to the list. When you add a user group, you will need to configure the method they will be using to access mail (Client Type), the profile of the user (how heavily they use email), and the size of their mailboxes. Add as many different test groups as you would like and click Continue when you are finished.

9. The Remote Configurations screen gives you the option of adding remote load generators. If you don't want to use remote load generators, then leave this screen at the default values and click Continue.

10. On the Configuration Summary screen, verify the settings that you want to use and click Start Initialization Followed By Simulation.

   The test will be initialized and the simulation will run for the time you specified.

Mitigating Risk

PART III

12

Securing Exchange Server

Mitigating Risk

PART III

Configure Security for Exchange Servers

One of the benefits of having servers with multiple roles in Exchange is that each role has its own type of functionality. This means the servers can all be secured in a way that best suits their purpose. Securing Exchange is a server-specific or role-specific process, but there is also a common set of security practices across all Exchange servers. In this section, you will discover how to secure different aspects of Exchange servers.

Secure Client Access Servers

Client Access servers (CASs) are potentially Internet-facing servers that your users use when accessing their mail. An externally accessible CAS can pose a threat to your organization. The primary method used for accessing the CAS externally is web services. Therefore, it's important to lock down both the server and the web services. The key items to secure the CAS role in this capacity are the Secure Sockets Layer (SSL) certificates used for Transport Layer Security (TLS) in the web services.

Configure a Certificate from a Certification Authority

Exchange Server uses X.509 certificates for securing the communications of Client Access servers. The web services used by the CAS should be SSL-enabled using a certificate. By default, CASs have a self-signed certificate installed that is valid for five years. This means that the CAS issues its own certificate. Using the default self-signed certificate can work fine in many instances. However, clients must trust the issuer of the certificate to ensure that the certificate is valid. And since the issuer of the self-signed certificate is the server itself, it is not trusted by clients by default. Therefore, self-signed certificates are difficult to deploy and manage in complex enterprise-wide deployments.

There are a couple of ways to deal with this situation:

Install the certificate into the list of trusted issuers on each client. This method of certificate deployment has some challenges. Also, you will need to issue the trusted certificate for every CAS in your organization.

Obtain a new certificate from a certificate authority.   Obtaining a certificate from a mutually trusted issuer—a certificate authority (CA)—is the more accepted way to solve the problem. There are several well-known and publicly trusted CAs that are trusted by default in Windows. Therefore, any certificate that is issued to your Client Access servers by these CAs is automatically trusted by your clients and considered valid. You can also issue a certificate from a CA that your organization already owns, instead of buying a certificate from a third party. In either case, here are the steps for using a trusted certificate from a CA:

1. Obtain the certificate.

2. Install the certificate in Exchange.

3. Ensure that the clients trust the issuer.

Obtain a Certificate

When you obtain a certificate for your Client Access servers, you will be required to prove your identity to the certificate issuer. How this process works is dependent on the issuer and will likely be different when you buy a certificate from an Internet-based CA compared to using a CA that is owned by your organization.

When you obtain your certificate, keep the following considerations in mind:

- You should obtain either a wildcard certificate or a certificate that supports *subject alternative names*. This ensures you can use the same certificate for verifying both internal and external identities of the server. For example, the internal name of the server may be contoso-cas1.corp.contoso.com, but the external name may be mail.contoso.com. You want the certificate to verify both identities.

- If the CA is not already trusted by your clients as a Trusted Root Certification Authority, you should determine how much extra work is needed to make it trusted. It may be worth using a publicly trusted CA if your clients don't already trust the CA that you want to use.

- You should ensure that your servers contain the certificate revocation list (CRL) specified on the certificate. This is typically done through HTTP, but you many need to open access on your firewall depending on your organization's security configuration.

To start the process of obtaining a certificate, you will need to create a certificate request from your Client Access server. This request will be stored in a file with a specific format, and the file will be transferred to the CA that is issuing you the certificate.

Mitigating Risk

PART III

You must specify of the following in your certificate request:

The Various Names That the Certificate Will Be Used For   Make sure that you include every name that clients will use to access the server when using SSL. For example, they may use both CAS1 and mail.contoso.com. The issuer will likely have a restriction on the number of names that you can use.

The Name of the File That the Request Will Be Saved In   The certificate request is saved to a file that you can give to the certificate authority for generating the certificate.

The Subject Name of the Certificate   When creating your subject name, ensure that the Organization name is the organization that owns the domain namespace for the certificate. Your issuer will verify that the organization owns the namespace before issuing your certificate.

TIP   When including the alternate names in the certificate request, make sure that you include all the potential identities of the server, including the names used for AutoDiscover. When generating the request, you can use the IncludeAutodiscover parameter to automatically include the AutoDiscover Fully Qualified Domain Names (FQDNs) in the request.

You can create the certificate request in the EMS using the New-ExchangeCertificate cmdlet. When running this cmdlet, the DomainName parameter will be used to list the FQDNs for the certificate's Subject Alternative Name field. You will use the SubjectName parameter to specify the subject name of the certificate. The output of this cmdlet is written to the screen, but you will want to capture it to a file instead by piping the command to the Set-Content cmdlet and specifying the name of the file. The following example command shows you how to use the cmdlet to generate the certificate request:

```
New-ExchangeCertificate -GenerateRequest -DomainName cas1, ↵
mail.contoso.com -PrivateKeyExportable $true -SubjectName ↵
"c=US, o=Contoso, cn=cas1.contoso.com" | ↵
Set-Content -Path c:\cert.req
```

When you contact the certificate issuer to purchase your certificate, you must provide them with the information in the file.

Install the Certificate

Once you've obtained your certificate from a trusted authority, you can install the certificate on your Client Access server. You will receive your certificate in the form of a file. To import the certificate, run the Import-Certificate cmdlet in the EMS, as shown here:

```
Import-Certificate -Path c:\contoso.cer
```

When you create the certificate request, the private key of the certificate is created during the request and stored on the server where the request was generated. If you want to use the same certificate on multiple servers (such as in a lab environment), you will need to import the certificate at the server on which the request was generated and then export the certificate with the private key. You can then import the exported certificate into other servers.

After importing the certificate, you must enable the certificate on the services for which your users will need to use a secure connection. On Client Access servers, you will enable the certificate for IIS at a minimum. If you are using IMAP or POP, you should enable the certificate for those protocols as well.

To enable the certificate for the user services, you can use the Enable-ExchangeCertificate cmdlet. You will need the thumbprint of the certificate, which can be obtained from the Get-ExchangeCertificate cmdlet. The following command enables the certificate on CAS1 for IIS, IMAP, and POP services:

```
Get-ExchangeCertificate -DomainName CAS1 | ↵
Enable-ExchangeCertificate -Services "IIS,IMAP,POP"
```

Ensure That Clients Trust the Issuer

In most cases, if you obtained your certificate from a well-known certificate authority, your client computers will already trust the certificate. However, if you used an internal certificate authority or another third-party CA, you may have to add the CA to the trusted CA list on your client computers. This is typically the case with self-signed certificates. You can do this manually by installing the CA's certificate on each of the client computers. Or, if your clients are joined to an Active Directory domain, you can use an Active Directory Group Policy Object (GPO) to issue the certificate.

To manually install the CAs certificate on your clients, use these steps:

1. Open the Microsoft Management Console (MMC) on the client by running `mmc.exe`.

2. In the MMC, choose File ➤ Add/Remove Snap-In.

3. In the Add Or Remove Snap-Ins dialog box, select the Certificates snap-in from the list on the left and click the Add button in the center of the dialog box.

4. You will be prompted with the Certificates Snap-In dialog box. This dialog box is asking you for the certificate store that you want to edit. Select the Computer Account option, as shown in Figure 12.1, and click Next.

Figure 12.1: Ensure that you open the certificate store for the computer.

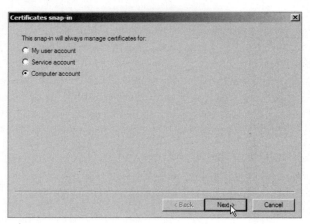

5. In the Select Computer dialog box, select Local Computer and click Finish.

6. When back in the Add Or Remove Snap-Ins dialog box, click OK to close the dialog box.

7. In the Certificates Snap-In in the MMC, use the tree in the left pane to browse to the Certificates (Local Computer) ➤ Trusted Root Certification Authorities ➤ Certificates node.

8. Choose Actions ➤ All Tasks ➤ Import to launch the Certificate Import wizard.

9. On the Welcome page of the wizard, click Next.

10. At the File To Import screen, click the Browse button to find the CA's certificate file. After you have selected the CA certificate file, click the Next button in the Certificate Import wizard.

11. On the Certificate Store page, ensure that the option Place All Certificates In The Following Store is selected.

12. Also make sure that Certificate Store is set to Trusted Root Certification Authorities, as shown in Figure 12.2. If not, you can change it using the Browse button. Click Next to continue.

Figure 12.2: Place the CA certificate in the Trusted Root Certification Authorities store.

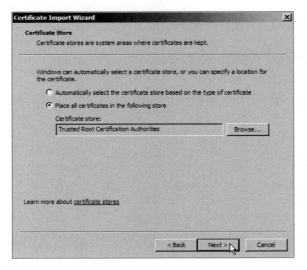

13. On the Completion page, click Finish to import the CA's certificate into the store.

14. You may be prompted with a Security Warning dialog box indicating that Windows could not validate that the certificate is from the CA that it says it's from. If you know that the certificate is really from the source CA, you can click the Yes button to continue. If you receive a dialog box indicating that the certificate import was successful, click OK.

You can also deploy the CA's certificate with an Active Directory GPO. Using Active Directory GPOs is outside of the scope of this book. However, if you are familiar with using GPOs in Active Directory, you can add the certificate to a domain GPO under Computer Configuration ➢ Windows Settings ➢ Security Settings ➢ Public Key Policies ➢ Trusted Root Certification Authorities. Any certificates that you import into this policy will be added to the Trusted Root Certification Authorities list in the certificate store on the computers that are affected by the Group Policy.

Secure the Transport Layer

Deciding how you are going to secure the Transport layer of your Exchange system is an important step. You can use the guidelines in this section to develop a good strategy of securing your transport environment.

Define a Transport Security Model

Exchange includes the Edge Transport role for the purpose of having a nondomain-joined Exchange server with advanced antispam functionality outside your network. This strategy of securing the outer layers of the network as a first line of defense is a great example of a concept known as *defense in depth*. Defense in depth ensures that there are multiple layers of security between your access points and the data. This is a risk mitigation approach. You can't guarantee that someone won't break through your first line of defense, but when there are many other fences to climb before reaching your backyard, the target looks less and less attractive.

Another consideration is that every message now flows through a Hub Transport server. Because of this, you may want to consider performing antivirus scanning at the Hub Transport server. Hub Transports are typically less utilized than other server roles, so the added burden of scanning messages for viruses will probably have a minimal impact on those servers. And since every message filters through a Hub Transport, you can be certain that every message is scanned. If you are concerned about scanning the data on the database side, one option is to rely on the antivirus software on the client computers instead of performing the virus scanning on a Mailbox server.

Install Antispam Functionality on Hub Transport Servers

By default, Edge Transport servers have antispam functionality enabled. However, Hub Transport servers do not have it enabled because they typically are not Internet-facing. If you have Internet-facing Hub Transport servers, however, you can enable antispam functionality for those servers.

Exchange exposes the ability to turn on the antispam features in Hub Transport servers through the use of an EMS script. This script, `Install-AntiSpamAgents.ps1`, is kept in the Scripts folder in the folder where the Exchange files are stored. You can use the following steps to enable the antispam capabilities on the Hub Transport servers:

1. Open the EMS and navigate to the Script folder under the location that the Exchange files are stored—for example, `C:\Program Files\Microsoft\Exchange Server\v14\Scripts`.

2. Run the script `Install-AntiSpamAgents.ps1` using the following command in the EMS:

    ```
    .\Install-AntiSpamAgents.ps1
    ```

3. After the antispam agents are installed, restart the transport service using the following EMS command:

    ```
    Restart-Service MSExchangeTransport
    ```

After the antispam configuration is complete, you will see the antispam settings appear in the EMC if you open the EMC and look under the Hub Transport nodes in the Organization Configuration and Server Configuration nodes.

Manage Permissions

In order for both administrators and users to use features and functionality in Exchange, they need to have the right access. The permission model in Exchange Server 2010 has changed dramatically. This section will help you understand this new permission model and guide you in using it.

Understand the Exchange Server 2010 Administrative Model

The administrative model changes in Exchange Server 2010 rank high in the list of significant changes from earlier versions of Exchange. The implementation of Role-Based Access Controls (RBAC) is more flexible and more granular, and provides some useful capabilities in specifying what administrators can do and where they can do it. In this section, you'll learn what RBAC is and how it works.

Understand Role-Based Access Control

RBAC is a completely different permission model than what was used in previous versions of Exchange. With RBAC, you are no longer assigning permissions to Exchange objects using access control lists. Instead, you use the built-in mechanisms of RBAC to delegate access.

Under RBAC, administrators have access to perform certain tasks in Exchange by being assigned a management role that has permissions to perform the task. For example, people assigned the Legal Hold role can put mailboxes on legal hold or take mailboxes off of legal hold. Administrators can be assigned these roles directly, or multiple roles can be grouped together into management role groups. One example of a management role group is the Discovery Management group. The Discovery Management group has the roles Legal Hold and Mailbox Search assigned to it. Therefore, anyone who is a member of the Discovery Management group has the ability to perform the tasks associated with the Legal Hold and Mailbox Search roles.

NOTE Management role groups are represented by universal security groups in the domain. Do not add users to these groups directly. Instead, use the supported methods described in this section.

Each management role consists of management role entries. A management role entry is an EMS cmdlet or a script that users in a management role can execute. For example, the Mailbox Import Export management role has three management role entries defined, as shown in Figure 12.3.

You will notice that each management role entry corresponds to an EMS cmdlet. The cmdlet parameters that the role-holder can use are also specified. If the parameter is not listed in the management role entry, the role-holder cannot use that parameter with the cmdlet. You can assign granular permissions with this type of access model.

Figure 12.3: Management role entries are defined for each management role.

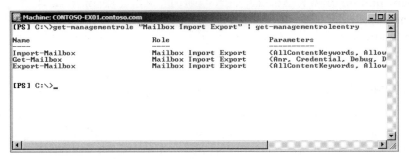

Management roles are assigned to management role groups using a management role assignment. The assignment not only specifies which roles are in which groups, but can also define the scope of the role. For example, a management role assignment can specify that administrators in the Baltimore Recipient Managers role group can only mail-enable recipients in the Baltimore OU.

Understanding the interaction between management role groups, management roles, management role entries, and management role assignments is the key to effectively using RBAC in your Exchange implement. Figure 12.4 summarizes the relationship between these components.

Review the Built-In Roles and Role Groups

Exchange Server 2010 comes with several roles and role groups already defined. If you want to view the list of role groups, you can run the Get-RoleGroup cmdlet in the EMS. This cmdlet can be run without any parameters to return a list of all of the role groups. If you specify the identity of an existing role group, the details of that role group are returned. For example, you can view the properties of the Help Desk role group using the following command:

```
Get-RoleGroup "Help Desk" | fl
```

Table 12.1 lists the default role groups that are created by Exchange.

PART III

Figure 12.4: Overview of the RBAC model in Exchange Server 2010

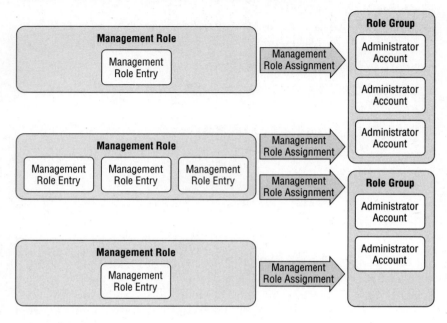

Table 12.1: The Default Role Groups

Role Group	Group Member Abilities
Delegated Setup	Install Exchange servers into the organization.
Discovery Management	Perform discovery functionality, such as placing users on legal hold and performing discovery searches.
Help Desk	Perform basic Help Desk functionality, such as changing user display names or other general information.
Hygiene Management	Perform message hygiene functions, such as configuring antivirus and antispam functionality.
Organization Management	Manage almost every aspect of Exchange. These are high-level administrators who are highly trusted.
Public Folder Management	Perform management of public folders and their databases.
Recipient Management	Add and remove recipients, as well as perform other tasks related to recipient management.

Table 12.1: The Default Role Groups *(continued)*

Role Group	Group Member Abilities
Records Management	Administer compliance and policy settings. These administrators have the ability to manage retention settings, journaling, and so forth.
Server Management	Administer all Exchange servers in the organization. This includes the management of databases, connectors, and virtual directories on each server.
UM Management	Administer the Unified Messaging functionality.
View-Only Organization Management	View Exchange configuration information and recipient data in a read-only fashion.

You can also view the various roles that Exchange creates by default. To view the entire list, run the `Get-ManagementRole` cmdlet with no parameters. If you want to see the details of a particular role, such as a list of the cmdlets that it allows role-holders to execute, you can provide the identity of the role as a parameter to the cmdlet. For example, the following command will display the cmdlets that can be executed by people who are in the Move Mailboxes role:

```
Get-ManagementRole "Move Mailboxes" | ↵
Get-ManagementRoleEntry
```

In the previous example, we're pipelining the `Get-ManagementRole` cmdlet into the `Get-ManagementRoleEntry` cmdlet. You can use the `Get-ManagementRoleEntry` cmdlet to get information about the specific role entry. If you recall from earlier, a role entry is a cmdlet or script that a people in a role can execute. You will also notice that the output from the previous command displays not only the cmdlets that can be executed, but also the parameters that can be used in the cmdlet.

Delegate Role-Based Permissions

One of the powerful benefits of RBAC is that you can tailor the access model to meet the needs of your organization at a granular level. You have the ability to edit the existing role groups as well as the ability to add new roles or role groups that you design. In this section, we'll walk through the process of both editing the existing RBAC configuration and creating and using your own roles.

Mitigating Risk

Customize Roles

Exchange Server 2010 comes with dozens of roles out of the box. These roles cover a wide variety of access permissions. Sometimes you might find that a built-in role handles everything you want but allows access to a cmdlet that you don't want users or administrators in the role to have access to. For example, one of the roles built into Exchange is called Mailbox Import Export. This role has permission to both export and import mail from mailboxes. But suppose that you want an administrator to be able to export mail but not import it.

If you only wanted to allow administrators to export mail, you must remove access to the `Import-Mailbox` cmdlet. However, you cannot modify the built-in roles. Instead, you must create a new role and give it access to the cmdlets that you want to use.

To create a new role, you can use the `New-ManagementRole` cmdlet. When you create the role, you will need to derive the role from an existing one. When you do this, there will be a parent/child relationship established between the roles. The child role (the one that you created) will allow all the cmdlets that the parent role allows. You will then need to go into the child role and remove the cmdlets that you don't want people with that role to have access to.

To create a custom role based on an existing role, do the following:

1. Create the new management role.

2. Determine which cmdlets you want to remove access to.

3. Modify the role that you created, removing access to the management role entries that you don't want your role-holders to use.

Using our example of exporting mail, we will make a child role and use the Mailbox Import Export role as the parent. The following command can be used to create a new child role called Mailbox Export that uses the existing built-in Mailbox Import Export role as its parent:

```
New-ManagementRole "Mailbox Export" -Parent ↵
"Mailbox Import Export"
```

After the role is created, you can view the cmdlets that the role is allowed to run. Remember that these cmdlets were derived from the role that you designated as the parent. The following command displays these cmdlets:

```
Get-ManagementRole "Mailbox Export" | ↵
Get-ManagementRoleEntry
```

You can go through the list and determine which cmdlets you want to remove access to. In our scenario, we will remove access to the `Import-Mailbox` cmdlet. To remove a role's access to a cmdlet, you can use the `Remove-ManagementRoleEntry` cmdlet. You must reference the identity of the role entry (the cmdlet) as *Role Name\Entry Name*. For example, the role entry that we are removing in the following command is `Mailbox Export\Import-Mailbox`. In most cases, the name of the role entry will be the name of a cmdlet. The following example removes access to the `Import-Mailbox` cmdlet without asking for confirmation:

```
Remove-ManagementRoleEntry "Mailbox Export\Import-Mailbox" ↵
-Confirm: $False
```

Assign Roles to Administrators

After you have your roles defined in the manner that best fits your needs, you must assign those roles to people. The process for assigning roles to administrators is different from the process for assigning roles to users. You will want to assign roles to role groups and then add your administrators to the appropriate role groups. Here's the process:

1. Determine if an existing role group already contains all of the roles that you want to use.

2. If needed, customize a role group to contain the roles that you need.

3. Add the administrator accounts to the appropriate role group.

Determine If You Can Use an Existing Role Group

If an existing role group meets your needs, it's simple to grant the roles to the administrators. You only need to make the administrator's account a member of the role group. But you first need to find out whether an existing group meets your needs. Table 12.1 earlier in this chapter provides an overview of the built-in role groups.

If you want to see for yourself what roles the existing role groups contain, you can use the EMS. The following command uses the `Get-RoleGroup` cmdlet to list each of the roles that the group holds:

```
Get-RoleGroup | ft Name, Roles
```

You can also get even more granular and view the list of cmdlets that a particular role has access to. The following command displays the cmdlets for the administrators in the Discovery Management role group:

```
Get-RoleGroup "Discovery Management" | foreach ↵
{ $_.Roles | Get-ManagementRole | Get-ManagementRoleEntry }
```

Use a Customized Role Group

After going through the roles available in the existing role groups, you may decide that none suit your needs and you want to customize a role group instead. When you customize a role group, you can add an existing built-in role or you can use a custom role that you created. Whether you decide to use a built-in role or your own customized role, the procedures for assigning these roles to a role group are the same.

If you recall from earlier, roles are associated with role groups using a role assignment. A role assignment assigns only one role to only one role group. Each time that role is assigned to another role group, another role assignment needs to be created. When you create the new role assignment, you can just specify the role that you want to assign and the role group that you want to assign it to. Exchange will automatically name the role assignment for you, and I recommend letting it do so.

You can create a new role assignment by using the New-ManagementRoleAssignment cmdlet in the EMS. For example, the following command assigns the Mailbox Export role to the Discovery Management role group:

```
New-ManagementRoleAssignment -SecurityGroup ↵
"Discovery Management" -Role "Mailbox Export"
```

You also have the option of creating a new role group if you don't want to use an existing one. To create a new role group, use the New-RoleGroup cmdlet in the EMS. The following example creates a new role group called Lawyers:

```
New-RoleGroup "Lawyers" -Roles "Mailbox Search", ↵
"Mailbox Import Export"
```

After you have created a custom role group, you can use the same process of creating a role assignment for the group in order to assign roles to it.

Add Administrators to a Role Group

You can add administrators to role groups in one of two ways:

- Add the administrator to the group through the Exchange Control Panel.
- Use the Exchange Management Shell to add the administrator with a cmdlet.

To add the administrator to the role group using the ECP, use the following steps:

1. Open the Exchange Control Panel by browsing to the ECP URL from an Internet browser. The URL is typically the URL of the Client Access server with /ecp—for example, `https://mail.contoso.com/ecp`.

2. Log on to the ECP with an account that has privileges to modify the membership of the role group.

3. When the ECP loads, ensure that the Select What To Manage box in the upper left of the page is set to My Organization. Then click the Administrator Roles icon.

4. In the list of role groups, select the group that you want to add the administrator to and click the Details button, as shown in Figure 12.5.

5. The Role Group dialog box will launch and list the roles that are assigned to the group. To add a member to the group, click the Add button in the Members section near the bottom of the dialog box.

6. In the Select Members dialog box, choose the accounts that you want to add to the role group and click the Add button. After you are finished selecting accounts, click OK to close the Select Members dialog box.

7. Back in the Role Group dialog box, the accounts that you selected should have been added to the list of members. Click the Save button to make the changes and close the Role Group dialog box.

You can also use the EMS to add administrators to a role group. You will use the `Add-RoleGroupMember` cmdlet to do this. Specify the name of the role group and use the Member parameter to specify the account that you are adding to the group, as shown in the following example:

```
Add-RoleGroupMember "Lawyers" -Member "Nora Shea"
```

Figure 12.5: Modify the membership of role groups using the ECP.

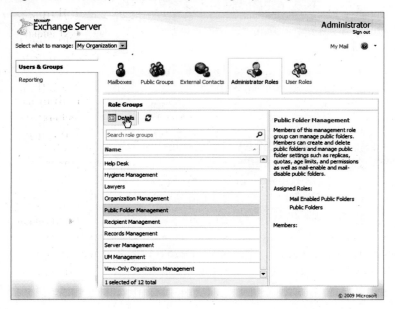

Assign Roles to Users

In addition to giving permissions to resources for administrators, RBAC is also used in Exchange Server 2010 to delegate access to end users. Your end users typically won't be modifying Exchange server settings or organization settings. However, they may need to modify their personal information, such as address or phone number, or they may need permissions to manage their own distribution groups. In order to do this, you will need to assign roles to your users.

Users aren't added to role groups like administrator accounts are. Instead users are assigned roles by using a role assignment policy. Each user account can have only one role assignment policy defined.

Exchange defines a default role assignment policy. The default role assignment policy allows users to manage OWA settings, contact information, voice mail, text messaging, and distribution group membership. In most cases, the default policy will suit your needs.

You have the option of creating your own role assignment policy and assigning your own roles to it. You can override the default policy for user accounts and use your custom policy instead. Using a custom role assignment policy involves three steps:

1. Create the new role assignment policy.
2. Add roles to the policy.
3. Assign the policy to the users who you want it to apply to.

Create a New Role Assignment Policy

To create a new role assignment policy, you can use the New-RoleAssignmentPolicy cmdlet in the EMS. You only need to specify the name of the policy. You will link the roles to the policy in a later step. The following example creates a custom role assignment policy:

```
New-RoleAssignmentPolicy "Enhanced User Role Policy"
```

You can determine whether you want your new policy to take the place of the existing default role assignment policy that is applied to new mailboxes. If you want to use the new policy as the default policy, add the IsDefault parameter to the command:

```
New-RoleAssignmentPolicy "Enhanced User Role Policy" ↵
-IsDefault
```

Add Roles to the Role Assignment Policy

After the policy is created, you can add roles to the policy. Similarly to RBAC for administrator roles, you use the New-ManagementRoleAssignment cmdlet to add the roles. For example, to add the custom management role called Extended Attribute Modification to the Enhanced User role policy, use the following command:

```
New-ManagementRoleAssignment -Role "Extended Attribute ↵
Modification" -Policy "Enhanced User Role Policy"
```

Assign the Role Assignment Policy to Mailboxes

The final step is to assign the policy to the users that you want the policy to apply to. If you set the policy as the default policy, it

Mitigating Risk

PART III

only applies to new mailboxes. Existing mailboxes will need to be changed manually.

To modify the role assignment policy for a mailbox, you must use the Set-Mailbox cmdlet with the RoleAssignmentPolicy parameter. The following sample command shows how to configure this:

```
Set-Mailbox lincoln -RoleAssignmentPolicy ↵
"Enhanced User Role Policy"
```

> **WARNING** Setting a role assignment policy on a mailbox overrides any existing role assignment policies that may be in place. Each mailbox can only have one role assignment policy assigned to it.

Configure Message Hygiene Options

The message hygiene options in Exchange Server 2010 help prevent you from receiving mail that you don't want. This mail is either about a subject that you don't want to hear about, or it's from a sender that you don't want to receive messages from. In either case, it's important to ensure that you understand how to fight this battle and come out on top. This section focuses on helping you block the mail that you don't want to receive.

Battle Unwanted Mail

One of the challenges of administering email systems is accurately filtering out messages that are unwanted. These messages, called *spam*, often appear in the form of advertisements or offensive content. Spam poses multiple risks to organizations by spreading viruses, bloating users' mailboxes with massive numbers of email messages, and using valuable storage. This section is about using the content filtering mechanisms in Exchange to battle this unwanted mail.

Understand the Spam Confidence Level

When messages come in from outside your organization, they can be assigned a number called the Spam Confidence Level (SCL) rating. This is a number between 0 and 9 that determines the likelihood that the message is spam. A high rating means that there is a high probability that the message is spam. The content filter determines the probability of a message's being spam and marks the message with the SCL rating. Depending on the SCL rating that is assigned to the message, certain actions can be taken. Table 12.2 describes these actions and the default thresholds for when these actions are taken on a message.

Table 12:2: Actions and Thresholds for Messages Marked as Spam

Action	Default Threshold
The message is not delivered to the user, but is instead placed in a quarantine mailbox.	9
A rejection is sent to the sender and the message is deleted.	7
The message is deleted without any notice.	9

Use Spam Quarantine

When a message has an SCL rating that is high enough to quarantine it, the message is moved to a quarantine mailbox. An administrator can monitor the quarantine mailbox for false positives. The administrator can have such messages sent to users. To use spam quarantining, use the following steps:

1. Configure the quarantine mailbox.

2. Monitor the quarantine mailbox.

3. Adjust the SCL thresholds as necessary.

Configure the Quarantine Mailbox

When configuring the mailbox used for spam quarantine, here are some considerations to keep in mind:

- Administrators will need to monitor this mailbox, so ensure that those administrators have permissions to the mailbox.

- The quarantine mailbox has the potential to get rather large, depending on the amount of spam that you except to receive. Therefore, you may want to place the quarantine mailbox in its own database and decide whether or not it is worth replicating it if you are using a DAG.

- Consider applying separate retention policies and a large quota to the quarantine mailbox. You probably don't want messages being removed before you've had a chance to review them.

To create the spam quarantine mailbox, follow the steps outlined for creating resource mailboxes in Chapter 4, "Administering Recipients."

After you have created the spam quarantine mailbox, you need to configure the mailbox in the Content Filter settings so that Exchange knows to send quarantined messages to that mailbox. You can make this configuration change using the `Set-ContentFilterConfig` cmdlet in the EMS, using the following command as an example:

```
Set-ContentFilterConfig -QuarantineMailbox ↵
quarantine@contoso.com
```

Make sure that you configure the quarantine mailbox on the Transport servers that will be performing the content filtering. If you are using Edge Transport servers, you must configure the quarantine mailbox on every Edge Transport server individually. For Hub Transport servers, you only need to configure the quarantine mailbox once, because Exchange uses Active Directory to ensure that every Hub Transport server uses the same spam quarantine configuration.

Monitor the Quarantine Mailbox

Administrators will need to monitor the quarantine mailbox to ensure that any false positives are caught and the messages are sent to the recipients. The easiest way to do this is for administrators to connect to the quarantine mailbox using Microsoft Outlook. In order to do this, you must ensure that the administrator has access to open the quarantine mailbox. The quarantine mailbox can be opened as a secondary mailbox in Outlook, so an additional Outlook profile does not need to be created.

When you come across a message in the quarantine mailbox that is a false positive, you can use the following steps to resend the message to the user:

1. In the list of messages in Outlook, open the NDR that represents the message that was falsely identified as spam.

2. In the message, select the Report tab.

3. On the Report tab, click the Send Again button. The original message will open in a new dialog box. When it does, click the Send button to have the message sent to the user.

Adjust the SCL Thresholds

After monitoring the quarantine mailbox for a while, you may notice that there are many false positives. If this is the case, you may want to increase the SCL threshold to a higher value when taking action on a message. To increase the SCL thresholds, you can use the `Set-ContentFilterConfig` cmdlet with a set of the parameters specified in Table 12.3.

Table 12.3: EMS Parameters for Setting the SCL Thresholds

Action	Feature Enable Parameter	Threshold Parameter
Quarantine the message	SCLQuarantineEnabled	SCLQuarantineThreshold
Reject the message	SCLRejectEnabled	SCLRejectThreshold
Delete the message	SCLDeleteEnabled	SCLDeleteThreshold

Remember that the threshold values can be anywhere from 0 to 9. So to set the SCL message quarantine threshold to 7, you would use the following command:

```
Set-ContentFilterConfig -SCLQuarantineEnabled $true ↵
-SCLQuarantineThreshold 7
```

Block Message Attachments

In Exchange, you have the ability to block file attachments in email messages that meet predefined criteria. In Exchange Server 2010, you have many more options for blocking attachments.

In Exchange Server 2010, attachment filtering is accomplished through a transport rule on the Transport servers. This no longer runs as an agent. If you want to use attachment filtering, you will need to create a transport rule for your Hub Transport servers. The following steps walk you through the process of creating a transport rule for attachment filtering:

1. Open the EMC and browse to the Organization Configuration ➢ Hub Transport node in the Console tree.

2. In the Actions pane, click the New Transport Rule action to start the New Transport Rule wizard.

Mitigating Risk

PART III

3. At the Introduction screen of the wizard, type a name for the attachment filter rule. Then click Next.

4. On the Conditions screen, select the check box When Any Attachment File Name Matches Text Patterns. This allows this transport rule to trigger when a file attachment name meets the criteria that you specify, such as a file extension.

5. While still on the Conditions screen, click the blue link in the bottom box that reads Text Patterns. This launches the Specify Text Patterns dialog box.

6. Type in the filename patterns that you want to block and click the Add button. For example, if you want to block all files that contain .EXE, type .**EXE** and click Next.

7. At the Actions screen, you can choose what to do with the message that contains the attachment that you want to block. Click the Next button after you have chosen your action.

8. On the Exceptions screen, you choose what exceptions you want to apply when blocking attachments. For example, you can choose to let messages through when they are sent by certain people, even if they contain an attachment that is usually blocked. Click Next when ready.

9. On the Create Rule screen, click the New button to create your attachment filter rule.

10. On the Completion screen, click the Finish button to close the wizard and return to the EMC.

Protect Against Unwanted Mail Sources

In addition to protecting your organization from messages that are considered spam or that have inappropriate content, you can also protect against specific mail sources. This is useful in situations where there is a specific attack against your organization or if there are senders you want to ignore at the organization level.

Block Mail from Specific IP Addresses

You can choose to block all messages sent from a specific set of IP addresses using an IP block list. IP block lists are typically configured on Edge Transport servers, since they are Internet-facing. However, if you install the antispam features on a Hub Transport server, you can configure IP block lists on the Hub Transport server as well.

When adding IP addresses to the IP block list, you can add a single address, a subnet, or a range of addresses. To block an IP address, you use the `Add-IPBlockListEntry` cmdlet in the EMS. The following command blocks connections from the 10.0.0.1 address. In this command, the `IPAddress` parameter is specified to indicate that we are blocking a single IP.

```
Add-IPBlockListEntry -IPAddress 10.0.0.1
```

When blocking a subnet or a range of IP addresses, you should use the `IPRange` parameter. The following example blocks everything coming from 10.0.0.1–10.0.0.100:

```
Add-IPBlockListEntry -IPRange 10.0.0.1-10.0.0.100
```

After you have configured the IP addresses to block, you can run the `Get-IPBlockListEntry` cmdlet to view the configuration. To remove IP addresses from the block list, use the `Remove-IPBlockListEntry` parameter and specify the blocked IP address entry that you want to remove.

Verify That Senders Are Valid

In Exchange, you can also block mail from specific senders. You can set up a filter based on the sender's IP address or domain name. In addition, you can check whether the sender of the message is valid and whether the message is spoofed. This functionality is exposed in the two Exchange features called Sender Filtering and Sender ID.

Sender Filtering and Sender ID are enabled as part of the antispam feature set in Exchange. These two features work together to ensure that the headers on an email message are not spoofed (that is, they verify that the message is really from who it says it's from) and that the message is from a sender you want to accept mail from.

Prevent Spoofed Messages

To ensure that messages aren't being spoofed, you can configure Sender ID. Sender ID will compare the sender's address against the Sender Policy Framework (SPF) record in the sender's DNS domain name. The Sender ID status is set on the message to indicate the results of the SPF record lookup. This status is used in the calculation of the SCL of messages.

Mitigating Risk

You can also configure the Transport server to perform certain actions based on the Sender ID status. You can have the server reject the message, delete the message, or just stamp the Sender ID value on the message. By default, Exchange just stamps the value onto the message.

You can configure these settings in the EMC by using the following steps:

1. Open the EMC and browse to either the Organization Configuration ➤ Hub Transport node or the Organization Configuration ➤ Edge Transport node in the Console tree, depending on which server you are using for transporting Internet email.

2. In the Work area, click the Anti-spam tab to open a list of available antispam options.

3. Double-click on Sender ID in the list. The Sender ID Properties dialog box is displayed.

4. Click the Action tab.

5. Select the option that represents what you want to happen after a Sender ID check takes place. In Figure 12.6, the Reject Message option is being configured. This will send a rejection notice to the sender of the message.

6. Click the OK button to close the Properties dialog box and make the change.

Figure 12.6: Configuring the Sender ID action

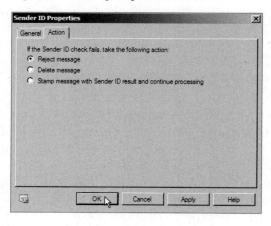

You can also configure the Transport server to reject spoofed messages by using the `Set-SenderIDConfig` cmdlet with the `SpoofedDomainAction` parameter. You can set this parameter to either `Reject`, `Delete`, or `StampStatus`. The following command will ensure that messages from spoofed domains are deleted:

```
Set-SenderIDConfig -SpoofedDomainAction Reject
```

Block Messages from Certain People or Organizations

Now that you've verified that the message isn't spoofed, you can choose to block messages from people or organizations that you don't want to hear from. To do this, you use the Sender Filtering feature. You can configure Sender Filtering to either flat-out deny the message or to accept the message and mark that it's from a blocked sender. The SCL of the message will be updated appropriately.

To configure which senders are blocked, use the following steps in the EMC:

1. Open the EMC and browse to either the Organization Configuration ➤ Hub Transport node or the Organization Configuration ➤ Edge Transport node in the Console tree, depending on which server you are using to receive mail from the Internet.

2. In the Work area, click on the Anti-spam tab to open a list of available antispam options.

3. Double-click on Sender Filtering in the list. The Sender Filtering Properties dialog box is displayed.

4. Click the Blocked Senders tab.

5. Click the Add button to add senders to the list that you want to block. This launches the Add Blocked Senders dialog box.

6. In the Add Blocked Senders dialog box, add individual email addresses that you want to block, or if you want to block an entire domain, select the Domain option and type the name of the domain, as shown in Figure 12.7.

7. When back in the Sender Filtering Properties dialog box, add any additional addresses that you want to block and then click OK to close the Properties dialog box. This configuration is illustrated in Figure 12.8.

Mitigating Risk

PART III

Figure 12.7: Blocking mail from an entire domain namespace

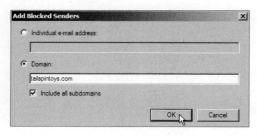

Figure 12.8: Setting the list of blocked senders on a Transport server

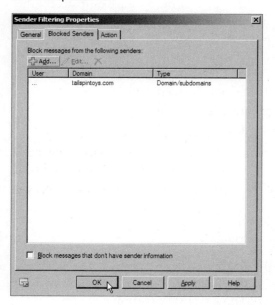

You can also use the `Set-SenderFilterConfig` cmdlet in the EMS to enable Sender Filtering and configure the addresses that you are blocking. You can block an entire domain using the `BlockedDomains` parameter or a single sender using the `BlockedSenders` parameter. The following command enables Sender Filtering and blocks messages from anyone in the `tailspintoys.com` domain:

```
Set-SenderFilterConfig -Enabled $true -BlockedDomains ↵
tailspintoys.com
```

Prevent Internet Users from Sending Email to Distribution Groups

You may have distribution groups inside your organization that you only want internal employees to have access to send email to. You can block these distribution groups from receiving Internet email by using Recipient Filtering to block messages from the Internet that are destined to a certain address. For example, suppose you have a distribution list called finance@ contoso.com that you don't want people on the Internet to send mail to. You can use the following steps in the EMC to ensure that Internet users can't send mail to the finance@contoso.com distribution group:

1. Open the EMC and browse to either the Organization Con-figuration ➤ Hub Transport node or the Organization Configuration ➤ Edge Transport node in the Console tree, depending on which server you are setting up the recipient filtering on.

2. In the Work area, click the Antispam tab to open a list of available antispam options.

3. Double-click on Recipient Filtering in the list. The Recipient Filtering Properties dialog box is displayed.

4. Click the Blocked Recipients tab.

5. Select the check box Block Messages Sent To The Following Recipients. Type the address of the distribution group in the field below the check box and then click the Add button (Figure 12.9).

6. Click OK to close the Properties dialog box and make the change.

Figure 12.9: Blocking Internet-based mail to an internal distribution group

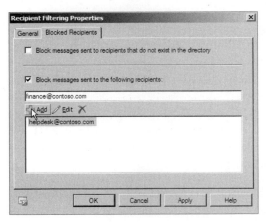

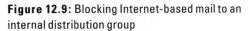

You can also add the distribution group to the recipient filtering list in the EMS. Use the `Set-RecipientFilterConfig` cmdlet with the `BlockedRecipients` parameter. The following EMS command accomplishes the same thing that we just performed in the EMC:

```
Set-RecipientFilterConfig -BlockListEnabled $true ↵
-BlockedRecipients finance@contoso.com
```

Index

Note to reader: **Bold** page numbers refer to definitions and main discussions of a topic. *Italicized* page numbers refer to illustrations.

forest, message flow inside
examining AD site topology, **236–239**, *237–239*
forcing mail to route through hub site, *241*, 241–242
modifying mail flow through, *240*, 240–241
forest(s)
adding Exchange, **56–57**
collecting data about Exchange, 57–58
preparing Active Directory, **14**
Format- cmdlets, 67–68, *68*
free-flowing mail. *See* routing topology health

G

Get-Help cmdlet
formatting options, *68*, 68
parameters for, 66–67
Global Address List, 122
global groups, 169
graphical user interface (GUI)
basic installation with, **21–23**, *22*, *24*
installing AD Management Tools, 11–13
installing Management Tools, *39*, 39–40
GUI. *See* graphical user interface (GUI)

H

hard quota, 372–373
Help links, context-sensitive, 52–53, *53*
Helpdesk folder, 319
hierarchy replication, **349–350**, *350*
Hourly Report, mobile device, 216
HTTP Redirect, 189–190
HTTP Status Report, mobile device, 217

HTTP URL, 191–192
hub sites, *241*, **241–242**
Hub Transport servers
blocking mail, 503
choosing for advanced installation, **26**, **26–27**
configuring quarantine mailbox, 500
for configuring receive connector permissions, *46*, 46
configuring to receive email, **253–255**, *254*
enabling Edge Subscription, 262–263
installing antispam functionality on, 487
internal message routing redundancy. *See* redundant Transport servers
required components, 18
role definition, **5**, **230**
transport rules, 390
in Transport security model, 486

I

If...Else conditional, 76–77
IMAP4
enabling for third-party clients, **226**
overview, 225
turning on access, **226–227**
using certificates with, **227**
index, Exchange Search, 281–282
installation, advanced
of Client Access Server role, **27–29**, *28*
of Edge Transport Server role, **30–32**, *31*
of Hub Transport Server role, **26**, **26–27**
of Mailbox Server role, *29*, **29–30**
overview, 24

enabling/disabling access,
197–199
enabling/disabling Exchange
ActiveSync, **197**, *198*
enforcing password
requirements, **206–209**
generating device reports,
216–218
managing synchronization
settings, **204–206**
overview, *196*
recovering password,
210–211, *211*
remotely wiping, **213–215**
retrieving list of, **215–216**
setting policy on users, **201–202**
monitoring communications
with email inspection, 396–398,
397–398
without detection, **398–399**, *399*
Mount-Database cmdlet, 334
multicast mode, 404
MX. *See* Mail Exchanger (MX)

N

name specifications, certificate
request, 482
Netdom query fsmo command, 13
Network Load Balancing (NLB)
adding additional nodes to
cluster, *408–409*, **408–409**
creating cluster/adding first node,
404–407, *405–407*
installing on Client Access
servers, **404**
New-AddressList cmdlet
creating address lists in EMS,
114–116
RecipientFilter property
of, 116
New Federation Trust, 98, 99
New-OrganizationRelationship
cmdlet, 107

New-PublicFolderDatabase cmdlet,
333–334
New Sharing Policy, *109*, 109
NLB. *See* Network Load
Balancing (NLB)
NTLM authentication, 221
$null variable, 73–74

O

Offline Address Book (OAB)
changing default for new users,
125–126
creating, **122–124**, *124*
distributing to specific users,
126–127, *127*
securing distribution,
127–129, *129*
version comparison, 122
virtual directory, *129*
one-liner, *65*
online maintenance window,
274–276, *275*
Organization Identifier,
103–104, *104*
organizational relationships
management
defining sharing policies. *See*
sharing policies
enabling data sharing. *See*
data sharing with other
organizations
out-of-office (OOF) messages, *248*,
248–249
Outlook Anywhere
AutoDiscover for, **223–225**, *225*
configuring SSL offloading,
220–221
enabling, **218–220**
modifying authentication
method, **221–222**
overview, 218
Outlook client access. *See*
Outlook Anywhere

Outlook Web App
(OWA) connectivity
configuring ECP external URL,
187–188
configuring external URL
manually, **186–187**, *187*
external, configuring on OWA
manually, *187*
overview, 183–184, *184*
redirecting default server URL to,
188–191, *189–190*
redirecting from HTTP to
HTTPS, **191–192**
setting same DNS name on CAS,
184–186, *185*
Outlook Web App (OWA) features
managing web-based document
viewing, **194–196**
modifying segmentation options,
192–194, *193*
output pane, in ISE, **71**, *71*
OWA connectivity. *See* Outlook
Web App (OWA) connectivity

P

parameters
cmdlet, **63–65**, *64*, 107
for configuring mobile device
policies, 203–204
for configuring mobile device
sync settings, 205–206
for creating client access
array, 410
for creating DAG network, 296
for creating journal rules, 377
for creating retention tags, 366
for database copy settings, 303
defining public folder limits, 322
distribution group
moderation, 174
for email address recipient types,
153–154
for Get-Help cmdlet, 66–67

mailbox access rights, 161
mailbox quota, 157
mailbox type, 142
for mobile device password
requirements, 208–209
for New-AddressList cmdlet, 115
for OWA segmentation options,
193–194
for reseeding databases, 299
setting public folder limits, 336
for setting SCL thresholds, 501
Tracking Log Explorer search,
453, *453*
for updating contact information,
140–141
passwords, mobile device
enforcing requirements, **206–209**
recovering, **210–211**, *211*
per-user message read state,
319–321, *320*
performance limitations tests.
See stress-testing
Performance Monitor
saving statistics for analysis,
469–471
viewing real-time statistics,
468–469, *469–470*
Performance Troubleshooter,
467–468, *468*
permissions
administrator, 328
client, 323–325, 327
management. *See* Role-Based
Access Control (RBAC)
public folder. *See* public
folder permissions
receive connector, *46*, 46–47
PFMC. *See* Public Folder
Management Console (PFMC)
pipe character, *65*
pipelining
cmdlets, **65–66**
for formatting command
output, 67–68